Masters of the
Nyingma Lineage

# Masters of the Nyingma Lineage

## Crystal Mirror Series
## Volume Eleven

CRYSTAL MIRROR SERIES

**Library of Congress Cataloguing-in-Publication Data**

Masters of the Nyingma Lineage
        p.   cm. — (Crystal mirror series ; v. 11)
    ISBN 0–89800–275–3 (pbk.)
  1. rNying-ma-pa lamas—biography    I. Series.
BQ 7662.9A236 1995   294.3 '923 0922–dc20   95-46695

Frontispiece: Guru Padmasambhava and the Twenty-Five Disciples. Courtesy of TNMC.

Photographs: Courtesy of TNMC.

Director and general editor of the Crystal Mirror Series:  Tarthang Tulku. Preface by Tarthang Tulku. Research, compiling, and manuscript preparation for *Masters of the Nyingma Lineage* by Leslie Bradburn in conjunction with the staff of the Yeshe De Project.

Typeset in Adobe New Aster with New Aster Outline titles and initials. Printed and bound by Dharma Press, 2910 San Pablo Avenue, Berkeley, CA 94702.

10   9   8   7   6   5   4   3   2   1

NYINGMA

ANCIENT ONES

CRYSTAL MIRROR

# The Crystal Mirror Series

Introductions to Buddha, Dharma, and Sangha
created by Tarthang Tulku
for Western Students of the Dharma

*Dedicated to the Future of Buddhism in the West*

*Homage to Guru Padmasambhava and the Twenty-Five Disciples*

# Contents

ix

PART THREE:
ERA OF ZUR-CHEN AND LCE-BTSUN SENG-GE DBANG-PHYUG
NINTH THROUGH ELEVENTH CENTURIES

PART FOUR:
ERA OF NYANG-RAL NYI-MA 'OD-ZER AND GURU CHOS-DBANG
TWELFTH AND THIRTEENTH CENTURIES

xvii

PART SIX:
ERA OF PHRENG-PO GTER-CHEN AND
RTSE-LE SNA-TSHOGS RANG-GROL
SIXTEENTH AND EARLY SEVENTEENTH CENTURIES

PART EIGHT:
ERA OF TSHE-DBANG NOR-BU AND 'JIGS-MED GLING-PA
EIGHTEENTH CENTURY

xxiii

# Illustrations

# Maps

# Line Drawings

# Preface

The teachings of the Buddha unfold the knowledge of full awakening that fulfills our destiny as human beings. Our world desperately needs such knowledge for we are living in an era of increasing suffering and growing loss of faith in the higher purposes of human being. The path of the Buddha has been studied, practiced, and explicated by Tibetan masters for twelve hundred years. Verifying the teachings in the texts with living experience, setting forth guidance and explanation of each step along the path, the lineage holders transmitted the light of understanding from master to disciple in an unbroken stream. This knowledge tradition has been gravely threatened since the Communist invasion of Tibet in the 1950s, which resulted in the destruction of monasteries and libraries and the loss of enlightened masters.

## PRESERVING THE TEXTS

As the Tibetans fled their homeland, they carried with them their most precious treasures, the sacred art and texts of the

Dharma. In India while I was a research fellow at Sanskrit University from 1962 to 1968, my friends and I set up a printing press to publish texts that the Tibetan lamas were beginning to gather together. Arriving in America, I founded Dharma Publishing in 1971 and the Yeshe De Project in 1983. Dharma Publishing has focused on translations of fundamental texts and resources for studying Dharma history and lineage, such as the Crystal Mirror Series, while Yeshe De is dedicated to Tibetan Buddhist text preservation. By 1983 we were able to bring out 128 volumes of the Nyingma Edition of the sDe-dge bKa'-'gyur and bsTan-'gyur, supplemented with 598 texts from other editions, the most comprehensive edition of the Tibetan Buddhist Canon ever produced.

Having completed this fundamental work, we turned to preserving the works of the rNying-ma tradition. Over many years, we had been gathering texts, which I now began to assemble into a collection called Great Treasures of Ancient Teachings. Texts came from about forty private libraries of lamas in exile. Additional texts were located in Bhutan and Nepal, and inside Tibet. Some were also found in Western libraries. Dharma Publishing has now assembled and printed a collection of 627 volumes of Tibetan texts, the first volumes appearing in 1991.

Great Treasures of Ancient Teachings contains ten sections. Five sections hold distinctive Vajrayāna teachings of the rNying-ma school: rNying-ma-rgyud-'bum editions, works by early lineage holders of the Inner Yogas, texts of the bKa'-ma, the Rin-chen gTer-mdzod, and the collected works of individual rNying-ma lamas and gTer-ma masters. These five sections fill over five hundred volumes.

The remaining five sections contain general works by authors of all schools. They include texts on the five śāstra subjects of Logic and Epistemology, Vinaya, Abhidharma, Madhyamaka, and Prajñāpāramitā; the arts and sciences, such as medicine, iconography, astrology, grammar, and poetry; history, lineage records, and biography; and renowned philosophical commentaries by masters of Tibetan Buddhism. Together these ten sections cover all fields of human knowledge, thus preserving sources for a comprehensive education.

In all, Great Treasures of Ancient Teachings contains 30,864 texts, composed by 424 rNying-ma authors, 240 authors of other Tibetan schools, and 128 Indian śāstra masters. The collection includes seventy-five percent of the rNying-ma texts I believe still to be extant. When we are able to access additional texts in various parts of the world, we expect to print several hundred more volumes.

In Tibet a collection as comprehensive as Great Treasures of Ancient Teachings never existed, for texts were distributed among the libraries of major monasteries, each preserving those important for their lineages. Generally, sacred books were the province of incarnate lamas and initiated masters, and were not widely accessible to the public, or even to scholars. Bringing the texts of the rNying-ma tradition together is a unique event in the history of Tibetan Buddhism. My intention is to preserve the texts and restore them to the lineage holders and monasteries where they can be put to best use. I hope that my decisions in assembling the texts have been appropriate, and I pray that the blessings of Padmasambhava's lineage grace this project.

## ADVANCED STUDIES

Publications such as Great Treasures of Ancient Teachings, which contain both basic and advanced teachings, raise important questions over which I have pondered at length. On the one hand, the survival of Buddhism depends on preserving this knowledge. On the other hand, few people are properly prepared to receive the advanced teachings of the Vajrayāna. Modern civilization does not provide the background for understanding the meanings and methods of practice connected with these esoteric teachings.

In Tibet, the tremendous power of the advanced teachings was deeply respected. Vajrayāna teachings were offered only to students who had received initiations and were capable of holding strict vows. Entering the Mantrayāna depends on a deep connection to a lineage holder with teaching experience who can supervise study and practice.

Undertaking the preliminary practices, comprehending the vows and initiations requires time, training, and the proper conditions. Mar-pa did not quickly bestow teachings on Mi-la Ras-pa and Vairotsana did not immediately teach Khri-srong lDe'u-bstan. Master and disciple worked carefully together, for unless the vows could be maintained, transmission could not take place; like a wire that carries no current, a practitioner without vows and initiations does not carry the living light of understanding.

The higher teachings cannot be grasped by ordinary mind. Vajrayāna teachings depend on Tantras, texts that have at least four levels of meaning: The meaning of the words (tshig-gi-don), the general meaning in context (spyi-don), the esoteric meaning (sbas-don), and the ultimate meaning (mthar-thug-gi-don). The Tantras use unconventional forms of expression, sections are not in sequential order, quotations have reversed meanings in certain contexts, and crucial instructions are hidden. Without the keys to the text, held by lineage masters who have undergone proper training and received complete transmission, the Tantra will remain incomprehensible. The reader who approaches the text with an ordinary mind 'just doesn't get it'. The tradition is vital for a genuine understanding.

Unaware of how carefully structured this system of advanced knowledge is, people today are impatient. They want the highest teachings first, hoping for quick results; they also want to find their own way, choosing what seems most relevant to them, and imagining that they can succeed without the transmission of the lineage. For their part, teachers may be tempted to make things easy, encouraging students to proceed with little preparation. According to Buddhist scriptures, entering the Mantrayāna without proper guidance and training brings negative rather than positive results and undermines the lineages of the Dharma.

## BUILDING A FOUNDATION

To lay the foundation for more advanced study of the Mantrayāna, it is essential to develop an attitude of faith and profound respect for Dharma, to study fundamental topics in the right order, and to practice step by step. Effective study and practice are based on authentic sources of knowledge: original Sūtras and śāstras, traditional basic practice texts, and reliable historical materials. These sources make it possible to develop a cohesive view, grounded in the understanding of where we are, where it is possible to go, and how to get there.

Specifically to meet this need, Dharma Publishing has published seventeen translations. They include *Path of Heroes* (a self-mastery text by Zhe-chen rGyal-tshab), *Wisdom of Buddha* (Saṁdhinirmocana Sutra), *Calm and Clear* (analytic meditation instructions of Lama Mi-pham), *Mind in Buddhist Psychology* (an Abhidharma work). In addition, Dharma Publishing has produced eleven volumes of the Crystal Mirror Series to introduce basic materials on history and lineage and to set forth the essential topics for study.

Among Dharma Publishing's translations are four biographies: *Voice of the Buddha* (Lalitavistara Sūtra, the Buddha's life story), *The Life and Liberation of Padmasambhava* (Padma Thang-yig), *Mother of Knowledge* (Ye-shes mTsho-rgyal's biography), and *The Marvelous Companion* (Jātakas that recount the previous lives of the Buddha). Biographies demonstrate how the path works and make it relevant to our lives, showing how the teachings are put into practice and what results are obtained. Seeing the steps taken as the Dharma is transmitted, we begin to appreciate the unbroken stream of enlightenment that runs through the centuries.

Several volumes of the Crystal Mirror Series have contained biographical notes on lineage holders. This eleventh volume presents brief biographical sketches of rNying-ma masters who are authors in the Great Treasures collection, with a few additional early lineage holders. These summaries are only preliminary notes for further research by the Yeshe De Project, based on historical sources such as 'Jigs-med Gling-pa's rNying-ma-rgyud-'bum dKar-chag and Kong-sprul Blo-gros mTha'-yas' Rin-chen gTer-mdzod dKar-chag, as well as bDud-'joms Rinpoche's rNying-ma'i-chos-'byung. The aim is to make these summaries available so that the names, dates, and key facts concerning these masters are preserved in English, and so that Dharma students can begin to understand the chronology of the masters and disciples. Dates and data are as accurate as we could make them based on available information.

Each biographical note contains references to the number of texts by that author in Great Treasures of Ancient Teachings, and particularly in the Rin-chen gTer-mdzod section. These counts may change as more texts are located and as texts are more thoroughly catalogued. These present summaries will also be indexed, expanded, and verified in the future, while notes on many hundreds of additional lineage holders will be added. It is my hope that in reading this material, Western Dharma students will glimpse the importance of lineage and find inspiration for their continued study and practice.

Tarthang Tulku
October, 1995
Berkeley, California

# Introduction to the rNying-ma School

The tradition of the rNying-ma School, known as the Ancient Ones, traces back to the Buddha in an unbroken lineage of enlightened masters of the Sūtrayāna and Mantra-yāna. Between the seventh and ninth centuries, the stream of these teachings flowed from India across the Himalayas into the Land of Snow. Guided by King Srong-btsan sGam-po, an Avalokiteśvara incarnation, King Khri-srong lDe'u-btsan, a Mañjuśrī incarnation, and King Ral-pa-can, a Vajrapāṇi incarnation, the Tibetan kingdom became a repository for the teachings of the Buddha.

## THE BUDDHIST TEACHINGS ENTER TIBET

The first Dharma texts appeared in Tibet during the reign of King lHa Tho-tho-ri in the fourth century C.E., together with mantras and a golden stūpa. lHa Tho-tho-ri venerated these precious objects, though he did not comprehend them. He received a prediction that in five generations one would arise who would understand their meaning.

Five generations later in the seventh century C.E., the first Dharma King, Srong-btsan sGam-po (569–650), prepared the way for the Dharma. Uniting the country, he established a constitution and laws based on Buddhist ethics. He foresaw the need to develop a written language for translation of sacred texts and to build temples to pacify the negative forces that would otherwise prevent the establishment of the teachings of enlightenment. To guarantee peace for his realm he married Buddhist princesses from the two great neighboring kingdoms of China and Nepal. These two embodiments of Tārā brought to Tibet remarkably beautiful and powerful statues of the Lord Buddha, together with other Dharma treasures. The compassionate actions of the king began to open the people's hearts to the Dharma, while his foresight set the stage for the full transmission of Buddhist teachings in the following century.

One hundred years later, the teachings were transplanted to Tibet. The time could not have been more auspicious, for the Buddhadharma was at its height in India: A strong monastic Sangha had established many thousands of monasteries, the Mahāyāna universities of Nālandā and Vikramaśīla were flourishing, and the siddhas were bringing forth the Vajrayāna teachings, which had been transmitted in secret through the centuries by the Vidyādharas (Knowledge Holders) to a few fortunate individuals.

Fulfilling an ancient vow to bring the teachings of the Lord Buddha to the wilds of Tibet, three great masters— Padmasambhava, the Guru of Oḍḍiyāna; Śāntarakṣita, the Abbot of Nālandā; and the second Dharma King Khri-srong lDe'u-btsan—established the Dharma in the Land of Snow. Renowned as mKhan-slob-chos-gsum (the Trio of Abbot, Guru, and King), in 762–63 C.E. they founded the first monastery, bSam-yas lHun-gyi-grub-pa gTsug-lag-khang, the Temple of bSam-yas, the Inconceivable Unchanging Perfect Creation. Over the next decade, bSam-yas was completed and consecrated with elaborate ceremony.

Thereafter, the abbot and twelve Sarvāstivādin masters from Kashmir ordained the first seven Tibetan monks who would transmit the Vinaya lineage. According to the decision of King Khri-srong lDe'u-btsan, which was respected by every master of later times, this Pratimokṣa lineage would be followed by all monks in Tibet.

Under the supervision of one hundred major paṇḍitas of the Mahāyāna, hundreds of specially trained Tibetan translators or lo-tsā-bas worked in the sGra-bsgyur rGya-gar-gling temple at bSam-yas to translate the Buddha's teachings on Vinaya, Sūtra, and Abhidharma, as well as the śāstras of the Indian Mahāpaṇḍitas. Thus, the textual transmission essential for the study and practice of the Śrāvakayāna and Bodhisattvayāna was established in Tibet.

## Types of Teachings Introduced

The Śrāvakayāna teachings form the basis for all Buddhist practice: the Four Noble Truths, the Twelve Links of Interdependent Origination, the laws of karma, and other First Turning teachings. The Bodhisattvayāna contains two divisions, the Sūtrayāna and the Mantrayāna. The Sūtrayāna teachings originate with the Prajñāpāramitā Sūtras of the Second Turning and the Tathāgatagarbha Sūtras of the Third Turning.

In India these Sūtras had inspired two great Mahāyāna currents of philosophy, the Madhyamaka, following the works of Nāgārjuna, and the Yogācāra, following the works of Asaṅga. These two outstanding authors of śāstras (commentaries), together with their major disciples, were renowned as spiritual guides able to systematize the views of the Mahāyāna and explain the practices of the ten stages of the Bodhisattva path, the actual 'engineering' of enlightenment. Due to their kindness and wisdom, the Mahāyāna was widespread in India.

In Tibet the Abbot Śāntarakṣita and the Kashmiri masters transmitted the Prajñāpāramitā, Abhidharma, Madhyamaka, and Yogācāra lineages to their disciples, the Tibetan translators sKa-ba dPal-brtsegs, Ye-shes-sde, Cog-ro Klu'i rGyal-mtshan, and others.

The Śrāvakayāna and Bodhisattvayāna teachings are the foundation for the path of the Mantrayāna, which is based on the teachings of the Tantras. The Tantric teachings offer ways to shorten the long path of the Bodhisattva so that enlightenment is attained not in aeons, but in lifetimes, or even within a single lifetime. The skillful means of the Tantras, explained in detail in the texts and commentaries, directly transcend obscurations and defilements.

Through the guidance of Guru Padmasambhava, Paṇ-chen Vimalamitra, Indian Vajrayāna master Buddhaguhya, and the Tibetan siddha Vairotsana, the Mantrayāna teachings were translated and transmitted to qualified disciples grounded in the Śrāvakayāna and Bodhisattvayāna—-gNubs-chen Sangs-rgyas Ye-shes, gNyags Jñānakumāra, Nam-mkha'i sNying-po, rMa Rin-chen-mchog, and the rest of twenty-five close disciples of Padmasambhava.

The lineages of the Buddha's teachings had taken firm root by the reign of the third of the great Dharma Kings, Ral-pa-can (814–836), an emanation of Vajrapāṇi. With the Dharma now well-established, this king employed his royal power to foster its growth. Deeply respecting the Sangha, he guaranteed their support through royal edicts. At Ral-pa-can's request, artisans from Khotan, China, Nepal, and Kashmir came to Tibet to create sacred art and temples such as 'U-shang-rdo, a nine-storied temple with a remarkable golden roof that was erected south of the capital of lHa-sa.

The king invited Mahāyāna scholars to Tibet and directed a commission of paṇḍitas and Tibetan translators to standardize terminology and establish a more systematic form of the Tibetan language for translation purposes. As part of this project, the commission prepared a Sanskrit-Tibetan lexicon, the Mahāvyutpatti, still used today. Thus, by the middle of the ninth century, under the auspices of the three Dharma Kings, the Sūtrayāna and Mantrayāna lineages were flourishing, and the enlightened wisdom of the Buddha was flowing into the heart of Tibetan civilization.

## NINE LEVELS OF TEACHINGS

According to the Sūtras, the Buddha's word contains 84,000 types of teachings to match as many types of mind, and there exist various classifications of three, nine, twelve, fourteen, and fifteen Yānas. Generally, the Buddha's teachings are classified into Three Yānas or Vehicles: the Śrāvakayāna, Pratyeka-buddhayāna, and Bodhisattvayāna, which includes Sūtrayāna and Mantrayāna. The teachings flow from the Enlightened One through the great Patriarchs and Arhats of the Śrāvakayāna, and through the Masters, Vidyādharas, and Siddhas of the Mahāyāna down through the centuries.

The rNying-ma elaborate six additional classifications of the esoteric teachings of the Mantrayāna to make nine levels of teachings presented according to levels of consciousness. The Three Outer Tantras are Kriyā, Caryā, and Yoga Tantras. The bKa'-'gyur and bsTan-'gyur contain hundreds of works related to these Tantras.

Yoga Tantra is further subdivided into Yoga Tantra and the more advanced Anuttara Yoga Tantra. Anuttara Yoga has three divisions of Father, Mother, and Neutral Tantras (these names do not refer literally to gender). Anuttara Tantras include the Tantras of the gSar-ma schools devoted to the Yi-dams such as Hevajra, Cakrasaṁvara, Kālacakra, and Guhyasamāja. For each one there are root Tantras (rtsa-brgyud), explanatory Tantras (bShad-brgyud), Branch Tantras (Yan-lag-brgyud), and Guidance Tantras (Man-ngag-brgyud).

The Three Inner Tantras belong to the rNying-ma tradition. Mahāyoga Tantra contains eighteen subsections, Anuyoga contains five, and Ati has three major sections. These teachings are transmitted in three ways: the Realization Transmission of the Buddhas, the Symbolic Transmission of the Vidyādharas (Knowledge Holders), and the Hearing Lineage of the Yogins.

The Three Inner Tantras are transmitted from the Ādibuddha through rDo-rje Sems-dpa' and the Bodhisattvas into the human realm. The Mahāyoga and Anuyoga were revealed first to King Indrabhūti within three decades of the Parinivāṇa of the Buddha. These teachings were transmitted through the Vidyādharas Kukkurāja, Līlāvajra, Buddhaguhya, Padmasambhava, and others. The Atiyoga flowed from the first human Vidyādhara dGa'-rab rDo-rje to Mañjuśrīmitra, Śrī Siṁha, Jñānasūtra, Vimalamitra, Padmasambhava, and others.

In Tibet, Padmasambhava, Vimalamitra, Buddhaguhya, and Vairotsana transmitted the Inner Tantras. In particular, the sixty-four hundred thousand teachings of rDzogs-pa-chen-po, obtained from Bodh Gayā in India and from other lands and realms by the Great Guru Padmasambhava, were brought to the Land of Snow.

## TRANSMITTING THE INNER TANTRAS IN TIBET

Once established in Tibet, the Inner Tantras flowed in two streams. The bKa'-ma transmission, an uninterrupted stream from master to disciple, is known as the long transmission, for it proceeds step by step through many individuals over a long period of time. The gTer-ma lineages are derived from teachings concealed by Padmasambhava and his disciple the Lady Ye-shes mTsho-rgyal, to be discovered by gTer-stons in future times. This is known as the short or close transmission because the teachings descend from the Great Guru Padmasambhava directly to the master who finds the treasure. The gTer-ma teachings guarantee a pure, unadulterated transmission to individuals of later centuries.

The bKa'-ma lineage flowed from gNubs, gNyags, and So to the tenth-century master Zur; from Zur it descended in stages to Rong-zom Mahāpaṇḍita in the eleventh century. From Rong-zom the teachings descended in stages to O-rgyan gTer-bdag Gling-pa and down to bKa'-ma masters of the present day.

As the Great Guru and Lady Ye-shes mTsho-rgyal journeyed throughout Tibet, they concealed the gTer-ma treasures and blessed the land: the twenty mountain peaks in mNga'-ris sKor-gsum in the west; the twenty-one wonderful meditation places in dBus and gTsang in the center; the twenty-five sacred places in mDo-khams in the east; the three supreme hidden valleys of the Upper, Lower, and Middle country; the five valleys; the three districts; and the one parkland. In each locale they practiced the Mantrayāna and hid treasures for recovery by future generations, planting the seeds of liberation for others.

The Lady Ye-shes mTsho-rgyal, King Khri-srong lDe'u-btsan, Vairotsana the translator, gNyags Jñānakumāra, gNubs-chen Sangs-rgyas Ye-shes, and rMa Rin-chen-mchog, together with the rest of the twenty-five disciples of Padmasambhava, were given responsibility for the transmission of the Dharma to future generations. Each of these disciples was reborn time and again as master of bKa'-ma and gTer-ma to guide and protect the lineages of the rNying-ma School.


BRIEF PERSECUTION OF THE DHARMA

The reign of the last Dharma King, Ral-pa-can, ended with his assassination in 836 C.E. His brother Glang Dar-ma, backed by followers of the Bon traditions and the discontented among the nobility, briefly seized the throne. Attempting to destroy all vestiges of the Dharma in Tibet, the anti-Buddhist king and his ministers closed monasteries and passed laws forcing monks to resume lay life.

The Tantric community of practitioners carried on quietly in hermitages and private residences, much as it had for centuries in India before the rise of the Mahāyāna, maintaining the complete transmission of texts and explanations during the time of persecution.

During these difficult times, the Mantrayāna lineages were protected by the disciples of Guru Padmasambhava and Vimalamitra. Manifesting a scorpion the size of an ox above the king's head, the accomplished siddha gNubs-chen Sangs-rgyas Ye-shes demonstrated to the king that the white-robed tantric Sangha was too powerful to challenge.

In contrast, the red-robed Sangha of monks was seriously endangered by Glang Dar-ma's closing of the Buddhist monasteries. The Vinaya lineage was preserved by three monks known as sMar, Rab, and gYo. Ordained by sBa Ratna, one of the first monks ordained by Śāntarakṣita, these three carried the precious Vinaya texts via the Turkish lands in Central Asia to the remote province of A-mdo in eastern Tibet, where the texts could be safely preserved. In A-mdo they ordained Bla-chen dGongs-pa Rab-gsal (832–915).

## DHARMA ACTIVITIES RESUME

The official persecution of Buddhism did not last beyond 841 or 842, ending with the assassination of Glang Dar-ma by a disciple of Padmasambhava, the monk lHa-lung dPal-gyi rDo-rje. For several generations, however, central Tibet was in turmoil, and Dharma activities had little support. To help revive the monastic tradition, ten men from the central provinces of dBus and gTsang traveled to the east in search of monastic ordination. Ordained by Bla-chen, these ten, led by Klu-mes Tshul-khrims Shes-rab, were able to return to central Tibet and successfully reestablish the monastic Sangha. These monks and their disciples soon restored old temples and founded new monasteries, such as La-mo, rGyal-lug-lhas, gZhu Kun-dga' Ra-ba, Sol-nag Thang-po-che, and Grwa-phyi Tshon-'dus.

By this time, panditas from Nepal and India were once more crossing the mountains into Tibet. Among the first of these was Smṛtijñānakīrti (892–975), a renowned master of the Abhidharma and an important paṇḍita of Nālandā, who was also well-versed in the Tantras. His interpreter, however, died en route to Tibet, forcing Smṛti to support himself as a shepherd until his identity became known. He spent the remainder of his life in Khams, teaching and translating Dharma texts and especially fostering the study of the Abhidharmakośa.


## THE LATER TRANSMISSION

By the tenth century, the Tibetan Empire had fragmented into small kingdoms, and central and western Tibet were ruled by Glang Dar-ma's descendents. These rulers did not persecute the Dharma and some may even have offered support. Toward the end of the tenth century, the king of Gu-ge in western Tibet became a monk, taking the name of Ye-shes-'od. He invited translators and teachers from Kashmir to his kingdom, and sent young men to Kashmir to study. Rin-chen bZang-po (958–1055), later known as the Great Translator, was one of these students.

Late in life, Ye-shes-'od was captured by the Turks, who asked for his weight in gold as ransom. When the gold was collected, Ye-shes-'od asked that it be used instead to invite Atīśa, the abbot of Vikramaśīla and the greatest living master of his time, to Tibet. Although Atīśa had previously refused the invitation to teach in Tibet, seeing Ye-shes-'od's sacrifice, he could refuse no longer. His arrival in Tibet in 1042 ushered in a new era for Tibetan Buddhism.

It is just at this juncture that the distinction between the Ancient School (rNying-ma) and the New Schools (gSar-ma) becomes meaningful. The period beginning with the work of Rin-chen bZang-po is known as the Later Spread of the Dharma, and the Tantras translated at this time became known as New Tantras. In contrast, the previous era, concluding with the translations of Smṛtijñānakīrti, is known as the Period of the Early Spread of the Dharma.

Transmitted in the eighth and ninth centuries, all the major Sūtrayāna teachings of the Buddha and the śāstras of the Mahāpaṇḍitas were preserved in revised and modified translations by the new schools and constitute a heritage shared by all schools. The texts of the Three Inner Tantras, translated in the early period and known as the Ancient Tantras, are the unique heritage of the rNying-ma School.

## DISTINCTIVE QUALITIES OF RNYING-MA

The distinctive qualities of the rNying-ma school, as enumerated by Rong-zom Mahāpaṇḍita, encompass six types of greatness, conditions that were not to be repeated again:

1. The three Dharma Kings were the Great Bodhisattvas Avalokiteśvara, Mañjuśrī, and Vajrapāṇi, acting in the world of men for the purpose of establishing the Dharma in Tibet. These kings offered the full support of their royal office to establish the Dharma. Sweeping power and long-range vision were the distinctive qualities of these kings.

2. The great Dharma center of bSam-yas, constructed as a mandala of the cosmos, provided the most sacred environment imaginable for the transmission of the Buddha's teachings. In specially appointed halls, temples, and libraries, hundreds of translators worked in concert with paṇḍitas to transmit the Dharma in a comprehensive fashion. Following the decrees of

the king, they were guided by the wisdom of the Abbot, and protected by the blessings of the Guru.

3. The translators were not ordinary individuals but emanations of Bodhisattvas, incarnations of enlightened beings knowledgeable in the transformation of human nature. Cog-ro Klu'i rGyal-mtshan, rMa Rin-chen-mchog, gNyags Jñāna-kumāra, and the other twenty-five disciples achieved the level of the Eighty-four Siddhas, utterly selfless in their love of Dharma and capable of transmitting it purely. Vairotsana, for example, who knew three hundred different dialects, had the same level of understanding as Padmsambhava. Comprehending beyond any doubt all levels of meaning, these enlightened ones devised precise terminology to convey the essence of the teachings in each type of text.

4. The founding fathers of the rNying-ma tradition possessed the eye of wisdom and the heart of unfailing compassion. Śāntarakṣita, Padmasambhava, and Vimalamitra were Bodhisattvas and even Buddhas, masters of the greatest masters of India and Oḍḍiyāna. Śāntarakṣita, renowned as Abbot Bodhisattva, remained on earth nine hundred years in order to transmit the Dharma to Tibet; immortal Padmasambhava embodies all the Buddhas of the three times; Kha-che Paṇ-chen Vimalamitra remains even today on this planet, residing, it is said, in a Body of Light at Wu-t'ai-shan, the mountain sacred to the Bodhisattva Mañjuśrī.

5. Because the Dharma patrons in the eighth and ninth centuries were the rulers of the land, they were able to make great offerings so that Tibet might receive enlightened teachings. Traditionally, in India, aspirants wishing to receive the highest doctrines of the Mantrayāna made gifts of gold to the master as a symbol of the value of the teachings. Likewise in the days of the early transmission, the royal coffers of Tibet were opened wide, demonstrating a deep appreciation for the teachings and supporting Dharma work that was never constrained by limited resources.

6. The Inner Tantras, the most profound teachings of the Lord Buddha transmitted in the days of the early translations, were unavailable to later masters. The texts and teachings of these precious Mantrayāna lineages had been transmitted in secret since the time of the Buddha, each Vidyādhara receiving the direct transmission of enlightened realization. Flowing from dGa'-rab rDo-rje down to Vairotsana, this stream of living understanding reached Tibet in the eighth century. When these teachings were brought to the Land of Snow, sometimes the sole remaining copies of ancient texts were granted to the Tibetan disciples. Moreover, the Great Guru Padmasambhava obtained Vajrayāna texts from Oḍḍiyāna and from other realms that had been under the protection of the ḍākinīs.

The efforts of these eighth- and ninth-century masters and disciples created the foundation for the Dharma in Tibet, laying the cornerstone of Tibetan Buddhist civilization, which endured for twelve centuries. Like Mount Kailaśa from which descend the four great rivers of Asia—the Glang-po-che Kha-'bab (Sutlej), the rTa-mchog Kha-'bab (gTsang-po-Brahma-putra), the rMa-bya Kha-'bab (Karnali), and the Seng-ge Kha-'bab (Indus)—the tradition of the Ancient Ones is the fountain-head from which flow the streams of the bKa'-gdams, bKa'-brgyud, Sa-skya, and dGe-lug traditions.

Over the centuries the lineages of the rNying-ma tradition were preserved by thousands of masters and hundreds of monasteries throughout Tibet. Independent and nonhierarchical, each major monastery was self-governing, and no one organization had authority over another. While all belonged to the tradition of mKhan-slob-chos-gsum, each had its own lineage holders and teachers, and each preserved distinctive bKa'-ma traditions and teachings of particular gTer-stons. In particular, the six monasteries of Kaḥ-thog, rDo-rje-brag, sMin-grol-gling, Zhe-chen, rDzogs-chen, and dPal-yul were repositories of Dharma and models of enlightened ways of living.

Hundreds of lineage holders arose in unbroken succession, a golden chain of light connecting the past to the present. The great rNying-ma masters of the past were so successful in their work for the Dharma that there could be no doubt about their enlightened understanding. The lives of more recent masters like 'Jigs-med Gling-pa and 'Jam-dbyangs mKhyen-brtse likewise demonstrate the purity and efficacy of Padmasambhava's lineage. The depth of their knowledge, compassion, and power confirm that in the midst of our world of confusion and suffering, the inner light of the Bodhisattva path still shines.

Masters of the
Nyingma Lineage

# Part One

# Vajrayāna Lineage

སྐལ་ལྡན་ཀྲི་རྒྱལ་པོ་ཛཿ

King Indrabhūti sKal-ldan rGyal-po Dza

# Knowledge Holders
## of the Ancient School

The teachings of the Mahāyāna were transmitted and protected by great Bodhisattvas since the time of the Lord Buddha. The Enlightened One predicted that shortly after his Parinirvāṇa, a master of the Dharma would appear to reveal the full extent of the teachings of the Mantrayāna. To traverse the way of the Bodhisattva in a single lifetime and fulfill the vision of complete Awakening proclaimed by the Sūtrayāna required the most skillful knowledge of the Mantrayāna, the Diamond Vehicle of the Vajrayāna.

Following the prophecy in the "Instructions of the Sūtra," the Lotus-Born Guru Padmasambhava arose to transmit the Mantrayāna teachings. These teachings were preserved for centuries by a lineage of Knowledge Holders, Vidyādharas foretold by the Buddha. As the time and conditions became suitable, the Mantrayāna teachings spread across Asia. When the Dharma reached Tibet, the Great Guru himself brought the Mantrayāna lineages to the Land of Snow.

སློབ་དཔོན་ཆེན་པོ་པདྨ་འབྱུང་གནས།

## The Great Guru Padmasambhava
### 5 years after the Parinirvāṇa
### 14 texts, 547 pages
### and innumerable gTer-ma texts

In his universal aspect, the Lotus-Born Padmasambhava is pure enlightened awareness encompassing all Buddhas and Bodhisattvas, the ḍākinīs who transmit their subtle teachings, and the Dharma protectors who protect them. As Guru Rinpoche, he manifests in the ten directions and in the three times, taking thousands of forms to benefit different beings. A channel of wisdom and compassion, he is a pure lotus of natural beauty that is inseparable from our own heart.

Master of the external, internal, and secret traditions of the Dharma, Padmasambhava transmitted the Inner Yogas of the Mantrayāna to Tibet. Arising in a miraculous manner five years after the Buddha's Parinirvāṇa, Padmasambhava appeared within a lotus in Lake Dhanakośa in the kingdom of Oḍḍiyāna. King Indrabhūti of Oḍḍiyāna adopted him as his son, but like Lord Buddha, he wished to renounce his kingdom. Contriving to be exiled, he departed for the cemetery grounds, where he received teachings from ḍākinīs, and then studied all Sūtras and Tantras under accomplished masters.

From Ānanda he requested the Sūtras; from Prabhahasti in Sa-hor, he received ordination and the name Śākyasiṁha; from dGa'-rab rDo-rje and Śrī Siṁha he obtained rDzogs-chen teachings of the highest Tantras; from Buddhaguhya he received Mahāyoga teachings. He was among the eight Great Vidyādharas who received and taught the heruka sādhanas: Hūṁkara, Mañjuśrīmitra, Nāgārjuna, Vimalamitra, Prabhahasti, Dhanasaṁskṛta, Śāntigarbha, and Padmasambhava. While each of these masters received one of the heruka teachings, the precious Guru Padmasambhava received all eight.

6

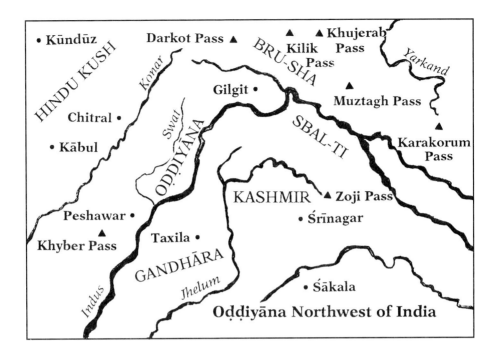

Oddiyāna Northwest of India

Together with the dākinī Mandāravā, Padmasambhava practiced longevity rites at Māratika Cave and gained power over the duration of his own life and the body of indestructible reality. When attempts were made to destroy him and the lady Mandāravā, he turned the funeral pyre into a lake. When the ministers of the kingdom of Oddiyāna tried to immolate him, he again transformed the fire into water.

Padmasambhava took many other forms throughout the history of the Dharma. He was the monk who converted King Aśoka; he was the siddhas Saroruha and Virūpa and numerous others. He taught in many lands and obtained teachings from many realms. Speaking all languages, touching the hearts of every being, Padmasambhava can best be understood as transcending all of the limits of ordinary time and space.

In Tibet Padmasambhava subdued the forces opposed to enlightenment and consecrated the land for the Dharma by blessing every hill and vale. Together with King Khri-srong lDe'u-btsan and the great Abbot Śāntarakṣita, he founded the first monastery of bSam-yas. To the twenty-five disciples, he

7

taught the highest teachings of the Mantrayāna, establishing the streams of the bKa'-ma and gTer-ma transmission that flowed through these disciples to future generations. He concealed countless treasures so that the pure teachings of the Mantrayāna could come forth at the appropriate times and places. Remaining in Tibet for fifty-five or more years, Guru Padmasambhava ensured the long-range success of the teachings of the Lord Buddha, which endured for twelve hundred years in the Land of Snow.

སྐལ་ལྡན་གྱི་རྒྱལ་པོ་ཛཿ

## sKal-ldan rGyal-po Dza King Indrabhūti
### 28 years after Parinirvāṇa
### 3 texts, 18 pages

Śākyamuni Buddha predicted that twenty-eight years after his Parinirvāṇa, a king called Dza but known also by many other names, among them Indrabhūti, would ensure the continuation of the Enlightened One's teachings in many world realms. The prophecy was fulfilled when King Indrabhūti became ruler of Sa-hor.

In a series of seven successive dreams or visions inspired by Vajrapāṇi, King Indrabhūti awakened to the wonder of the Mahāyoga Tantras. Thereafter the Mahāyoga teachings rained down from the heavens and a statue of Vajrapāṇi appeared in the palace courtyard. Having understood portions of the texts, the noble Indrabhūti prayed and practiced so successfully that he received the transmission of the Mahāyoga directly from the Mahābodhisattva Vajrapāṇi.

Completely comprehending the Tantras, Indrabhūti first taught Uparāja, a renowned scholar, but Uparāja could not fully understand the teachings, so the king transmitted the lineage to the siddha Kukkurāja. Vajrapāṇi then appeared to Kukkurāja, granting him empowerment, and urging the siddha to seek out Licchavi Vimalakīrti for further instruction. Eventually Kukkurāja divided the Mahāyoga Tantras into the eighteen great sections and taught them to the king. Although King Indrabhūti already possessed complete understanding, he demonstrated the ordinary path to realization by relying on Kukkurāja as his teacher.

This king was also the essential link in the Anuyoga transmission. Empowered by Vajrapāṇi, and relying once again on Licchavi Vimalakīrti, Indrabhūti received the Anuyoga teachings of the 'Dus-pa'i-mdo and associated Tantras. At Śrī Dhānyakaṭaka in southern India and at Ksemākara, he bestowed the Tantras upon Uparāja and his own three sons: Śākyaputra, Nāgaputra, and Guhyaputra.

Renowned as Indrabhūti the Younger and as the siddha Kambalapāda, Śākyaputra instructed his entourage, all of who became Vidyādharas. In particular, he empowered Siṁhaputra and the later Kukkurāja, who in turn taught dGa'-rab rDo-rje. These early lineage holders all achieved the radiant realm of reality and vanished completely. Great Treasures of Ancient Teachings contains three texts by this master.

གྲུབ་ཆེན་ཀུ་ཀུ་ར་ཛ

### Mahāsiddha Kukkurāja
1st century after Parinirvāṇa

One of the Eighty-four Mahāsiddhas, Kukkurāja, the "King of Dogs," received the entire body of Mahāyoga teachings from King Indrabhūti. After his vision of Vajrapāṇi, he went to live in a forest where it is said he felt no fear of even the most ferocious beasts, and instilled no fear in even the most timid creature. During the day he appeared as a master of yoga, and at night he taught the Mahāyoga Tantras in many places throughout the world. He taught for twelve years, and one hundred thousand of his students became enlightened. Thereafter the Mahāyoga lineage spread to many realms.

The lineage transmitted by Kukkurāja passed through Śākraputra, the king's son, to Siṁharāja and then to Uparāja, who taught the Princess Gomadevī. Princess Gomadevī in turn taught the renowned scholar and teacher, Līlavajra. Another lineage passed from King Dza and Kukkurāja to sPrul-sku dGa'-rab rDo-rje and Bhāsita, who then taught Prabhahasti. Eight texts authored under the name of Kukkurāja are preserved in the bsTan-'gyur.

སྤྲུལ་བའི་སྐུ་དགའ་རབ་རྡོ་རྗེ

sPrul-ba'i-sku dGa'-rab rDo-rje
166 years after the Parinirvāṇa
11 texts, 108 pages

Born in Oḍḍiyāna northwest of India near the lake where Guru Padmasambhava first appeared in the world, dGa'-rab rDo-rje is considered the first human Vidyādhara or Knowledge Holder of the Atiyoga lineage. An emanation of Vajrasattva, dGa'-rab rDo-rje was conceived in a vision to Sudharmā, the daughter of King Uparāja, who had become a renunciate. Out of shame and fear at his illegitimacy, the princess placed her newborn son in a dust-heap but returned after three days to discover him healthy and radiant. Realizing that he was an incarnation, she took him back to the palace.

When dGa'-rab rDo-rje was a youth, his grandfather experienced such great joy in his presence that he named the boy dGa'-rab rDo-rje, Joyous Vajra. He was also known as Ro-lang bDe-ba, Blissfully Arisen from the Dead. dGa'-rab rDo-rje was initiated into all the Tantras by Vajrapāṇi and began to teach at age seven. In a debate on the nature of the path, he put forth arguments from the viewpoint of the goal to defeat five hundred learned masters whose viewpoint was that of the starting point. He then instructed the assembly in the Atiyoga, so astonishing them that they fell to their knees around him.

After thirty-two years in solitary meditation on a mountaintop, dGa'-rab rDo-rje went to live in a cemetery, where he transmitted the Atiyoga teachings to a great number of disciples. He manifested numerous unusual powers, such as enveloping his body in light. All who came into his presence were inspired with great faith and devotion. On the summit of Mount Malaya, assisted by three heavenly ḍākinīs, dGa'-rab rDo-rje recorded the teachings of the Atiyoga and arranged the six million four hundred thousand verses. In Śitavana cemetery he taught Mañjuśrīmitra for seventy-five years.

dGa'-rab rDo-rje also received the Anuyoga transmission from Kukkurāja, and in turn bestowed these teachings on Vajrahāsya in the Uttarasāra forest and on Prabhahasti (Śākyaprabha) on the banks of the Indus river. This lineage descended to Śākyamitra and Śākyasiṁha (a manifestation of Padmasambhava).

After dGa'-rab rDo-rje had passed away in a Rainbow Body of brilliant light, he appeared in a vision to Mañjuśrīmitra and gave him a golden box with his final teachings. Mañjuśrīmitra transmitted the Atiyoga lineage to his disciple Śrī Siṁha. Śrī Siṁha in turn transmitted the lineage to Padmasambhava, Vimalamitra, and Vairotsanarakṣita, all of whom carried these precious teachings to Tibet. The Anuyoga lineage was passed to Vajrahasya and Prabhahasti. Great Treasures of Ancient Teachings contains eleven texts by this master.

# བྱང་སེམས་མཁན་ཆེན་ཞི་བ་འཚོ

mKhan-chen Zhi-ba-'tsho Abbot Śāntarakṣita

1st century B.C.E.–8th century

7 texts, 170 pages

Born the son of rGyal-po Dza (Indrabhūti), King of Sa-hor, five hundred and fifty years after the Parinirvāṇa of the Lord Buddha, Śāntarakṣita awaited the fulfillment of an ancient prophecy: During the reign of Khri-srong lDe'u-btsan he would work with Guru Padmasambhava and the king to establish the Dharma in Tibet. Traditional accounts record that he lived nine hundred years.

While still a youth, Śāntarakṣita realized that the worldly life is a source of misery and traveled to Nālandā. There he was ordained by the abbot Jñānagarbha, under whom he studied Sarvāstivādin Abhidharma. From Vinayasena he heard the Prajñāpāramitā, the Abhisamayālaṁkāra and other commentaries, and mastered the works of Nāgārjuna. He received the Vinaya lineage of Rāhula and Nāgārjuna, which was transmitted through Jñānagarbha. Renowned for his comprehensive knowledge, he eventually succeeded Jñānagarbha as abbot of the university of Nālandā.

Among his major works are the Madhyamakālaṁkāra, an explication of the Madhyamaka, and the Tattvasaṁgraha, a comprehensive work that summarizes the positions of both Buddhist and non-Buddhist schools. Heir to all lineages of the śāstra tradition and consummate master of philosophy and logic, Abbot Śāntarakṣita synthesized Mahāyāna philosophies into an integrated system that later became known as the Yogācāra-madhyamaka-svātantrika.

Arriving in Tibet in the mid-eighth century, this great abbot began to lay the foundation for the first monastery in Tibet. There he found the forces opposing Dharma so strong that he recommended the king invite the Vajra Guru Padmasambhava. Fulfilling the ancient prophecy, together the Abbot, the Guru, and the King (mKhan-slob-chos-gsum) established bSam-yas. Śāntarakṣita then ordained the first seven Tibetan monks into the Vinaya lineage that would be followed by all schools of Tibetan Buddhism. Abbot Śāntarakṣita guided the translation of the Sūtras and śastras, and transmitted Mahāyāna lineages to fortunate disciples. His major disciples included Haribhadra and Kamalaśīla. Seven of his works are preserved in Great Treasures of Ancient Teachings.

སློབ་དཔོན་ཆེན་པོ་འཇམ་དཔལ་བཤེས་གཉེན་

'Jam-dpal bShes-gnyen Mañjuśrīmitra
1st–3rd century C.E.
4 texts, 8 pages

An emanation of the Bodhisattva Vajrapāṇi, Mañjuśrīmitra was the second Vidyādhara of the Atiyoga lineage. Prophesied to be as wise as the Bodhisattva Mañjuśrī, this master was born as the son of the brahmin Sādhuśāstrī and his wife Pradīpālokā at Dvikrama, a village west of Vajrāsana. Even as a youth, he mastered the Vedas, Sanskrit, linguistics, philosophy, logic, and art. In a vision he was instructed by Mañjuśrī to proceed to the cremation ground at Śītavana, where he would find an enlightened teacher who would instruct him in the direct path to realization.

Mañjuśrīmitra attended dGa'-rab rDo-rje for seventy-five years and received the complete Atiyoga lineage and other Dharma teachings. He divided the six million four hundred thousand verses into three sections: Sems-sde, Klong-sde, and Man-ngag-gi-sde; he subsequently divided the Man-ngag-gi-sde

13

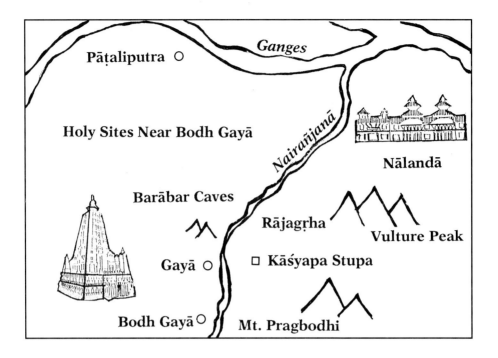

into the sNyan-brgyud (aural tradition) and the bShad-brgyud (exegesis tradition).

Awaiting the auspicious time for their transmission, he concealed these texts at Bodh Gayā beneath the Diamond Throne (Vajrāsana). This holy place is said to be the most powerful on the earth, the site where Siddhārtha Gautama and the three preceding Buddhas of this aeon attained complete enlightenment in past and present eras. He then returned to the cremation ground, where he is said to have remained in meditation for one hundred and nine years.

Mañjuśrīmitra transmitted all of the Atiyoga teachings to the great siddha Śrī Siṁha, who in turn transmitted the lineage to Padmasambhava, Vimalamitra, and Vairotsana. He himself also taught the Atiyoga to Guru Padmasambhava and Buddhajñānapāda, and to Āryadeva, among others.

Mañjuśrīmitra achieved a level of realization indistinguishable from the noble Mañjuśrī, who, as Yamāntaka, empowered Mañjuśrīmitra in the Yamāntaka heruka practices. After discovering the written texts of these practices at Mount Malaya, Mañjuśrīmitra reconcealed these north of Vajrāsana. Known also as Sārasiddhi and the Brahmin Sāra, who was the father of Jetāri, Mañjuśrīmitra was the master of the brahmins Jñānavajra and Bodhivajra, and of Amoghavajra, who became an expert in the Yamāntaka practices. Great Treasures contains four texts by this master.

རིག་འཛིན་ཆེན་པོ་ཤྲི་སིཾ་ཧ

## Rig-'dzin Chen-po Śrī Siṁha
### 3rd–8th century C.E.
### 16 texts, 61 pages

Śrī Siṁha was born in Sho-khyam (Suofeng?) in western China or Khotan as the son of dGe-ba'i Yid-can and his wife sNang-ba gSal-ba Rab-tu mKhyen-ma. After mastering the ordinary sciences under Haribhala, he became ordained and studied the Outer and Inner Tantras with the master Bhelakīrti at Ri-bo rTse-lnga, the Five-Peaked Mountain sacred to Mañjuśrī in eastern China. Later he traveled to India, where it had been prophesied he would receive the highest teachings. Under the inspiration of the Mahābodhisattva Avalokiteśvara, Śrī Siṁha went to the cremation ground of Sosadvīpa, where he met the great Vidyādhara Mañjuśrīmitra, who instructed him for twenty-five years.

Finally, assured of his disciple's success, Mañjuśrīmitra dissolved into multi-hued light. In a vision, Mañjuśrīmitra gave Śrī Siṁha final instructions and a jeweled box containing the sGom-nyams-drug-pa (Six Meditation Experiences). Upon receiving this teaching, Śrī Siṁha attained full realization.

At Vajrāsana, Śrī Siṁha discovered the Man-ngag-gi-sde of the Atiyoga concealed there by Mañjuśrīmitra. He divided the

Man-ngag-gi-sde into four parts: the outer cycle (Phyi-skor), the inner cycle (Nang-skor), the secret cycle (gSang-skor), and the most inner secret cycle (gSang-ba-bla-na-med-pa'i-skor). Having concealed the first three cycles at Bodh Gaya and the last cycle at bKra-shis Khri-sgo in China, Śrī Simha entered contemplation in the cremation ground of bSil-byin.

Disciples of Śrī Simha included the masters Vimalamitra, Jñānasūtra, Padmasambhava, Vairotsana, and Buddhaguhya. Great Treasures contains sixteen texts by this master.

ཁ་ཆེ་པཎ་ཆེན་པི་མ་ལ་མི་ཏྲ

Kha-che Paṇ-chen Vimalamitra
6th–8th century C.E.
40 texts, 406 pages

The master Vimalamitra was born in Glang-po'i-sgang (probably Hastināpura) near the land of Kuru south of Kashmir. His father was Sukhacakra and his mother was Ātmaprakāśā. He studied the Vinaya, Sūtra, and śāstra traditions at Bodh Gaya with five hundred paṇḍitas. After receiving the Mahāyoga transmission from Buddhaguhya, he traveled to Byang-chub-shing temple in China, where he studied with Śrī Simha for twenty years. Upon his return to India, Vimalamitra instructed Jñānasūtra, who had been born in eastern India at the same time that Vimalamitra was born in the west. Jñānasūtra then journeyed to see Śrī Simha and studied with him for many years.

When Vimalamitra was over one hundred years old, he traveled to the Bha-sing cemetery, where Jñānasūtra transmitted to him the precious teachings of the Atiyoga sNying-thig. Ten years after empowering Vimalamitra, Jñānasūtra was enveloped by a brilliant light and vanished, at which time

Vimalamitra received his last testament. Vimalamitra made three copies of the Atiyoga texts, one set being preserved at Oḍḍiyāna, one set in Kashmir, and the third in the cremation ground of Prabhāskara.

Vimalamitra became the master of King Haribhadra of Kāmarūpa and guru to King Dharmapāla of Bhirya. While he was residing at Oḍḍiyāna, he was visited by emissaries from the king of Tibet, who invited him to teach the Dharma in the Land of Snow. Although more than two hundred years old, Vimalamitra departed for Tibet, where he taught, translated, and transmitted the teachings for thirteen years, working closely with Padmasambhava's Tibetan disciples.

Renowned in Tibet as the Kashmiri Master, Vimalamitra translated many rNying-ma Tantras and transmitted the lineages to his Tibetan disciples. He conferred the highest Atiyoga teachings, the sNying-thig transmission of the Guidance Section (Man-ngag-gi-sde) upon five disciples: King Khri-srong lDe'u-btsan, the king's son Mu-ne bTsan-po, Myang Ting-nge-'dzin, sKa-ba dPal-brtsegs, and Cog-ro Klu'i rGyal-mtshan. Several translations of these Atiyoga texts were concealed at mChims-phu near bSam-yas for the sake of future generations and were recovered later. His translations are contained in the bKa'-'gyur and bsTan-'gyur and in the rNying-ma-rgyud-'bum.

After completing his work in the Land of Snow, Vimalamitra resided in China at the Five-Peaked Mountain sacred to Mañjuśrī (Wu-ta'i-shan or Ri-bo rTse-lnga). Promising to remain in the world as long as the Buddha's teachings endure, Vimalamitra has returned to Tibet every century to ensure the purity of the Dharma transmission. Forty texts composed by this master have been preserved in the Great Treasures of Ancient Teachings.

གཁས་པ་ཆེན་པོ་ཡེ་ཤེས་མདོ

mKhas-pa Chen-po Ye-shes-mdo Jñānasūtra

6th–7th century C.E.

Born in eastern India to an outcaste family, Jñānasūtra was the son of Śāntihasta and Kalyāṇacittā. Inspired by a vision of Vajrasattva, and encouraged by Vimalamitra, Jñānasūtra became intent on meeting Śrī Siṁha, whom he finally encountered in the bSil-byin cremation ground. For three years he served the master, finally requesting instruction. Over the next twelve years, Śrī Siṁha bestowed upon him the Hearing Lineage, the texts, and the empowerments. At Mount Kosala, the master gave him additional profound empowerments, and Jñānasūtra practiced devotedly for sixteen years.

After Śrī Siṁha had passed away in a rainbow body, Jñānasūtra had a vision of his teacher in which he received his last testament, the seven essential teachings of the rDzogs-pa-chen-po (gZer-bu-bdun) and instructions on the locations of hidden texts. Following these instructions, Jñānasūtra recovered texts concealed by Śrī Siṁha at bKra-shis Khri-sgo. He remained in the Bha-sing cemetery in India for many years, teaching the ḍākas and ḍākinīs and receiving numerous other teachings from Śrī Siṁha, who taught him through visions. Vimalamitra came to Bha-sing to receive the most profound teachings, and Jñānasūtra bestowed the texts and empowerments upon him. When this great master vanished in light, he transmitted his final testament to Vimalamitra. Works composed by Jñānasūtra have not been located in recent times.

sGeg-pa'i-rdo-rje Līlavajra
7th–8th century C.E.
8 texts, 90 pages

Born in a region known as Saṃsara and ordained in the land of Oḍḍiyāna, Līlavajra was an accomplished Vidyādhara of the Three Inner Yogas, and of Mahāyoga in particular. Also known as the siddha Viśvarūpa for his ability to change his form, he imparted his lineages to the foremost Mantrayāna masters of his day, ensuring the widespread transmission of these teachings. He was known to have resided at Nālandā and also in Oḍḍiyāna.

Līlavajra was a central link in the transmission of the Guhyamūlagarbha Tantra (gSang-ba'i-snying-po), the root text of the Mahāyoga teachings, receiving the lineage from Princess Gomadevī, and in turn passing it on to the Vajrayāna master Buddhaguhya. Līlavajra transmitted this lineage widely in Oḍḍiyāna. Although he never journeyed to Tibet, his disciples included Buddhaguhya, Padmasambhava, and Vimalamitra, all of whom carried the teachings to the Land of Snow.

Līlavajra wrote numerous commentaries on the Inner Tantras, including a particularly important commentary on the gSang-ba'i-snying-po. The bsTan-'gyur preserves nineteen of his works. Eight of these texts are also contained in Great Treasures of Ancient Teachings.

Sangs-rgyas gSang-ba Buddhaguhya
7th–8th century C.E.
32 texts, 551 pages

Born in Magadha, Buddhaguhya entered the monastic order at Nālandā, where he became a renowned paṇḍita. Having received the lineages of the Outer Tantras, together with Ānandagarbha and Śākyamitra, he became one of the most important masters in this lineage. He traveled to the land of Oḍḍiyāna, where he also received the Mahāyoga lineage of the Guhyamūlagarbha Tantra from Līlavajra. Buddhaguhya also received the shorter lineage of the Mahāyoga from King Indrabhūti.

With Buddhaśānti, he journeyed to Mt. Potalaka where together they received teachings directly from the Bodhisattvas. At the urging of both Mañjuśrī and Tārā, Buddhaguhya took up residence at Mt. Kailaśa, the holy mountain overlooking Lake Manasarowar on the far western edge of the Tibetan plateau. Although he declined invitations from Mes-ag-tshoms (Khri-srong lDe'u-btsan's father) to journey to the Tibetan capital, Buddhaguhya bestowed teachings on Tibetan disciples who came to Mt. Kailaśa. He greatly assisted the Outer Tantra and Mahāyoga transmissions by teaching dBas 'Jam-dpal, Bran-ka Mukti, and gNyags Jñānakumāra, who in turn passed these precious teachings on to their disciples.

A master of the Outer and Inner Tantras, Buddhaguhya wrote many commentaries that are still extant, and passed on to Padmasambhava and Vimalamitra his lineage of the Mahāyoga. Buddhaguhya himself translated the Guhyamūlagarbha Tantra into Tibetan and wrote an extensive commentary on Mahāyoga teachings for his students. Thirty-two texts by this master are preserved in Great Treasures of Ancient Teachings.

# སློབ་དཔོན་ཆེན་པོ་ཀ་མ་ལ་ཤཱི་ལ

Slob-dpon Chen-po Kamalaśīla

8th century C.E.

18 texts, 500 pages

Disciple of Śāntarakṣita, Mahācarya Kamalaśīla received all the lineages of his master and brought this living wisdom to Tibet at a crucial time. Predicting that heretical doctrines would soon be introduced to Tibet, Śāntarakṣita had advised King Khri-srong lDe'u-bstan to rely on Kamalaśīla in time of need. When controversies did indeed arise between the followers of Śāntarakṣita and the followers of the Hwa-shang view promulgated by Chinese masters, the king sent for Kamalaśīla.

In an historic debate at bSam-yas, Kamalaśīla defeated the advocates of the Hwa-shang view. By order of the king, the doctrine expounded by Śāntarakṣita became the basis for the Dharma in Tibet. During the debate, Kamalaśīla composed three texts known as Bhāvanākramas that set forth the path to enlightened understanding. He also wrote commentaries on Mahāyāna Sūtras, as well as learned explications of the Tattvasaṁgraha and the Madhyamakālaṁkāra. More than thirty of his texts were translated into Tibetan and preserved in the bsTan-'gyur. Great Treasures of Ancient Teachings contains eighteen of his works.

# Part Two

# Era of the
# Dharma Kings

བྱང་སེམས་ཆོས་རྒྱལ་ཁྲི་སྲོང་ལྡེའུ་བཙན

Dharma King Khri-srong lDe'u-btsan

# Seventh through Ninth Centuries

Between the seventh and ninth centuries, the teachings of the Enlightened Ones reached the Land of Snow and took firm root in Tibetan soil. Tibetan civilization was completely transformed by the efforts of the Dharma kings and the remarkable masters, yogins, paṇḍitas, and translators who planted the seeds, cultivated the Dharma, and brought it to complete fruition.

Under the guidance of these same kings, Tibet became a vast empire that encompassed parts of northern India, the rich oasis states of central Asia, the borderlands of T'ang China in the east, and the fringes of the Arab conquests in the west. Though the empire began to fragment about 850 C.E., the Dharma survived and flourished. The ancient tradition of the Buddha had been successfully transplanted to its new home, where it would blossom for twelve hundred years. The enlightened lineages spread far and wide throughout the land and have continued unbroken to the present day.

ཆོས་ཀྱི་རྒྱལ་པོ་སྲོང་བཙན་སྒམ་པོ

Chos-rgyal Srong-btsan sGam-po
569–649 C.E.
28 texts, 864 pages

Early in the seventh century, King Srong-btsan sGam-po, an emanation of Avalokiteśvara, the Bodhisattva of Great Compassion, resolved to create the conditions for the pure transmission of the Dharma to Tibet. During his reign the Tibetan principalities were unified, and the kingdom became an influential force in Central Asia, expanding in all directions. To develop political stability and to bring the blessings and influence of the Dharma directly into his court, Srong-btsan sGam-po married two Buddhist princesses, who are considered emanations of Green and White Tārā. Bṛkuṭī or Khri-btsun was the daughter of the Nepalese King Aṁśuvarman (r. 576–621), while Kong-jo was the relative of the second T'ang Emperor T'ai-tsung (r. 627–649).

The princesses brought with them revered statues, the Jo-bo Chen-po, for which the temple of Ra-mo-che in lHa-sa was built, and the Jo-bo Chung-ba, or little Jo-bo, for which the temple of gTsug-lag-khang was built. Altogether, the king built more than one hundred temples throughout his empire. At locations carefully chosen to help control forces hostile to the Dharma, he erected twelve land-taming temples that were envisioned as pinning down a demoness: sKa-tshal and Khra-'brug on her shoulders; gTsang Gram and Gram-pa rGyangs on her legs; Kong-po Bu-chu and lHo-brag Khom-mthing on her elbows; sKa-brag and Bra-dum-rtse on her knees; Rlung-gnod and Klong-thang sGrol-ma on her hands; and Byams-sprin and sPa-ro sKyer-chu on her feet.

Having sent his minister Thon-mi Sambhoṭa to India to devise a script for Tibetan, the king was now able to inaugurate the keeping of official records and to devise a written code of

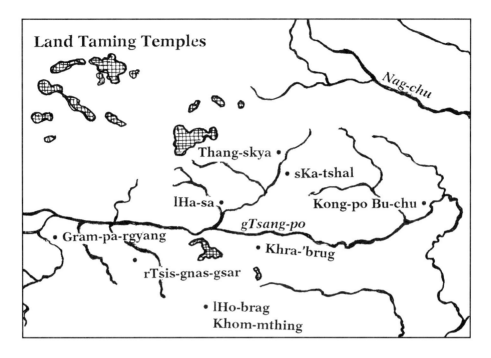

**Land Taming Temples**

Nag-chu

Thang-skya •

• sKa-tshal

lHa-sa •

Kong-po Bu-chu •

gTsang-po

• Gram-pa-rgyang

• Khra-'brug

rTsis-gnas-gsar

• lHo-brag
Khom-mthing

laws. The king himself created the six codices of the constitution, including a code of ethics based on Dharma principles known as the Sixteen Pure Guidelines. He wrote a number of texts in the new Tibetan script, the most famous of which is the Maṇi-bka'-'bum, considered the first indigenous Tibetan treatise on the Dharma. It contains instructions on meditation, prayers, and visualizations, as well as historical and cultural narratives. Several copies of this text were hidden to assure their preservation; copies were found in later centuries, one in a pillar of the Jo-khang temple.

The king and Thon-mi Sambhoṭa taught eighty individuals the essentials of the Dharma, especially focusing on practices relating to Avalokiteśvara. When Srong-btsan sGam-po died, he left a prediction that in another five generations a king would appear who would build a great mansion of the Dharma upon the foundations he had so carefully prepared. The works of this king and his minister are preserved in Great Treasures of Ancient Teachings.

ཆོས་བློན་ཆེན་པོ་ཐོན་མི་སཾ་བྷོ་ཊ

Chos-blon Chen-po Thonmi Sambhoṭa
7th century C.E.
2 texts, 2 pages

State minister of the Dharma King Srong-btsan sGam-po, Thon-mi Sambhoṭa was known as the first learned scholar in the Land of Snow. He was a courageous and brilliant advisor to the king, who entrusted him single-handedly with the task of forming a Tibetan system of writing suitable for translating the Buddhist scriptures into Tibetan. The king dispatched him to India to study Sanskrit and to learn different scripts. On his return, Thon-mi composed eight treatises on Tibetan grammar and spelling, setting forth rules and giving examples. Two extant texts together with later commentaries provide the foundation for Tibetan language studies.

Working together with the king and several other translators, Thon-mi began translating the texts that had appeared in Tibet during lHa Tho-tho-ri's reign. The most important was the dPang-skong-phyag-brgya-pa, a text on offering and confession, which has been preserved in the Tibetan Canon. Thon-mi also translated from the Sanskrit the Sūtra of Golden Light and several texts on Avalokiteśvara, and wrote and translated other texts as well. He himself became a practitioner of the Avalokiteśvara teachings and with the king, quietly taught eighty others who became the first Dharma practitioners in Tibet. The two surviving grammar texts composed by this master are preserved in Great Treasures of Ancient Teachings.

# བོད་ཆོས་རྒྱལ་ཁྲི་སྲོང་ལྡེའུ་བཙན།

## Dharma King Khri-srong lDe'u-btsan
### 742–797 C.E.
### 1 text, 17 pages

As predicted in the Mañjuśrīmūlatantra, four generations after Srong-btsan sGam-po, King Khri-srong lDe'u-btsan was born as the son of Khri-lde gTsug-btsan and Kim-sheng, his Chinese queen. Ascending the throne in 756 C.E. at age thirteen, he ruled in the traditional manner until the age of seventeen, at which time the holy lineage within him awakened, and he conceived of the wish to build a great temple. The young king invited to Tibet the Abbot Śāntarakṣita, who attempted to lay the foundation but was unable to tame the land. The Abbot urged the king to invite Guru Padma.

Fulfilling the ancient vow, Guru Padma arrived in Tibet in 762 C.E when the king was twenty. Once the Great Guru vanquished inner obstacles, Mi-'gyur lHun-gyi Grub-pa'i gTsug-lha-khang, Inconceivable Unchanging Perfect Creation, the Temple of bSam-yas, was successfully founded by the renowned trio of the Abbot, the Guru, and the King (mKhan-slob-chos-gsum) in 762 or 763 and completed and consecrated twelve years later in 775.

Twelve Sarvāstivādin monks from Kashmir were invited to Tibet, and the abbot now ordained the first seven monks. The king dispatched messengers to invite one hundred paṇḍitas and organized the training of hundreds of translators. Together they translated all the major Sūtrayāna teachings of the Buddha and the śāstras of the Mahāpaṇḍitas, as well as the precious Inner Yogas of Mahā, Anu, and Ati. The king sent twelve divisions of the Tibetan army to India to obtain Buddha relics, erected one hundred and eight temples, and encouraged the spread of the teachings of the Enlightened One to all corners of his kingdom.

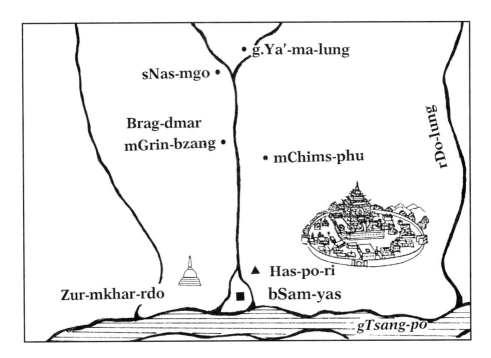

Khri-srong lDe'u-btsan received the transmission of the Sūtras and śāstras from Abbot Śāntarakṣita, while Vimalamitra and Padmasambhava offered him the precious teachings of the Inner Yogas of the Mantrayāna. Padmasambhava bestowed upon him the eight heruka sādhanas, practices of the three roots (guru, deva, ḍākinī), and the three essential cycles of guru sādhanas, rDzogs-chen teachings, and Avalokiteśvara practices (Bla-rdzogs-thugs-gsum).

At bSam-yas mChims-phu in Brag-dmar Ke'u-tshang Cavern, the Great Guru Padmasambhava opened the mandala of the bKa'-brgyad-bde-gshegs-'dus-pa. As the king's flower fell upon the center of the mandala, the Guru initiated him into the Che-mchog heruka sādhanas, which he mastered to perfection. Khri-srong lDe'u-btsan composed numerous texts on fundamental Dharma teachings, one of which is preserved in Great Treasures of Ancient Teachings.

Thus the deeply compassionate Mañjuśrī, playing the role of King Khri-srong lDe'u-btsan, Lord of Men, enacted deeds of wisdom in the kingdom of Tibet. Out of unparalleled kindness, the king took birth time and again: His Body incarnation was Nyang-ral Nyi-ma 'Od-zer; his Speech incarnation was Guru Chos-dbang; his Heart incarnation was Paṇ-chen Padma dBang-rgyal; his Qualities incarnations were mDo-sngags Gling-pa mKhyen-brtse'i dBang-phyug and bKra-shis sTobs-rgyal; and his Action incarnation was rGyal-dbang lNga-pa rDo-rje Thogs-med, the Fifth Dalai Lama.

གུ་ནེ་བཙད་པོ་མུ་རུམ་བཙད་པོ་སད་ན་ལེགས་

རྒྱལ་སྲས་ལྷ་རྗེ་དང་ལྔ་ལྔག་པདྨ་གསལ་

The Tibetan Princes and Princesses
Mu-ne, Mu-rum, Sad-na-legs,
rGyal-sras lHa-rje, and Padma gSal
8th century C.E.

According to various well-known accounts, King Khri-srong lDe'u-btsan had three sons. The eldest was Mu-khri bTsad-po or Mu-ne bTsan-po; the middle son was Mu-rum bTsad-po or lHa-sras Dam-'dzin Rol-pa Ye-shes-rtsal; and the youngest was Mu-tig bTsad-po or Sad-na-legs mJing-yon. All three were Heart Sons of the Great Guru, deeply devoted to Padmasambhava, who had been their spiritual master since the princes' early childhood.

Blessed by the Oḍḍiyāna Guru, these princes were later able to return to Tibet to protect the Dharma. Mu-ne's later incarnations included 'Bri-gung Chos-rgyal Rin-chen Phun-tshogs and Yongs-dge Mi-'gyur rDo-rje. lHa-sras incarnated again and again, retaining both yogic knowledge and power, as gTer-chen Sangs-rgyas Gling-pa, lHa-btsun sNgon-mo, Zhig-po Gling-pa, mChog-gyur Gling-pa, and many others.

Mu-tig Sad-na-legs' incarnations included Guru Jo-tshe and others; Mu-tig's son was the renowned Dharma King Ral-pa-can, who protected both kingdom and religion. This king revised the language of translation, built the temple of 'U-shang-rdo, and spread the holy teachings widely in Tibet.

The son of Sad-na-legs was rGyal-sras lHa-rje, the very next incarnation of King Khri-srong lDe'u-btsan, who passed away in 797 C.E. Relying on the amazing compassion of Guru Padma, lHa-rje incarnated thirteen times. He returned as Sangs-rgyas Bla-ma, rGya Lo-tsā-ba rDo-rje bzang-po, Mang-yul Nyi-ma Seng-ge, O-rgyan Gling-pa, Chos-rje Gling-pa, Gar-dbang 'Chi-med rDo-rje, 'Jigs-med Gling-pa, and mNga'-bdag rJe Bla-ma Padma 'Od-gsal mDo-sngags Gling-pa ('Jam-dbyangs mKhyen-brtse).

King Khri-srong lDe'u-btsan's young daughter, lHa-lcam Padma gSal, played a crucial role in the transmission of the sNying-thig teachings. When she passed away at the age of eight, her father was desolate and begged Padmasambhava to bring her back to life. The Great Guru did revive the child and then blessed her with the highest instructions of the mKha'-'gro-snying-thig. Empowered by Padmasambhava to bring forth this doctrine in later rebirths, Padma gSal returned to Tibet as Padma Las-'brel-rtsal, Kun-mkhyen Klong-chen-pa, and Padma Gling-pa.

# མཁའ་འགྲོའི་རྗེ་མོ་ཡེ་ཤེས་མཚོ་རྒྱལ

## mKha'-'gro'i rJe-mo Ye-shes mTsho-rgyal
### 8th–9th century C.E.

Born in sGrags as the daughter of dPal-gyi dBang-phyug of the mKhar-chen clan and gNubs-mo dGe-ba-mtsho, Ye-shes mTsho-rgyal was an incarnation of Vajravārāhī. After her birth the little lake on the family estate grew larger; because of this auspicious event, she was named mTsho-rgyal (The Lake Conquers). Even as a child, she desired a religious life. When her beauty led to strife among powerful suitors, King Khri-srong lDe'u-btsan married her in order to restore peace in his kingdom. At the royal court she met the Guru Padmasambhava and became his disciple. Through her exemplary devotion and utter determination, she attained profound realization. She received the teachings of the Vajra Guru so purely that all his knowledge became hers, as if the water from one vessel were poured into another.

Having received the Vajrakīla teachings from the Great Guru, she practiced and accomplished them in the cave of Ne-ring Seng-ge rDzong in Mon-kha. Her Vajrakīla transmission is known as Phur-pa-jo-mo-lugs, the Noble Lady's Vajrakīla tradition. At gZho Ti-sgro and other places, she received extensive teachings from Guru Padmasambhava, including the mKha'-'gro-snying-thig, and practiced until she reached the heights of accomplishment. She meditated especially at the three Tiger Dens (sTag-tshangs), caves in geomantically powerful locations in Bhutan, Khams, and Nepal.

Ye-shes mTsho-rgyal is said to have remembered every word spoken by the Great Guru. Out of kindness for generations to come, she wrote down all of his teachings, including his biographies such as the Padma Thang-yig (*The Life and Liberation of Padmasambhava*, Dharma Publishing, 1978). Many teachings were concealed by her and by the Great Guru as treasures intended for later recovery.

After Padmasambhava departed from Tibet, the "Mother" Ye-shes mTsho-rgyal remained for two hundred years, guiding hundreds of disciples to realization, and providing stability and continuity for the Sangha. At the end of her life, without abandoning her body, she rejoined the Guru at the Copper-Colored Mountain. Out of inconceivable kindness, she guides the gTer-ma transmission, manifesting to the great gTer-stons and empowering their search for the concealed teachings. Her later incarnations include the women masters Jo-mo sMan-mo and mKha'-'gro-ma Kun-dga'-'bum.

Lo-tsā-chen-po Vairotsana
8th–9th century C.E.
2 texts, 14 pages

Born as the son of Pa-gor rDo-rje rGyal-po and the Lady Bran-ka sGron-skyid, Lo-chen Vairotsana was Tibet's first Knowledge Holder. Some sources say he was born in sNye-mo Bye-mkhar near 'U-yug in central Tibet, while others say his birthplace was in Nyang. Ordained as one of the first seven monks by the Abbot Śāntarakṣita, he is also known as Vairotsanarakṣita, sNam-par sNang-mdzad Srung-ba.

Skilled in hundreds of dialects and languages, he was sent by the Tibetan king to India, where he sought out the finest masters. He then traveled to Khotan, China, Nepal, Zhang-zhung, and other lands, receiving teachings from twenty-five masters. His root teacher was Śrī Siṁha, who bestowed the Atiyoga teachings upon him; dGa'-rab rDo-rje became his master as well, teaching him in visions.

Returning to Tibet, Vairotsana followed the instructions of Śrī Siṁha, teaching philosophy to the court during the day and Atiyoga privately to the king at night. Jealous of his close relationship with the king, a queen and several court ministers cast aspersions on Vairotsana's teachings. These accusations led to Vairotsana's exile to rGyal-mo-rong. There Vairotsana met gYu-sgra sNying-po, who became his close disciple, and the Buddha's teachings began to spread in eastern Tibet.

In the meantime, Vimalamitra had arrived in the Land of Snow, and the king found to his amazement that Vimalamitra taught doctrines very similar to those of Vairotsana. Convinced by Vimalamitra that these teachings had great value, the king invited Vairotsana to return and to resume teaching and translating. Padmasambhava granted him Mahāyoga heruka teachings and instructed him to practice at gYa'-ma-lung.

One of the three closest disciples of Padmasambhava (rje-'bangs-grogs) together with the king and the lady Ye-shes mTsho-rgyal, Vairotsana is hailed as the foremost translator of Dharma texts in Tibetan history, and his skills are recognized by all schools of Tibetan Buddhism.

He was the principal transmitter of the Sems-sde and Klong-sde divisions of Atiyoga, and the translator of five major Sems-sde texts. This lineage flowed to five disciples: gYu-sgra sNying-po, who practiced in a meditation retreat at rGyal-mo-rong; gSang-ston Ye-shes Bla-ma, who resided in the hermitage of sTag-rtse-mkhar; Pang-gen Sangs-rgyas mGon-po, who practiced at the settlement of Brag-dmar-rdzong; gNyags Jñānakumāra; and the Khotanese lady Shes-rab sGron-ma, who invited Vairotsana to visit Khotan.

After a long life of service to the Dharma, Vairotsana passed away in Nepal's Bha-sing Forest. Three major lineages developed from his teachings: one through gNyags Jñānākumāra and Sog-po dPal-gyi Ye-shes, a second through Sog-po dPal-gyi Seng-ge and gNubs-chen Sangs-rgyas Ye-shes, and a third through rTsangs Śāk-dor and sPang Rakṣita, which was received by sGro-sbug-pa.

In succeeding centuries, Vairotsana returned to Tibet as gTer-chen rDo-rje Gling-pa, Kun-skyong Gling-pa, mChog-ldan mDo-sngags Gling-pa, Phreng-po Shes-rab 'Od-zer, Rig-'dzin gTer-bdag Gling-pa, Rong-ston bDe-chen Gling-pa, and Kong-sprul Blo-gros mTha'-yas. Vairotsana translated many of Śrī Siṃha's texts and other Mantrayāna works, as well as Sūtras, including parts of the 100,000-line Prajñāpāramitā. The exact number of his translations cannot now be determined because later translators did not always preserve the names of the original translators. Several of his treatises are preserved in Great Treasures of Ancient Teachings.

སྔགས་པའི་རྒྱལ་པོ་གནུབས་ཆེན་སངས་རྒྱས་ཡེ་ཤེས

sNgags-pa'i rGyal-po gNubs-chen Sangs-rgyas Ye-shes
785–896 C.E.
4 texts, 467 pages, Rin-chen gTer-mdzod: 17 texts

Proclaimed in the Sūtras to be a Bodhisattva of the fourth stage, gNubs-chen Sangs-rgyas Ye-shes was the great charioteer through whom the entire transmission of the Inner Yogas flowed to future generations. He was born in lower sGrags at gNubs-rong-yul as the son of gSal-ba dBang-phyug and mChims-mo bKra-shis-mtsho when King Khri-srong lDe'u-btsan was forty-two. Over the course of his long life, he was known by three names: rDo-rje Khri-gtsug, rDo-rje Yang-dbang-gter, and Sangs-rgyas Ye-shes.

At age seven, Sangs-rgyas Ye-shes entered the Dharma and soon after began to receive empowerments and teachings from Guru Padmasambhava and Vimalamitra. In his youth, Padmasambhava bestowed upon him the Vajrakīla and

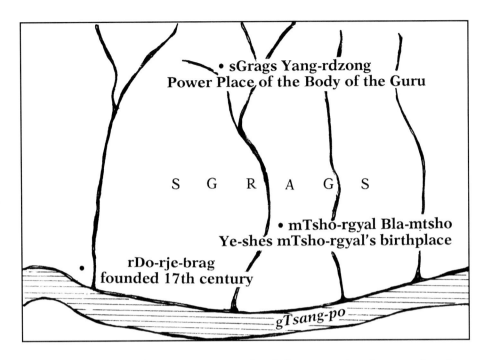

• sGrags Yang-rdzong
Power Place of the Body of the Guru

S   G   R   A   G   S

• mTsho-rgyal Bla-mtsho
Ye-shes mTsho-rgyal's birthplace

rDo-rje-brag
founded 17th century

gTsang-po

Yamāntaka heruka practices, which he practiced to perfection at sGrags Yang-rdzong, the powerful holy place associated with the Enlightened Body of the Guru.

Seven times he traveled to India, Nepal, and Bru-sha, where he received teachings from Śrī Siṁha, Paṇ-chen Vimalamitra, Kamalaśīla, Khrag-'thung Nag-po, Dhanadhala, Śāntigarbha, Dhanasaṁskṛta, and Śākyadeva. Master of the Mahāyoga, Anuyoga, and Atiyoga, gNubs-chen in particular brought the Anuyoga lineages to Tibet, having obtained them from Vasudhara in Nepal, from Prakāsālaṁkāra in Vārāṇasī, and from Dhanarakṣita, Dharmabodhi, and Dharmarāja and Che-btsan-skyes in Bru-sha. He achieved great levels of realization and attained wondrous powers such as clairvoyance, passing through rock, and walking on water.

In Tibet, he resided at sGrags Yang-rdzong, where he received teachings from gNyags and his disciple Sog-po dPal-gyi Ye-shes, and from Zhang rGyal-ba'i Yon-tan, the disciple of rMa Rin-chen-mchog and gNyags Jñānakumāra. Unable to bear the suppression of the Buddha's teaching during the reign of Glang Dar-ma, gNubs-chen, who was then in his sixties, deliberately terrified the king with his yogic powers until Glang Dar-ma promised not to harm or obstruct the White Sangha.

gNubs-chen Sangs-rgyas Ye-shes preserved and passed on the major transmission lineages of the Inner Tantras to five disciples: sPa-gor Blon-chen 'Phags-pa received the root teachings, Bru Legs-pa'i-sgron-ma the leaves, Ngan Yon-tan-mchog received the flowers, and So Ye-shes dBang-phyug the fruit. Yon-tan rGya-mtsho received the entire tree. From these disciples the lineages passed to Zur-po-che and flowed in an unbroken stream down to the present day.

Master of time, gNubs lived one hundred and twelve years or perhaps one hundred and thirty until the reign of dPal-'khor (r. 906–924). This Bodhisattva passed from the world in radiant light, but returned to Tibet in succeeding centuries as Dum rGya Zhang-khrom, the gTer-stons gTsug-lhag dPal-dge and rGya-ston Seng-ge Dar, O-rgyan Dri-med Kun-dga', rTsa-gsum gTer-bdag Gling-pa, gSang-bdag Phrin-las lHun-grub, and other bKa'-ma and gTer-ma masters.

gNubs-chen Sangs-rgyas Ye-shes translated a large number of Tantras and authored a famous commentary on the root Tantra of the Anuyoga, which was transmitted in an extraordinary way to the nineteenth-century master Kaḥ-thog Si-tu. He composed a treatise on the Atiyoga known as the bSam-gtan-mig-gi-sgron-me, as well as a Mahāyoga commentary. Great Treasures of Ancient Teachings contains four of his works and numerous texts in the Rin-chen gTer-mdzod.

# དན་ལམ་རྒྱལ་བ་མཆོག་དབྱངས་

## Ngan-lam rGyal-ba mChog-dbyangs
### 8th–9th century C.E.

Near 'Phan-yul north of lHa-sa, rGyal-ba mChog-dbyangs was born into the clan of Ngan-lam. Among the first seven monks ordained by Abbot Śāntarakṣita, he was known as one of the nine excellent leaders of Tibet. Working with the Great Guru Padmasambhava, he translated Avalokiteśvara sādhanas preserved in the bsTan-'gyur.

Initiated by Guru Padmasambhava into the heruka sādhana of Hayagrīva, rGyal-ba mChog-dbyangs meditated at the sacred site of mChims-phu. He became so accomplished that during his practice, the head of a horse appeared upon his own head and the sound of neighing filled the Three Realms, summoning beings to the Dharma. Mounting the horse of non-action, he cut through all karmic bonds. Perfectly comprehending the inseparability of form and formlessness, he radiated light and even fire from his body.

He served King Khri-srong lDe'u-bstan throughout his reign and supported the Dharma activity of Kings Sad-na-legs and Ral-pa-can. Master of time, he lived for many generations until the days of King dPal-'khor (r. 906–924), whom he cured of illness. To disseminate and protect the rNying-ma teachings, he returned to Tibet in succeeding centuries as gTer-ston rGya-ston Padma dBang-phyug, Guru Tshe-brtan rGyal-mtshan, bDud-'dul Gling-pa, Dri-med Gling-pa, and the renowned Karma Pakṣi.

དགེ་སློང་ནམ་མཁའི་སྙིང་པོ

dGe-slong Nam-mkha'i sNying-po
8th–9th century C.E.
2 texts, 14 pages

Nam-mkha'i sNying-po was born into the clan of gNubs in Lower gNyal at Nyang dKar-mda' Sham-bu. Renowned as a scholar, siddha, and translator, he became one of the most important early masters. On the order of King Khri-srong lDe'u-btsan, as a youth he traveled to India with a hundred other young men, and there learned the art of translation and studied the Dharma with Indian masters. Upon his return, he was ordained by the Abbot Śāntarakṣita.

Together with Vairotsana and several others, he journeyed a second time to India. While Vairotsana studied with Śrī Siṃha, Nam-mkha'i sNying-po became the disciple of the great siddha Hūṃkāra. Under Hūṃkāra's direction, he mastered the Yang-dag heruka practices, achieving the heights of wisdom and depths of courage.

Returning to Tibet, Nam-mkha'i sNying-po and the other disciples of the Dharma met with slander and intrigues stirred up by factions opposed to the king's new religion. Fortunately, when Nam-mkha'i sNying-po cured his sovereign of an illness and reassured him of the truth and power of the Vajrayāna teachings, the king offered him protection. Though the ministers were demanding Nam-mkha'i sNying-po's death, the king sent him into exile at lHo-brag mKhar-chu. This was the very land that Padmasambhava had recommended for Nam-mkha'i sNying-po's retreat, after having empowered him in the heruka sādhana practice of Yang-dag-thugs.

Nam-mkha'i sNying-po became so accomplished that he could ride the rays of the sun across the sky. Pebbles blessed by this miracle-worker yielded fruit and flowers when planted. He could turn rocks into turquoise and leave hand-prints in the rocky cliffs as signs of his accomplishments.

An outstanding lo-tsā-ba who was ranked with Vairotsana, he collaborated with sKa-ba dPal-brtsegs to prepare the lDan-dkar-ma dKar-chag, a catalogue of the texts translated during the reign of Khri-srong lDe'u-btsan. This catalogue is preserved in the Nyingma Edition of the bKa'-'gyur and bsTan-'gyur. Two rare biographies of this master are preserved in the Great Treasures of Ancient Teachings.

Assisting Guru Padma and the Lady Ye-shes mTsho-rgyal, Nam-mkha'i sNying-po concealed treasures for future generations. Together with rGyal-ba Byang-chub and other disciples of the Great Guru, he wrote down and concealed the biography of Ye-shes mTsho-rgyal (*Mother of Knowledge*, Dharma Publishing, 1983). He was a Vidyādhara of the Mahāmudrā, who departed this life flying up into the sky without abandoning his body. For the sake of Tibet, he returned as the gTer-ston Mang-po Byang-chub Gling-pa and as Kaḥ-thog Rig-'dzin Tshe-dbang Nor-bu.

 སྙགས་པའི་རྒྱལ་པོ་གཅུགས་ལ་ཡེ་ཤེས་གཞོན་ནུ

### gNyags Ye-shes gZhon-nu Jñānakumāra
### 8th–9th century C.E.

Among Padmasambhava's twelve closest disciples was gNyags Jñānakumāra, through whom the Inner Yoga flowed to gNubs-chen and thus to future generations. He was born in 'Phyos at Yar-lung, the son of sTag-sgra lHa-snang of the gNyags clan and Sru-bza' mGon-skyid. At birth his neck was marked with a double rdo-rje, which inspired his parents to name him Intelligence of Buddha, rGyal-ba'i Blo-gros.

Ordained by Śāntarakṣita, Ye-shes gZhon-nu received one of the eight heruka sādhanas from Padmasambhava and then practiced at Yar-lung Shel-brag, the sacred power place connected with the Guru's Enlightened Qualities. Once at Yer-pa, he took the form of a crow and landed in the meditation cave of rGyal-ba mChog-dbyangs, who recognized him and warmly welcomed him. Even today that cave is famous as Crow Fortress (Bya-rog-rdzong). An expert in both Vajramṛta practices and the Vajrakīla practices that he had received from Vimalamitra, he could cause water to flow from rocks. His lineage of Vajrakīla practices was known as gNyags-lugs-phur-pa.

A key link in the Mahāyoga transmission, gNyags received Padmasambhava's teachings and the Great Guru's famous commentary, the Man-ngag-lta-ba'i-phreng-ba. He assisted Vimalamitra in translating the Guhyamūlagarbha Tantra, the root text of the Mahāyoga, the lineage of which he received from this great master. Through gNyags the Sems-sde and Klongs-sde Atiyoga teachings flowed to master Sog-po dPal-gyi Ye-shes and 'O-bran dPal-gyi Zhon-nu, both of whom taught gNubs-chen Sangs-rgyas Ye-shes.

Having received teachings from Guru Padmasambhava, Vimalamitra, Vairotsana, and gYu-sgra sNying-po, Jñāna-kumāra held all the major Vidyādhara lineages of the Three Inner Yogas and all four streams of instructions: the textual explanations, the Hearing lineage, the blessings and empowerments, and the rites and practices. Thus it is said that the rNying-ma teachings descended first to gNyags, then to gNubs, and finally to Zur.

Altogether, gNyags Jñānakumāra had eight glorious disciples: dPal-gyi Ye-shes, O-'bran dPal-gyi gZhon-nu, gNyan-chen dPal-dbyangs, Thag-bzang dPal-gyi rDo-rje, Lam-mchog dPal-gyi rDo-rje, Dar-rje dPal-gyi Grags-pa, Dra dPal-gyi sNying-po, and lHa-lung dPal-gyi rDo-rje.

A brilliant translator as well as siddha and scholar, he translated both Sūtras and Tantras. Twenty of his translations are preserved in the bKa'-'gyur and bsTan-'gyur and one in the rNying-ma rGyud-'bum. In later centuries the compassionate gNyags Jñānakumāra returned to Tibet as the gTer-ma masters Ra-mo Shel-sman and Byar-rong E-yi sMan-pa.

## 'Brog-mi dPal-gyi Ye-shes
### 8th–9th century C.E.

Born at Yar-'brog-sgang in the clan of 'Brog-mi, dPal-gyi Ye-shes was initiated into the Tantras by the Great Guru. As he mastered the Ma-mo practices among the heruka teachings, the female spirits became his servants and assistants. He practiced at Yar-lha Sham-po, the peak rising at the southern end of the Yar-lung valley, the residence of one of Tibet's four most powerful mountain gods. There he achieved the level of Vidyādhara, whereupon he taught many disciples and trained translators who sought him out.

Working with Buddhaguhya, 'Brog-mi dPal-gyi Ye-shes translated Mahāyoga teachings such as the Sangs-rgyas mNyams-sbyor and the Ma-mo cycles, which are included in Great Treasures of Ancient Teachings. His famous incarnations include Ra-shag Chos-'bar and three embodiments of bDe-chen Gling-pa.

རྣས་དཔལ་གྱི་སེངྒེ

Rlangs dPal-gyi Seng-ge
8th–9th century C.E.

Born into the divine clan of Rlangs, dPal-gyi Seng-ge was the  son of A-mnyes Byang-chub 'Dre-khol. His father was a disciple of Guru Padmasambhava and an accomplished sub-duer of demons who had spent years in Oḍḍiyāna. His mother was Jo-mo sKal-ldan-ma.

Possessed of amazing magical powers, dPal-gyi Seng-ge was one of the Heart Sons of Padmasambhava, who initiated him into the heruka practices of 'Jig-rten-mchod-bstod. He resided at sTag-tshang Tiger Den in sPa-ro in the land of Bhutan, where he tamed wild spirits that became his servants. He taught the Dharma to all and obtained the two kinds of sid-dhis (yogic powers and ultimate realization). From his family clan arose the renowned Phag-mo-gru rulers. Out of compas-sion for the people of Tibet, dPal-gyi Seng-ge reincarnated as Rwa-ston sTobs-ldan rDo-rje in a later century.

སྣ་ནམ་རྡོ་རྗེ་བདུད་འཇོམས

sNa-nam rDo-rje bDud-'joms
8th–9th century C.E.

Born at gTsang-rong in the family of King Khri-srong lDe'u-bstan's state minister (Zhang-blon) sNa-nam, rDo-rje bDud-'joms became a state minister of religious affairs (Chos-blon) at a young age. One of the delegation dispatched by the king to invite Padmasambhava to Tibet, he entered the gate of the Mantrayāna due to the kindness of the Great Guru.

Initiated by Guru Padma into Tantric practices, he practiced especially at Rong-gi Brag-dmar near Yar-'brog lake. He became master of mind and breath, skilled in the Vajrakīla sādhanas. This yogin penetrated to ultimate realization, ornamented by such accomplishments as the ability to pass through solid rock and travel to other lands in a split second.

Working for both bKa'-ma and gTer-ma traditions, rDo-rje bDud-'joms assisted the Great Guru in concealing the gTer-ma treasures for future generations. Through him, the instructions of Padmasambhava flowed in an unbroken stream to mKharchen dPal-gyi dBang-phyug, descending to Rong-zom Mahāpaṇḍita's father, and thus to the great Rong-zom. Another stream flowed through Bal-po A-hūṁ and others. His reincarnation lineage includes Rig-'dzin rGod-ldem, one of the three most outstanding gTer-ma masters of Tibet, and the succeeding incarnations in this stream such as Legs-ldan mGon-po, Ngag-gi dBang-po, and Padma Phrin-las.

 སློབ་དཔོན་ཡེ་ཤེས་དབྱངས།

## Slob-dpon Ye-shes-dbyangs
### 8th–9th century C.E.

Born into the clan of sBa, Ye-shes-dbyangs was also known as Ācārya Ye-shes or simply Ācārya, and renowned for his clarity and precise expression. He was one of eight disciples who assisted the Great Guru in preparing the written manuscripts for the gTer-ma treasures. Ye-shes-dbyangs' awareness extended beyond space and time; within this expanse of non-thought, he could travel to the realms of the ḍākinīs and comprehend the secret codes of the gTer-ma. He lived as befitted one who held the Triple Vajra Saṁvara vows.

With the guidance of Padmasambhava, he concealed the gTer-ma treasures in specially selected locations on rocky mountainsides, in pools of water, hidden caves, and even in the sky. At the end of his life, he simply rose up into the sky and disappeared from view. Out of great kindness to living beings, he returned to Tibet at a later time as the gTer-ma master Kunbzang bDe-chen rDo-rje.

## གྲུབ་ཆེན་སོག་པོ་ལྷ་དཔལ་

Grub-chen Sog-po lHa-dpal
8th–9th century C.E.

The layman and siddha, lHa-dpal the Sogdian, was born in Yar-'brog. A blacksmith by trade, he was recognized as a potential siddha by gNyags Jñānakumāra, who trained him in the Outer Tantras and then in the Inner Tantras. Possessing great faith in his teacher, lHa-dpal offered him all he owned—his smithy tools—and took up the practice of Vajrakīla, completely purifying his mind and developing extraordinary powers and courage.

Able to seize savage beasts by the neck and crush the attacks of ordinary men, Sog-po lHa-dpal risked his life for his master gNyags. On three occasions he protected gNyags from mortal danger, once even breaking him out of prison. lHa-dpal became one of gNyags' eight glorious experts of the Vajrakīla practices and his most distinguished disciple. It was through Sog-po lHa-dpal that the Inner Yoga transmission of gNyags Jñānakumāra flowed to the great gNubs-chen Sangs-rgyas Ye-shes and forward to future generations.

sNa-nam Ye-shes-sde
8th–9th century C.E.
3 texts, 25 pages

Zhang Ye-shes-sde, also known as the Lo-tsā-ba Jñānasena, was born into the clan of sNa-nam. He possessed both the knowledge of an outstanding scholar and the abilities of an accomplished siddha. One of the four greatest rNying-ma translators of all time, he ranked with Lo-tsā-bas Vairotsana, Cog-ro Klu'i-rgyal-mtshan, and sKa-ba dPal-brtsegs. A siddha who had cut through all illusory appearances, Ye-shes-sde was able to liberate body, speech, and mind and could fly like a bird in the expanse of the sky.

Holder of the Triple Vajra Saṁvara vows, he became a disciple of the Great Guru, who bestowed the Vajrakīla teachings upon him. This teaching lineage later became known as the sNa-nam Phur-pa tradition.

Working with the Kashmiri paṇḍitas Jinamitra, Dānaśīla, Surendrabodhi, Munivarman, Prajñākaravarman, and Śīlendrabodhi, he helped translate over three hundred texts preserved in the bKa'-'gyur and bsTan-'gyur. Expert in all fields of Buddhist thought, he could translate Sūtra works of Prajñāpāramitā, Avataṁsaka, and Ratnakūṭa, śāstras on logic, Cittamātra, and Yogācāra, as well as Tantras. Playing a key role in the transmission of the Abhidharma and the Prajñāpāramitā, Ye-she-sde passed these teachings on to lHa-lung dPal-gyi rDo-rje, Zla-ba rDo-rje, and dBas rGyal-ba Ye-shes. It was sBas who preserved the lineage of the Abhidharmasamuccaya in Khams during the brief but destructive reign of Glang Dar-ma.

Appointed to the committee led by sKa-ba dPal-brtsegs to standardize translation terms, sNa-nam Ye-shes-sde assisted in the revision of the literary language. Later compilers of the

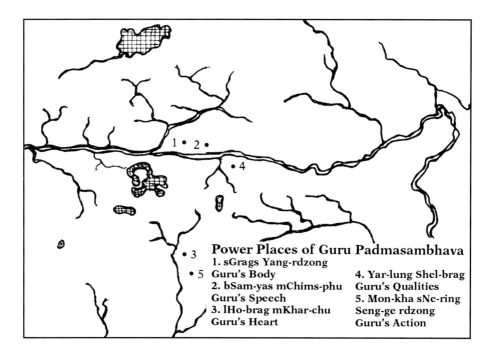

**Power Places of Guru Padmasambhava**
1. sGrags Yang-rdzong
   Guru's Body
2. bSam-yas mChims-phu
   Guru's Speech
3. lHo-brag mKhar-chu
   Guru's Heart
4. Yar-lung Shel-brag
   Guru's Qualities
5. Mon-kha sNe-ring
   Seng-ge rdzong
   Guru's Action

Tibetan Canon honored Ye-shes-sde by including three of his compositions in the bsTan-'gyur. These three works are also preserved in Great Treasures of Ancient Teachings.

 མཁར་ཆེན་དཔལ་གྱི་དབང་ཕྱུག

## mKhar-chen dPal-gyi dBang-phyug
### 8th–9th century C.E.

Brother of Lady Ye-shes mTsho-rgyal, dPal-gyi dBang-phyug often accompanied his sister and Guru Padma in their travels through Tibet. He became one of the Great Guru's Heart Sons, deeply imbued with the teachings. Living as a lay Mantrayāna master, he truly manifested as a "Powerful Lord" (dbang-phyug) whose actions were possessed of magical force. An accomplished expert in the Vajrakīla practices, he could subdue illusion with the blade of discriminating awareness and defeat enemies by simply brandishing his dagger. He held the Vajrakīla lineage that had passed through his sister, Ye-shes mTsho-rgyal, and disseminated the teachings widely.

The stream of Padmasambhava's instructions that passed through sNa-nam rDo-rje bDud-'joms came to dPal-gyi dBang-phyug, who in turn transmitted them to Dom Atsara dPal-me-tog, from whom they eventually descended to Rong-zom Mahāpaṇḍita. In later centuries, this Mantrayāna master returned to Tibet as the gTer-ston Matiratna.

ཡོ་ཆེན་ལྡན་མ་གཙེ་མང་

Lo-chen lDan-ma rTse-mang
8th–9th century C.E.

Born in lDan-ma in Khams, lDan-ma rTse-mang became an accomplished expert in calligraphy, creating elegant scripts and types of annotation that remained in use even in the nineteenth century. With these skills he assisted the Great Guru in preparing the manuscripts of the gTer-ma texts.

As a translator, he was ranked among the Three Major and Three Minor Lo-tsā-bas and was especially skilled in deciphering and translating the commentarial notes appended to the texts. Many texts written in his handwriting survive today. Among them are the bKa'-brgyad bDe-gshegs-'dus-pa teachings that lDan-ma had copied for King Khri-srong lDe'u-btsan. Hidden as a gTer-ma at lHo-brag sMra-bo-cog, these works were recovered by Nyang-ral Nyi-ma 'Od-zer.

lDan-ma rTse-mang received abundant Mantrayāna teachings from the Great Guru, all of which he remembered perfectly by virtue of his power of complete retention. He practiced in the valley behind bSam-yas at gYa'-ma-lung, in one of the eight most sacred and powerful meditation caves blessed by Padmasambhava. Here Ye-shes mTsho-rgyal received her first initiations and Vairotsana went on retreat. Bringing his understanding to fruition, he reached a high level of accomplishment. lDan-ma rTse-mang returned to Tibet in later centuries as the gTer-ston O-rgyan bZang-po.

ༀཆེན་སྐ་བ་དཔལ་བརྩེགས

## Lo-chen sKa-ba dPal-brtsegs Rakṣita
### 8th–9th century C.E.
### 5 texts, 110 pages

Recognized by Guru Padmasambhava as the reincarnation of an Indian Mahāpaṇḍita, sKa-ba dPal-brtsegs took birth in Tibet for the purpose of translating the texts of the Dharma. He became one of the four foremost translators of the Ancient School, together with Vairotsana, Cog-ro Klu'i rGyal-mtshan, and Zhang Ye-shes-sde.

Born in dBu-ru 'Phan-yul north of lHa-sa as the son of sKa-ba Blo-ldan and 'Bro-bza' mDzes-ma, dPal-brtsegs was among the first seven monks ordained by Abbot Śāntarakṣita. He became the disciple of the greatest masters in Tibet: Guru Padmasambhava, Vimalamitra, and Vairotsana. Under the guidance of Padmasambhava, dPal-brtsegs' mind was completely freed from obscuration and obstruction, and he obtained yogic powers of clairvoyance. He practiced especially at Brag Yer-pa in the cliffs east of lHa-sa where King Khri-srong lDe'u-btsan had established a Tantric retreat center.

sKa-ba dPal-brtsegs was one of the great calligraphers of the Tibetan language, and his style of writing became popular throughout the land. Translating more than one hundred texts that now appear in twenty-seven divisions of the Tibetan

Canon, dPal-brtsegs worked with the paṇḍitas Jñānagarbha, Vidyākārasiṁha, Vidyākāraprabha, and Jinamitra. Especially learned in Prajñāpāramitā, Madhyamaka, Logic, and Abhidharma, he received the transmission of these teachings from the paṇḍitas with whom he collaborated and passed these lineages to his disciples. His knowledge of Chinese enabled him to translate important texts from this language as well.

Together with Cog-ro Klu'i rGyal-mtshan and rMa Rin-chen-mchog, he traveled to Oḍḍiyāna to invite Vimalamitra to Tibet at the request of King Khri-srong lDe'u-btsan. From Vimalamitra, he received the precious sNying-thig teachings, the heart of the Atiyoga transmission.

Working together with Vimalamitra and Padmasambhava, dPal-brtsegs translated many Tantras that were preserved in the rNying-ma-rgyud-'bum. With Nam-mkha'i sNying-po, he prepared the lDan-dkar-ma dKar-chag, the catalogue of the texts translated during the reign of Khri-srong lDe'u-bstan. Later he headed the committee established by Dharma King Ral-pa-can to standardize translation terminology. He was renowned as a commentator and writer of discourses on the sacred texts. Four of his works are preserved in Great Treasures of Ancient Teachings, while the lDan-dkar-ma dKar-chag is preserved in the bKa'-'gyur and bsTan-'gyur.

Shud-pu dPal-gyi Seng-ge
8th–9th century C.E.

Counted as one of the eight greatest Tibetan scholars, Shud-pu dPal-gyi Seng-ge had formerly been a minister of the interior for the king. Born into the same clan as King Khri-srong lDe'u-btsan, dPal-gyi Seng-ge became knowledgeable in the ancient Tibetan traditions of the Bon, Grung, and lDe'u (shamans, bards, and singers). One of the messengers dispatched by Khri-srong lDe'u-btsan to invite Padmasambhava to the Land of Snow, he learned the art of translation to support the transmission of the Dharma to Tibet. He translated texts relating to gShin-rje, Ma-mo, and phur-pa teachings and many other rNying-ma Tantric works.

dPal-gyi Seng-ge specialized in the practice of Vajrakīla and Ma-mo, which brought him supernormal powers: He was able to separate the waters of a river or make it run backwards with the touch of his phur-pa. On the grounds of bSam-yas, he constructed the White Stupa, which remains to this day. Shud-pu dPal-gyi Seng-ge returned to Tibet on numerous occasions as a Kalyānamitra, a kind spiritual friend working for the liberation of others. He reincarnated as the gTer-ma master Grwa-pa mNgon-shes in the eleventh century and as the renowned gTer-ston gNam-chos Mi-'gyur rDo-rje in later times.

འབྲེ་རྒྱལ་བའི་བློ་གྲོས་

'Bre rGyal-ba'i Blo-gros
8th–9th century C.E.

Formerly a member of King Khri-srong lDe'u-btsan's court known as mGon-po, the Protector, rGyal-ba'i Blo-gros took the religious vows of a Triple Vajra Saṁvara Holder and was trained as a Lo-tsā-ba. Sent to India, he studied numerous teachings with the great siddha Huṁkāra, especially the Yang-dag-chos-skor, and became an accomplished yogin. Granted one of the eight heruka sādhanas by Padmasambhava, he practiced most often at mChims-phu, the sacred place of power associated with the Enlightened Speech of the Guru.

Through his wizardry, he was actually able to rescue his mother and other beings from the hell realms, fending off the denizens of Yama with magical armies. After he had perfected the teachings of Guru Padmasambhava, he gained even more wondrous abilities and was able to turn corpses into gold. According to Guru Padma's instruction, he then deposited these golden treasures in secret places for recovery by gTer-stons of later times. Eventually he obtained even the power of longevity and lived until the days of Rong-zom Mahāpaṇḍita in the eleventh century. There exists an account describing how Rong-zom heard teachings directly from rGyal-ba'i Blo-gros.

 གྲུབ་ཆེན་ཁྱེའུ་ཆུང་ལོ་ཙ།

## Grub-chen Khye'u-chung Lo-tsā
### 8th–9th century C.E.

An incarnation of an Indian paṇḍita, Khye'u-chung was born into the clan of 'Brog-mi. Since he knew the art of translation from a very young age, he was called Khye'u-chung Lo-tsā-ba, "Child Translator." Living as a white-robed layman with long braided hair, Khye'u-chung received all the Tantric teachings from Guru Padmasambhava and achieved both profound realization and yogic powers. He practiced in the wilds of the north at Byang-gi gNam-mtsho lake. By means of magical gestures he was able to attract birds from the sky to hear him preach the Dharma. Out of compassion, he reincarnated in later centuries as the incomparable bDud-'dul rDo-rje, Lord of the Ten Stages of the Bodhisattva Path.

# དྲན་པ་ནམ་མཁའ

Dran-pa Nam-mkha'
8th–9th century C.E.
Rin-chen gTer-mdzod: 1 text

Originally a master of Bon teachings, Dran-pa Nam-mkha' was present at the debate between the Buddhists and the Bon-pos at bSam-yas, after which he became the disciple of Padmasambhava and received the Triple Vajra Saṁvara vows. He offered numerous Bon-po teachings to the Great Guru, who concealed them as gTer-ma.

Guru Padmasambhava granted Dran-pa Nam-mkha' many Tantric teachings and instructed him to practice at Byang-gi gNam-mtsho lake. Reaching a state of realization beyond distinctions, he proclaimed, "There is no need to introduce distinctions into the shining knowledge of the mutual sphere of sentient beings." He became learned in translation and so accomplished in yogic powers that he could stop wild yaks with a gesture of his hand.

In the succeeding centuries, he reincarnated several times as gTer-ma masters, including Rig-'dzin Phrin-las Lhun-grub, who was an incarnation of both Dran-pa Nam-mkha' and gNubs-chen. One Dharma text connected with Bla-chen Dran-pa Nam-mkha' is included in the Rin-chen gTer-mdzod section of Great Treasures of Ancient Teachings.

ཨོ་བྲན་དཔལ་གྱི་དབང་ཕྱུག

'O-bran dPal-gyi dBang-phyug
8th–9th century C.E.

Born in 'U-yug as the son of dPal-gyi 'Byung-gnas, dPal-gyi dBang-phyug became one of the Heart Sons of Guru Padmasambhava. His master granted him teachings on the heruka sādhanas and sent him to practice at Brag Yer-pa. There in the caves in the white cliffs east of lHa-sa, where the Dharma King Srong-btsan sGam-po and the Great Guru Padmasambhava had practiced, dPal-gyi dBang-phyug meditated wholeheartedly. He became very skilled in methods of the Mantrayāna and achieved the signs of yogic acomplishment. Completely fearless in any kind of river or lake, he was able to swim like a fish. A lay practitioner, dPal-gyi dBang-phyug and his descendents preserved many precious bKa'-ma traditions, together with initiations and explanations, in an uninterrupted stream that flowed through nearly fifty generations of rNying-ma masters down to recent times.

ལོ་ཆེན་རྨ་རིན་ཆེན་མཆོག

Lo-chen rMa Rin-chen-mchog
8th–9th century C.E.

One of the nine most excellent Tibetan leaders, rMa Rin-chen-mchog achieved the stage of Vidyādhara and established the major transmission lineage of the Mahāyoga teachings in Tibet. Born in 'Phan-yul north of lHa-sa, Rin-chen-mchog possessed the sharpest intellect in the land. A disciple of both Padmasambhava and Vimalamitra, he was ordained by Śāntarakṣita as one of the first seven Tibetan monks. He completely understood the inner meaning of the teachings of Nāgārjuna, and during the bSam-yas debate, defended Abbot Śāntarakṣita's view of the path to complete enlightenment.

An outstanding translator and practitioner, rMa was chosen by the Tibetan king to travel to Oḍḍiyāna to invite the master Vimalamitra to Tibet. Upon their return, rMa became one of Vimalamitra's closest disciples, assisting him in the translation of the Guhyamūlagarbha Tantra. Vimalamitra gave the main Mahāyoga lineage to both rMa Rin-chen-mchog and gNyags Jñānakumāra.

Assisting Guru Padmasambhava and the Lady Ye-shes mTsho-rgyal, rMa Rin-chen-mchog prepared and concealed various gTer-ma texts. For many years he practiced at mChims-phu, the sacred site associated with the Enlightened Speech of the Guru, where he undertook the discipline of staying alive by transforming rocks and minerals into food.

After the death of Glang Dar-ma, rMa proceeded to Khams where he bestowed the Mahāyoga teachings upon gTsug-ru Rin-chen gZhon-nu and Kye-ra mChog-skyong. These two both taught Dar-rje dPal-gyi Grags-pa and Zhang rGyal-ba'i Yon-tan, who instructed gNubs-chen. This stream of teachings was later known as the Khams-lugs of Mahāyoga.

rMa Rin-chen-mchog is said to have translated an ocean of Sūtra and Tantra. Some of his translations are preserved in the rNying-ma-rgyud-'bum and fifteen in the bKa'-'gyur and bsTan-'gyur, including important commentaries by his masters, such as Vimalamitra's treatises on the Guhyamūlagarbha Tantra. He himself composed numerous commentaries on the works of Padmasambhava, Vimalamitra, and Buddhaguhya, expressing the essence of the Atiyoga, though these do not appear to have survived to the present day.

ༀ་ལྷ་ལུང་དཔལ་གྱི་རྡོ་རྗེ

lHa-lung dPal-gyi-rdo-rje
8th–9th century C.E.

Born at Gung-mo-che in upper 'Gram in dBu-ru, dPal-gyi rDo-rje was known in his youth as sTag-nya-bzang. To protect the kingdom of Tibet, he departed for the eastern borderlands, where for years he endured the harshest conditions. Eventually filled with deep sorrow at the suffering of samsara, he returned with his brothers to central Tibet in search of liberation. Here at bSam-yas the great Vimalamitra ushered him into the Dharma, and Guru Padmasambhava gave him the Bodhisattva vows.

From Jinamitra and sKa-ba dPal-brtsegs, he received the teachings of the Lower and Higher Abhidharma and disseminated these widely in Khams giving rise to a lineage that has continued to the present. He was a key link in the Sems-sde and Klong-sde lineage that descended from Vairotsana through gNyags. Receiving the initiations and oral instructions for the Mantrayāna teachings, he practiced for a long time at Grib-kyi dKar-mo Valley. One day he was carried off by the wind to a realm of perfect harmony where his being was clarified and completely awakened. Upon his return, he could pass freely through mountains of rock and fly from peak to peak.

Horrified at the reign of the evil king Glang Dar-ma, dPal-gyi rDo-rje resolved to protect the Dharma and free the king from further bad karma by taking the ruler's life. Disguised as a Bon-po magician, dPal-gyi rDo-rje approached the king during a festival and shot him down with an arrow. After fleeing to safety in the far northeast, he resided in the mountains at Tan-tig for many years, praying for the liberation of all sentient beings. At the end of his life, this accomplished yogin dissolved in radiant light.

ལང་གྲོ་དཀོན་མཆོག་འབྱུང་གནས

Lang-gro dKon-mchog 'Byung-gnas
8th–9th century C.E.

Born in gTsang at gYas-ru Byang rTa-nag, dKon-mchog
'Byung-gnas was one of King Khri-srong lDe'u-btsan's
ministers of the interior, known as Lang-gro. Later he received
the religious name of dKon-mchog 'Byung-gnas. Learned in
both Sanskrit and Tibetan, he assisted in the translation of
Dharma texts. Receiving empowerments and oral instructions
from Guru Padma, he practiced devotedly to the point where
he was able to manifest the signs of accomplishment.

Living as befitted a holder of Mantrayāna vows, he continued to perfect his attainment until his mind was so powerful
and firm that he could hurl thunderbolts like arrows. Blessed
by the Great Guru and acknowledged as his Heart Son,
dKon-mchog 'Byung-gnas became lord and master of the
ocean of Mantrayāna methods. The valley of Shangs was his
favorite place of practice. His family lineage remained in
nearby rTa-nag until recent times. Reincarnations of the great
Lang-gro include Ratna Gling-pa, Klong-gsal sNying-po, and
rJe-drung Phrin-las Byams-pa 'Byung-gnas and others.

ལ་གསུམ་རྒྱལ་བ་བྱང་ཆུབ

La-gsum rGyal-ba Byang-chub
8th–9th century C.E.

Considered one of the nine most excellent leaders of Tibet,
rGyal-ba Byang-chub was among the first seven monks
ordained by Abbot Śāntarakṣita. Journeying to India many
times, he perfected his skills as a translator and translated both

Sūtra and Tantra texts. Because his knowledge was vast like an ocean, he became known as the Bodhi King (Byang-chub rGyal-ba). Padmasambhava initiated him into the Hayagrīva practices and sent him to practice in Shangs valley. Having received empowerments and oral instructions from the Great Guru, he developed extraordinary powers: He could sit cross-legged in the sky, a lord of yogins.

After Padmasambhava departed from Tibet, rGyal-ba Byang-chub and ten other disciples received teachings from Ye-shes mTsho-rgyal at Zab-bu-lung in Shangs for ten years. Just before leaving the Land of Snow, mTsho-rgyal bestowed on these disciples additional teachings to lead them to the radiant light of complete liberation. She revealed at this time that rGyal-ba Byang-chub had been Ācārya Sa-le, her consort of early days, and that he would be a great siddha in thirteen future lives. It was this disciple, especially blessed by the Lady mTsho-rgyal, who, with Nam-mkha'i sNying-po, prepared the manuscript of her biography, which was then concealed as gTer-ma for the benefit of future generations. This biography, discovered in the seventeenth century by the gTer-ston sTag-sham Nus-ldan rDo-rje, is preserved in Great Treasures of Ancient Teachings. Its translation is published as *Mother of Knowledge* (Dharma Publishing, 1983).

## rGyal-mo gYu-sgra sNying-po
### 8th–9th century C.E.

Born in rGyal-mo-rong in eastern Tibet, gYu-sgra sNying-po became the chief disciple of Vairotsana, whom he met while this great master was exiled in the eastern borderlands. Vairotsana recognized rGyal-mo gYu-sgra sNying-po as the reincarnation of a fellow scholar who had traveled with him to Bodh Gayā. Closely guiding his new disciple, he introduced him to the practice of the Inner Tantras, whereupon gYu-sgra sNying-po developed a profound understanding, and his yogic powers manifested.

gYu-sgra sNying-po later made his way to lHa-sa, where he learned that Vimalamitra was in Tibet and teaching at the king's invitation. Attending one of Vimalamitra's discourses, gYu-sgra sNying-po asked why the master was teaching on so low a level and refraining from conveying the most profound teachings. When Vimalamitra learned that gYu-sgra's teacher was his own disciple Vairotsana, who had been unjustly exiled, Vimalamitra personally reassured Khri-srong lDe'u-btsan of the authenticity of Vairotsana's teachings. The king then invited Vairotsana to return to lHa-sa.

Accomplished both as a scholar and a siddha, gYu-sgra sNying-po was among the translators who worked together at bSam-yas. He assisted Vimalamitra in translating the thirteen Sems-sde Atiyoga texts, which are preserved in the rNying-ma-rgyud-'bum section of Great Treasures of Ancient Teachings. From Guru Padmasambhava he received the precious commentary, the Man-ngag-lta-ba'i-phreng-ba, and other instructions. Thereafter his yogic powers became extraordinary. He practiced especially at mChims-phu, the sacred power site associated with the Enlightened Speech of the Great Guru, where Padmasambhava had initiated the twenty-five disciples into the heruka sādhanas.

Having fully comprehended the rDzogs-pa-chen-po teachings, gYu-sgra sNying-po became the central pillar of the Klong-sde and Sems-sde Atiyoga transmission to Tibet. After the reign of Glang Dar-ma, he transmitted Sems-sde teachings to Bla-chen dGongs-pa Rab-gsal. In order to revitalize and protect the teachings of the Ancient Ones in later centuries, he and his master Vairotsana returned to Tibet as the incomparable brothers of sMin-grol-gling: gYu-sgra sNying-po as Lo-chen

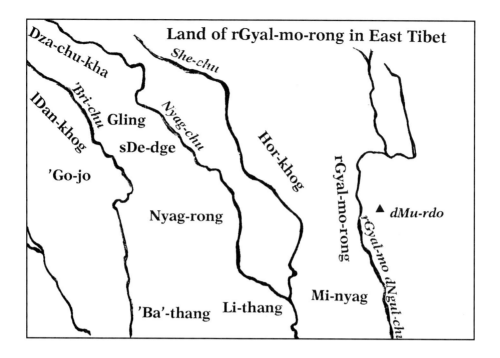

**Land of rGyal-mo-rong in East Tibet**

Dharmaśrī and Vairotsana as gTer-bdag Gling-pa. He also
manifested as Brag-gsum gTer-ston rDo-rje Thogs-med
(known as bsTan-'dzin Zla-'od rDo-rje) and other compassionate and wise spiritual guides.

Cog-ro Klu'i rGyal-mtshan
8th–9th century C.E.
1 text, 238 pages

Recognized by the Guru Padmasambhava as a reincarnate
Bodhisattva destined to assist in the transmission of the
Dharma to Tibet, Klu'i rGyal-mtshan was brought to lHa-sa as
a young man and trained by order of the king. He became one

of Tibet's four finest translators, together with Vairotsana, sKa-ba dPal-brtsegs, and Zhang Ye-shes-sde.

After studying in India, he was ordained by the Abbot Śāntarakṣita and set to work first with the Kashmiri paṇḍita Jinamitra. While they translated Vinaya and commentaries on the Abhidharmasamuccaya, Klu'i rGyal-mtshan received the lineages of Asaṅga and Maitreya. Working with the paṇḍita Jñānagarbha, he translated Madhyamaka texts by Nāgārjuna and Bhavya, and became learned in these teachings.

With sKa-ba dPal-brtsegs, he journeyed to Oḍḍiyāna to invite Vimalamitra to Tibet. From this great master paṇḍita, he received the precious sNying-thig teachings. Working with Vimalamitra and Vairotsana, he translated numerous Tantras and received from them the lineage of the root text of the Mahāyoga, the Guhyamūlagarbha (gSang-ba'i-snying-po). He studied intensively with gYu-sgra sNying-po, from whom he received further teachings. Assisting Padmasambhava, he transcribed and concealed gTer-ma texts. He practiced especially at dPal Chu-bo-ri, one of the powerful sacred sites where King Khri-srong lDe'u-btsan established a Tantric retreat center.

Klu'i rGyal-mtshan transmitted the lineages of Vinaya, Abhidharma, Madhyamaka, Cittamātra and Mantrayāna to his disciples. He ordained Rab, dMar, and gYo, the three monks who preserved the Vinaya lineage during the disruption of the Dharma in the time of Glang Dar-ma.

More than thirty of his translations are preserved in the bKa'-'gyur and bsTan-'gyur, while his Tantra translations are in the rNying-ma-rgyud-'bum section of Great Treasures. His own commentary on the Saṁdhinirmocana Sūtra, honored with inclusion in the bsTan-'gyur, is also preserved in Great Treasures of Ancient Teachings. In order to reveal precious gTer-ma texts, he returned to Tibet in the fourteenth century as the incomparable Karma Gling-pa.

# འཇའ་ལུས་པ་མྱང་བན་ཏིང་ངེ་འཛིན་བཟང་པོ

’Ja’-lus-pa Myang-ban Ting-nge-’dzin bZang-po

8th–9th century C.E.

Myang Ting-’dzin bZang-po was one of the major disciples of the master Vimalamitra. As guardian and advisor to King Khri-srong lDe’u-btsan from the time the king was a young child, he recommended inviting Vimalamitra to Tibet. Becoming a disciple of both the Great Guru Padmasambhava and Vimalamitra, Myang Ting-nge-’dzin received the full transmission of the Atiyoga Man-ngag-sde from Vimalamitra. One line of transmission descended from Myang-ban Ting-nge-’dzin bZang-po to Khu Byang-chub-’od to Khyung-po dByig-’od, and eventually to Rong-zom Mahapandita.

During the reign of King Ral-pa-can, Myang built Zhwa’i lHa-khang temple where he himself concealed these precious teachings, known as the Bi-ma-snying-thig, Vimalamitra’s Heart Drop Instructions, and gave instructions to ’Brom Rin-chen-’bar. Myang disappeared in rainbow light fifty-five years after Vimalamitra departed from Tibet, and lDang-ma lHun-rgyal later recovered some of the texts.

The Bi-ma-snying-thig texts are preserved in the Great Treasures of Ancient Teachings, while eight texts translated by Myang-ban are preserved in the bKa’-’gyur and bsTan-’gyur. It is said that Myang-ban Ting-’dzin bZang-po had completely realized the fruit of the Vajrayāna and was supreme among the one hundred and eight disciples of Guru Padmasambhava. Out of great kindness he returned to Tibet as the monk and gTer-ma master ’Ja’-tshon sNying-po.

ད་ཕྲེངས་ཕྱུག་ལབྟ་རབ།

Mandāravā

8th century C.E.

Aḍākinī of long-life who was born as the daughter of the king of Sa-hor, Mandāravā was a disciple of the Great Guru Padmasambava. When the Guru arrived in Sa-hor to instruct her, he found her engaged in retreat with her attendents and bestowed Mantrayāna precepts upon them all. Mandāravā's father was outraged that his daughter was in seclusion with Padmasambhava and ordered the Guru burned at the stake. Unscathed by the flames, Padmasambhava transformed the funeral pyre into a lake, inspiring deep faith in the king, who converted to the Dharma. Mandāravā and Padmasambhava both received the nectar of immortality through the blessings of Amitāyus while she and the Great Guru were practicing together. Undying and endlessly compassionate, Lady Mandāravā manifests in many guises to lead beings to liberation. Texts by Mandāravā have not yet been located, but her biography, concealed as a gTer-ma, was discovered by sTag-sham Nus-ldan rDo-rje in the seventeenth century and is preserved in Great Treasures of Ancient Teachings.

ཤཱཀྱ་གི་བལ་མོ་ཤུ་ཀྱུ་དེ་བྷི།

Śākyadevī

8th century C.E.

Born in Nepal as the daughter of the king, Śākyadevī was abandoned by her father after her mother died in childbirth. Nourished by monkeys in the cemetery, she survived, and was later discovered by the Great Guru, who recognized her as a ḍākinī. Filling her heart and mind with Dharma instructions, he accepted her as his disciple and enlightened consort. Śākyadevī resided in Nepal at Asura cave and Yang-le-shod, where she and Lady Ye-shes mTsho-rgyal met and exchanged teachings. A great siddha, at the end of her life she manifested the Vajra Body of Rainbow Light.

གོས་དཀར་མོ་བལ་འབངས་ཀུ་ལ་སིདྡྷི

### Kālasiddhī
### 8th century C.E.

Born in India in the land of rNga-thub-can at Bal-bong to a family of weavers, Kālasiddhī was also abandoned as a child when her mother died in childbirth. Taken to the cemetery by her father and left alone with the body of her dead mother, she was rescued by the Lady Mandāravā. Appearing as a tigress, Mandāravā nursed the baby and raised her. Later the Great Guru, taking the form of the monk So-kya Deva, bestowed teachings upon her and brought her to complete spiritual maturity. She worked for the Dharma in the land of Nepal and at the end of her life, achieved enlightenment.

དམ་ཚིགས་སྒྲོལ་མ་མོན་མོ་བཀྲ་ཤིས་ཁྱེའུ་འདྲེན

### bKra-shis Khye'u-'dren
### 8th century C.E.

Born in Mon near the border with Nepal as the daughter of King Ham-ra Bya-ba, bKra-shis Khye'u-'dren was blessed by the ḍākinīs from early childhood. Recalling her past lives, she knew she must travel to Tibet to find Ye-shes mTsho-rgyal. mTsho-rgyal took her to meet the Great Guru at La-yag Mon-mkhar, where he bestowed teachings upon her and made her one of his enlightened consorts. Able to transform herself into a tigress, bKra-shis Khye'u-'dren is the wild beast that rDo-rje Gro-lod rides when he manifests at sPa-ro sTag-tshang to tame negative forces opposing enlightenment. Being a karma yoga ḍākinī, she assisted the Guru in concealing the gTer-ma treasures. At the end of her life, without abandoning her body, she traveled to Copper Mountain to rejoin Padmasambhava.

## སྦ་གསལ་སྣང་ཡེ་ཤེས་དབང་པོ་

sBa gSal-snang Ye-shes dBang-po
8th century C.E.
1 text, 40 pages

One of King Khri-srong lDe'u-btsan's earliest supporters in his efforts to bring the Dharma to Tibet was gSal-snang of the sBa clan. He traveled to India to visit Bodh Gayā and Nālandā, where he heard reports of the outstanding master, Śāntarakṣita. Meeting the abbot in Nepal, he became his disciple, receiving from his new master the name Ye-shes dBang-po. Upon his return to Tibet, he recommended Śāntarakṣita to the king, who then dispatched gSal-snang and two others to invite the abbot to the Land of Snow. After the founding of bSam-yas and the passing of Śāntarakṣita, gSal-snang urged the king to invite Kamalaśīla to the historic debate at bSam-yas. gSal-snang authored an eye-witness account of the founding of bSam-yas, known as the sBa-bzhed, which Bu-ston and later historians relied upon in their works. The sBa-bzhed is preserved in Great Treasures of Ancient Teachings.

གཡུ་ཐོག་ཡོན་ཏན་མགོན་པོ

gYu-thog Yon-tan mGon-po
8th–9th century C.E.
30 texts, 416 pages

The famous court physician of King Khri-srong lDe'u-btsan, gYu-thog Yon-tan mGon-po the Elder was born as the son of gYu-thog Khyung-po rDo-rje and Lady rGya-sa Chos-kyi sGron-me in the same year as the king. From a young age he had visions of the medicine Buddhas and mastered the medical arts even as a youth. The most outstanding eighth-century Tibetan physician, he studied all the foreign systems of medicine known in Tibet and traveled to India three times. Working from a comprehensive understanding of the rGyud-bzhi and its supplementary works, he compiled all the medical treatises extant in Tibet and wrote compendia of instructions on curing disease. gYu-thog lived one hundred and twenty-five years.

His eleventh-century reincarnation, Yon-tan mGon-po the Younger, was born in gTsang. An outstanding physician like his predecessor, he went to India six times and also to Ceylon. Returning to Tibet, he contributed substantially to the Tibetan medical tradition. Altogether thirty texts by these two masters are included in Great Treasures of Ancient Teachings, which contains a total of one hundred and eighty-one medical texts.

# Part Three


# Era of Zur-chen and lCe-btsun Seng-ge dBang-phyug

སྔགས་པའི་རྒྱལ་པོ་ཟུར་ཆེན་ཤཱཀྱ་འབྱུང་གནས

sNgags-pa'i rGyal-po Zur-chen Śākya 'Byung-gnas

# Ninth through Eleventh Centuries

In this era disciples of the founding fathers of the rNying-ma tradition spread the Inner Yogas throughout Tibet. The lineages of So, Zur, gNubs and gNyags preserved the bKa'-ma transmission, while several important Atiyoga lineages flowed through the disciples of Vairotsana and Myang Ting-nge-'dzin. gTer-stons such as Sangs-rgyas Bla-ma appeared to discover the treasures concealed by Guru Padmasambhava. In this era, Jo-bo-rje Atīśa and other Indian masters were invited to Tibet, and their disciples began to found the gSar-ma schools.

Following the dissolution of the empire of the Dharma Kings, descendents of Glang Dar-ma's sons 'Od-srung and Yum-brtan ruled small kingdoms in central and western Tibet. A scion of the mGar clan, A-mnyes Byams-pa'i-dpal, settled in Gling in the east, where later the kingdom of sDe-dge would rise. In the far northeast, Tsong-kha was ruled by Prince rGyal-sras (997–1065). North of Tsong-kha the kingdom of Mi-nyag (Hsi-hsia) was established in 990 by King Se-hu and endured two hundred and sixty years.

# སྔགས་པའི་རྒྱལ་པོ་སོ་སྟོན་ཡེ་ཤེས་དབང་ཕྱུག

## sNgags-pa'i rGyal-po So-ston Ye-shes dBang-phyug
## and the Disciples of gNubs-chen
## 9th–10th century C.E.

The five major disciples of gNubs-chen Sangs-rgyas Ye-shes were: sPa-gor Blon-chen 'Phags-pa, who was expert in the Tantras; Sru-ston Legs-pa'i sGron-me, who was accomplished in the nectar of immortality; Dan-gyi Yon-tan-mchog, who was learned at replying to objections; So Ye-shes dBang-phyug, who was learned in the essential doctrines of the view; and Khu-lung-pa Yon-tan rGya-mtsho.

So had the following disciples: Ngan-thung Byang-chub rGyal-mtshan, Kong-btsun Shes-rab Ye-shes, and Ra-thung Shes-rab Tshul-khrims. Some sources say that Nyang Shes-rab-mchog was also a disciple of So as well as a disciple of Yon-tan rGya-mtsho and lHa-rje Hūṁ-chung. Nyang's disciple Ye-shes 'Byung-gnas in turn passed the lineage to Zur-po-che. While So Ye-shes dBang-phyug played an essential role in the transmission of the Inner Tantras, no texts by this great lineage holder have been located in recent times.

# ཁུ་ལུང་པ་ཡོན་ཏན་རྒྱ་མཚོ

## Khu-lung-pa Yon-tan rGya-mtsho
## 9th century C.E.

Heart Son of the great gNubs-chen Sangs-rgyas Ye-shes, Yon-tan rGya-mtsho was born at Khu-lung, which is just across the gTsang-po river from 'U-yug. He was first instructed by the Indian master Dhanadhala, who had been his elder brother in a previous life. Upon his advice, Yon-tan rGya-mtsho built his retreat center of gTsug-rum lTa-bu at the particularly powerful geomantic site of mKhar-gdong Yon-mo.

At the age of thirty, Yon-tan rGya-mtsho met gNubs-chen and received from him the Tantras, empowerments, instructions, and rituals of the Inner Yogas. An enormously successful yogin, he achieved the two great accomplishments, enlightened understanding and yogic powers, such as control of the elements of nature.

His son and principal disciple, Ye-shes rGya-mtsho, became master of all Yon-tan rGya-mtsho's transmissions, which he passed on to his own son and disciple, lHa-rje Hūṁ-chung. Hūṁ-chung taught Nyang Shes-rab-mchog, who in turn instructed Nyang Ye-shes 'Byung-gnas of Chos-lung, Zur-po-che's root guru.

འཇའ་ལུས་པ་སྤངས་མི་ཕམ་མགོན་པོ་

## 'Ja'-lus-pa sPangs Mi-pham mGon-po
## 8th–9th century C.E.

Vairotsana transmitted the Atiyoga Klongs-sde precepts known as the Diamond Bridge to sPangs Mi-pham mGon-po at Brag-dmar-rdzong when Mi-pham mGon-po was eighty-five years of age. Mi-pham mGon-po had not had the opportunity to practice the Dharma when he was a young man, but once he received the precepts, he practiced with diligence, using a meditative cord and chin support to help keep his body erect. It is said that his practice of meditation transformed his entire being, enabling him to live to the age of more than one hundred years.

sPangs Mi-pham mGon-po transmitted the Diamond Bridge precepts to Ngan-lam Byang-chub rGyal-mtshan, a monk of sixty-seven, who passed away at age 172 without leaving his body behind. Ngan-lam transmitted the precepts to Za-dam Rin-chen-dbyig, who reached the age of 144 and also passed away without leaving his body behind. His disciple was Khu-'gyur gSal-ba'i-mchog, who passed away at age 117 in the same manner as his teacher.

Khu-'gyur gSal-ba'i-mchog taught the monk Nyang Byang-chub-grags, who possessed the ability to transform himself into the various elements. His disciple was Nyang Shes-rab 'Byung-gnas, who passed on the teachings to sBa-sgom Ye-shes Byang-chub. sBa-sgom, who lived to the age of ninety-eight, transmitted the Diamond Bridge teachings to 'Dzeng Dharma-bodhi, establishing an uninterrupted lineage of teachers who attained the Rainbow Body of light. Works composed by these masters have not been located, but the Klongs-sde Tantras are preserved in the rNying-ma-rgyud-'bum section of Great Treasures of Ancient Teachings.

## 'Dzeng Dharmabodhi
### 1052–1168 C.E.

When just a young boy, 'Dzeng Dharmabodhi met the Indian siddha Pha Dam-pa Sangs-rgyas, who blessed him and predicted he would meet with the Diamond Bridge teachings. When he was thirty-five, 'Dzeng received the secret instructions of the Diamond Bridge from sBa-sgom Ye-shes Byang-chub, upon which his mind merged with the sky. 'Dzeng's other famous teachers included disciples of Atīśa, Ma-gcig Lab-sgron, Yu-mo, and sGam-po-pa.

Known for his miraculous deeds, austere practices, cease-less meditation, and detailed interpretations of the basic texts,

'Dzeng lived to the age of 117. His students included 'Dzeng Jo-sras, who taught Kun-bzang, whose son sPrul-sku 'Od-'bar continued the lineage. From this time on, the Hearing Lineage of the Diamond Bridge was widely spread. The transmission of the Diamond Bridge descended through sKye-tshe Ye-shes dBang-phyug to Śākya rGyal-po and 'Gos Lo-tsā-ba in the fifteenth century and eventually to gTer-bdag Gling-pa in the seventeenth century. No texts composed by these earlier lineage holders have been located in recent times.

ལྡང་མ་ལྷུན་གྱིས་རྒྱལ་མཚན་

## lDang-ma lHun-gyis-rgyal-mtshan
### 9th–10th century C.E.
### Rin-chen gTer-mdzod: 1 text

One hundred years after Myang Ting-nge-'dzin passed away, lDang-ma lHun-grub rGyal-mtshan (also known as lHun-gyis rGyal-mtshan), an incarnation of Vimalamitra, was born in Upper dBus at gZho near 'Bri-gung as the son of lDang-ma dGe-mchog. He became the disciple of sBas Blo-gros dBang-phyug, a disciple of Myang Ting-nge-'dzin.

To all appearances, he was a simple temple attendant at Zhwa'i lHa-khang, the temple founded by Myang Ting-nge-'dzin. There he discovered Vimalamitra's Heart Drop teachings (Bi-ma-snying-thig), the treasures that had been concealed earlier by Myang. He also received the oral instructions from sBas Blo-gros and perfected the practices.

Fifteen years later, lDang-ma lHun-rgyal transmitted these teachings in seven stages to lCe-btsun Seng-ge dBang-phyug and to Kha-rag sGom-chung, who became completely liberated. When lDang-ma passed away, the skies were filled with rainbows, much to the astonishment of all, for no one had realized that he was a remarkable individual.

In the future, these teachings proceeded as a bKa'-ma transmission through sBas Blo-gros dBang-phyug and a gTer-ma transmission through numerous gTer-stons, beginning with lCe-btsun Seng-ge dBang-phyug. One text associated with this great master is preserved in the Rin-chen gTer-mdzod section of Great Treasures, while the Bi-ma-snying-thig teachings are preserved in several other sections.

ཁོད་ལུས་གྲུབ་པ་ལྕེ་བཙུན་སེ་ངེ་དབང་ཕྱུག

'Od-lus Grub-pa lCe-btsun Seng-ge dBang-phyug

10th–11th century C.E.

Rin-chen gTer-mdzod: 1 text

The siddha lCe-btsun Seng-ge dBang-phyug was born in Myang-ro in gTsang as the son of lCe Thub-pa'i dBang-po. He met lDang-ma lHun-grub rGyal-mtshan, who transmitted the Bi-ma-snying-thig to him, telling him to copy the precious texts he had found at Zhwa'i lHa-khang and hide them. lCe-btsun concealed the texts in three locations: at 'U-yug, at Lang-gro'i 'Chad-pa sTag-'dra, and in the upper valley of Byar.

Inspired by a vision, lCe-btsun proceeded to mChims-phu where he located additional texts. Soon afterward, Vimala-mitra appeared, gave him the complete empowerments for these teachings, and returned to Wu-t'ai-shan, the mountain in China sacred to the Bodhisattva Mañjuśrī. lCe-btsun practiced intensively for seven years at 'U-yug, where he transformed the five skandhas and attained complete liberation.

lCe-btsun bestowed teachings on Nyang bKa'-gdams-pa of Mal-dro, who practiced in the caves at gZho Ti-gro (one of

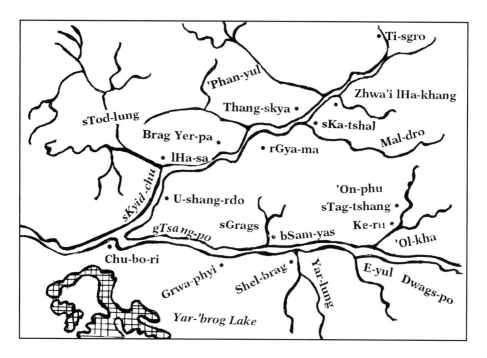

Ye-shes mTsho-rgyal's favorite practice sites). After two years, Nyang's body disappeared without leaving behind a trace. To Zhang-ston bKra-shis rDo-rje, who had discovered sNying-thig texts at mChims-phu, lCe-btsun granted the complete instructions. It was this disciple who continued the major stream of these teachings. Thus by the eleventh century there were three gTer-stons associated with the Bi-ma-snying-thig: lDang-ma lHun-rgyal, lCe-btsun Seng-ge dBang-phyug, and Zhang-ston bKra-shis rDo-rje.

At the age of one hundred and twenty-five, lCe-btsun disappeared in a mass of rainbow light. Thirty years after lCe-btsun Seng-ge dBang-phyug concealed the texts, lCe-sgom Nag-po discovered some texts at 'U-yug, Shangs-pa Ras-pa discovered others at Lang-gro, and Zhang discovered the ones at Byar. From that time forward, they propagated the Bi-ma-snying-thig teachings widely. The Bi-ma-snying-thig transmission descended to the great master Klong-chen-pa, who joined these teachings together with the mKha'-'gro-snying-thig. These

77

teachings are preserved in several sections of Great Treasures of Ancient Teachings.

The transmission of related teachings occurred once again in the nineteenth century when 'Jam-dbyangs mKhyen-brtse dBang-po was traveling through 'U-yug. Here, in the very place where the great lCe-btsun Seng-ge dBang-phyug had attained realization, mKhyen-brtse recalled his previous life as lCe-btsun and his passing away in a body of light. Thus he received the lCe-btsun-snying-thig teachings, which he later bestowed upon the master A-'dzom 'Brug-pa.

སྤྲུལ་སྐུ་ཨ་རོ་ཡེ་ཤེས་འབྱུང་གནས

sPrul-sku A-ro Ye-shes 'Byung-gnas
9th–10th century C.E.
24 texts, 166 pages

The incarnation A-ro Ye-shes 'Byung-gnas appeared in the tenth century in eastern Tibet in Khams at Klong-thang sGrol-ma, the temple built by King Srong-btsan sGam-po. He held rDzogs-chen lineages that flowed from seven successive masters of India and seven successive masters of China. He received the Sems-sde lineage from gNyags Jñānakumāra. Ye-shes 'Byung-gnas manifested in the world by taking the form of a small boy and concealing himself in the sand at the springs of Ring-mo, where he was found and cared for by a nun. As a child he began teaching Dharma to the monks; amazed by the doctrines that the boy knew, the monks named him Ye-shes 'Byung-gnas, Fountainhead of Primordial Wisdom.

He lived a long life and had many disciples including Ya-zi Bon-ston, Bru-sha rGyal-bu of Kha-rag, Grum-shing Shes-rab sMon-lam from dBus, and Cog-ro Zangs-dkar mDzod-khur of gTsang. Cog-ro Zangs-dkar and Ya-zi Bon-ston transmitted this precious lineage to Rong-zom Mahāpaṇḍita. It became known as the Khams tradition of rDzogs-chen or the A-ro-lugs. Great Treasures of Ancient Teachings preserves twenty-four texts of this tradition.

སྔགས་པའི་རྒྱལ་པོ་ཟུར་ཆེན་ཤཱཀྱ་འབྱུང་གནས

## sNgags-pa'i rGyal-po Zur-chen Śākya 'Byung-gnas
### b. 954 C.E.
### 154 texts, 484 pages

Zur-po-che Śākya 'Byung-gnas was born in mDo-khams at Yar-rdzong into a family that had originated in India. He was the first of the three great masters known as the Three Zur and the principal Vidyādhara of his time for the Mahāyoga and Anuyoga tantric systems. He also continued the lineage of the heruka sādhanas brought to the Land of Snow by Guru Padmasambhava. So profound was his realization of these powerful teachings that his disciples often observed him manifesting in heruka form.

Ordained by Bla-chen dGongs-pa Rab-gsal, Zur-po-che, also known as Zur-chen or as Zur-po-che Heruka, studied the Mahāyoga and the Atiyoga Sems-sde with Nyang Ye-shes 'Byung-gnas, the disciple of Nyang Shes-rab-mchog, and with sPa-gor Blon-chen 'Phags-pa, the direct disciple of gNubs-chen. He obtained the bDud-rtsi heruka teachings from Śākya-mchog. From gNyan-nag dBang-grags of Yul-gsar he obtained the secret initiation and other inner practices, and from Thod-dkar Nam-mkha'-sde, Zhu-ston bSod-nams Śākya, and other masters he received the Anuyoga teachings. From Rog Śākya 'Byung-gnas of mChims-phu he obtained initiation into the Yang-dag cycle, and 'Bre Khro-chung-pa of Upper Nyang gave him additional teachings.

Zur-po-che classified the Tantras, arranging the root Tantras and the explanatory Tantras, grouping the Tantras with their commentaries and corresponding sādhanas, and the sādhanas with their ritual manuals. Through devoted practice he applied and fully realized every one of these teachings. Residing and meditating in a cave in 'Ug-pa-lung (Canyon of Owls), he became known as 'Ug-pa-lung-pa, the Guru of Owl Canyon. Here he constructed a temple filled with images of deities and a mandala of stupas filled with images of herukas.

Zur-po-che guided at least one hundred and eight disciples to liberation. His five principal disciples were known as the Four Summits and the Summit Ridge. Among the Four Summits was Shes-rab Grags-pa of the clan of Zur, who became widely known as Zur-chung-pa, the Younger Zur. It is said that Zur-po-che planted the roots of the teaching of the rNying-ma tradition, his disciple Zur-chung-pa extended its branches, and Zur-chung's disciple sGro-sbug-pa cultivated its leaves and fruit. At the end of his life, Zur-po-che disappeared in a blaze of radiant light. Great Treasures of Ancient Teachings contains a collection of one hundred and fifty-four texts associated with the Zur tradition.

gTer-ston Sangs-rgyas Bla-ma
late 10th–early 11th century C.E
Rin-chen gTer-mdzod: 2 texts

The earliest gTer-ma master and the first of thirteen incarnations of rGyal-sras lHa-rje, Sangs-rgyas Bla-ma was born at La-stod mTsho-bar in central Tibet during the period of the early life of Rin-chen bZang-po (late 10th century). He lived as a shaven-headed upholder of the Mantrayāna tradition, traveling widely in dBus and gTsang. In mNga'-ris he discovered treasure texts focusing on the three essential cycles of guru sādhanas, rDzogs-chen teachings, and Avalokiteśvara practices (Bla-rdzogs-thugs-gsum) and on the practices of the three roots of guru, deva, and ḍākinī. Later he also found Hayagrīva sādhanas. Although these very early treasures did not survive the succeeding centuries, with the blessings of Padmasambhava, the great 'Jam-dbyang mKhyen-brtse was able to restore the most important practices. Kong-sprul Blo-gros mTha'-yas received these teachings and preserved two works in the Rin-chen gTer-mdzod.

རྒྱ་བན་རྡོ་རྗེ་དབང་ཕྱུག་གི་འོད་

## rGya-ban rDo-rje dBang-phyug-gi-'od
### 10th century C.E.
### Rin-chen gTer-mdzod: 2 texts

The gTer-ston known as rDo-rje dBang-phyug-gi-'od was born at the end of the early transmission of the Dharma in gTsang at Nyang-ro. He lived as a master of the Mantrayāna known as A-khu sTon-pa. On the way to the sacred place of lHo-brag mKhar-chu, he met 'Brog-mi dPal-gyi Ye-shes, father and son, disciples of the Great Guru. At mKhar-chu he discovered alchemical treasures which he himself practiced, completely transforming his physical embodiment to that of a youth. Though he is said to have lived three hundred years, it is certain that he lived at least one hundred and fifty. Kong-sprul Blo-gros mTha'-yas received these teachings and preserved two texts in the Rin-chen gTer-mdzod.

གཏེར་སྟོན་གཙུག་ལག་དཔལ་དགེ།

gTer-ston gTsug-lag dPal-dge
late 10th century C.E
Rin-chen gTer-mdzod: 1 text

Born in the later period of the life of Sangs-rgyas Bla-ma,
gTsug-lag dPal-dge was said to be an incarnation of the
great gNubs Sangs-rgyas Ye-shes. Born at Grong-khyer-sun
along the Nepal-Tibet border, he lived in the Newari manner as
a holder of the Mantrayāna vows. He discovered gTer-ma in
Nepal at E Vihara, a monastery in the Kathmandu valley where
Padmasambhava had taught. Ye-shes mTsho-rgyal had met the
Anuyoga master Vasudhara at E Vihara while searching for her
yoga partner, Ācārya Sa-le. The texts uncovered by gTsug-lag
dPal-dge did not continue, but with the blessings of gNubs-
chen Sangs-rgyas Ye-shes, 'Jam-dbyangs mKhyen-brtse was
able to recover their essential meanings. Kong-sprul Blo-gros
mTha'-yas preserved one text in the Rin-chen gTer-mdzod.

གཏེར་སྟོན་གུ་རུ་ཧཱུྃ་འབར།

gTer-ston Gu-ru Hūṁ-'bar
late 10th century C.E.

Born into the Bon-po family at sTag-sde, Guru Hūṁ-'bar
lived as a holder of Mantrayāna vows. He discovered a
treasure text in a Hayagrīva statue in the temple at mTho-lding
in mNga'-ris built by lHa Bla-ma Ye-shes-'od (c. 975), the king
of Pu-hrang. Guru Hūṁ-'bar gave the texts to lHa Bla-ma
Ye-shes-'od, who was deeply pleased. The king bestowed the
teachings on others, and the lineage gradually spread. One text

was located by Kong-sprul Blo-gros mTha'-yas and preserved in the Rin-chen gTer-mdzod.

ཁྱུང་པོ་དཔལ་དགེ།

Khyung-po dPal-dge

early 11th century C.E.

1 text, 1 page Rin-chen gTer-mdzod: 1 text

An incarnation of Vairotsana born in La-stod in gTsang into the clan of Khyung-po, dPal-dge was a contemporary of lHa Bla-ma Ye-shes-'od. He lived as a holder of Mantrayāna vows in an era when unethical practices and misuse of yogic powers were passing for the Dharma in some quarters. From Mon Bum-thang he extracted texts of both Bon and Buddhist teachings, and at Has-po-ri, the mountain ridge east of bSam-yas, he found Dharma teachings, together with Bon texts and numerous medical and astrological works. While not all of these very early discoveries survived, the essentials of these treasures came to 'Jam-dbyangs mKhyen-brtse, which enabled Kong-sprul Blo-gros mTha'-yas to preserve one text in the Rin-chen gTer-mdzod.

Lo-tsā-ba Sha-mi Go-cha

early 11th century C.E.

Known as rDo-rje rGyal-po and Lo-tsā-ba Sha-mi, the gTer-ma master Sha-mi Go-cha took birth through the blessings of gNyags Jñānakumāra. His family belonged to the clan of Sha-mi, residing in Shangs at Sha-mi Pra-du. Living as a holder of the Mantrayāna vows, he became known as Sha-mi sTon-pa (teacher), due to his extensive knowledge of both the Sūtras and Tantras.

At Has-po-ri he discovered the large cycle of the dGongs-don-zab-tig-'gro-ba-kun-sgrol. He found many other treasures, but none have survived to the present time. There does still remain a text known as the dGongs-don-zab-tig, which is the long version of the commentary on Padmasambhava's Man-ngag-lta-ba'i-phreng-ba, a Mahāyoga Lam-rim describing all the vehicles of enlightenment.

In later centuries rJe-btsun sGrol-ba'i mGon-po (the historian Tārānatha) discovered the medium-sized version and Thang-stong rGyal-po discovered a short version at mChims-phu. The essentials of the long version also came to 'Jam-dbyangs mKhyen-brtse as a Reconcealed Treasure. Through the blessings of Thang-stong rGyal-po, Lord 'Jam-dbyangs mKhyen-brtse also received five cycles of condensed sādhanas as a Realization Treasure. He set down these Vajra words, which possessed wondrous power, and bestowed this treasure on Kong-sprul to preserve in the Rin-chen gTer-mdzod.

gTer-ston dPon-sras Khyung-thog-rtsal
early 11th century C.E.
Rin-chen gTer-mdzod: 1 text

During the time of lHa-btsun Byang-chub-'od in the eleventh century, the gTer-ma master Khyung-thog-rtsal was born in La-stod at lHa-rtse into a family of Bon adherents. With the blessings of Vairotsana, he located texts on medicine and astrology at Ru-lag Gram-pa rGyang, the land-taming temple erected by King Srong-bstan sGam-po. Although these early discoveries disappeared over the centuries, 'Jam-dbyangs mKhyen-brtse recovered them as Reconcealed Treasures and Kong-sprul Blo-gros mTha'-yas preserved one work in the Rin-chen gTer-mdzod.

This yogi lived in remote solitude a long time, bringing benefits to sentient beings. At the end of his days, he disappeared in light. Another gTer-ston also known as dPon-sras Khyung-thog lived in the time of Chos-rje Gling-pa (seventeenth century).

གཏེར་ཆེན་གྲྭ་པ་མངོན་ཤེས།

## gTer-chen Grwa-pa mNgon-shes
### 1012 C.E.
### 4 texts, 151 pages, Rin-chen gTer-mdzod: 2 texts

An incarnation of both Shud-pu dPal-gyi Seng-ge and Vairotsana, Grwa-pa mNgon-shes was born at sKyid in the Grwa valley into the family descended from mChims rDo-rje sPre'u-chung. Since his affinity for the Dharma awakened at an early age, as a youth he received the Triple Vajra Saṁvara vows at bSam-yas from Yam-shud rGyal-ba-'od, a disciple of Klu-mes Tshul-khrims, and was given the name dBang-phyug-'bar. He was called Grwa-pa after his native place, and he was known as mNgon-shes because he was extremely learned in Abhidharma.

When he was twenty-six he discovered in the main temple at bSam-yas several Tantric practice texts and the four basic medical texts known as the rGyud-bzhi, which had been translated by Vairotsana in the eighth century. From Grwa-pa these precious teachings descended through Yar-lung dGe-bshes Khu-ston Dar-ma-grags to gYu-tog Yon-tan mGon-po the Later, the second King of Physicians. The rGyud-bzhi became the

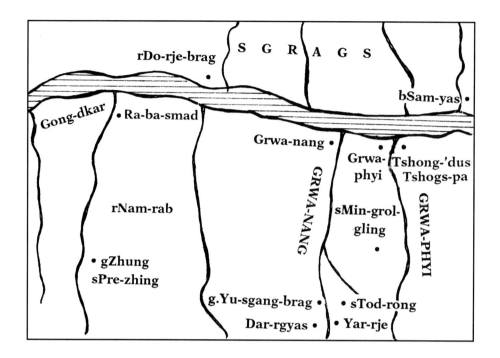

Map showing locations including rDo-rje-brag, SGRAGS, bSam-yas, Gong-dkar, Ra-ba-smad, Grwa-nang, Grwa-phyi, Tshong-'dus Tshogs-pa, rNam-rab, GRWA-NANG, sMin-grol-gling, GRWA-PHYI, gZhung sPre-zhing, g.Yu-sgang-brag, sTod-rong, Dar-rgyas, Yar-rje

basis of various branches of Tibetan medicine, and their incalculable benefits have continued to the present day. Grwa-pa mNgon-shes founded several monasteries including the one at Grwa-thang in Grwa-nang, where he served as abbot while also maintaining his duties as abbot of bSam-yas. Great Treasures preserves the medical texts discovered by Grwa-pa mNgon-shes in the arts and sciences section, and the Tantric practices in the Rin-chen gTer-mdzod section.

དགེ་བཤེས་དྲ་ང་རྡོ་རྗེ་ཀུན་གྲགས

dGe-bshes Dra-nga rDo-rje Kun-grags

11th century C.E.

This gTer-ston discovered Dharma protector rites that later were practiced at Ngor monastery, but the stream of the actual texts no longer remained in the time of Kong-sprul Blo-gros mTha'-yas.

རིག་སྔགས་འཛིན་པ་རོང་ཟོམ་མཱ་ཧཱ་པཎྜི་ཏ་ཆོས་ཀྱི་བཟང་པོ

Rig-sngags 'Dzin-pa
Rong-zom Mahāpaṇḍita Chos-kyi bZang-po
1012–1131 C.E.
29 texts, 578 pages, Rin-chen gTer-mdzod: 1 text

Rong-zom Mahāpaṇḍita is famous as the Great Paṇḍita of Tibet. Born in Lower gTsang at sNar-lung-rong, he was the son of Rong-ban Rin-chen Tshul-khrims. It is said that he was an incarnation of Smṛtijñānakīrti, an Indian paṇḍita who had recently died in Khams, or of Paṇḍita Ācārya Phra-la Ring-mo. At the time the gSar-ma lineages began to flow into Tibet, Rong-zom became the peerless master of the lineages of the early transmission. His scholarship and visionary foresight maintained the integrity of the older lineages and preserved their teachings intact.

From childhood his intellect was unobstructed, his awareness was both quick and profound, and he spoke Sanskrit and other languages. The great Atīśa met Rong-zom when the boy was only six years old and saw in the remarkable child his master Kṛṣṇācārya. Rong-zom mastered all doctrines upon hearing them once and defeated in debate not only his classmates but also the most famous of Tibetan scholars. Thus even as a youth he became known as an incarnation of Mañjuśrī.

At the age of thirteen years, he traveled to India, where he studied the gSar-ma Tantras under such distinguished Indian masters as Mañjuśrīvarma, Mañjuśrījñāna, Devakaracandra, Parasura, Aśokavajra, and Buddhakarabhadra, all of whom acclaimed him as the most outstanding translator of gSar-ma Tantras. Lama Mi-pham relates that Rong-zom's understanding of Sanskrit and Madhyamaka and his skill in logic were unmatched; established scholars in India accepted him as the greatest among them, and Dharmabhadra requested that he write for the purpose of saving numerous beings.

It is said that Rong-zom was like Dignāga in his awareness, like Dharmakīrti in his analytic understanding, like Ācārya Vasubandhu in learning, like Candragomin in speech, and like Āryadeva in his writing. The eight great treasures of brilliance were unleashed within him, bringing him unobstructed ability to comprehend and communicate the Dharma. Among Tibet's many accomplished scholars, his equal had never been seen.

From his father, Rong-zom received lineages transmitted by Guru Padmasambhava, and from Ya-zi Bon-ston he received Vairotsana's Sems-sde lineage transmitted through gYu-sgra sNying-po and Bla-chen dGongs-pa Rab-gsal. From Ya-zi Bon-ston, the Khams tradition (A-ro-lugs) of the Atiyoga lineage descended to him. He also received Vimalamitra's lineages transmitted through Myang Ting-nge-'dzin, rMa Rin-chen-mchog, and gNyags Jñānakumāra.

An outstanding scholar, debator, and translator, Rong-zom Mahāpaṇḍita was also a powerful guru who could directly transmit the deeper meanings of the Mantrayāna texts and practices. He wrote texts containing the secret precepts, treatises on the Atiyoga doctrines, and important commentaries on the Mahāyoga Tantras.

As a result of the power of his compassion and blessings, his sādhanas are so powerful that even lacking the hearing lineage, one who follows them carefully can obtain siddhi through their practice. His teachings were continued in two major lineages, one transmitted through his physical sons, and the other transmitted through his disciples. Of the numerous works known to have been composed by this great enlightened master, only twenty-nine texts have been located and preserved in Great Treasures of Ancient Teachings.

སྲུགས་པའི་རྒྱལ་པོ་ཟུར་ཆུང་ཤེས་རབ་གྲགས་པ

## Zur-chung Shes-rab Grags-pa
### 1014–1074 C.E.

Zur-chung Shes-rab Grags-pa was born in gYas-ru gTsang as the son of Thags-pa sGom-chen and Ma-jo Shes-rab-skyid. He continued Zur-po-che's work, firmly establishing 'Ug-pa-lung as a center for study and practice of the transmitted teachings. By following the instructions of Zur-po-che in every detail, he obtained unusual powers that enabled him to benefit beings. Like a fine vase filled to overflowing, Zur-chung-pa came to possess all wisdom of the lineage.

Obtaining the fruit of the practice of the Vajrasattva sādhana, he understood reality as the pure Dharmakāya and became able to abide in effortless meditation. As his mind was free of attachment to thoughts, he was unmatched in debate. Hundreds of disciples gathered around him, attracted by the power of his presence. All the yogins of Tibet paid him homage; even the gSar-ma masters who had vowed not to bow to him saw him as a heruka, not as a human, and prostrated themselves before him. His spiritual heir was his physical son Zur Śākya Seng-ge, known as the master sGro-sbug-pa. No works composed by this great lineage holder have been located.

ཞང་བཙུན་དར་མ་རིན་ཆེན

## Zhang-btsun Dar-ma Rin-chen
### early 11th century C.E.
### Rin-chen gTer-mdzod: 1 text

Born in Pu-hrang mNga'-ris in western Tibet, Dar-ma Rin-chen discovered texts associated with Dharma protector practices, which have been transmitted continuously from the days of the first Karmapa Dus-gsum mKhyen-pa (1110–1193) to the present. These practices formed the major Dharma protector rites of the bKa'-rgyud Kam-tshang school. Kong-sprul Blo-gros mTha'-yas preserved one text in the Rin-chen gTer-mdzod.

རྡོར་འབུམ་ཆོས་ཀྱི་གྲགས་པ

rDor-'bum Chos-kyi Grags-pa

early 11th century C.E.

Rin-chen gTer-mdzod: 3 texts

Born in mNga'-ris in western Tibet into a wealthy family, this gTer-ma master was known as rDo-rje 'Bum because on the day of his birth his family sponsored the production of golden copies of the Vajracchedika (rDo-rje gCod-pa) and the 100,000-line Prajñāpāramitā (known as the 'Bum). He held the vows of the Triple Vajra Saṁvara, and his religious name was Chos-kyi Grags-pa. Later he discovered medical texts in the statues of the temple of Bra-dum-rtse built by Srong-btsan sGam-po in the seventh century. The transmission of these texts has remained unbroken to the present day, bringing immeasurable benefits to the land of Tibet. Three works are preserved in the Rin-chen gTer-mdzod.

# འབྲོག་པ་སྣ་ནམ་ཐུབ་པ་རྒྱལ་པོ

'Brog-pa sNa-nam Thub-pa rGyal-po
early 11th century C.E.
Rin-chen gTer-mdzod: 2 texts

An incarnation of Vairotsana, this gTer-ma master was born in Khams at dGe-rgyal Byang-rong into the family of Zhang sNa-nam. Living as a member of the White Sangha holding Mantrayāna vows, he journeyed to the ancient temple of Tārā at Klong-thang in lDan-khog. Here he discovered medical and astrological works as well as Dharma texts, but by the nineteenth century, only teachings on rituals survived.

With the blessings of Guru Padmasambhava, 'Jam-dbyangs mKhyen-brtse was able to recover some of these teachings, and Kong-sprul Blo-gros mTha'-yas preserved two works in the Rin-chen gTer-mdzod. The reincarnation of 'Brog-pa Thub-rgyal was sNye-mo Zhu-yas gNod-sbyin-'bar, the rDzogs-chen gTer-ma master.

# གཏེར་སྟོན་སངས་རྒྱས་འབར

gTer-ston Sangs-rgyas-'bar
early 11th century C.E.

Born in La-stod into the same family as the first gTer-ston, Sangs-rgyas Bla-ma, Sangs-rgyas-'bar discovered heruka sādhanas, Mantrayāna practice instructions, sādhanas to the Four Guardian Kings, and other texts at La-stod Kha-chu and at Glo-bo Thang-'bar. Unfortunately, the transmission of these very old treasure teachings did not successfully continue through the centuries.

ལྷ་རྗེ་གནུབས་ཆུང་པ

lHa-rje gNubs-chung-pa
early 11th century C.E.
Rin-chen gTer-mdzod: 1 text

Born in gTsang-rong at Khu-lung as the son of gNubs Ye-shes rGya-mtsho, lHa-rje gNubs-chung, also known as Huṁ-chung, was an expert in powerful mantras. He played an essential role in the bKa'-ma lineages transmitted through gNubs-chen Sangs-rgyas Ye-shes and in the gTer-ma lineages. lHa-rje's grandfather was Yon-tan rGya-mtsho, the son of gNubs-chen Sangs-rgyas Ye-shes. Yon-tan rGya-mtsho had received from his father empowerment as master of all the Tantras and instructions. Perfecting the practices and sādhanas, he had profound visions and achieved extraordinary occult powers. He bestowed his knowledge on his two sons, Padma dBang-rgyal and lHa-rje. lHa-rje became the first teacher of rJe-btsun Mi-la Ras-pa, instructing him in rites of sorcery and mantras.

At Srong-btsan sGam-po's land-taming temple of lHo-brag Khom-mthing, lHa-rje gNubs-chung discovered gNubs-chen's teachings on powerful mantras, which were eventually transmitted to rGya Zhang-khrom. These have remained the essential protective rites of the teachings of the Ancient Ones. They also descended to 'Bri-gung Chos-kyi Grags-pa, who spread them very widely. One gTer-ma discovered by gNubs-chung is included in the Rin-chen gTer-mdzod, while several additional texts that descended through him have been placed in Great Treasures of Ancient Teachings.

lHa-rje's main disciple was Nyang Shes-rab-mchog, who taught Nyang Ye-shes 'Byung-gnas, who in turn taught Zur-po-che. The bKa'-ma lineage that descended through these masters became known as the Rong-lugs or the Nyang-lugs, and it flourished in central Tibet until recent times.

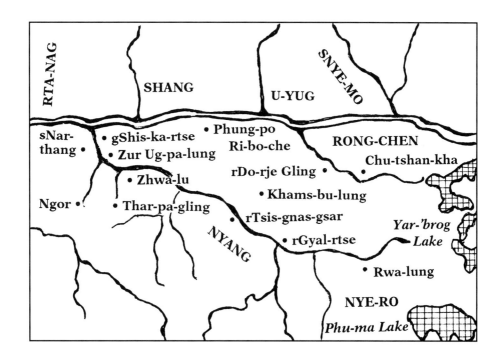

दुम་རྒྱ་ཞང་ཁྲོམ་རྡོ་རྗེ་འོད་འབར་ཞབས

Dum-rgya Zhang-khrom rDo-rje 'Od-'bar-zhabs
early 11th century C.E.
268 texts, 1,776 pages, Rin-chen gTer-mdzod: 7 texts

This gTer-ma master took birth according to the heartfelt intention of the great gNubs Sangs-rgyas Ye-shes. Born into the rGya clan at gTsang-rong Dum-pa Chu-tshan-kha, he lived as a lay practitioner of the Mantrayāna. His ordinary name was Zhang-khrom and his secret name was rDo-rje 'Od-'bar. At first, he lived in deliberate poverty and went forth like a beggar asking alms. At gTsang-chu'i Nya-mo temple, he met a yogi who gave him a list of treasures, inspiring him to follow the path of a gTer-ston. From the sacred site of Phung-po Ri-bo-che where Padmasambhava had practiced, he drew forth his first discovery, which was followed by many others at gYung-ge rDza-lhud-mo, the two land-taming temples at Bra-dum-rtse and lHo-brag, and at mChims-phu.

Among all the teachings recovered from these holy places, the most powerful were Yamāntaka practices, Atiyoga teachings, and a collection of instructions by gNubs-chen. These precious teachings later passed to 'Gyur-med Yid-bzhin dBang-rgyal and other sMin-grol-gling masters, while the gTer-ston's descendents continued to transmit them in gTsang-rong. In addition to seven texts in the Rin-chen gTer-mdzod section, Great Treasures of Ancient Teachings preserves another two hundred and sixty-eight works by rGya Zhang-khrom.

དྲག་སྔགས་མཁན་པོ་སེ་སྟོན་རིང་མོ

## Drag-sngags mKhan-po Se-ston Ring-mo
### early 11th century C.E.

Born in the early eleventh century, Se-ston Ring-mo was known as Drag-sngags mKhan-po, the Expert in Powerful Mantras. He received an index of treasures that had belonged to lHa-btsun sNgon-mo. lHa-btsun had given this list to two monks who had tried to obtain treasures hidden at sPa-ro in Bhutan. While these two had failed to obtain the texts and had lost their lives in the attempt, Se-ston Ring-mo was able to recover the treasures from their place of concealment. One special cycle of mantras became very famous, but this was lost by the time that Kong-sprul assembled the texts of the Rin-chen gTer-mdzod. No texts discovered by this gTer-ma master have been found in recent times.

རྒྱ་ཕུར་བུ་མགོན།

rGya Phur-bu-mgon
early 11th century C.E.
Rin-chen gTer-mdzod: 2 texts

Born in lHo-brag into the clan of rGya, the gTer-ston known as Phur-bu-mgon lived as a member of the White Sangha of Mantrayāna practitioners. The treasures he discovered traced back to Khri-srong lDe'u-btsan, the Dharma King of the eighth century. For the sake of future generations, the king had concealed at Mon-yul Bum-thang and at sPa-ro sKyer-chu in Bhutan Guru Padmasambhava's teachings and ritual objects that had particularly protected the king's life. Bla-ma rGya Phur-bu discovered both of these precious treasures and combined them. From Bla-ma rGya Phur-bu they passed in an unbroken lineage to Rig-'dzin rGod-ldem and Byang-bdag bKra-shis sTobs-rgyal, and from them through masters down to the present day. Kong-sprul Blo-gros mTha'-yas received this lineage and included two texts discovered by rGya Phur-bu-mgon in the Rin-chen gTer-mdzod.

གཏེར་སྟོན་ལྷ་འབུམ་གུ་རུ་རྣོན་རྩེ།

gTer-ston lHa-'bum Guru rNon-rtse
early 11th century C.E.
Rin-chen gTer-mdzod: 1 text

A shared incarnation of Vairotsana and Dran-pa Nam-mkha', lHa-'bum took birth in rTa-nag in Shangs about the same time as 'Brom-ston (1004–1064). His family was Bon-po and he lived as a practitioner who became known as Guru rNon-rtse. At Dung-phor-brag in rTa-nag he discovered treasures of the three essential practices of guru sādhanas, rDzogs-chen teachings, and Avalokiteśvara practices (Bla-rdzogs-thugs-gsum), as well as Bon texts, and works on astrology and medicine that had been concealed in the time of Padmasambhava. The Bon texts survived, while most of the astrology works were lost. In later centuries the Dharma treasure lHa-'bum had discovered was obtained by 'Jam-dbyangs mKhyen-brtse as a Reconcealed Treasure and preserved by Kong-sprul Blo-gros mTha'-yas in the Rin-chen gTer-mdzod.

## sNgags-'chang rGya-ston brTson-'grus Seng-ge-dar
### early 11th century C.E.

Born into the clan of rGya, brTson-'grus Seng-ge-dar was an incarnation of gNubs Sangs-rgyas Ye-shes. From their place of concealment in Bhutan at sPa-ro sTag-tshang Tiger Den, this gTer-ma master recovered several treasures including Yamāntaka texts and instructions. Another of his discoveries was later prized by the 'Brug-pa bKa'-'bryud as their most excellent Dharma protector rites. But most of the texts did not survive to the nineteenth century.

## gTer-ston lCe-sgom Nag-po
### early 11th century C.E.

A key link in the Bi-ma-snying-thig lineage of lDang-ma lHun-grub and lCe-btsun Seng-ge dBang-phyug was the master lCe-sgom Nag-po. Thirty years after lCe-btsun concealed the texts of this transmission in three separate locations, lCe-sgom Nag-po discovered one set of teachings at 'U-yug. He practiced these intensively and taught them to others, especially to the young bKra-shis rDo-rje, who later became famous as Zhang-ston and continued the transmission lineage.

བྱང་ཆུབ་སེམས་དཔའ་ཟླ་བ་རྒྱལ་མཚན

Byang-chub Sems-dpa' Zla-ba rGyal-mtshan
mid-11th–late 11th century C.E
1 text, 7 pages, Rin-chen gTer-mdzod: 1 text

Among the gTer-ma masters renowned for Pure Visions and Realization Treasures is Zla-ba rGyal-mtshan. An incarnation of Avalokiteśvara, he was born during the same era that Mi-la Ras-pa (1040–1123) lived, and became known as the Bodhisattva Zla-ba rGyal-mtshan. With the blessings of Guru Padmasambhava, this extraordinary individual received the teachings of Hayagrīva and other sādhanas. A text discovered by Zla-ba rGyal-mtshan was preserved in the Rin-chen gTer-mdzod, and this lineage remained intact until the present.

གཏེར་སྟོན་ལྷ་བཙུན་སྔོན་མོ

gTer-ston lHa-btsun sNgon-mo
mid-11th–late 11th century C.E.
Rin-chen gTer-mdzod: 1 text

Incarnation of Mu-rum bTsad-po lHa-sras Dam-'dzin Rol-pa Ye-shes-rtsal (King Khri-srong lDe'u-btsan's middle son), lHa-btsun sNgon-mo was born at bSam-yas into the later lineage of the royal dynasty. His father was lHa-btsun Bodhirāja, the seventh generation in the line of Yum-brtan, the eldest son of Glang Dar-ma. lHa-btsun Bodhirāja met Atīśa at bSam-yas, and it was there that his son, Rig-pa rGya-mtsho Glog-gi Phreng-ba, went to study. Rig-pa rGya-mtsho became known as lHa-btsun because he was a Mantrayāna vow holder descended from a divine clan.

lHa-btsun sNgon-mo became learned in the entire Tripiṭaka and established the teachings at the bSam-yas Chos-'khor chen-mo. Having invited to bSam-yas both the Lo-tsā-ba Pa-tshab Nyi-ma-grags (b. 1054), translator of Madhyamaka and Abhidharma, and mKhas-pa Shud-ke Dar-ma rDo-rje, lHa-btsun studied and received instructions from them. Working together, they translated Sūtras and Tantras.

In the main central temple of bSam-yas and in the caves at sGrags Yang-rdzong, the sacred power site connected with the Enlightened Body of the Guru, this master discovered many gTer-ma that described medical techniques to protect beings from infections and create antidotes for poisons. He is known to have had in his hands lists of all the major gTer-ma to be found in the kindgom of Tibet.

From 'U-shangs-rdo, the nine-storied temple built by King Ral-pa-can in the ninth century, he took out seven treasures of Zhi-byed teachings. Some treasures he reconcealed at sGrags Yang-rdzong above the door of the large meditation cave, where eight hundred years later, they were found by the renowned mChog-gyur bDe-chen Gling-pa, another incarnation of lHa-sras (Mu-rum bTsad-po). mChog-gyur bDe-chen Gling-pa gave these treasures to mKhyen-brtse Rinpoche, who brought forth teachings of wondrous benefit. Kong-sprul Blo-gros mTha'-yas received these works and preserved them in the Rin-chen gTer-mdzod together with his own explanatory notes.

གཏེར་སྟོན་ཉི་མ་སེང་གེ

gTer-ston Nyi-ma Seng-ge
mid-11th–late 11th century C.E.
Rin-chen gTer-mdzod: 1 text

Born near dPal-mtsho in Mang-yul, gTer-ston Sūrya Siṁha, also known as Nyi-ma Seng-ge, was the next rebirth of rGya Lo-tsā-ba. He lived as a holder of Mantrayāna vows, perfecting his understanding of the Sūtras and Tantras. At Mang-yul Byams-pa-sprin, a land-taming temple built by King Srong-btsan sGam-po in the seventh century, he discovered treasures of the three major cycles of guru sādhanas, rDzogs-chen teachings, and Avalokiteśvara practices (Bla-rdzogs-thugs-gsum). But the conditions were not harmonious and it was not possible for him to make these teachings available. Other gTer-stons, however, rediscovered some of these treasures. In particular, eight centuries later, 'Jam-dbyangs mKhyen-brtse was able to recover a condensed version of the essentials of the Avalokiteśvara teachings and transmitted them to Kong-sprul Blo-gros mTha'-yas, who preserved them in the Rin-chen gTer-mdzod.

ཟུར་ཤཱཀྱ་སེང་གེ་སྒྲོ་སྦུག་པ

Zur Śākya Seng-ge sGro-sbug-pa
1074–1134 C.E.

An incarnation of the Bodhisattva Vajrapāṇi, Zur Śākya Seng-ge, also known as sGro-sbug-pa, was the son of Zur-chung-ba. He grew up in mDa'-phu and then proceeded to Chu-bar to receive teachings in the Mahāyoga from Glan Śākya bZang-po. From his father's spiritual heirs, known as the Four

99

Pillars, he obtained the complete transmission of the Inner Yogas, including the instructions, rites, sādhanas, empowerments, and advice. After practicing intently at sGro-sbug in Nya-ri, he became an immensely powerful yogi with great charisma. His enlightened activity upheld the traditions of the Ancient School for many years. People came from far and wide to hear him teach. Among his ten thousand disciples, twelve outstanding masters transmitted his teachings and were known as the Four Black Ones, the Four Teachers, and the Four Grandfathers. No texts by this great lineage holder have been located in recent times.

གཏེར་སྟོན་སར་བན་ཕྱོགས་མེད

gTer-ston Sar-ban Phyogs-med
mid-11th–late 11th century C.E.
Rin-chen gTer-mdzod: 2 texts

The reincarnation of Guru Padmasambhava's consort Jo-mo Shel-bza' sGron-skyid, Sar-ban was born near Mon sPa-gro and lived in the manner of an upholder of Mantrayāna vows. At sTag-tshang Seng-ge cave, he discovered precious rDzogs-chen gTer-ma, which spread widely over the years. In later times, Kong-sprul Blo-gros mTha'-yas could not find all the texts discovered by this gTer-ston, but was able to place a few in the Rin-chen gTer-mdzod.

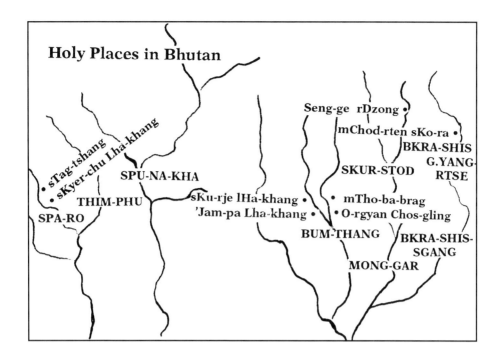

Holy Places in Bhutan

sTag-tshang •
sKyer-chu Lha-khang
SPU-NA-KHA
• sKu-rje lHa-khang •
'Jam-pa Lha-khang •
• THIM-PHU
SPA-RO
Seng-ge rDzong •
mChod-rten sKo-ra •
BKRA-SHIS
G.YANG·
SKUR-STOD RTSE
• mTho-ba-brag
• O-rgyan Chos-gling
BUM-THANG
BKRA-SHIS-
SGANG
MONG-GAR

ར་ཤག་གཏེར་སྟོན་ཆོས་འབར་བསོད་ནམས་རྡོ་རྗེ།

Ra-shag gTer-ston Chos-'bar bSod-nams rDo-rje

mid-11th–late 11th century C.E.

Rin-chen gTer-mdzod: 3 texts

An incarnation of both Vairotsana and 'Brog-mi dPal-gyi Ye-shes, sPrul-sku Ra-shag was born in Yar-'brog-sgang into the clan of gNyan. He was known as Ra-shag Chos-'bar or bSod-nams rDo-rje. Having studied medicine and divination from the time he was young, he continually expanded his knowledge. A great yogin of the Mantrayāna, he had obtained the level of a deathless Vidyādhara. He discovered treasures of the Ma-mo sādhanas at sPa-gro in Bhutan and also found medical texts, divination texts, and Bon teachings. The divination teachings became very famous, while the Ma-mo practices

101

were difficult to locate in later times. Kong-sprul included three texts in the Rin-chen gTer-mdzod, together with practice instructions that he himself had composed.

sPrul-sku Ra-shag was also associated with the teachings of the Five Goddesses of Long Life, transmitting the lineage to rJe-btsun Mi-la Ras-pa. It was he who actually gave these gTer-ma texts to Mi-la Ras-pa and explained their origin.

དབུ་རུ་སྟོན་པ་ཤཱཀྱ་འོད་

dBu-ru sTon-pa Śākya-'od
mid-11th–late 11th century C.E.
Rin-chen gTer-mdzod: 1 text

Born in 'Phan-yul north of lHa-sa in the district of dBu-ru, Śākya-'od was an incarnation of Vairotsana and Lang-gro dKon-mchog 'Byung-gnas. He lived as a holder of Mantrayāna vows, studying the Sūtras and Tantras so thoroughly that he became renowned as the Teacher of dBu-ru. From Byang Bra-dum-rtse, the land-taming temple built by Srong-btsan sGam-po, he withdrew many gTer-ma treasures. He found more precious treasures at gYu-mdo-brag and at Ra-sa 'Phrul-snang, the temple built in lHa-sa by the Nepalese wife of King Srong-btsan sGam-po. With the blessings of 'Jam-dbyangs mKhyen-brtse, a few texts were recovered and Kong-sprul placed one work in the Rin-chen gTer-mdzod. In the same lHa-sa temple, this gTer-ston also discovered texts associated with the Maṇi-bka'-'bum of King Srong-btsan sGam-po. Great Treasures contains numerous Maṇi-bka'-'bum texts in the collected works of this king.

gTer-ston Brag-tshal rDo-rje-'bar

mid-11th–late 11th century C.E.

Rin-chen gTer-mdzod: 1 text

Born in gTsang-rong Zar into a Bon-po family, rDo-rje-'bar was an incarnation of Vairotsana and dPal-gyi Seng-ge. He lived as a holder of Mantrayāna vows. Because he was so physically powerful, he became known as Brag-tshal, Splinter of Rock, while his secret name was rDo-rje-'bar. At Bum-thang rTsis-lung, in the Temple of the Three Jewels with the bronze statues of the Buddhas of the three times, this master discovered precious rDzogs-chen texts that later flowed into the Byang-gter lineage of Northern Treasures. rDo-rje-'bar also found precious phur-pa teachings and Dharma protector teachings that were known and practiced even in the nineteenth century. Though the complete transmission did not continue, the great 'Jam-dbyangs mKhyen-brtse held lineages of related teachings. One treasure discovered by rDo-rje-'bar is preserved in the Rin-chen gTer-mdzod.

gTer-ston gNyal-pa Jo-sras

late 11th–mid-12th century C.E.

The Black Master of gNyal, gNyal-pa Jo-sras, also known as gNyal-ston Nag-po, discovered texts hidden by Guru Padmasambhava in the Black Stupa at bSam-yas. Although these teachings became quite renowned, the lineage did not continue down to the present time.

གཏེར་སྟོན་བླ་མ་ཟངས་རི་རས་པ

gTer-ston Bla-ma Zangs-ri Ras-pa
late 11th–mid-12th century C.E.

Born in La-stod in the territory of gTsung-pa, Zang-ri Ras-pa became the disciple of rJe-btsun Ras-chung-pa, the disciple of Mi-la Ras-pa. He was known as Zangs-ri Ras-pa because he practiced at Mount Zangs; he was also known as 'Go-ston dBang-phyug rDo-rje. Dus-gsum mKhyen-pa, the first Karmapa, took Zangs-ri Ras-pa as his lama. At Yer-pa, the valley northeast of lHa-sa where disciples of Padmasambhava had practiced in the caves, he discovered the Yer-pa dKar-chag. It remained in circulation for centuries, but by the time of Kong-sprul not a single copy could be found.

རྒྱ་གོང་རི་པ་སྙེ་མོ་སངས་རྒྱས་དབང་ཆེན

sNye-mo rGya-gong Ri-pa Sangs-rgyas dBang-chen
mid-11th–late 11th century C.E.
Rin-chen gTer-mdzod: 2 texts

Born at sNye-mo, Sangs-rgyas dBang-chen lived as a holder of Mantrayāna vows. He was also known as sNye-mo rGya-gong Ri-pa. He discovered Hayagrīva sādhanas. In accord with predictions of the Great Guru, this lineage later descended to sKyer-sgang-pa Chos-kyi Senge. This stream of gTer-ma became known as the rTa-mgrin sKyer-sgang tradition and eventually spread to all the schools. Kong-sprul Blo-gros mTha'-yas received these teachings and preserved them in the Rin-chen gTer-mdzod together with the notes and comments made by Tibetan masters over the centuries.

## ར་མོ་ཤེལ་སྨན་ཡེ་ཤེས་བཟང་པོ

Ra-mo Shel-sman Ye-shes-bzang-po
mid-11th–late 11th century C.E.
Rin-chen gTer-mdzod: 3 texts

An incarnation of gNyags Jñānakumāra, Ra-mo Shel-sman was born in Yar-lung at Ra-mo sMan-chu-kha. He lived as a doctor and Mantrayāna practitioner who was known as Ye-shes bZang-po. At Yar-lung Shel-brag Padma-brtsegs, the Cave of Padma at Crystal Rock, one of the five sacred sites especially connected to Guru Rinpoche, he discovered teachings of the three essential cycles of guru sādhanas, rDzogs-chen teachings, and Avalokiteśvara practices (Bla-rdzogs-thugs-gsum). At sMan-chu 'Od-gsal-rdzong and many other places, he found works on medicine and healing practices that over the centuries brought inconceivable benefits to beings and set many on the path of liberation. Not all of the texts survived, but fortunately the ḍākinīs transmitted some of them to 'Jam-dbyangs mKhyen-brtse. Thus two such works were preserved in the Rin-chen gTer-mdzod, together with notes added by Kong-sprul and one original gter-ma discovered by Ra-mo Shel-sman.

## གཏེར་སྟོན་སྙེ་མོ་ཞུ་ཡས་གནོད་སྦྱིན་འབར

gTer-ston sNye-mo Zhu-yas gNod-sbyin-'bar
late 11th–mid-12th century C.E.

Master of Tantra, sNye-mo Zhu-yas was a great Vajrayāna lineage holder whose enlightened activity met with success. Born in gTsang at sNye-mo into the old Bon-po clan of Zhu-yas, gNod-sbyin-'bar was an incarnation of Vairotsana and the next incarnation after sNa-nam Thub-pa rGyal-po.

Having received a treasure list from the gTer-ma master Brag-tshal, he proceeded to Rong-po 'Dam-gyi-snying. Here from a crystal rock, he was able to withdraw twenty-five precious rDzogs-chen teachings belonging to the sPyi-ti division, which he bestowed on mNga'-bdag Nyang-ral. Later, these were preserved in the rNying-ma-rgyud-'bum and included in Great Treasures of Ancient Teachings in the rGyud-'bum section.

གཏེར་སྟོན་ཆུ་ཕོ་རྟོགས་ལྡན་

gTer-ston Chu-pho rTogs-ldan
late 11th–mid-12th century C.E.
Rin-chen gTer-mdzod: 1 text

Born in rGyal-mo-rong at Chu-pho Nor-bu-gling, Chu-pho rTogs-ldan lived as a sage though it is not certain he was a renunciate. He was known as dGe-'dun rGyal-mtshan. In upper gSer at 'Brong-ri sMug-po mountain, he discovered Dharmapāla practices that had been concealed by Vairotsana. These teachings, which were known for their great efficacy, were joined together with the related bKa'-ma texts from Vairotsana's lineage and eventually preserved in the Kaḥ-thog tradition as their main protective rites. The Rin-chen gTer-mdzod section of Great Treasures preserves this treasure together with related texts by lDi-ri Chos-grags.

# སྤྲུལ་སྐུ་བ་མཁལ་སྨུག་པོ་

sPrul-sku Ba-mkhal sMug-po
late 11th–mid-12th century C.E.
Rin-chen gTer-mdzod: 2 texts

Ba-mkhal sMug-po was an incarnation of the middle son of King Khri-srong lDe'u-bstan, Mu-rum bTsad-po or lHa-sras Dam-'dzin Rol-pa Ye-shes-rtsal. He was born about the same time as Nyang-ral Nyi-ma 'Od-zer in lHo-brag. He lived as a holder of Mantrayāna vows, and as he resided at sMug-po, he became known as sPrul-sku sMug-po-gdong or Ba-mkhal sMug-po. At Mang-yul he discovered the rNam-thar of Guru Padmasambhava that describes his birth as a human being (womb-born rather than lotus-born), together with a commentary on a famous prayer (Bar-chad-lam-sel), and Vajrakīla teachings. The prayer spread to all the schools, and later mChog-gyur bDe-chen Gling-pa, who was also an incarnation of lHa-sras, discovered at the same place in Mang-yul the closely related prayers of the Thugs-sgrub Bar-chad-kun-sel. Merged into a single stream of blessings, these two prayers have remained precious and powerful practices to the present time. Two texts are preserved in the Rin-chen gTer-mdzod.

# གཏེར་སྟོན་སུམ་པ་བྱང་ཆུབ་བློ་གྲོས།

gTer-ston Sum-pa Byang-chub Blo-gros
late 11th–mid-12th century C.E.

Major lineage holder of the gTer-ma transmission and Heart Incarnation of the Great Guru Padmasambhava, Byang-chub Blo-gros took birth at Sum-pa in sMar-khams-sgang, which is one of the three mountain ranges of mDo-khams. Thus he was known as Sum-pa Byang-chub Blo-gros. His ordination name was bSod-nams rGyal-mtshan. When the Great Guru was preparing to depart from Tibet for India, King Khri-srong lDe'u-btsan offered him a golden begging bowl filled with nectar and a golden mandala as large as a warrior's shield, holding eight pieces of turquoise the size of pigeons. Padmasambhava bestowed on the king twenty wrathful forms of prayerwheels with detailed instructions on using the power of the wind to remove obstacles.

Sum-pa Byang-chub Blo-gros discovered these instructions beneath the big toe of the Vajrapāṇi statue at bSam-yas. In the statue of Mahādeva, he discovered other minor teachings. The precious wind-power instructions spread throughout Khams and from north to south across central Tibet. While the stream of teachings remained unbroken, Kong-sprul Blo-gros mTha'-yas was unable to obtain any texts and so none were preserved in the Rin-chen gTer-mdzod.

གཏེར་སྟོན་མངའ་བདག་མོལ་མི་འཁྱིལ

### gTer-ston mNga'-bdag Mol-mi-'khyil
late 11th–mid-12th century C.E.
Rin-chen gTer-mdzod: 1 text

Rebirth of Ta-mi Nātha, the meditator from Mon who was a disciple of Padmasambhava, Mol-mi-'khyil was born into the same clan as mNga'-bdag Nyang in the southern part of Upper gTsang. He led the life of a holder of Mantrayāna vows. According to predictions, at Bra-dum-rtse temple, one of the seventh-century land-taming temples built by Dharma King Srong-btsan sGam-po, he discovered precious texts relating to Hayagrīva and Pe-har, and other treasures. These teachings spread in early days, but later became much more rare.

Fortunately ḍākinīs entrusted the old manuscripts to the care of 'Jam-dbyangs mKhyen-brtse, who with the blessings of Guru Padmasambhava, brought forth some of the teachings once again. Kong-sprul preserved the Hayagrīva teachings in the Rin-chen gTer-mdzod.

གཏེར་སྟོན་ཀུ་ས་སྨན་པ་པདྨ་སྐྱབས་ཀུན་སྤངས་ཟླ་འོད།

gTer-ston Ku-sa sMan-pa Padma-skyabs
Kun-spangs Zla-'od
late 11th–mid-12th century C.E.
Rin-chen gTer-mdzod: 1 text 1164

An incarnation of Vairotsana, Ku-sa sMan-pa took birth in lHo-brag and lived as a doctor and Mantrayāna follower. Spending long periods of time on retreat, he became known as Zla-'od the Ascetic (Kun-spangs Zla-'od) and Doctor Padma the Refuge (sMan-pa Padma-skyabs). He was called Ku-sa for the name of his native region and sTon-pa or teacher for his vast knowledge of the texts. Ku-sa sMan-pa was one of the greatest hidden yogis.

At sPa-gro in Bhutan he discovered four wonderful treasures: teachings of Dharma, Bon, medicine, and astrology. The Dharma discoveries included the early transmission of the dKon-mchog-spyi-'dus, which was also conveyed in "middle" and "later" transmissions. The essential elements of the early transmission were recovered by 'Jam-dbyangs mKhyen-brtse as Reconcealed Treasure.

The middle transmission flowed through the sixteenth-century gTer-ma master 'Ja'-tshon sNying-po, and the later one was discovered at Padma Shel-ri as earth gTer-ma by 'Jam-dbyangs mKhyen-brtse. The lineages of the dKon-mchog-spyi-

'dus teachings have continued to the present time and are a specialty of the dPal-yul tradition. One text associated with this gTer-ma master is contained in the Rin-chen gTer-mdzod.

གཏེར་སྟོན་བྱར་རོང་ཨེ་ཡི་སྨན་པ

### gTer-ston Byar-rong E-yi sMan-pa
### late 11th–mid-12th century C.E.

Born in Byar-gyi-rong E-yul at Rig-pa'i 'Byung-gnas, the gTer-ston E-yi-sman-pa was one of two incarnations of gNyags Jñānakumāra. He lived as a physician and a holder of Mantrayāna vows. Because he was a doctor, he was called sMan-pa, while his personal name was Nyi-'od-gsal.

On the border of lHo-brag and Tibet at rDza-rong Bhi, he discovered rDzogs-chen teachings and medical texts. At 'Bri-thang Ko-ro-brag, he found many pilgrimage guides to holy places. From the rocks at Byar-rong, he extracted gNyags Jñānakumāra's own copies of healing practices, which existed in four sections: a large, medium, small, and essence-only. E-yi sMan-pa was known as a healer and siddha with the power to extend life and protect against the forces of death, and yet the full enlightened activity of this gTer-ston was not able to manifest. Some related teachings on sādhanas to the medicine Buddha survived as Realization Treasures received by the great 'Jam-dbyangs mKhyen-brtse.

ལྕེ་སྟོན་རྒྱ་ནག

## lCe-ston rGya-nag
## 1094–1148 C.E.

Disciple of sGro-sbug-pa, lCe-ston rGya-nag was among the famous students known as the Four Black Ones. He was born in Nyang and resided at his family residence at sKyil-mkhar southwest of Nyang. For many years, he studied Abhidharma, Prajñāpāramitā, and Logic. At the age of thirty he took sGro-sbug-pa as his guru and received from him doctrines and teachings more complete than those received by any other disciple. Ordained as a monk at age forty, he continued his studies of Vajrakīla Tantras and the Khams tradition of rDzogs-chen (A-ro-lugs). His main disciple and successor was his nephew Yon-tan-gzungs (1126–1195). No texts by this lineage holder have been located.

དག་པ་སེ་སྦྲག་པ

## Dam-pa Se-sbrag-pa (Ton-Śāk of dBus)
## late 11th–mid-12th century C.E.

Dam-pa Se-sbrag-pa was a major lineage holder of the Zur tradition. Belonging to the family of gZad-kyi gCer-pa Wang-thung, he studied with sGro-sbug-pa and the master lCe-ston rGya-nag. These two transmitted to him all of the rNying-ma Tantras, which he cultivated in meditation in the northern mountains of gTsang at Yol-ba rock and then in Gung-thang. A lord of yogins, he possessed realization so profound that he transcended the physical body entirely and was unharmed by lightning and avalanches. He established a

Tantric college and had many disciples, including Zhig-po bDud-rtsi. No texts by this master have been located.

གཏེར་སྟོན་ཞང་སྟོན་བཀྲ་ཤིས་རྡོ་རྗེ

## gTer-ston Zhang-ston bKra-shis rDo-rje
### 1097–1167 C.E.

Born in Yar-'brog Do-nang, the island in the middle of Lake Yar-'brog, Zhang-ston was an essential link in the transmission of the Bi-ma-snying-thig, the Atiyoga transmission that descended from Vimalamitra. As a youth, he requested teachings from lCe-sgom, and later studied with many masters until he became learned in the Tripiṭaka and the Tantras. Blessed with visions of Bodhisattvas and protected by the Dharmapālas, he proceeded to 'U-yug to a cave where he located a list of treasures. Soon at mChims-phu he found the texts of Vimalamitra, and the great Vimalamitra actually appeared to him in visions and bestowed instructions on him. At Shangs rTa-nag, he later met lCe-btsun Seng-ge dBang-phyug, who granted him the complete teachings. Later he recovered the texts lCe-btsun had concealed at Byar.

A master of forms, Zhang-ston sometimes appeared as the Buddhas of the five families, and it was said that his body never cast a shadow. When he taught rDzogs-chen, rainbows filled the sky. The miraculous signs that accompanied his enlightened actions inspired hundreds of individuals with faith and encouraged them to practice the Dharma.

Zhang-ston had one son, Nyi-'bum, who was his closest disciple and major transmitter of the Bi-ma-snying-thig. Zhang-ston bKra-shis rDo-rje passed away at the age of seventy-one amidst rainbows, a shower of flowers, and the roll of cymbals. He once stated that had he not gathered a circle of disciples, his body would have vanished without a trace. No texts by this master have been located.

ཨ་ཁས་པ་ཟངས་གླིང་དབང་ཕྱུག

mKhas-pa Zangs-gling dBang-phyug
late 11th–mid-12th century C.E.?
Rin-chen gTer-mdzod: 1 text

The gTer-ma master mKhas-pa Zangs-gling dBang-phyug discovered texts associated with Yamāntaka practices that became widespread, but his life story and time of birth are not known. Kong-sprul included several of his treasure texts in the Rin-chen gTer-mdzod.

འབས་སྟོན་པ་ཡེ་ཤེས་རྡོ་རྗེ

'Bas-ston-pa Ye-shes rDo-rje
12th century C.E.
5 texts, 317 pages

Author of commentaries on texts by Buddhaguhya, Ye-shes rDo-rje is thought to have lived in the twelfth century, but his life story requires further research. Five related commentaries are preserved in Great Treasures of Ancient Teachings.

Part Four


Era of Nyang-ral
Nyi-ma 'Od-zer and
Guru Chos-dbang

གཏེར་ཆེན་མངའ་བདག་ཉང་རལ་ཉི་མ་འོད་ཟེར

gTer-chen mNga'-bdag Nyang-ral Nyi-ma 'Od-zer

# Twelfth and Thirteenth Centuries

In the twelfth and thirteenth centuries, the first two of five great gTer-ston Kings established the Upper and Lower Treasures. With the founding of Kaḥ-thog monastery, transmission of the Three Inner Yogas grew very strong in the east, while Dharma centers such as 'Ug-pa-lung continued the transmission unbroken in central Tibet. In this era, masters of the bKa'-gdams, bKa'-brgyud, and Sa-skya traditions were developing these new schools.

Small principalities in central Tibet continued to proliferate. In the east the kingdom of Gling was flourishing, while 'Bru lHa-rgyal founded the kingdom of 'Gu-log. In 1197 Nālandā was destroyed by Afghano-Turkish invasions. Ten years later Genghis Khan united the Mongol tribes, which engulfed China in 1215, Russia in 1236. After Sa-skya Paṇḍita negotiated Tibet's peaceful entrance into the Mongol Empire in 1247, central Tibet was divided into thirteen myriarchies and the Sa-skya lamas rose to political prominence in the Land of Snow.

# ཆོས་རྗེ་ཀཿདམ་པ་བདེ་གཤེགས

## Chos-rje Kaḥ-dam-pa bDe-gshegs
## 1122–1192 C.E.
### 2 texts, 26 pages, Rin-chen gTer-mdzod: 1 text

Kaḥ-dam-pa bDe-gshegs was born in Khams at Bu-'bur-sgang as the son of gTsang-pa dPal-sgra of the sGa clan. His mother was the sister of the mother of the bKa'-brgyud-pa teacher, Phag-mo-gru-pa. Ordained as a novice at 'Phan-yul by Bla-ma Byang-chub Seng-ge, and given the name Shes-rab Seng-ge, he studied Vinaya very seriously. Then he mastered Mahāyoga and Atiyoga teachings under the guidance of 'Dzam-ston 'Gro-ba'i-mgon-po, a disciple of sGro-sbug-pa.

Kaḥ-dam-pa also studied the Cakrasaṁvara, Hevajra, and Guhyasamāja Tantras with various gSar-ma masters. He became the major disciple of the Karmapa and with him studied the Six Doctrines of Nāropa. One of his masters said that Kaḥ-dam-pa could achieve the rainbow body if he would spend the rest of his life in practice; if he chose instead to teach, he would greatly extend the Dharma.

Kaḥ-dam-pa decided to teach; returning to Khams, he founded the monastery of Kaḥ-thog in 1159. This great center of learning soon attracted students from all across southern and eastern Tibet, and even from Nepal. Kaḥ-dam-pa taught all of the Three Inner Tantras of the rNying-ma, including the major and minor commentaries and texts, as well as the five Maitreya texts and the Bodhicaryāvatāra. Some sources indicate he was the incarnation of Śāntideva, the Indian siddha and scholar. Kaḥ-dam-pa was in direct communion with the Bodhisattva Mañjuśrī and could discuss the doctrine with the great Bodhisattvas. He passed away in 1192, having established the foundation for the Mantrayāna in eastern Tibet. His important texts include a work on the nine vehicles of the rNying-ma

tradition. Two texts are preserved in the Great Treasures of
Ancient Teachings.

His disciples included the three brilliant students Shes-rab
rGyal-mtshan, Shes-rab dPal-ba, and Shes-rab rDo-rje; and the
four supreme students 'Bru-tsha sGang-pa, Nam-mkha' rDo-rje,
rMog-ston 'Jam-dpal Seng-ge, and Maṇi Rin-chen. These masters took the Khams lineages back to central Tibet. His closest
disciple was gTsang-ston rDo-rje rGyal-mtshan.

གཙང་སྟོན་པ་རྡོ་རྗེ་རྒྱལ་མཚན་

gTsang-ston-pa rDo-rje rGyal-mtshan
1126–1216 C.E.
2 texts, 253 pages

The lineage holder gTsang-ston was born in Bu-'bur-sgang
and met Kaḥ-dam-pa at the age of seventeen. Traveling
with Kaḥ-dam-pa in eastern Tibet ten years before Kaḥ-thog
was built, rDo-rje rGyal-mtshan lived and practiced meditation
in the valley where the monastery would be founded. Kaḥ-
dam-pa bDe-gshegs recognized that his disciple was extraordinary, an incarnation of an Indian siddha, and transmitted
to him all the Inner Yogas of the rNying-ma tradition. Later,
gTsang-ston composed an explanation for a profound text written by Padmasambhava. Great Treasures of Ancient Teachings
contains this work and one other by this master.

At the age of fifty-six, gTsang-ston became the abbot of
Kaḥ-thog monastery, where he propagated the Three Inner
Yogas according to the tradition of Kaḥ-dam-pa. gTsang-ston
rDo-rje rGyal-mtshan was renowned even in his own time as a
Bodhisattva advanced on the path. He passed away at the age
of ninety in 1216. His major disciple was Kaḥ-thog-pa
Byams-pa-'bum (1179–1252).

# གཏེར་ཆེན་མངའ་བདག་ཉང་རལ་ཉི་མའོད་ཟེར

## gTer-chen mNga'-bdag Nyang-ral Nyi-ma 'Od-zer
### 1124–1192 C.E.
### 550 texts, 5,073 pages, Rin-chen gTer-mdzod: 43 texts

First of the five renowned gTer-ston Kings, and first of the Three Supreme Incarnations, Nyang-ral Nyi-ma 'Od-zer was an incarnation of King Khri-srong lDe'u-btsan. Born in southern Tibet at gTam-shul in lHo-brag, he was the son of Nyang-ston Chos-kyi 'Khor-lo and Padma bDe-ba-rtsal. Guru Padmasambhava and Ye-shes mTsho-rgyal blessed him with visions and empowerments that began during his childhood.

Padmasambhava actually appeared to Nyang-ral as the yogi dBang-phyug rDo-rje and gave him guidance on finding treasures. Nyang-ral also received the treasure indexes of Grwa-pa mNgon-shes and Ra-shag gTer-ston. Within the Vairotsana statue at Khom-mthing in lHo-brag, the land-taming temple built by Dharma King Srong-btsan sGam-po in the seventh century, Nyang-ral found the largest of the teachings on the eight heruka sādhanas (bKa'-brgyad-bde-gshegs-'dus-pa). The personal copies of Khri-srong lDe'u-btsan, these texts were in the handwriting of Vairotsana and lDan-ma Tsemang. At mChims-phu and at Srin-bya rock in gNam-skas-can in lHo-brag, he discovered more treasures.

Among his discoveries were teachings on the Great Compassionate One, the peaceful and wrathful aspects of the guru, a cycle of Mahākāla, a ḍākinī cycle, and the Hundredfold Dialogue of the Ḍākinī, which he received directly from the Lady Ye-shes mTsho-rgyal. The siddha dNgos-grub possessed bKa'-ma teachings related to the bKa'-brgyad cycles, which he gave to Nyang-ral, enabling Nyang-ral to combine the streams of gTer-ma and bKa'-ma. This siddha also bestowed on mNga'-bdag Nyang-ral the special Avalokiteśvara practices of the great

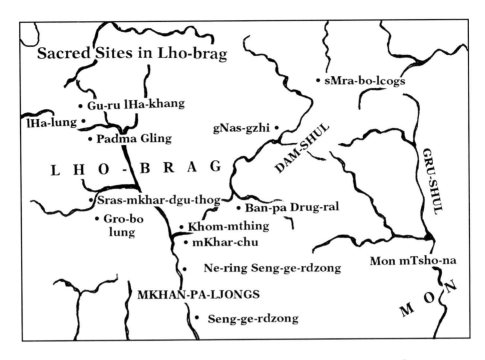

Sacred Sites in Lho-brag

- sMra-bo-lcogs
- Gu-ru lHa-khang
- lHa-lung
- Padma Gling
- gNas-gzhi
- DAM-SHUL
- GRU-SHUL
- LHO - BRAG
- Sras-mkhar-dgu-thog
- Gro-bo lung
- Ban-pa Drug-ral
- Khom-mthing
- mKhar-chu
- Mon mTsho-na
- Ne-ring Seng-ge-rdzong
- MKHAN-PA-LJONGS
- MON
- Seng-ge-rdzong

King Srong-btsan sGam-po (texts that belong to the Maṇi-bka'-'bum), which he had discovered in lHa-sa.

Nyang-ral Nyi-ma 'Od-zer's teachers included his father Nyang-ston, rGya-smyon-pa Don-ldan, Zhig-po Nyi-ma Seng-ge, Mal Ka-ba-can-pa, and sTon-pa Kha-che. Padmasambhava blessed and instructed him, and Ye-shes mTsho-rgyal took him to Śītavana cemetery where he received empowerment in the bKa'-brgyad teachings directly from the eight Vidyādharas.

Nyang-ral's consort was Jo-'bum, an emanation of Ye-shes mTsho-rgyal. Their two sons continued this stream of teachings, which is called the Upper Treasures. Nyang-ral founded the monastery of sMra-bo-cog in lHo-brag, where the Son Lineage later made its seat. The Son Lineage passed through Nyang-ral's son 'Gro-mgon Nam-mkha' dPal-ba, an emanation of Avalokiteśvara (who taught Guru Chos-dbang), Nyang-ral's grandson mNga'-bdag Blo-ldan Shes-rab, an emanation of Mañjuśrī, and Nyang-ral's great grandson mNga'-bdag bDud-'dul, an emanation of Vajrapāṇi.

121

Nyang-ral's foremost disciples included gNyos Grags-rgyal, the renowned Zhig-po bDud-rtsi, and sMan-lung-pa Mi-bskyod rDo-rje. These lineages have been maintained to the present day. Great Treasures of Ancient Teachings contains five hundred and fifty texts by this gTer-ston king, with an additional forty-four gTer-ma texts in the Rin-chen gTer-mdzod section.

གྲུབ་ཐོབ་དངོས་གྲུབ

## gTer-ston Grub-thob dNgos-grub
### late 11th–mid-12th century C.E.

An incarnation of Lo-chen Vairotsana, gTer-ston dNgos-grub was born in gTsang and lived as a Vajrayāna lineage holder. He mastered the forces of life and death and thus remained in the human realm for three hundred years.

This master bestowed upon mNga'-bdag Nyang-ral Nyi-ma 'Od-zer the bKa'-ma transmission of teachings related to the eight heruka sādhanas (bKa'-brgyad). Grub-thob dNgos-grub discovered many precious treasures at gTsang Ri-bo-che. He also found the Avalokiteśvara teachings of the Dharma King Srong-btsan sGam-po, which had been conccalcd at Ra-sa 'Phrul-snang temple in lHa-sa. These texts on the Great Compassionate One descended to Nyang-ral and were included in the king's collected works known as the Maṇi-bka'-'bum. Grub-thob dNgos-grub is the most important of the several gTer-stons who discovered sections of the Maṇi-bka'-'bum, which is preserved in Great Treasures of Ancient Teachings.

བྲུ་གུ་ཡང་དབང་

Gru-gu Yang-dbang
late 11th–mid-12th century C.E.
Rin-chen gTer-mdzod: 12 texts

Belonging to the incarnation stream of the great mNga'-bdag Chen-po, Nyang-ral Nyi-ma 'Od-zer, Gru-gu Yang-dbang was born in mDo-khams Gru-gu and lived as a great upholder of the Mantrayāna traditions. He was known as Yang-dbang-gter or rDo-rje gTer-bzhad-rtsal. In his lifetime, three transmissions of the precious sPyi-ti Atiyoga teachings were simultaneously flowing: one through sNye-mo Zhu-yas, a second in the texts transmitted through mNga'-bdag Nyang, and a third in the powerful mantra instructions transmitted through Yang-dbang. At Brag-dmar 'Om-bu-tshal Gru-gu Yang-dbang-gter discovered this section of mantras, together with the empowerments, texts, and instructions. This transmission continued undiminished to the time of Kong-sprul, who received all of it. Twelve texts are preserved in the Rin-chen gTer-mdzod section of Great Treasures of Ancient Teachings.

Zhig-po bDud-rtsi
b. 1143–1199 C.E.

A lineage holder of the Zur tradition, Zhig-po bDud-rtsi was born in gZad, a valley close to the sKyid-chu river near Shug-gseb in central Tibet. His father was Sangs-rgyas Dwags-chung, a follower of Dwags-po rGya-ras, and his mother was Jo-mo dBang-mo. His uncle was Se-sbrag-pa. At sKyil-mkhar lHa-khang southwest of Nyang, Zhig-po bDud-rtsi studied extensively with Yon-tan-gzungs (1126–1195), the disciple of lCe-ston rGya-nag. He focused in particular on the Sems-sde of rDzogs-chen. He guided the Dharma activity of Chos-sding monastery in 'On, 'Ug-skad monastery in gZad, and Se-sbrag-pa's monastery in the district of gTsang. He attended on all the translators and paṇḍitas who came to the Land of Snow in this era. Free of all worldly thoughts, he worked entirely for the Dharma. Among his countless disciples were six who became his spiritual heirs, the foremost being rTa-ston Jo-ye (1163–1230). No texts by this lineage holder have been located.

## rTa-ston Jo-ye
## 1163–1230 C.E.

Foremost disciple of Zhig-po bDud-rtsi, rTa-ston Jo-ye was the son of rTa-ston Jo-'bum, a nobleman of gYo-ru, who abandoned his wealth and property for the Dharma. Jo-'bum mastered the Mantrayāna traditions of the Ancient School with gNyos Chu-bo Ri-pa and received teachings from the bKa'-brgyud master Phag-mo-gru (1110–1170).

His son Jo-ye began study and practice of the Dharma as a child and grew very learned in the gSar-ma and rNying-ma Tantric traditions. At age twenty-five, Jo-ye became a disciple of Zhig-po bDud-rtsi at 'Ug-skad monastery. Under his guidance, Jo-ye attained profound realization, and Zhig-po bDud-rtsi en-trusted his monastery to his care. At the request of his guru, Jo-ye worked endlessly for the benefit of others, abandoning even his heartfelt wishes to go on retreat. His selfless action removed all his obscurations and his realization deepened until Jo-ye experienced no more personal sorrow of any kind. His younger brother rTa-ston Jo-bsod (1167–1197), a disciple of Zhig-po bDud-rtsi and of Yon-tan-gzungs, received the lineages of the Inner Yogas.

རོག་བན་ཤེས་རབ་འོད་ཟེར

Rog-ban Shes-rab 'Od-zer
1166–1244 C.E.
2 texts, 121 pages

Following in the Zur tradition, Rog Shes-rab-'od was a great scholar who held both the Mahāyoga and Anuyoga lineages from the disciples of the three Zur: Rog-ston bsTan-po, lHab-dres-ma Gong-pa, Yam-shud dNgos-grub, So Darma Seng-ge, and Myang Nag mDo-pa. He promulgated the Atiyoga system of So Ye-shes dBang-phyug (So-lugs). Author of several commentaries, including an important one on the Guhyagarbha, he wrote explanations and detailed notes on key texts that were found to greatly aid in the teaching of the rNying-ma Tantras.

His own lineage of the Mahāyoga is known as the system of Rog (Rog-lugs). These lineages were preserved at Kaḥ-thog and at Dan-bag, where, in the fourteenth century, Klong-chen-pa studied them. Two works are preserved in Great Treasures of Ancient Teachings, including a Grub-mtha' text that clarifies and compares the doctrines of different schools.

གཉལ་པ་ཉི་མ་ཤེས་རབ

gNyal-pa Nyi-ma Shes-rab
mid-12th–early 13th century C.E.
Rin-chen gTer-mdzod: 3 texts

Taking birth at gNyal, Nyi-ma Shes-rab was one of the four main disciples of Zangs-dkar Lo-tsā-ba 'Phags-pa Shes-rab, and became learned in the Yoga Tantras. Nyi-ma Shes-rab first studied with Zangs-dkar Lo-tsā-ba in lHa-sa and then journeyed with him to Nepal. He later received teachings from Mang-nang-pa and sKyi-mor Jñāna.

Nyi-ma Shes-rab established the foundation for the Dharma in gNyal, building many temples and shrines to the Buddha Vairocana and turning the wheel of the Dharma throughout the region. During his lifetime, the Yoga Tantras spread very widely due to his great kindness and intention to bring benefits to sentient beings.

In the temple at Bya-rgod-gshong he discovered wonderful treasures: a statue hidden by Blon-chen lHa-bzang Klu-dpal in early times, the banner of one of the Guardian Kings, as well as the associated sādhana practices that had been given by the Great Guru to Khri-srong lDe'u-bstan. Kong-sprul Blo-gros mTha'-yas was able to locate and preserve in the Rin-chen gTer-mdzod several texts that Khro-phu Lo-tsā-ba (1173–1225) had originally helped arrange.

གཏེར་སྟོན་འབྲེ་ཤེས་རབ་བླ་མ།
གཏེར་སྟོན་རྐྱང་པོ་གྲགས་པ་དབང་ཕྱུག
གཏེར་སྟོན་སུམ་པ་བྱང་ཆུབ་ཚུལ་ཁྲིམས།

gTer-ston 'Bre Shes-rab Bla-ma
gTer-ston rKyang-po Grags-pa dBang-phyug
gTer-ston Sum-pa Byang-chub Tshul-khrims
mid-12th–early 13th century C.E.
Rin-chen gTer-mdzod: 1 text

These three gTer-ma masters discovered hidden treasures associated with the herukas at the holy site of Yer-pa Se-ba-lung This transmission did not flourish, for the conditions were not right: rKyang-po was struck with leprosy,

Sum-pa passed away, and 'Bre lost his senses. Fortunately, the teachings came into the hands of a siddha who was expert in these types of practices, and so survived the centuries. Kong-sprul Blo-gros mTha'-yas located one text and included it in the Rin-chen gTer-mdzod.

གཏེར་སྟོན་གཡས་བན་ཡ་བོན།

gTer-ston gYas-ban Ya-bon
mid-12th–early 13th century C.E.

Born into a Bon-po family in the period of the latter part of the life of gNyan Lo-tsā-ba Dar-grags, gYas-ban Ya-bon discovered gTer-ma treasures at the ancient temple of Bra-dum-rtse built by Srong-btsan sGam-po in the seventh century. Transmitted for centuries, the texts had been lost by the time of Kong-sprul Blo-gros mTha'-yas, and so none were preserved in the Rin-chen gTer-mdzod.

གཏེར་སྟོན་གཡག་ཕྱར་སྟོན་མོ་རྡོ་རྗེ་འབུམ།

gTer-ston gYag-phyar sNgon-mo rDo-rje-'bum
mid-12th–early 13th century C.E.
Rin-chen gTer-mdzod: 3 texts

An incarnation of Lo-chen Vairotsana, gYag-phar was born into a Bon-po family in 'U-yug. He lived as a holder of Mantrayāna vows known as rDo-rje-'bum. Near his birthplace of gYag-lce Khra-mo in 'U-yug, he discovered precious treasure texts concealed by Vairotsana associated with the three essential cycles of guru sādhanas, rDzogs-chen, and Avalokiteśvara practices (Bla-rdzogs-thugs-gsum) and collected sādhanas. He also located Bon teachings, but the stream of these did not continue in the future.

The collection of sādhanas included practices focused on Tārā's giving protection from fear, which he reconcealed at Yer-pa. Later Rong-pa bDud-'dul Gling-pa discovered these and concealed them once again. 'Jam-dbyangs mKhyen-brtse received these teachings and out of his great kindness made them available. Kong-sprul Blo-gros mTha'-yas was able to include three texts in the Rin-chen gTer-mdzod, together with one he composed to augment these practices.

## བལ་པོ་ཨ་ཧཱུྃ་འབར་

Bal-po A-Hūṁ-'bar
mid-12th–early 13th century C.E.
Rin-chen gTer-mdzod: 1 text

Apparently the incarnation of sNa-nam rDo-rje bDud-'joms, Bal-po A-Hūṁ was born in southern gTsang, where he lived as a holder of Mantrayāna vows. He proceeded to sPa-gro in Bhutan where he discovered instructions and practices hidden as treasure texts. Gradually the lineages of these teachings spread from dPal dGa'-ba-lung-pa. In early times the texts and the practices remained intact, but in the era of Kong-sprul, copies of the texts could no longer be found. Fortunately, the ḍākinīs bestowed on 'Jam-dbyangs mKhyen-brtse an ancient copy of the text, and Kong-sprul included this in the Rin-chen gTer-mdzod together with his own supplementary notes.

# ཟུར་མཁར་ཨ་ཇོ་དཔལ་པོ

A-jo dPal-po
mid-12th–early 13th century C.E.
Rin-chen gTer-mdzod: 1 text

Zur-mkhar A-jo dPal-po was born near bSam-yas at Zur-mkhar, where five small white stupas dedicated to the five Buddha families mark the spot where King Khri-srong lDe'u-btsan first met Guru Padmasambhava. A-jo dPal-po lived as a Mantrayāna practitioner. In the pillar of the temple at Mon Bum-thang, he found precious treasure texts and prayers. The prayers were still recited by everyone in the time of Kong-sprul Blo-gros mTha'-yas seven hundred years later. This gTer-ma teaching is preserved in the Rin-chen gTer-mdzod. A-jo dPal-po also found sādhanas to the Three Protector Sisters at sGrags Yang-rdzong, the powerful sacred place connected with the Enlightened Body of the Guru. At bSam-yas he found more treasure texts. None of these were extant in the time of Kong-sprul Blo-gros mTha'-yas and so could not be included in the Rin-chen gTer-mdzod.

# དབང་ཕྱུག་ཆེན་པོ་འདར་ཕྱར་རུ་པ

dBang-phyug Chen-po 'Dar-phyar Ru-pa
mid-12th–early 13th century C.E.
Rin-chen gTer-mdzod: 2 texts

An accomplished yogin, master 'Dar-phyar Ru-pa practiced at Jo-mo Nags-rgyal in gTsang. Guru Padmasambhava appeared in person to direct the fortunate yogi to Yer-pa, the sacred place of power where in the eighth century the Great Guru had hidden the Vajrakīla teachings. There, in the Moon

Cave, Padmasambhava arrived each morning to instruct him in the Vajrakīla practices, and 'Dar-phyar Ru-pa actually found the kīla dagger concealed there by the Great Guru.

In gTsang, 'Dar-phyar Ru-pa met Sa-skya Paṇḍita, who informed him that his way of reciting the mantra was not correct. Having already attained great accomplishment with his practice of Vajrakīla, 'Dar-phyar Ru-pa displayed his powers, thrusting the kīla dagger into solid rock. Sa-skya Paṇḍita immediately asked him to accompany him to a debate with some non-Buddhists led by Haranandin.

After thirteen days of argumentation, Sa-skya Paṇḍita was victorious, but Haranandin demanded competition in yogic powers to confirm the victory. When the non-Buddhist rose in the sky, Sa-skya Paṇḍita turned to 'Dar-phyar Ru-pa for assistance. The great yogi thrust his kīla into the shadow of the extremist, who fell to the earth like a bird struck with a stone. After that time, non-Buddhist philosophies were no longer propagated in the Land of Snow. 'Dar-phyar Ru-pa was the holder of the gTer-ma lineage of the Vajrakīla practices, which were also transmitted as a bKa'-ma lineage through numerous masters. Two texts are preserved in the Rin-chen gTer-mdzod.

Du-gu Rin-chen Seng-ge
gTsang-pa Lab-ring-mo
mid-12th–early 13th century C.E.
Rin-chen gTer-mdzod: 1 text

Born in dBus, Du-gu Rin-chen Seng-ge discovered gTer-ma treasures in an old stupa erected at a seventh-century temple. These Tantric teachings had first been given by Guru Padma to the king and five disciples during the period when Vairotsana was in exile in rGyal-mo-rong. The king was instructed to conceal them at Bra-dum-rtse, a land-taming temple built by King Srong-btsan sGam-po. Rin-chen Seng-ge obtained the treasure list at bSam-yas and then proceeded north to Bra-dum-rtse. Many difficulties beset the gTer-ston and his student gTsang-pa Lab-ring-mo as they tried to obtain the texts, and both men eventually lost their lives. The texts were preserved by the gTer-ston's daughter 'Od-ldem, however, and the teachings spread and endured. Kong-sprul included these extensive works in the Rin-chen gTer-mdzod.

## སྤྲུལ་སྐུ་སྟོད་དམར་པོ

### sPrul-sku La-stod dMar-po
### mid-12th–early 13th century C.E.
### Rin-chen gTer-mdzod: 2 texts

Dam-pa dMar-po, also known by the name of sPrul-sku La-stod dMar-po, discovered one gTer-ma treasure in Bhutan at sPa-gro near the rock shaped like a lion. From the Black Stupa at bSam-yas, he obtained very powerful mantras of sorcery belonging to the tīrthikas, which had been concealed there by Guru Padma. From Yer-pa, the valley northeast of lHa-sa filled with practice caves of eighth-century siddhas, he obtained a dkar-chag written in the handwriting of Kong-jo, the Chinese princess. At Mang-mkhar Mu-gu-lung, he discovered many more gTer-ma treasures.

The first treasure from sPa-gro was later practiced intensely by the great Thang-stong rGyal-po, who thereby attained yogic powers. But unfortunately most of these teachings were no longer available in the time of Kong-sprul Blo-gros mTha'-yas, who included only two texts in the Rin-chen gTer-mdzod.

ཤངས་པ་སྐྱེར་སྒང་ཆོས་ཀྱི་སེང་གེ

## Shangs pa sKyer-sgang Chos-kyi Seng-ge
### mid-12th–early 13th century C.E.
### Rin-chen gTer-mdzod: 2 texts

An incarnation of the Mahābodhisattva Avalokiteśvara, sKyer-sgang-pa Chos-kyi Seng-ge was the second of the seven great masters of the Shangs-pa bKa'-brgyud tradition that was established on the basis of teachings of 'Khyung-po rNal-'byor (978–1079). Chos-kyi Seng-ge was born in sTod-lungs gNam into the clan of 'Bal and at age seventeen was ordained by his uncle 'Bal Thams-cad mKhyen-pa. He soon received teachings on Avalokiteśvara sādhanas, which he practiced intensively at sKyer-sgang for a number of years until he saw the face of the Bodhisattva.

He set out for La-stod to find Tsā-ri sGom-pa, a disciple of Ras-chung-pa. There he received the complete precepts of Ras-chung-pa. Then he studied with Bla-ma sPen-phug in 'U-yug and received the Tantras of Lord Atīśa. Thereafter he became the devoted disciple of rMog-cog-pa, one of the chief disciples of 'Khyung-po rNal-'byor.

Later he returned to sKyer-sgang where he built stupas and acted as abbot, though most of his labors for others were accomplished within his meditation practice. Completely prescient, he was able to benefit many beings. He could simply vanish from sight and arrive at a destination; in this way he proceeded to the renowned eight cemeteries in India, where he practiced the teachings of Dhanasaṁskṛta, the master of one of the heruka sādhanas.

132

sKyer-sgang-pa's major disciple was Sangs-rgyas gNyan-ston Chos-kyi Shes-rab, who later became such a powerful teacher that a single meeting with him was sufficient to produce eventual liberation.

sKyer-sgang-pa was able to travel to Zangs-mdog dPal-ri, the Copper-Colored Mountain of Padmasambhava, where he requested special Hayagrīva teachings from the Great Guru in order to tame demonic forces. This stream of precious teachings was joined with the gTer-ma of sNye-bo Sangs-rgyas dBang-chen; together these lineages generated tremendous blessings. They pervaded both gSar-ma and rNying-ma traditions, and remained extant down to present times. Kong-sprul Blo-gros mTha'-yas included two texts discovered by sKyer-sgang-pa in the Rin-chen gTer-mdzod.

## Zhang-ston Nyi-ma-'bum
### 1158–1213 C.E.

An emanation of Vajrapāṇi, Nyi-'bum was born as the son of Zhang-ston bKra-shis rDo-rje and rGyal-mo gYang. He was an essential link in the transmission of the Bi-ma-snying-thig, the Atiyoga transmission that descended from Vimalamitra. He was named Nyi-ma-'bum (One Hundred Thousand Suns) by his father, who predicted he would illuminate the darkness of ignorance. His father transmitted to him the empowerments, explanations, and guidance for the Bi-ma-snying-thig teachings, which Nyi-'bum mastered completely.

Nyi-ma-'bum studied the gSar-ma Tantras with the bKa'-brgyud-pa master rNgog rGyal-rtse, and Sa-skya teachings with Sa-skya Grags-pa rGyal-mtshan and others. He received the teachings of the Cakrasaṁvara Tantra from Kha-rag

'Brug-ston sGrags-pa, and teachings from Bla-ma Zhang gYu-brag-pa. He is known to have composed at least one text, but it has not been located in recent times. His disciple was Guru Jo-'ber, who taught 'Khrul-zhig Seng-ge-rgyab.

ཀཿཐོག་པ་བྱམས་པ་འབུམ་

## Kaḥ-thog-pa Byams-pa-'bum
## 1179–1252 C.E.

An incarnation of the Indian siddha Kṛṣṇacārin, Byams-pa-'bum was the disciple of Kaḥ-dam-pa bDe-gshegs and gTsang-ston. He continued the glorious tradition of Kaḥ-thog monastery in the thirteenth century, emphasizing both the Mahāyoga and the Atiyoga teachings. He ordained the Second Karmapa, Karma Pakṣi, giving him instructions in Great Perfection and Mahāyoga teachings. He also gave teachings to the Sa-skya master 'Phags-pa. On his return from Mongolia, 'Phags-pa offered Kaḥ-thog monastery a large bronze stupa and seven great altar bowls. Following Byams-pa-'bum, a succession of enlightened abbots guided Kaḥ-thog monastery in a series known as the "Thirteen Generations," which ended with the master Kaḥ-thog-pa Ye-shes rGyal-mtshan (born 1395). Texts by Byams-pa-'bum have not been located in recent times.

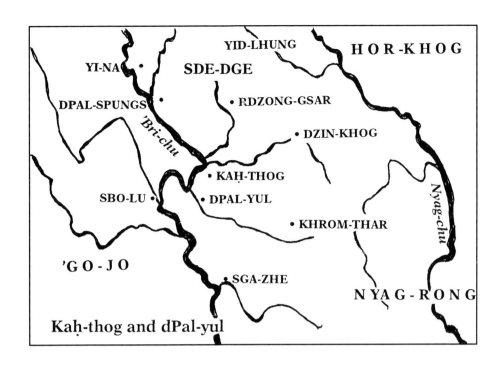

Kaḥ-thog and dPal-yul

གུ་རུ་ཇོ་འབེར

Gu-ru Jo-'ber
b. 1196 C.E.

Gu-ru Jo-'ber was a key link in the transmission of the Bi-ma-snying-thig lineage that descended eventually to the Omniscient Klong-chen-pa. He was born as the son of his master Nyi-'bum's younger brother Zla-ba-'bum. He lived with his uncle Nyi-ma-'bum, receiving the complete teachings and empowerments for the Bi-ma-snying-thig. At the age of nineteen he also studied Sa-skya doctrines with the great Sa-skya Paṇḍita. By the time he was thirty-six he had studied Logic and Madhyamaka, Mahāmudrā, and many different Tantras. He lived sixty years, guiding disciples and transmitting the lineage of the Bi-ma-snying-thig to 'Khrul-zhig Seng-ge-rgyab. No texts by this master have been located in recent times.

# གཏེར་ཆེན་གུ་རུ་ཆོས་ཀྱི་དབང་ཕྱུག

## gTer-chen Guru Chos-kyi dBang-phyug
### 1212–1270 C.E.
### 463 texts, 2,212 pages, Rin-chen gTer-mdzod: 40 texts

The second of the five Discoverer Kings, gTer-chen Guru Chos-kyi dBang-phyug was the second great incarnation of King Khri-srong lDe'u-btsan. Born in lHo-brag as the son of the siddha sPang-ston Grub-pa'i sNying-po and the ḍākinī dKar-bza' mGon-skyid, Guru Chos-dbang was a remarkable child. Having mastered grammar, divination, medicine, history, music, drama, and art, he studied and mastered all the Dharma disciplines including Abhidharma, Zhi-byed, both Ancient and New Tantras, Mahāmudrā, and rDzogs-chen.

Inspired by a vision of Vajrasattva at the age of thirteen, he soon obtained a list of gTer-ma locations that had been discovered by Grwa-pa mNgon-shes. His father concealed the list, fearing its great power since all who had handled it had met with misfortune. Chos-kyi dBang-phyug later found the list and followed it, discovering nineteen sets of teachings, including the three essential cycles of guru sādhanas, rDzogs-chen teachings, and Avalokiteśvara practices. These teachings became known as the Lower Treasures.

Guru Chos-dbang found treasures at sacred sites such as gNam-skas-can in lHo-brag, Brag-dmar near bSam-yas, rTa-mgrin-zhabs at bSam-yas, upper Mon-kha, rTa-mgrin, dBen-rtsa'i-sgo, sGrom-cho-la, Mi-la Ras-pa's tower at Sras-mkhar, sKya-bo Phugs-ring, Phyag-mtheb-ma, bSam-yas Ārya, lCags-phur, Mon Bum-thang, rTsis-ki temple, Rong-brag, and bSam-yas Ha-bo-sgang.

Chos-kyi dBang-phyug, renowned as the "Moon" among all gTer-stons, became an incomparable siddha. Padmasambhava appeared to him and transmitted the full empowerment of the eight heruka sādhanas (bKa'-brgyad). His teachers included Nyang-ral Nyi-ma 'Od-zer's son 'Gro-mgon, and Sa-skya Paṇḍita, who gave him Bodhisattva vows.

He built the temples of Tshong-'dus mGur-mo and bSam-'grub bDe-ba-chen. At La-yag Gu-ru lHa-khang, his main seat in lHo-brag, scholars and disciples from all parts of Tibet gathered to hear him teach. All the Dharma masters of the Land of Snow, both gSar-ma and rNying-ma, revered Chos-kyi dBang-phyug as their guru. The noted gTer-ston Jo-mo sMan-mo became his consort, and the two adepts benefited one another greatly. The Son Lineage flowed through Padma dBang-chen and gNyal Nyi-ma 'Od-zer. His main disciples were Mi-bskyod rDo-rje and Newar Bha-ro gTsug-'dzin, the Nine Worthy Sons, and Kaḥ-thog Maṇi Rin-chen. Through them the lineage of the Lower Treasures was transmitted in Tibet, Nepal, and throughout the Himalayas.

Four hundred and sixty-three of his works are preserved in Great Treasures of Ancient Teachings. Forty additional gTer-ma are included in the Rin-chen gTer-mdzod section.

གཏེར་སྟོན་དུང་མཚོ་རས་པ་སྔ་མ།

## gTer-ston Dung-mtsho Ras-pa the Earlier
### early 13th–mid-13th century C.E.

The rebirth of Ye-shes rDo-rje, a disciple of sGam-po-pa, and an incarnation of Myang-ban Ting-nge-'dzin bZang-po, Dung-mtsho Ras-pa was born in Yar-lung and named Shes-rab rGya-mtsho. Early in life, he resided at gDan-sa-mthil, where he was ordained by sGam-po rDor-blo and given the religious name Rin-chen bZang-po.

At Kha-rag gYu-mtsho he undertook ascetic practices with instructions from 'Khrul-zhig Khams-pa Rinpoche. In his hermit's hut of straw, he discovered a list of gTer-ma texts that led him to a frozen lake in sGam-po. There Dwags-po Rinpoche sGam-po-pa and Ye-shes rDo-rje had hidden a gTer-ma, which Dung-mtsho Ras-pa now discovered beneath the ice. These precious teachings spread extensively in early times and were preserved in the Zur-mang Hearing Lineage. At gNyal, the birthplace of Dwags-po Rin-po-che, Dung-mtsho Ras-pa built many temples and stupas. His disciples included sTag-tshang Ras-pa, Tsā-ri Ras-pa, Bye-ma Ras-pa, and 'Khrul-zhig sNa'u-pa, sGrod-lung-pa, and others. He later reincarnated as Dung-mtsho Ras-pa the Later.

ཟུར་པཀྵི་ཤཱཀྱ་འོད་

## Zur Pakṣi Śākya 'Od
### early 13th–mid-13th century C.E.

A descendent of the Zur clan, Pakṣi Śākya 'Od was the son of Zur dBang-chen 'Od-po-che, an accomplished practitioner. When the great Śākya Śrī was visiting Tibet in 1204, 'Od-po-che invited him to 'Ug-pa-lung, the ancestral residence of the Zur clan, and the master predicted the birth of two sons who would uphold the Mantrayāna traditions of Zur.

The younger of these two was Śākya 'Od, who was obviously a remarkable individual even as a child. Studying with masters whose lineages traced back to sGro-sbug-pa, he became an extraordinary yogin and an expert in powerful mantras. The Mongol Emperor Qubilai Khan was intent on receiving the water of longevity from Śākya 'Od, for he was capable of locating and extracting such treasure. Having obtained the elixir, the great Khan granted Śākya 'Od the title of Pakṣi and bestowed lands and honors upon him. Śākya 'Od's main disciple was rTa-nag bDud-'dul, who taught mDa' Śākya 'Phel, the master of Zur Byams-pa Seng-ge. No texts by these masters have been located in recent times.

ཟུར་ཉི་མ་སེང་གེ

## Zur Nyi-ma Seng-ge
### early 13th–mid-13th century C.E.

The son of Mes-po Pakṣi, a great master of the Inner Yogas in the lineage of sGro-sbug-pa, Nyi-ma Seng-ge was ordained at Khro-phu by Khro-phu Lo-tsā-ba Byams-pa-dpal (1173–1225). He was firmly committed to the Bodhisattva path and to the practice of Bodhicitta, and had highly developed yogic powers. He worked for the benefit of beings during a period of invasions by Mongol troops, and protected many people from fear. In particular he defended the Sa-skya rulers from enormous Mongol armies. He was renowned for bringing droughts to an end and for building temples and filling them with sacred images, books, and stupas. His son was Byams-pa Seng-ge, lineage holder of the Three Inner Yogas in the Zur tradition, who was the teacher of the masters gYung-ston rDo-rje-dpal and sGrol-ma-ba bSam-'grub rDo-rje. No works composed by the master have been located.

# ཟུར་བྱམས་པ་སེང་གེ

## Zur Byams-pa Seng-ge
### 1283 C.E.

An essential link in the Inner Yoga lineages that descended from sGro-sbug-pa, Byams-pa Seng-ge was the son of Nyi-ma Seng-ge. He studied first at Khro-phu, where he discoursed on the Dharma even at the age of fourteen. At 'Ug-pa-lung he studied under mDa' Śākya 'Phel and other masters, receiving the entire transmission of the Zur traditions. From Thar-pa Lo-tsā-ba he learned grammar and logic, and from many other gurus he received gSar-ma Tantras. So powerful was this master's realization that the perception of all those who came into his presence was transformed.

Though he lived only to the age of twenty-seven, he trained sixteen major disciples and taught countless others. His foremost disciples were gYung-ston rDo-rje-dpal and sGrol-ma-ba bSam-'grub rDo-rje, both of whom regarded their master as omniscient. No works by this lineage holder have been located in recent times.

# འཁྲུལ་ཞིག་སེང་གེ་རྒྱབ

## 'Khrul-zhig Seng-ge-rgyab
### early 13th century–mid-13th century C.E.

A crucial link in the transmission of the Bi-ma-snying-thig lineages, 'Khrul-zhig Seng-ge-rgyab was born in Grwa valley. By the age of twelve he had become completely disillusioned with samsara. In a vision, Avalokiteśvara urged him to seek out the teachings of the sNying-thig; from that day forward unbounded compassion arose within his heart. At the age of twenty he was ordained by mKhan-po lDe'u sGang-pa.

Later, at Śrī Zhal Seng-ge-rgyab, 'Khrul-zhig Rinpoche met numerous masters who taught him Mantrayāna. Guru Jo-'ber bestowed upon him the sNying-thig teachings; practicing intently at Khro-bo-ma, 'Khrul-zhig developed complete understanding. He lived for sixty-four years, firmly connecting many disciples to the path of liberation. His closest disciple was Me-long rDo-rje. No texts by this master have been found in recent times.

## sKyid Chos-kyi Seng-ge
### early 13th century–mid-13th century C.E.

Chos-kyi Seng-ge was the disciple of Sangs-rgyas-grags, also known as rDo-thogs-pa, whose own master was a disciple of sGro-sbug-pa. He was invited to the court of Qubilai Khan, where his yogic powers were tested by his being confined within a locked stupa for an entire year. When the stupa was opened, the heroic lord of yogins had transformed into Vajrakīla. The Mongol Emperor bestowed many gifts and properties upon him.

Master of the Mahāyoga and Anuyoga, Chos-kyi Seng-ge transmitted these lineages to his disciple sMan-lung-pa Śākya 'Od and to Phung-po rGya Ye-shes mGon-po. The nephew of Phung-po rGya was rDo-rje rGyal-mtshan, who composed learned commentaries on Mahāyoga. No works by Chos-kyi Seng-ge, Ye-shes mGon-po, or rDo-rje rGyal-mtshan have been found in recent times.

སྨན་ལུང་པ་མི་བསྐྱོད་རྡོ་རྗེ

# sMan-lung-pa Mi-bskyod rDo-rje
## 1239 C.E.
## 5 texts, 235 pages

The master Mi-bskyod rDo-rje, who was also known as Śākya 'Od of sMan-lung, was the oldest of five sons born to mNyam-med-pa, the son of Nyang-ston Chen-po. He studied under the Mahāyoga and Anuyoga master sKyid Chos-kyi Seng-ge. He later studied with the great scholar of Glan, bSod-rgyal, who was the son of Glan rDo-rje 'Od-po. One of the foremost disciples of both Nyang-ral Nyi-ma 'Od-zer and Guru Chos-dbang, sMan-lung-pa Mi-bskyod rDo-rje was learned in both bKa'-ma and gTer-ma traditions. He authored a set of commentaries on the root Tantra of the Mahāyoga, the gSang-ba'i-snying-po.

He had many disciples in Dwags-po to whom he taught Inner Yogas. Later he became the guru of the ruler of 'Go-jo and preached the Dharma extensively in Khams. His major disciples included Śākya 'Bum-pa (1265–1310), who was the son of Yar-lung sPrul-sku, Dwags-po Sangs-rgyas Gong-la-ba, mKhas-grub Chos-dpal-pa (father and son), Dwags-po Bla-ma gNyan, Yar-lung Lo-tsā-ba Grags-pa rGyal-mtshan, and Yang-dgon-pa (1213–1258), who was the disciple of rGod-tshang-pa mGon-po rDo-rje (1189–1258). Five of his texts are preserved in Great Treasures of Ancient Teachings.

སྐལ་ལྡན་བྱིས་པ

sKal-ldan Byis-pa

early 13th–mid-13th century C.E.

Rin-chen gTer-mdzod: 2 texts

This gTer-ma master, who worked in Gu-ge in mNga'-ris, discovered healing practices that helped protect against diseases. These protective rites were passed in an unbroken stream that eventually reached Kong-sprul Blo-gros mTha'-yas, who preserved several texts in the Rin-chen gTer-mdzod.

གཏེར་སྟོན་བླ་མ་གྲུམ

gTer-ston Bla-ma Grum

early 13th–mid-13th century C.E.

Rin-chen gTer-mdzod: 1 text

Bla-ma Grum, together with his patron Nag-po mKhar, discovered a treasure in Bhutan at sPa-sgro sKyer-chu temple, one of the edifices built by Srong-btsan sGam-po in the seventh century to tame the land. These teachings, which were sādhanas and protective rites to avert various dangers, gradually became renowned and were transmitted in an unbroken stream to the present. These sādhanas were especially revered and practiced by Kumārādza (1266–1343), the great protector able to alleviate the misfortunes of beings in all realms. Kong-sprul Blo-gros mTha'-yas preserved one text with these teachings in the Rin-chen gTer-mdzod.

## ཁམས་པ་གཏེར་སྟོན་ཉི་མ་གྲགས་པ

Khams-pa gTer-ston Nyi-ma Grags-pa
early 13th–mid-13th century C.E.

Born in Upper Khams, Nyi-ma-grags was known as Khams-stod Dwags-po gTer-ston or sometimes Khams-pa gTer-ston. He should not be confused with another gTer-ston known as Nyi-ma-grags, who was born in later times. Khams-pa gTer-ston Nyi-ma-grags was the incarnation of lHa-lung dPal-gyi rDo-rje. Behind sGam-po gDar mountain in Dwags-po was Srin-po Srin-mo rDo-rje-rdzong, a hidden valley very difficult to enter. In that secret location, Nyi-ma-grags discovered Yamāntaka practices, seven sets of powerful mantras, and many other gTer-ma treasures

Beset by difficult conditions, this gTer-ston did not live long enough to establish the teachings, and most of the texts were not available later. The seven sets of mantras came to 'Jam-dbyangs mKhyen-brtse as a Reconcealed Treasure.

## གཏེར་སྟོན་གུ་རུ་ཚེ་བརྟན་རྒྱལ་མཚན

gTer-ston Gu-ru Tshe-brtan rGyal-mtshan
early 13th–mid-13th century C.E.
1 text, 2 pages, Rin-chen gTer-mdzod: 3 texts

One of two incarnations of rGyal-ba mChog-dbyangs, Tshe-brtan rGyal-mtshan was born at sNar-thang in Upper Mon La-mo. He was known as Chos-kyi Blo-gros and as Guru Tshe-brtan rGyal-mtshan. He lived as an ordained up-holder of the Mantrayāna.

His extensive understanding of both Sūtra and Mantra teachings made him an outstanding spiritual guide. As predicted by Padmasambhava, in a cave by a rock formation shaped like a dancing goddess in the region of Mon, and in several other locations, he discovered treasures concealed by Ye-shes mTsho-rgyal. In particular, he found the practices of peaceful and wrathful aspects of the guru, texts relating to Tārā and Amitābha, prophecies, works on rDzogs-chen, and many other precious gTer-ma.

All his discoveries remained in circulation in the time of gTer-bdag Gling-pa, but most could not be found by Kong-sprul Blo-gro mTha'-yas in the nineteenth century. The Rin-chen gTer-mdzod preserves three texts.

གཏེར་སྟོན་རཀྵི་སྟོན་པ

## gTer-ston Rakṣi sTon-pa
### early 13th–mid-13th century C.E.

An incarnation of Rlangs dPal-gyi Seng-ge, Rakṣi sTon-pa was born at gNyal. He lived as a holder of Mantrayāna vows in the days when the Sa-skya-pa had risen to power in central Tibet. On the border of Tibet and Glo, he discovered treasures of medical and astrological texts, Bon works, and Dharma teachings, but the texts did not all remain in circulation in later times. No works were located by Kong-sprul.

# གྲུབ་ཆེན་མེ་ལོང་རྡོ་རྗེ

## Grub-chen Me-long rDo-rje
### 1243–1303 C.E.

M e-long rDo-rje was born in sGrags as the son of the yogi bSam-yas. Grub-thob Za-lung-pa and mKhan-po Se-lung-pa gave him the Triple Vajra Saṃvara vows, and he spent years of his youth reciting Prajñāpāramitā Sūtras and deepening his understanding of the nature of reality. He studied both gSar-ma and rNying-ma Tantras, made pilgrimages to many holy places, and practiced austerities. From Sang-rgyas Ras-pa, he received gTer-ma teachings of rDo-rje Phag-mo.

Me-long rDo-rje received the Dharma from thirteen gurus. In particular, 'Khrul-zhig Seng-ge-rgyab, who was the disciple of Guru Jo-'ber, granted him rDzogs-chen teachings. Blessed by numerous visions of the great Bodhisattvas and founders of the lineage, Me-long rDo-rje was directly empowered in the Atiyoga teachings by Vajrasattva. Me-long rDo-rje's major disciple was the master Kumārādza to whom he transmitted the Bi-ma-snying-thig teachings.

At sGrags Yang-rdzong, the holy place associated with the Guru's Enlightened Body, he discovered precious instructions of Vimalamitra (Bi-ma-la'i-thugs-thig), which became known as the Me-long-snying-thig. These did not survive the centuries but later came to 'Jam-dbyangs mKhyen-brtse as Reconcealed Treasure.

Renowned for his yogic powers, possessed of impeccable conduct, Me-long rDo-rje served living beings in the hidden valleys of mKhar-chu, Seng-ge rDzong, mKhan-pa-gling, mKhan-pa-ljongs, and other places until he passed away, accompanied by masses of rainbow light. No works by this remarkable lineage holder have been located.

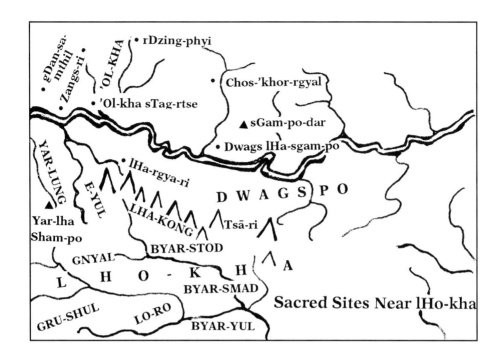

གཏེར་སྟོན་ཆེན་མོ་ཇོ་མོ་སྨན་མོ

## gTer-ston Chen-mo Jo-mo sMan-mo
### 1248–1283 C.E.

One of the two most renowned incarnations of the lady Ye-shes mTsho-rgyal, Jo-mo sMan-mo was born near the sacred site of gZar-mo-lung in E-yul into the family of the Mantrayāna practitioner rDo-rje rGyal-po of Dwags-po and Padma dPal-'joms, who was descended from a line of ḍākinīs. The child's parents called her Padma mTsho-skyid. At thirteen she entered the cave called Khyung-chen-lding at gZar-mo-lung, which had been one of Guru Padmasambhava's practice places. There she received empowerment from the ḍākinīs in the teachings known as Gathering All the Secrets of the Ḍākinīs (mKha'-'gro-ma'i-gsang-ba-kun-'dus), and the actual book was given to her.

147

Her understanding of reality blossomed, and she sponta-neously taught Dharma in song and dance. But as many local people thought her mad, she departed for lHo-brag, where she met Guru Chos-dbang and became his prophesied consort. Great benefit flowed from their union: Guru Chos-dbang be-came able to bring forth the meanings of gTer-ma previously unclear and Jo-mo received essential teachings of maturation and liberation. The great Guru Chos-dbang advised her not to make known the ḍākinī volume but to practice it secretly.

Jo-mo wandered throughout central Tibet, practicing and deepening her understanding. She met Gling-rje Ras-pa and opened his understanding to a profound depth. At last she rose bodily into the sky and flew to the Copper-Colored Mountain. The text of the Gathering All the Secrets of the Ḍākinīs came to 'Jam-dbyangs mKhyen-brtse as a Recollection Treasure, for he had in a previous lifetime been the individual known as Guru Chos-dbang. Thus, Kong-sprul Blo-gros mTha'-yas was able to include this treasure in the Rin-chen gTer-mdzod.

ब্রংর্তিক্রুল্যক্ষিগাব্যর্নু

Brang-ti rGyal-nye mKhar-bu
early 13th–mid-13th century C.E.
Rin-chen gTer-mdzod: 1 text

Brang-ti rGyal-nye mKhar-bu was born into the clan of Brang-ti as one of a succession of Brang-ti physicians. At bSam-yas he discovered some of the teachings on methods of healing hidden by King Khri-srong lDe'u-btsan and Padma-sambhava. Practicing the associated sādhanas, he became well-known for his healing powers. From the thirteenth cen-tury on, the lineage continued, descending through Brang-ti 'Jam-dpal bZang-po. A portion of these teachings has been preserved in the medical collection known as the gYu-thog-snying-thig and included in the Rin-chen gTer-mdzod.

gTer-ston sGom-chen 'Brug-pa
gTer-ston gNyan-ston Dzambhala
gTer-ston Don-grub Seng-ge
gTer-ston Padma Grags-pa
early 13th–mid-13th century C.E.

These four gTer-stons were assistants to the great Guru Chos-dbang and helped him locate his treasures. In particular, sGom-chen 'Brug-pa assisted in obtaining the large treasure from Sras-mkhar tower built by Mi-la Ras-pa, while gNyan-ston assisted in locating treasures at lHo-brag mKho-mthing, the seventh-century temple built by King Srong-btsan sGam-po. Don-grub Seng-ge and Padma Grags-pa also assisted at Sras-mkhar. The numerous treasures of Guru Chos-dbang are noted above.

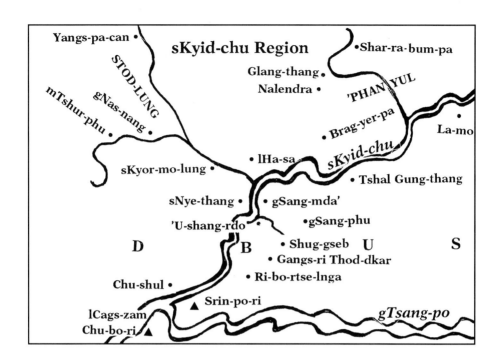

sKyid-chu Region

Yangs-pa-can •
STOD-LUNG
mTshur-phu •
gNas-nang •
Shar-ra-bum-pa
Glang-thang •
Nalendra •
'PHAN-YUL
Brag-yer-pa •
La-mo
sKyor-mo-lung •
• lHa-sa
sKyid-chu
• Tshal Gung-thang
sNye-thang •
• gSang-mda'
'U-shang-rdo •
•gSang-phu
D
B
• Shug-gseb
U
S
• Gangs-ri Thod-dkar
Chu-shul •
• Ri-bo-rtse-lnga
lCags-zam
▲ Srin-po-ri
Chu-bo-ri ▲
gTsang-po

རྒྱ་སྟོན་པདྨ་དབང་ཕྱུག

rGya-ston Padma dBang-phyug
early 13th–mid-13th century C.E.
Rin-chen gTer-mdzod: 1 text

Onc of two incarnations of Guru Padmasambhava's disciple Lo-tsā-ba rGyal-ba mChog-dbyangs, Padma dBang-phyug was born at Byar-yul into the clan of rGya. He became known as sTon-pa, or teacher, because of his extensive learning in both the Sūtras and Tantras. He lived as holder of the Triple Vajra Saṁvara vows. Within a cave in E-yul at Rig-pa 'Byung-gnas, he discovered treasures relating to the three essential practices of guru sādhanas, rDzogs-chen teachings, and Avalokiteśvara practices (Bla-rdzogs-thugs-gsum); precious substances; and sādhanas explicated by the Great Guru Padmasambhava. Most of the treasures had been lost by the time of Kong-sprul Blo-gros mTha'-yas except for some of the

150

sādhanas, which he preserved in the Rin-chen gTer-mdzod. 'Jam-dbyangs mKhyen-brtse also received related texts from the ḍākinīs as Reconcealed Treasure.

གཏེར་སྟོན་གུ་རུ་ཇོ་ཚེ

gTer-ston Gu-ru Jo-tshe

early 13th–mid-13th century C.E.

Rin-chen gTer-mdzod: 2 texts

An incarnation of one of Dharma King Khri-srong lDe'u-btsan's sons, either Mu-rum bTsad-po or Sad-na-legs, the gTer-ston Gu-ru Jo-tshe was born near the sKyid-chu river at sNye-mda' in sKyi-smad into a family of long-time Mantrayāna practitioners. For this reason, he became known as Guru, and also was called Tshe-dbang Dar-po.

He discovered gTer-ma in his homeland of sKyi-smad at Ri-bo rTse-lnga, the Five-Peaked Mountain of the Gods in the place known as Zang-yag-brag, where in later times a nunnery was built. From Padmasambhava's practice cave there, he withdrew Buddha relics, more than thirty volumes of texts, one hundred and eight statues of Padmasambhava, and the phur-pa Guru Rinpoche had used in the eighth century to tame the demons at bSam-yas. This phur-pa miraculously multiplied itself, creating five hundred daggers. Guru Jo-tshe discovered many other famous treasures, but Kong-sprul found only two texts and the wondrous phur-pas, which were housed at sTod-lung-mda' dNgos-grub-sdings and continued to multiply. These two texts are preserved in the Rin-chen gTer-mdzod.

རིག་འཛིན་ཀུ་མ་ར་ཛ

## Rig-'dzin Kumārādza
## 1266–1343 C.E.

Disciple of Me-long rDo-rje, Rig-'dzin Kumārādza was born in 'On-bar gSar-rdzing-kha in gYo-ru and named Thar-pa-rgyan. His early masters included Bla-ma dGyes-rdor of Kong-po, mKhan-po gTsang-pa, mNga'-ris-pa, mKhan-po Yer-ba-pa. mTshar sTengs-pa, and Rinpoche Grags-pa Ye-shes. He also met the siddha O-rgyan-pa and received instruction from Nam-mkha'i rDo-rje and Chos-kyi Seng-ge.

From the great Me-long rDo-rje he received the sNying-thig teachings and served this master with intense devotion at mKhar-chu. He later offered these teachings to the Karmapa Rang-byung rDo-rje and Klong-chen-pa, who were his foremost disciples in the Great Perfection teachings. Thus, the long-range benefits of his Dharma activity can scarcely be measured. No works by this lineage holder have been located.

ཀཪྨ་པ་རང་བྱུང་རྡོ་རྗེ

## Karmapa Rang-byung rDo-rje
## 1284–1339 C.E.
## 22 texts, 544 pages, Rin-chen gTer-mdzod: 5 texts

The actual incarnation of Avalokiteśvara, Karmapa Rang-byung rDo-rje took birth as the son of a yogin and a yoginī. No one else but the Lord Buddha had such clear recollection of past lives. Rang-byung rDo-rje discovered the elixir of immortality near bSam-yas at mChims-phu, which is the holy site associated with the Guru's Enlightened Speech, and at gYa'-ma-lung, one of the eight sacred places for practice.

Vimalamitra himself revealed the Bi-ma-snying-thig to him, and so this compassionate protector of beings had no need of masters. Nevertheless, to demonstrate how to receive the highest teachings in our world, he became the disciple of Kumārādza, who bestowed upon him the entire sNying-thig doctrines and practices. Thereafter, Guru Padmasambhava appeared to him and offered guidance and the most esoteric instructions. Rang-byung rDo-rje also received the oral teachings from rGyal-sras Legs-pa at the sacred mountain of Tsā-ri.

His disciples spread the sNying-thig teachings throughout Tibet and even into China and Mongolia: sMan-lung-pa Śākya gZhon-nu, gYung-ston rDo-rje-dpal, Ye-rgyal-ba, Ye-shes rGyal-mtshan, and sPrul-sku-ba. Five of his gTer-ma are preserved in the Rin-chen gTer-mdzod section of Great Treasures of Ancient Teachings, while twenty-two other works are contained in other sections.

 གཁས་གྲུབ་ཆེན་པོ་གཡུང་སྟོན་རྡོ་རྗེ་དཔལ་བཟང

mKhas-grub Chen-po gYung-ston rDo-rje dPal-bzang
1284–1365 C.E.
2 texts, 171 pages

Born in Tshong-'dus into the clan of Glang, rDo-rje dPal-bzang became the disciple of Zur Byams-pa Seng-ge. As a youth he mastered the Abhidharma and studied both Old and New Tantras. From Zur Byams-pa Seng-ge he received the teachings of the three Inner Yogas in their entirety and composed a commentary on the gSang-ba'i-snying-po Tantra. An extraordinary adept, he once saved Zur Byams-pa Seng-ge's life by the power of his invocations. Invited to China by the Mongol Emperor, gYung-ston impressed the court with his divination skills and received lavish rewards for making rain fall to end a severe drought.

gYung-ston-pa studied the Kālacakra with Bu-ston Rin-chen-grub and perfected his study and practice of rDzogs-chen with Karmapa Rang-byung rDo-rje. Toward the end of his life, he became a monk and resided at sPa-gro in Bhutan at Phung-po Ri-bo-che, where Guru Padmasambhava had practiced; at other places in Bhutan gYung-ston continued to teach the Dharma until the end of his days.

gYung-ston composed a treatise on the differences between descriptions of Buddhahood according to the Sūtrayana and the Mantrayāna, which has not been located in recent times, and a text on rDzogs-chen preserved in the Great Treasures of Ancient Teachings, together with his gSang-ba'i-snying-po commentary.

# སྤྲུལ་སྐུ་བཟང་པོ་གྲགས་པ

## sPrul-sku bZang-po Grags-pa
### mid-13th–early 14th century C.E.
### Rin-chen gTer-mdzod: 2 texts

An incarnation of lHa-sras Mu-khri bTsad-po, Khri-srong lDe'u-btsan's son, sPrul-sku bZang-po-grags was born in southern La-stod. He lived as a monk of the bKa'-brgyud school, undertaking many retreats and practicing intently until his understanding opened profoundly.

With the blessings of Guru Padmasambhava, who actually appeared as a yogin and trained him, he was able to discover treasures, including Hayagrīva practices and Maitreya sād-hanas, at the seventh-century temple of Gram-pa rGyang built by Srong-btsan sGam-po. At Yon-po-lung he located Vajrapāṇi sādhanas, pilgrimage guides, and guides for finding gTer-ma. His most important discovery was the Le'u-bdun-ma, the Prayer in Seven Chapters, the "Unmistaken Vajra Speech of Orgyan Guru Padmasambhava." The Seven-Chapter Prayer became very famous, spreading throughout central Tibet and to Khams, its blessings as endless as the skies.

He gave the gTer-ma guides to gTer-chen Rig-'dzin rGod-ldem, who was then able to obtain the great treasure of the dGongs-pa-zang-thal from a cave at Zang-zang lHa-brag. Kong-sprul Blo-gros mTha'-yas preserved the prayer and another gTer-ma in the Rin-chen gTer-mdzod.

གཏེར་སྟོན་བཛྲ་མ་ཏི

## gTer-ston Vajramati
### mid-13th–early 14th century C.E.
### Rin-chen gTer-mdzod: 1 text

Known as the gTer-ston who came from India, mKhas-grub Vajramati discovered gTer-ma, including rDzogs-chen teachings and protective mantras and rites, in Nepal at Li-shan-ti. These treasures were taken to Tibet by Tshal Gung-thang-pa gZhon-nu bSam-gtan, who actually met Vajramati in Nepal. This lineage flowed through Bla-ma dPal-'byor and down to later masters, but by the time of Kong-sprul Blo-gros mTha'-yas only one text remained, which he preserved in the Rin-chen gTer-mdzod.

# Part Five

# Era of Kun-mkhyen Klong-chen-pa and the Great Gling-pas

རྒྱལ་བ་ཀུན་གཟིགས་ཀློང་ཆེན་རབ་འབྱམས།

rGyal-ba Kun-mkhyen Klong-chen Rab-'byams

# Fourteenth and Fifteenth Centuries

During these centuries, Klong-chen-pa promoted the Atiyoga teachings, gTer-ma master Rig-'dzin rGod-ldem revealed the Northern Treasures, and Ratna Gling-pa assembled the Ancient Tantras into the rNying-ma-rgyud-'bum. Renowned gTer-ma masters O-rgyan Gling-pa, Sangs-rgyas Gling-pa, rDo-rje Gling-pa, Padma Gling-pa, and Karma Gling-pa brought forth major Dharma treasures. In this era, the Sa-skya monastery at sDe-dge was founded (fourteenth century), while the earliest dGe-lugs-pa monasteries were built (fifteenth century) by Tsong-kha-pa and his disciples. Copies of the bKa'-'gyur (Yung-lo edition) were first printed in 1410.

As Mongol influence waned in Asia, political power in central Tibet shifted from the Sa-skya lamas to the dynasty of Phag-mo-gru (1354–1436) with Byang-chub rGyal-mtshan's rise to prominence. He reintroduced Srong-btsan sGam-po's code of laws and fostered appreciation for Tibet's history. In the following century, Don-yod rDo-rje and three generations of Rin-spungs-pa princes ruled central Tibet (1436–1565).

གཏེར་ཆེན་པདྨ་ལས་འབྲེལ་རྩལ།

gTer-chen Padma Las-'brel-rtsal
b. 1231 or 1291 C.E.
88 texts, 181 pages, Rin-chen gTer-mdzod: 6 texts

An incarnation of King Khri-srong lDe'u-btsan's daughter lHa-lcam Padma gSal, who had received the rDzogs-chen sNying-thig teachings from Guru Padmasambhava, Padma Las-'brel-rtsal was born in gNyan-rong 'Bri-thang and received the Triple Vajra Saṁvara vows at Lo-ro. He belonged to the Nyang clan and was known as Rin-chen Tshul-rdor and as Tshul-khrims rDo-rje, his religious name. When he was sixteen, an old monk who was actually a manifestation of Guru Padmasambhava gave him lists of treasure locations and predictions that he would discover gTer-ma.

When he was twenty-one, gTer-ston Rin-chen Gling-pa gave him additional treasure lists that he had discovered at 'Bri-thang Ko-ro-brag. At twenty-three he proceeded to Dwags-po to lDang-lung Khra-mo-brag where he found the rDzogs-pa-chen-po mKha'-'gro-snying-thig and other treasures, including Yamāntaka and Hayagrīva teachings and various protective rites. He bestowed the blessings of the mKha'-'gro-snying-thig teachings on Karmapa Rang-byung rDo-rje, and having established these teachings, transmitted them to sPrul-sku Rin-chen Gling-pa and rGyal-sras Legs-pa.

Padma Las-'brel-rtsal practiced these teachings secretly until he passed away in his twenty-fifth year at lower Byar at Phying-dkar. His next birth was as the incomparable All-knowing Klong-chen-pa. Some sources say Padma Las-'brel-rtsal was the same individual as the master known as sPang-sgang-pa Rin-chen rDo-rje. Eighty-eight of Padma Las-'brel-rtsal's texts are preserved in Great Treasures of Ancient Teachings, as well as six texts in the Rin-chen gTer-mdzod.

# ཤྭ་བན་རྒྱལ་སྲས་ལེགས་པ་

Shwa-ban rGyal-sras Legs-pa
1230–1306 or 1290–1366 C.E.
Rin-chen gTer-mdzod: 5 texts

An incarnation of rNying-ma Lo-tsā-ba Rin-chen bZang-po and Shel-dkar-bza', rGyal-sras Legs-pa was born in gNyal at Se-ba-lung. His family belonged to the clan of Shwa (or Sho-bo), and his father was the healer dBang-phyug rGyal-po. From a young age, his understanding and mental dexterity were great. His uncle Sho Thams-cad mKhyen-pa and others were his teachers, instructing him in gSar-ma and rNying-ma teachings. His understanding grew profound, and his virtuous qualities became immeasurable.

When he was twenty-eight, he received the mKha'-'gro-snying-thig from Padma Las-'brel-rtsal, who named him the lineage holder of these highest Atiyoga teachings. At Byar in the south of Tibet, he discovered numerous gTer-ma. At the sacred mountain of Tsā-ri, one of the twenty-four key power places in the Tantric tradition, he found treasures on protective rites that later flowed into the bKa'-brgyud Kam-tshang tradition.

Invited to the district of Kong-po, rGyal-sras Legs-pa bestowed the sNying-thig teachings on Karmapa Rang-byung rDo-rje. The Karmapa in turn granted him precious teachings such as his Zab-mo-nang-don, the rGyal-ba-rgya-mtsho, and his collection of Jātakas. rGyal-sras Legs-pa also gave the sNying-thig transmission to Klong-chen-pa. Although Klong-chen-pa's understanding was already complete, this great one approached rGyal-sras Legs-pa in order to demonstrate the proper way of relying on a spiritual master to receive Mantrayāna teachings.

The lineage of the precious sNying-thig teachings has continued unbroken to the present. The Rin-chen gTer-mdzod preserves two other gTer-ma of rGyal-sras Legs-pa, while the sNying-thig teachings are found in other sections of Great Treasures of Ancient Teachings.

གཏེར་སྟོན་མེ་བན་རིན་ཆེན་གླིང་པ

gTer-ston Me-ban Rin-chen Gling-pa
mid-13th–early 14th century C.E.
Rin-chen gTer-mdzod: 3 texts

An incarnation of Vairotsana and the Indian paṇḍita Prajñākāra, Rin-chen Gling-pa was born in an ox year in southeastern Tibet at Tshe-khro-kha in Lo-ro dKar-po as the son of rDo-rje rGod-rdor-'bum and Bal-mo gYang-'bum. His Dharma name was Rin-chen rGyal-po dPal-bzang-po. At rTing-pa Lo-tsā-ba's residence he exhaustively studied general Mahāyāna teachings. At Lo-ro Drug-ral monastery, he received Ras-chung-pa's teachings, which he practiced until signs of achievement arose. At Za-stod Deng-ri, he met Byang-sems Kun-dga', who gave him a gTer-ma list. Following it, he arrived at 'Brin-thang Ko-ro-brag cave, where he discovered treasure teachings in five sections. As he put all the instructions into practice, visionary experiences and Pure Visions arose.

Rin-chen Gling-pa became able to travel to Copper-Colored Mountain, where Padmasambhava welcomed him. He then traveled magically to India to Pha-wang Nag-po (Black Bat), where he discovered precious rDzogs-chen and Mahāyoga treasures. From Sha-'ug, by the rock shaped like a five-pronged rdo-rje, he brought forth more treasures, including sādhanas, predictions, practices, and explanations. In Tibet at Kong-po and Tsā-ri he again made discoveries of teachings, which he undertook as his own practice.

Rin-chen Gling-pa became the disciple of Padma Las-'brel-rtsal, receiving sNying-thig teachings from this master. Living to the age of eighty, he protected innumerable beings from suffering. His incarnations transmitted his gTer-ma; gZhon-nu lHun-grub, rGyal-mtshan dPal-bzang, and Chos-dbang lHun-grub in particular were leaders of rNying-ma. The next incarnation was gTsug-lag 'Phreng-ba, succeeded by the gTsug-lag sPrul-skus, all of whom were incomparable Karma Kam-tshang lineage holders. The Rin-chen gTer-mdzod pre-serves three of Rin-chen Gling-pa's gTer-ma texts, including very extensive rDzogs-chen teachings, the lineage of which descended to the nineteenth-century master 'Jam-dbyangs mKhyen-brtse'i dBang-po.

སྒྲོལ་མ་པ་བསམ་འགྲུབ་རྡོ་རྗེ་

## sGrol-ma-pa bSam-'grub rDo-rje
### 1295–1376 C.E.
### 1 text, 32 pages

Born at rTa-nag gNas-gsar into an old family of rNying-ma yogins and practitioners, bSam-'grub rDo-rje became the disciple of Zur Byams-pa Seng-ge, and studied Atiyoga and Mahāyoga extensively. The master Glan Nya-tshal-pa bSod-nams mGon-po instructed him in the Mahāyoga teachings. bSam-'grub rDo-rje remained in complete solitude most of his life, perfecting the rDzogs-chen sNying-thig practices until he reached the limits of awareness.

His disciples included Zur Śākya 'Byung-gnas and Bla-ma Seng-ge-pa of 'Ug-pa-lung, both of whom he had cared for since childhood. Glan gSal-ba, whose learning was said to result from the blessing of bSam-'grub rDo-rje, was also his disciple.

Two lineages flowed from this immeasurably great master: the Zur-brgyud, the Zur lineage through Ham Śākya 'Byung-gnas; and the Sras-brgyud, the son lineage through his son Sangs-rgyas Rin-chen rGyal-mtshan dPal-bzang-po (1350–1431). One text by this outstanding yogin, a commentary on the root Mahāyoga Tantra, gSang-ba'i-snying-po, is preserved in Great Treasures of Ancient Teachings.

ཟུར་ཆུང་སྐྱུར་ཆུང་གནས

## Zur Ham Śākya 'Byung-gnas
### mid-13th–early 14th century C.E.

Śākya 'Byung-gnas was the son of Zur bZang-po-dpal, an accomplished yogin who possessed occult powers. Much sought after by the Mongol lords and princes, bZang-po-dpal traveled to China where he deeply impressed Emperor Buyantu (r. 1311–1320), to whom he offered precious Tantric teachings. bZang-po-dpal used the generous gifts received from the Mongols to print rNying-ma texts, bringing long-range benefits to the Ancient School.

bZang-po-dpal's son Śākya 'Byung-gnas lived from age seven at the monastery of 'Ug-pa-lung. Ordained by Bla-ma Kun-spangs-pa and later by bSod-nams Grags-pa, he became a disciple of sGrol-ma-ba bSam-'grub rDo-rje and studied with all the Zur lineage holders, mastering the Inner Yogas. He also became learned in the gSar-ma traditions, under the guidance of Sa-bzang Mati Paṇ-chen and other Sa-skya masters. Though Zur Ham composed numerous works, including an Anuyoga commentary, none have been located in recent times.

In the early fourteenth century, Zur Ham and his sister Zur-mo dGe-'dun-'bum were the key lineage holders of the empowerments of the Anuyoga Tantras, which they had received from sGrol-ma-ba. Zur-mo dGe-'dun-'bum resided in lower Nyang in a remote hermitage where she transmitted these teachings to Śākya bShes-gnyen. This lineage passed to rMog-ston rDo-rje dPal-bzang-po of Kaḥ-thog monastery in Khams. From him the Anuyoga empowerments eventually flowed through several masters down to gTer-bdag Gling-pa. Zur Ham empowered Nyi-sbug-pa, whose disciple transmitted the lineage to 'Jam-dbyangs Rin-chen, the father of mNga'-ris Paṇ-chen. Thus mNga'-ris Paṇ-chen and his brother Legs-ldan-rje became Anuyoga lineage holders.

ནམ་མཁའི་རིན་ཆེན་

Nam-mkha'i Rin-chen
mid-13th–early 14th century C.E.
1 text, 259 pages, Rin-chen gTer-mdzod: 2 texts

Author of a commentary on the gSang-ba'i-snying-po, this master may have lived in the early fourteenth century, but his life story requires further research.

# rGyal-ba Kun-mkhyen Klong-chen Rab-'byams
## 1308–1363 C.E.
### 177 texts, 5,058 pages, Rin-chen gTer-mdzod: 10 texts

Revered as an incarnation of Mañjuśrī, Vimalamitra, and Padma gSal, the daughter of Khri-srong lDe'u-btsan, Klong-chen-pa was the next birth of Padma Las-'brel-rtsal. He was born in the village of sTod-grong in the Grwa valley of gYo-ru into the clan of Rog. His father was bsTan-pa-gsung, the twenty-fifth generation of the family of rGyal-ba mChog-dbyangs, the disciple of Padmasambhava. His mother was 'Brom-bza' bSod-nams-rgyan, descended from the family of 'Brom-ston rGyal-ba'i 'Byung-gnas.

At bSam-yas Klong-chen-pa received the Triple Vajra Saṁvara vows from bSam-'grub Rin-chen and Kun-dga' 'Od-zer. He entered gSang-phu Ne'u-thog (founded in 1073 by rNgog Legs-pa'i Shes-rab), where he first studied all the śāstra traditions intensively. He then trained in Vinaya and received empowerments and teachings in the Outer Tantras, Zhi-byed, and Lam-'bras. So broad was his intelligence that he became known as Klong-chen Rab-'byams-pa, Extraordinary Learning, Vast Like Space.

Four rNying-ma masters granted him the teachings of the Inner Yogas and the rNying-ma-rgyud-'bum. The Karmapa Rang-byung rDo-rje bestowed on him the Six-limbed Yoga and Nāropa teachings, while Sa-skya Bla-ma bSod-nams rGyal-mtshan blessed him with Sa-skya teachings. In this way he thoroughly mastered all the philosophical systems in Tibet.

From the great Vidyādhara Kumārādza, he received the full empowerment of Vimalamitra's sNying-thig transmission. While residing at sNye-phu Shug-gseb, he received from 'Od-zer Go-cha, his own disciple, the texts of the mKha'-'gro-snying-thig that Padma Las-'brel-rtsal had discovered. At mChims-phu, through the blessings of Padmasambhava, he received the direct transmission of the mKha'-'gro-snying-thig. From rGyal-sras Legs-pa he received the oral sNying-thig teachings. In a vision, Vimalamitra himself empowered Klong-chen-pa to transmit his teachings. Klong-chen-pa then created his own commentaries on the mKha'-'gro-snying-thig and Bi-ma-snying-thig and summarized them. These precious texts and the commentaries together are renowned as the Ya-bzhi, which Klong-chen-pa arranged at Gangs-ri Thod-dkar, his favorite place of retreat.

At Vimalamitra's request, Klong-chen-pa reconstructed Zhwa'i lHa-khang, the temple in central Tibet founded by Myang Ting-nge-'dzin in the ninth century, and there he taught many who flocked to him. He spent ten years in sPa-gro, Bhutan, founding eight retreat centers for the practice of the sNying-thig teachings. Returning to Tibet, he restored the monastery of bSam-yas and strengthened several other monastic settlements. He spent his final years in meditation in Padmasambhava's cave at mChims-phu.

While Klong-chen-pa was honored by many nobles in central Tibet, including T'ai Situ, and had thousands of disciples, his most accomplished students were mKhas-grub Khyab-brdal lHun-grub, mKhas-grub Chos-kyi Grags-pa, and mKhas-grub bDe-legs rGya-mtsho.

Through an unbroken series of masters, his sNying-thig lineage descended to the sMin-grol-gling master O-rgyan gTer-bdag Gling-pa. Having united the sNying-thig teachings of Padmasambhava with the sNying-thig teachings of the master Vimalamitra, Klong-chen-pa bestowed them upon his disciple mKhas-grub Khyab-brdal lHun-grub. These precious teachings passed in a continuous lineage from the fourteenth century to the seventeenth century through these masters in succession: Grags-pa 'Od-zer, Sang-rgyas dBon-po, Zla-ba Grags-pa, Kun-bzang rDo-rje, rGyal-mtshan dPal-bzang, sNa-tshog Rang-grol, and bsTan-'dzin Grags-pa, down to mDo-sngags bsTan-'dzin, Rig-'dzin Phrin-las lHun-grub, and gTer-bdag Gling-pa.

In the eighteenth century Klong-chen-pa inspired 'Jigs-med Gling-pa in a series of visions at mChims-phu. Through this transmission 'Jigs-med Gling-pa thoroughly understood the great ocean of teachings. From among Kun-mkhen Klong-chen-pa's many works, three trilogies—the Ngal-gso-skor-gsum, the Mun-sel-skor-gsum, and the Rang-grol-skor-gsum—are among the most famous, together with his mDzod-bdun (Seven Treasures) and the renowned Ya-bzhi. The lineages of these teachings have continued unbroken since the fourteenth century. One hundred and seventy-seven of his texts are preserved in Great Treasures of Ancient Teachings, including two recently located rare texts, one on logic and the other a Tantric commentary.

gTer-ston O-rgyan Gling-pa
1323 C.E.
3 texts, 266 pages, Rin-chen gTer-mdzod: 12 texts

The seventh reincarnation of rGyal-sras lHa-rje, O-rgyan Gling-pa was born near Yar-rje in the Grwa-nang valley not far from Klong-chen-pa's birthplace. He belonged to a family of Mantrayāna practitioners and lived as a holder of Mantrayāna vows. As a young man, he became learned in the ordinary arts and sciences such as medicine and astrology.

At age twenty-three he found important treasure texts at Yar-lung Shel-brag Crystal Cave, where Padmasambhava had practiced: three essential cycles of guru sādhanas, rDzogs-chen teachings, and Avalokiteśvara practices, as well as the biography of Padmasambhava (Padma-thang-yig), and many other texts. Not far from his birthplace, he made more discoveries at gYu-gong rock in Grwa, in Guru Padma's practice cave on the cliffs behind sDings-po-che. At bSam-yas he found the Five Sections of Pronouncements (bKa'-thang-sde-lnga), which recount the religious history of the era of the Dharma kings. From the eighth-century stupas of the five Buddha families at Zur-mkhar-mdo, where King Khri-srong lDe'u-btsan and Guru Padma first met, he recovered Avalokiteśvara texts. At Brag-po-che in Grwa-phyi and at 'On-phu sTag-tshang Tiger Den, a powerful practice place of Guru Padmasambhava, he discovered more treasures.

O-rgyan Gling-pa discovered over one hundred volumes of treasures; most were reconcealed by the gTer-ston, and others survived until the days of gTer-bdag Gling-pa but were then lost. Those remaining in circulation, such as the biography of the Great Guru, the religious history, and a few others, are preserved in Great Treasures of Ancient Teachings. O-rgyan Gling-pa fell into disfavor with the ruler of central Tibet, T'ai Si-tu Byang-chub rGyal-mtshan, so he removed himself to Dwags-po and E-yul. The fortunate conditions for his work in Tibet having been interrupted, he passed away not long thereafter. His relics were said to possess extraordinary blessings.

### brGyud-'dzin Nyi-zla Sangs-rgyas
### mid-13th–early 14th century C.E.
### Rin-chen gTer-mdzod: 1 text

Born in Dwags-po, Lineage Holder Nyi-zla Sangs-rgyas was the reincarnation of King Khri-srong lDe'u-btsan's minister of religious affairs, Chos-blon Nyi-ma. He found precious gTer-ma teachings on the transference of consciousness at the time of death ('Pho-ba), which had been concealed at Black Mandala Lake (mTsho Mandal Nag-po) behind the mountain of sGam-po. Since he offered these teachings to the nāgas of the lake, the water had curative and liberating properties.

This accomplished master was actually able to travel to Copper-Colored Mountain to meet Guru Padmasambhava and receive instruction in these teachings, which he then passed to others. In time, the Hearing Lineage became very famous, and even gTer-bdag Gling-pa composed commentaries on this treasure. Nyi-zla Sangs-rgyas also discovered a self-arisen statue of the eleven-faced Avalokiteśvara at Tsā-ri Turquoise Lake.

Some sources say Nyi-zla Sangs-rgyas lived two hundred and twenty years; it is certain he lived at least to the age of one hundred. His son was the renowned gTer-ston Karma Gling-pa, whom he assisted in bringing forth gTer-ma. The 'Pho-ba treasure teachings have endured to this day, bringing incalculable benefit to beings. Kong-sprul preserved one text in the Rin-chen gTer-mdzod.

འགྲོ་མགོན་དུང་མཚོ་རས་པ་ཕྱིམ།

'Gro-mgon Dung-mtsho Ras-pa the Later
mid-13th–early 14th century C.E.
129 texts 656 pages, Rin-chen gTer-mdzod: 2 texts

Born in southern La-stod at Ding-ma-brin, Dung-mtsho Ras-pa was the reincarnation of the master known as the earlier Dung-mtsho Ras-pa. His father was Zhang dKon-ne Bya-ba and his mother was mGron-za sGron-skyid. Because he clearly recalled his previous life as Dung-mtsho Ras-pa, he became known as Dung-mtsho Ras-pa the Later.

Having studied Sūtra and Tantra very widely, at the age of twenty-three he went to Mi-nyag Ras-pa for instruction and initiations in gSar-ma and rNying-ma teachings. Practicing in lonely retreat places, he met O-rgyan Guru Padmasambhava face to face and received predictions to proceed to Kong-po and dBus. In 'On he met Kun-dga'-'bum, who became his sacred consort.

He began to discover gTer-ma treasures at Khyung-rdzong Gangs-ra in Mon and at lHa-stod Srin-po-rdzong, including Zhi-byed treasure texts and longevity practices. In particular, on the shores of Lake Mandal Nag-po that lies behind sGam-po mountain, Dung-mtsho Ras-pa discovered the precious treasure of the Yang-ti-nag-po, rDzogs-chen teachings that led many fortunate individuals to the achievement of the Body of Light ('Od-lus).

Dung-mtsho Ras-pa taught countless people and protected even more through his inconceivable enlightened activities. His gTer-ma discoveries have been transmitted over the centuries, descending through an unbroken stream of rNying-ma masters. Kong-sprul preserved some texts in the Rin-chen gTer-mdzod, while one hundred and twenty-nine texts have been included in Great Treasures of Ancient Teachings.

གཏེར་སྟོན་མཁའ་འགྲོ་མ་ཀུན་དགའ་འབུམ་པ

gTer-ston mKha'-'gro-ma Kun-dga'-'bum-pa
mid-13th–early 14th century C.E.
Rin-chen gTer-mdzod: 7 texts

An incarnation of Ye-shes mTsho-rgyal, mKha'-'gro Kun-dga'-'bum was born in the monkey year at bKra-shis rDo-mkhar in 'On. Her father was gTsang-pa rDo-rje dBang-phyug and her mother was lHa-skyid dPal-'dzom, an incarnation of Padmasambhava's disciple Shel-dkar-bza' rDo-rje 'Tsho'i-skyid. rNying-ma Bla-ma Grags-pa rGyal-mtshan gave her refuge vows, and she entered into the Dharma, relying on many masters. She received instruction and initiations in both gSar-ma and rNying-ma Tantras and practiced intensively.

She proceeded to sGrags Yang-rdzong, the holy place associated with the Enlightened Body of the Guru where both Ye-shes mTsho-rgyal and gNubs-chen Sangs-rgyas Ye-shes had meditated. There she received predictions from the ḍākinīs and practiced one-pointedly for seven years. Instructed by rDo-rje Phag-mo, she discovered treasures of rDzogs-chen teachings in the cave where she was meditating. She bestowed these teachings on many fortunate beings in dBus, leading them to liberation. When she became the consort of 'Gro-mgon Dung-mtsho Ras-pa, he spread these teachings near and far. At the end of her life, this master achieved the Rainbow Vajra Body.

By the days of Kong-sprul Blo-gros mTha'-yas, the discoveries of Kun-dga'-'bum had become very difficult to find. But he located an ancient copy at Yar-lung Shel-brag, while the great gTer-ston mChog-gyur Gling-pa received the transmission directly through the blessings of the lineage. Yet another copy appeared at sGrags Yang-rdzong due to the blessings of the ḍākinīs. Kong-sprul Blo-gros mTha'-yas preserved these precious teachings in the Rin-chen gTer-mdzod.

## gTer-ston Shes-rab Me-'bar
### mid-13th–early 14th century C.E.

Born in Khams, Shes-rab Me-'bar discovered rDzogs-chen treasure texts in Kong-po rGya-la'i rBa-dong and other treasures at sTag-rtse rock, but they could not be completely deciphered. His disciple 'Khrul-zhig sTag-tshang Ras-pa taught Karmapa Rang-byung rDo-rje and many learned ones, but none of these masters were able to decipher the treasure. At last Shes-rab Me-'bar asked the assistance of the great gTer-ston rDo-rje Gling-pa, the incarnation of Vairotsana the Translator, master of an enormous number of scripts, dialects, and languages. rDo-rje Gling-pa clarified all the meanings and continued this rDzogs-chen lineage.

Shes-rab Me-'bar proceeded to Mon-yul in Bhutan where he discovered more treasures, which were, however, reconcealed. Soon Padma Gling-pa rediscovered them, but they were not completely transmitted to future generations. Some of Shes-rab Me-'bar's rDzogs-chen gTer-ma were preserved among the treasures of the seventeenth-century gTer-ston sTag-sham Nus-ldan rDo-rje, which are included in the Great Treasures of Ancient Teachings.

### gTer-ston Do-ban rGya-mtsho-'od
### mid-13th–early 14th century C.E.

Fourth of the thirteen incarnations of rGyal-sras lHa-rje mChog-grub rGyal-po, rGya-mtsho-'od was born in Yar-'brog near the lake by that name. Because he was a Bhande and holder of Mantrayāna vows, he was known as Do-ban. He was the disciple of Zur Pakṣi Śākya 'Od and lived during the earlier part of rDo-rje Gling-pa's life.

He discovered rDzogs-chen and guru sādhana treasures at Mu-tig sPa-mo-gong in lower Yar-'brog; at sGrags Yang-rdzong, the sacred site associated with the Guru's Enlightened Body, he found many teachings on powerful mantras. But by the time of Kong-sprul Blo-gros mTha'-yas, none of these remained. 'Jam-dbyangs mKhyen-brtse was able to recover the essence of the guru sādhanas. No associated texts, however, are preserved in Great Treasures of Ancient Teachings.

གྲྭ་སྒོམ་ཆོས་ཀྱི་རྡོ་རྗེ

Grwa-sgom Chos-kyi rDo-rje
mid-13th–early 14th century C.E.
110 texts, 244 pages, Rin-chen gTer-mdzod: 1 text

The fifth incarnation of rGyal-sras lHa-rje mChog-grub rGyal-po was Khyung Nag Śākya Dar, who discovered Dharma, medicine, and astrology texts. The sixth incarnation was Chos-kyi rDo-rje, who was born at Grwa-nang. He lived as a holder of Mantrayāna vows, engaged intently in yogic practice, and so became known as Grwa-sgom (Meditator of Grwa). This gTer-ston made many discoveries at Bu-tshal gSer-khang.

Though many treasures were lost, his Vajrakīla teachings came to 'Jam-dbyangs mKhyen-brtse as Reconcealed Treasure. Great Treasures of Ancient Teachings preserves one hundred and ten texts on healing and overcoming negative forces, as well as one text in the Rin-chen gTer-mdzod. An earlier gTer-ston in mDo-khams was also known as Grwa-sgom, and he obtained some texts, but these treasures were not transmitted to future generations.

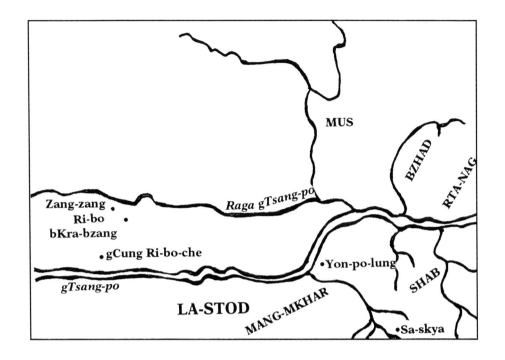

སྤྲུལ་བའི་གཏེར་སྟོན་ཆེན་པོ་རིག་འཛིན་རྒོད་ལྡེམ།

sPrul-ba'i gTer-ston Chen-po Rig-'dzin rGod-ldem
1337–1408 C.E.
780 texts, 4,519 pages, Rin-chen gTer-mdzod: 49 texts

The great gTer-ston Rig-'dzin rGod-ldem was the body incarnation of Padmasambhava and the incarnation of sNa-nam rDo-rje bDud-'joms. He is renowned as one of the Three Supreme Emanations, together with Guru Chos-dbang and Nyang-ral Nyi-ma 'Od-zer. Rig-'dzin rGod-ldem is the discoverer of the Byang-gter, or Northern Treasures, which include important rDzogs-chen teachings that were widely disseminated in Tibet and transmitted in an unbroken stream to the present day.

Rig-'dzin rGod-ldem was born near Ri-bo bKra-bzang in western gTsang just north of gCung Ri-bo-che into the household of sNa-mo-ring. His father was Slob-dpon bDud-'dul, who belonged to a long line of Vajrakīla practitioners descended from Mongol lords. At the age of twelve, three vulture feathers grew from the crown of his head, with five more appearing at age twenty-four. Thus he was known as rGod-ldem-can.

Having received the treasure list from bZang-po Grags-pa, he went first to Mount bKra-bzang, where he discovered the keys for the treasures. Just to the east of a cave at Zang-zang lHa-brag, he discovered five hundred gTer-ma, the foremost among them being the dGongs-pa-zang-thal, which is the distilled essence of a hundred thousand Tantras. Other renowned treasures included the eight heruka sādhanas, one of the three major bKa'-'brgyad cycles.

Rig-'dzin rGod-ldem became the guru of the ruler of Gung-thang and also worked in Sikkim, where he opened up secret power places in the hidden kingdom. Through the powerful blessings of the Northern Treasures, not only were individuals liberated, but wars were averted, illnesses dispelled, and harvests increased; the land of Tibet flourished.

The Northern Treasures have been transmitted to the present day by three unbroken lineages through Rig-'dzin rGod-ldem's son, his consort, and his reincarnations (Legs-ldan-rje, Ngag-gi dBang-po, and Padma Phrin-las). Ngag-gi dBang-po established the seat of the Northern Treasures at Thub-bstan rDo-rje-brag, which became one of the six major rNying-ma monasteries. A total of seven hundred and eighty of this master's works have been preserved in Great Treasures of Ancient Teachings, together with nearly fifty texts in the Rin-chen gTer-mdzod.

ཟངས་རྒྱས་རིན་ཆེན

# Sangs-rgyas Rin-chen
## 1350–1431 C.E.

The son of sGrol-ma-pa bSam-'grub rDo-rje, Sangs-rgyas Rin-chen was born at gNas-gsar when his father was fifty-six. He studied the Mahāyoga Tantras extensively with Zur Śākya 'Byung-gnas and under the guidance of his father. After raising a family, he took complete ordination at Chos-'khor-sgang and perfected his understanding. He composed a commentary on the gSang-ba'i-snying-po Tantra and several other works that are no longer available today.

The Son Lineage of the Inner Yogas flowed through Sangs-rgyas Rin-chen to the renowned 'Gos Lo-tsā-ba gZhon-nu dPal (1392–1481), who in turn taught the Karmapa Chos-grags rGya-mtsho (1454–1506) and the Zhwa-dmar-pa sPyan-snga Rinpoche Chos-kyi Grags-pa (1453–1525). Zhwa-dmar-pa in turn bestowed the precious teachings of the Ancient School on 'Bri-gung Rin-chen Phun-tshogs. In particular, the Anuyoga lineage flowed through Sangs-rgyas Rin-chen.

He resided at bDe-chen sGrol-ma hermitage in rTa-nag, where all the succeeding Anuyoga lineage holders later practiced. Sangs-rgyas Rin-chen taught Zhang-ston Nam-mkha' rDo-rje, who taught Sha-mi rDo-rje rGyal-mtshan, who in turn instructed Rig-'dzin gYu-'brug rDo-rje. gYu-'brug rDo-rje was the guru of Sog-bzlog-pa Blo-gros rGyal-mtshan, who was the next lineage holder of the Anuyoga teachings. No texts by Sangs-rgyas Rin-chen, Nam-mkha' rDo-rje, Sha-mi rDo-rje rGyal-mtshan, or gYu-'brug rDo-rje have been located recently.

# གཏེར་ཆེན་ཀརྨ་གླིང་པ

gTer-chen Karma Gling-pa
mid-14th–late 14th century C.E.
160 texts, 982 pages, Rin-chen gTer-mdzod: 3 texts

An incarnation of the great eighth-century translator Cog-ro Klu'i rGyal-mtshan, Karma Gling-pa was born at Khyer-grub in Dwags-po as the son of Rig-'dzin Nyi-zla Sangs-rgyas. An upholder of the Mantrayāna traditions, he embodied unobstructed enlightened activity, possessed supernormal powers, and displayed innumerable virtues.

At sGam-po-gdar mountain, Karma Gling-pa discovered numerous treasures. While he transmitted the Padma-zhi-khro'i-chos-skor to his fourteen principal disciples, the Zhi-khro-dgongs-pa-rang-grol he transmitted only to his son Nyi-zla Chos-rje, with instructions that it be bestowed on only one master for each of three generations. Within a century his gTer-ma treasures became widespread in Tibet. Karma Gling-pa's most widely-known discovery is the Bar-do-thos-grol-chen-po (translated into English as *The Tibetan Book of the Dead*). The lineages of this teaching continue strongly today.

Kong-sprul Blo-gros mTha'-yas received the Zhi-khro-dgongs-pa-rang-grol teachings of Karma Gling-pa and included several texts in the Rin-chen gTer-mdzod, supplemented by explanations that he himself composed. The great master Karma Chags-med also created commentaries on the works of Karma Gling-pa. One hundred and sixty of Karma Gling-pa's works are preserved in the Great Treasures of Ancient Teachings collection.

Nyi-zla 'Od-zer
mid-14th–late 14th century C.E.
5 texts, 30 pages

The son of Karma Gling-pa, Nyi-zla 'Od-zer, who was also known as Nyi-zla Chos-rje, received from his father the Zhi-khro-dgongs-pa-rang-grol gTer-ma teachings. Following his father's instructions, he transmitted these precious teachings to only a single disciple, who again bestowed them on only a single disciple, Nam-mkha' Chos-kyi rGya-mtsho. This master in turn disseminated the teachings throughout central and eastern Tibet, where they benefited countless people for centuries. Great Treasures of Ancient Teachings contains five texts composed by Nyi-zla 'Od-zer, including outlines and summaries of the texts his father discovered.

ཕྱོ་བྲག་གྲུབ་ཆེན་ལས་ཀྱི་རྡོ་རྗེ

lHo-brag Grub-chen Las-kyi rDo-rje
1326–1401 C.E.
48 texts, 227 pages, Rin-chen gTer-mdzod: 1 text

Nam-mkha' rGyal-mtshan Las-kyi rDo-rje was the son of Nam-mkha'i rGyal-po of the ancient clan of Shud-bu, the twenty-fifth siddha in an unbroken series of rNying-ma practitioners tracing back to Padmasambhava's disciple Shud-bu dPal-gyi rGyal-mtshan. His mother was Rin-chen-rgyan. As a young child he remembered his past lives and had visionary experiences. Ordained by mKhan-chen rGyal-sras and mKhan-chen Rin-chen bKra-shis, he studied intensively day and night until he no longer had a single ordinary thought. Not bound by the cords of hope and fear, he was able to visit the land of Oḍḍiyāna in the company of ḍākinīs and ḍākas. There he met Padmasambhava and received innumerable teachings.

A great spiritual master of both rNying-ma and bKa'-gdams traditions, Las-kyi rDo-rje was the root guru of Tsong-kha-pa. The Fifth Dalai Lama and gTer-bdag Gling-pa made great efforts to preserve and transmit his teachings, some of which eventually became established in the dGe-lugs-pa tradition. Great Treasures contains forty-eight texts, plus an additional text in the Rin-chen gTer-mdzod section. His later reincarnations include the eighteenth-century gTer-ma master Sle-slung rJe-drung bZhad-pa'i rDo-rje.

གཏེར་ཆེན་ཨོ་རྒྱན་སངས་རྒྱས་གླིང་པ

gTer-chen O-rgyan Sangs-rgyas Gling-pa
1340–1396 C.E.
403 texts, 4,197 pages, Rin-chen gTer-mdzod: 43 texts

Sangs-rgyas Gling-pa was an incarnation of lHa-sras Dam-'dzin Rol-pa Ye-shes-rtsal, Khri-srong lDe'u-bstan's middle son, Mu-rum bTsad-po. He was born in the Nyang-po district of Kong-po in southeastern Tibet as the son of the Hayagrīva emanation Khams-zhig sTag-lung sMyon-pa.

When he was five years old, Sangs-rgyas Gling-pa took lay vows with mKhan-po gZhon-nu dPal. Byang-chub rDo-rje and Śākya Ye-shes ordained him as a novice and gave him the name Sangs-rgyas bZang-po. They bestowed upon him the texts and teachings of the bKa'-ma. Karmapa Rol-pa'i rDo-rje watched over him and prophesied that he would guide many living beings to liberation.

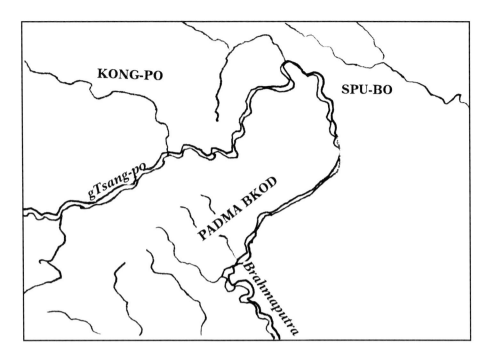

Inspired by visions of Avalokiteśvara, Sangs-rgyas Gling-pa began a solitary retreat at lHun-grub-steng valley in Tsā-ri, guided by Bla-ma Chos-kyi Blo-gros. One night in 1364, empowered by Guru Padmasambhava, he recovered from a cave a portion of the teachings known as the Bla-ma-dgongs-'dus. Later he discovered more of this treasure in Kong-po. He became the first master of these teachings, which he divided into thirteen volumes. There were twenty great streams of transmission of this cycle alone.

Between the ages of twenty-five and thirty-two, he located eighteen great treasure troves including teachings on the heruka sādhanas, divination charts, additional Avalokiteśvara texts, Vajrapāṇi teachings, sādhanas for longevity, alchemical texts, prophecies, ritual works, and ceremonies. Sangs-rgyas Gling-pa founded bDe-chen bSam-grub monastery at sNyi-phu in Kong-po and had many disciples. These included his own teacher, Karmapa Rol-pa'i rDo-rje, Zhwa-dmar Karmapa mKha'-spyod dBang-po, Yag-sde Paṇ-chen, 'Bri-gung Chos-kyi-rgyal-po, Sa-skya Bla-ma Dam-pa bSod-rnams rGyal-mtshan, and other illustrious individuals.

His gTer-ma spread throughout Tibet and especially in Khams. The lineage has been passed down through Sangs-rgyas Gling-pa's son, Ye-shes rDo-rje, and through Sangs-rgyas Gling-pa's chief disciple, Bya-khyung-pa dPal-ldan Seng-ge, through the masters of rTse-le monastery in Dwags-po in central Tibet, and through Ta-bla-ma Padma Mati at Kaḥ-thog monastery in Khams. Sangs-rgyas Gling-pa's treasures reached China when the fifth Karmapa, bDe-bzhin gShegs-pa, visited the Ming court in the fifteenth century. Acceding to the request of the emperor, he presented the sovereign with a manuscript of the Bla-ma-dgongs-'dus.

Later, Sangs-rgyas Gling-pa's teachings spread to Bhutan, where Zhab-drung Ngag-dbang rNam-rgyal became master of them. These teachings remain very influential in Bhutan even today. Great Treasures of Ancient Teachings preserves four hundred and three texts, as well as over forty texts in the Rin-chen gTer-mdzod, and two works by Bya-khyung-pa.

## gTer-ston Dri-med Kun-dga'
### 1347 C.E.
### 39 texts, 254 pages, Rin-chen gTer-mdzod: 5 texts

Renowned as one of the three gTer-stons called Dri-med (Spotless), Dri-med Kun-dga' was an incarnation of the great gNubs-chen Sangs-rgyas Ye-shes. He was born amidst wonderful auspicious signs as the son of dPal-'byor bZang-po and dGos-dgos 'Dzom-ma. His birthplace was Grwa-phyi, the valley of the river that joins the gTsang-po on the south side just west of Yar-lung. His family derived from a long line of Tantric practitioners, and he himself lived as a great Vajradhara of the Mantrayāna traditions. At Grwa-phyi he perfected his study and practice of the Vinaya under the master Chu-bzang-pa Chen-po, who gave him the name Shes-rab rGyal-mtshan.

Following predictions by ḍākinīs, he practiced devotedly at mChims-phu, where Guru Padmasambhava and Lady Ye-shes mTsho-rgyal actually appeared and gave him initiations, teachings, predictions, and lists of gTer-ma. Near mChims-phu at the lion-faced peak called Seng-ge gDong-can, he discovered treasure texts of the three essential subjects of guru sādhanas, rDzogs-chen teachings, and Avalokiteśvara practices (Bla-rdzogs-thugs-gsum), as well as bKa'-brgyad texts and other treasures. These Bla-rdzogs-thugs-gsum teachings brought benefits to many beings in dBus and gTsang, and in the south at lHo-brag and Mon-yul.

In Kong-po, Dri-med Kun-dga' founded the Tantric community of lHun-grags dGon. When he reached the end of his enlightened activity in this lifetime, he departed for the pure Buddha realms. His Heart Son was his older brother gZhon-nu Sangs-rgyas, who continued his lineage at his main seat, which became known as lHun-grags dKar-po. As its Dharma activity increased, the lineage through his descendents became famous in the region of Kong-po, in accord with predictions from the ḍākinīs, although it disappeared in later times.

A very condensed version of the Bla-rdzogs-thugs-gsum teachings was hidden again by Dri-med Kun-dga' at Brag-dmar mGrin-bzang, the site where the Dharma King Srong-btsan sGam-po had been born in the seventh century. In the nineteenth century, 'Jam-dbyangs mKhyen-brtse rediscovered these teachings and bestowed them on Kong-sprul. Five texts are preserved in the Rin-chen gTer-mdzod and another thirty-nine in Great Treasures of Ancient Teachings.

གཏེར་ཆེན་ཨོ་རྒྱན་རྡོ་རྗེ་གླིང་པ

# gTer-chen O-rgyan rDo-rje Gling-pa
## 1346–1405 C.E.
### 392 texts, 2,976 pages, Rin-chen gTer-mdzod: 20 texts

The third of the Five gTer-ston Kings was the renowned rDo-rje Gling-pa. An incarnation of Vairotsana, he was born in central Tibet at dBen-rtsa in the Grwa-nang valley west of Yar-lung, into a family that had long been followers of the Mantrayāna traditions. He was the son of Karma rGyan and Khu-ston bSod-nams rGyal-mtshan. rDo-rje Gling-pa mastered the Sūtras and the Tantric teachings of both the rNying-ma and gSar-ma schools at an early age and began discovering gTer-ma treasure texts at thirteen.

At Khra-'brug, the temple founded by Srong-btsan sGam-po in the seventh century, and at 'O-dkar-brag in Bying, rDo-rje Gling-pa made forty-three great discoveries, totaling one hundred and eight greater and lesser treasures. He met Guru Padmasambhava thirteen times; guided by Lady Ye-shes mTsho-rgyal, he retrieved teachings of the three essential subjects (guru sādhanas, rDzogs-chen teachings, and Avalokiteśvara practices). He found statues of Tārā, Avalokiteśvara, and Vajrasattva, Bon texts, and medical and astrological works. He performed many miracles and traveled to the eight great cemeteries where he received teachings directly from the eight great Vidyādharas.

Among rDo-rje Gling-pa's disciples were his son Chos-dbyings-pa (an incarnation of gNubs gSangs-rgyas Ye-shes) and the Fourth Karmapa, Rol-pa'i rDo-rje (1340–1383). His principal seat was at Gling-mo-kha in Bhutan. His teachings spread widely through descendents who resided at O-rgyan Chos-gling in Mon Bum-thang, and also through 'Jam-dbyangs mKhyen-brtse'i dBang-po, who later received some teachings directly. Great Treasures of Ancient Teachings preserves three

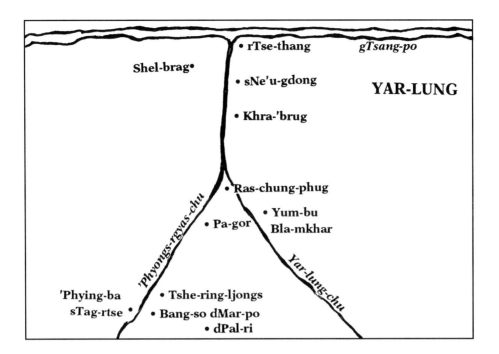

hundred and ninety-two texts, as well as twenty texts in the Rin-chen gTer-mdzod section. A later incarnation of his son Chos-sbyings-pa, mKha'-khyab rDo-rje, composed four texts that are also included in Great Treasures. Another disciple was Bya-btang sNgon-po, who composed three texts that are preserved in Great Treasures of Ancient Teachings.

gTer-ston O-rgyan bZang-po
mid-13th–early 14th century C.E.

A disciple of the gTer-ma Master rDo-rje Gling-pa, O-rgyan bZang-po is counted as one of the "Twenty-One Lesser gTer-stons." An incarnation of lDan-ma Tshe-mang, he was born at Mon Bum-thang Chos-'khor bDe-chen in Bhutan. He restored sKu-rje lHa-khang, the temple erected near the practice cave of Padmasambhava, constructing a marvelous mandala on the ceiling of this temple. An accomplished yogin, he was able to take the form of a bird and fly to Copper-Colored Mountain, perform wonders, and benefit beings. Though he discovered rDzogs-chen teachings and longevity practices, unfortunately, none of his discoveries survived the centuries.

དྲི་མེད་ལྷུན་པོ་རྣམ་པར་སྣང་མཛད་འོད་

Dri-med lHun-po rNam-par sNang-mdzad-'od

1352 C.E.

Rin-chen gTer-mdzod: 3 texts

An incarnation of Ācārya Sa-le, the practice partner of Ye-shes mTsho-rgyal, Dri-med lHun-po was born in 'Or valley in Kong-po as the son of Phyag-rdor and Padma mTsho. His birth was attended by wonderful omens. Since it was predicted that he would become a protector of beings, he became known as rNam-par sNang-mdzad-'od. Even as a child his supernormal powers began to develop, and he preached the Dharma without any difficulty. In visions Padmasambhava and Ye-shes mTsho-rgyal blessed him and gave him teachings.

At thirteen he discovered treasure texts, relics, and lists of gTer-ma at the stupa on the cliffs in mChims. He was given the Triple Vajra Saṁvara vows by mKhan-po Chos-kyi Blo-gros and then complete ordination by Sa-skya dPal-ldan Bla-ma. Having quickly reached a level of expertise in the five ordinary sciences, he began to focus on rDzogs-chen study and practice.

Finding the treasure lists for one hundred and thirty gTer-ma, he located the majority of them, including wondrous statues and King Khri-srong lDe'u-btsan's "Red Copy" of the 100,000-line Prajñāpāramitā. The king had blessed this Tibetan translation by giving his blood to mix with the ink. So accomplished was this master that he received predictions of reaching the complete and perfect enlightenment of a Buddha.

rGyal-dbang Rol-pa'i rDo-rje (1340–1383) was his main Dharma heir. Dri-med lHun-po's most famous teaching (Don-tig-'gro-ba-kun-sgrol) was included by Kong-sprul Blo-gros mTha'-yas in the Rin-chen gTer-mdzod. Many other texts were lost by the nineteenth century.

གྲུབ་ཆེན་ཐང་སྟོང་རྒྱལ་པོ

Grub-chen Thang-stong rGyal-po
1385–1510 C.E.
217 texts, 1,810 pages, Rin-chen gTer-mdzod: 4 texts

Born at 'Ol-ba lHa-rtse in upper gTsang, the great siddha Thang-stong rGyal-po is regarded as an embodiment of both Avalokiteśvara and Hayagrīva. Master gTer-ston and siddha, dramatist and engineer, he lived for one hundred and twenty-three years. Traveling widely, he heard the Dharma from more than five hundred teachers, receiving the Northern Treasures from Kun-spangs Don-yod rGyal-mtshan and the Shangs-pa teachings from Bla-ma rDo-rje gZhon-nu. He journeyed to many different realms and received direct teachings from Padmasambhava.

Master of geomancy, he constructed temples at important locations to protect Tibet from invasions and built fifty-eight iron suspension bridges and one hundred and eighteen ferry crossings still in use today. He founded gCung Ri-bo-che monastery on the gTsang-po river and his own residence of lCags-zam Chu-bo-ri monastery at the confluence of the gTsang-po and sKyid-chu rivers near one of his most famous iron bridges. Statues of this siddha, who was known as "the Great Engineer," are regularly used in dedication rites of new construction projects and modest houses alike. His dramatic works include plays such as A-lce-lha-mo that illustrate the lives of Bodhisattvas and religious kings.

He discovered gTer-ma teachings on longevity and Avalo-kiteśvara practices at sacred sites such as mChims-phu, one of the power places associated with the Enlightened Speech of the Guru; Grams-pa lJongs in western gTsang; sGrub-mtsho Padma Gling in lHo-brag, one of Tibet's four holiest lakes; sPa-ro sTag-tshang in Bhutan; and the hidden valleys of Tsā-ri. Thang-stong rGyal-po attained the state of a deathless aware-ness-holder and many of his disciples attained the power of longevity. Thang-stong rGyal-po's disciple Nyi-ma bZang-po continued his teachings, which are revered by both the rNying-ma and gSar-ma schools.

In later generations, he incarnated as mNga'-ris Siddha Tshul-khrims bZang-po and as mDo-khams siddha Phyar-thul-can. In the nineteenth century, through the blessings of Thang-stong rGyal-po, 'Jam-dbyangs mKhyen-brtse'i dBang-po became his direct disciple and received an array of precious teachings that became known as the Grub-thob-snying-thig. These works are preserved in the Rin-chen gTer-mdzod together with two hundred and seventeen texts in other sections of Great Treasures of Ancient Teachings.

 རྒོད་ལྡེམ་ཡང་སྤྲུལ་དཔལ་ལྡན་འཇམ་དབྱངས་བླ་མ་

rGod-ldem Yang-sprul dPal-ldan 'Jam-dbyangs Bla-ma
mid-14th–late 14th century C.E.
Rin-chen gTer-mdzod: 2 texts

An incarnation of Rig-'dzin rGod-ldem, 'Jam-dbyangs Bla-ma was born in gTsang at Upper Nyang, which is west of Yar-'brog lake along the Nyang-chu river in the region of rGyal-rtse. From his youth he resided with the rNying-ma Sangha and was able to clear away all doubt or confusion about Sūtra and Tantra teachings. In upper Nyang in a secret ḍākinī treasure cave, he discovered gTer-ma teachings that included precious prayers to the three roots (guru, deva, ḍākinī). Over the centuries, these powerful prayers liberated thousands of individuals.

He especially benefited those who lived in the Shangs, rTa-nag, and 'U-yug districts of gTsang. The stream of these teachings flowed into the Northern Treasures lineages and remained unbroken even in the time of Kong-sprul, who included several texts in the Rin-chen gTer-mdzod and composed supplementary explanations to accompany them.

གཏེར་སྟོན་ལང་པོ་པ་དཔལ་གྱི་རྒྱལ་མཚན་བྱང་ཆུབ་གླིང་པ

gTer-ston Lang-po-pa dPal-gyi rGyal-mtshan
Byang-chub Gling-pa
mid-14th–late 14th century C.E.
6 texts, 20 pages, Rin-chen gTer-mdzod: 6 texts

Born in upper mNga'-ris as the son of Klung-ston 'Jam-dbyangs mGon-po, Byang-chub Gling-pa was a reincarnation of Nam-mkha'i sNying-po. dPal-gyi rGyal-mtshan was his religious name, but later he became famous as Byang-chub Gling-pa. He departed from his homeland in western Tibet for the central regions, where he studied and practiced until all his questions were completely answered.

Relying on a gTer-ma list that had belonged to Guru Tshe-brtan rGyal-mtshan, he located sādhanas and a vajra wielded by Padmasambhava in the rocks by lHa-mtsho Srin-mtsho lake west of dPal-mo dPal-thang. Following predictions that he had found in the gTer-ma, he erected a statue to promote the happiness of future generations. The remarkably beautiful statue was consecrated perfectly, filled with holy substances he had found as gTer-ma. gTer-chen Sangs-rgyas Gling-pa (1340–1396) met Byang-chub Gling-pa, in whom he had great confidence. The transmission of all the gTer-ma texts did not continue in later centuries, but 'Jam-dbyangs mKhyen-brtse received the teachings directly in a Close Lineage, and so Kong-sprul was able to preserve six texts in the Rin-chen gTer-mdzod. Six other texts are preserved in Great Treasures.

 གཏེར་སྟོན་ཆག་བྱང་ཆུབ་གླིང་པ

gTer-ston Chag Byang-chub Gling-pa
late 14th–mid-15th century C.E.

Born in lHo-brag gTam-shul, Byang-chub Gling-pa was a follower of Padma Gling-pa. Although he discovered some gTer-ma, the transmission of these treasures did not continue. It appears that his monastery, Chag Byang-chub Gling in eastern lHo-brag, remained active in the time of gTer-bdag Gling-pa's father, Phrin-las lHun-grub, and had not been deserted even in the days of Kong-sprul in thc nineteenth century, when it was supervised by sMin-grol-gling.

ཉང་པོ་གཏེར་སྟོན་མཆོག་ལྡན་རྡོ་རྗེ

Nyang-po gTer-ston mChog-ldan rDo-rje
1437 C.E.
Rin-chen gTer-mdzod: 1 text

The incarnation of Ācārya Sa-le, Ye-shes mTsho-rgyal's practice partner, mChog-ldan rDo-rje was born at rGya-shod. He received Triple Vajra Saṁvara vows from rGya-ston Blo-bzang Grags-pa. As he applied himself to study and practice, the signs of knowledge and accomplishment became dramatically evident. When the ruler of Byar tried to burn him alive, he remained unharmed by the raging fire. Inspired by Guru Padmasambhava, whom he actually met many times, he was able to discover treasures in Nyang-po at the site known as Brag-dkar lHa-chu.

These precious rDzogs-chen, sNying-thig, and Hayagrīva teachings were later much esteemed by sTag-sham Nus-ldan rDo-rje and Chos-rje Gling-pa, who explained and clarified them. Some treasures remained until the time of Kong-sprul Blo-gros mTha'-yas, and he was able to preserve the Hayagrīva teachings in the Rin-chen gTer-mdzod. No other works of this master have been found in recent times.

སྔགས་འཆང་ལས་འཕྲོ་གླིང་པ

sNgags-'chang Las-'phro Gling-pa
late 14th–mid-15th century C.E.

A disciple of rDo-rje Gling-pa, a gTer-ston known as Las-'phro Gling-pa was born at Do-la. At Zab-lung Me-tsho ḍākinī cave he discovered treasure texts, but these did not continue in later times. A set of related sādhanas was recovered by 'Jam-dbyangs mKhyen-brtse as Reconcealed Treasure.

191

གཏེར་སྟོན་འགྲོ་འདུལ་ལས་འཕྲོ་གླིང་པ

gTer-ston 'Gro-'dul Las-'phro Gling-pa
late 14th–mid-15th century C.E.
Rin-chen gTer-mdzod: 3 texts

Las-'phro Gling-pa was an incarnation of two of Guru Padmasambhava's disciples: Lady Shel-dkar-bza' rDo-rje-mtsho and Rin-chen bZang-po, who was one of the one hundred and eight rNying-ma translators. Las-'phro Gling-pa was born in Upper gNyal in the clan of sNyi-ba as the son of dPal-'byor rGyal-po and bKra-shis lHa-mo.

He began to have Pure Visions at a young age and at sixteen received a list of gTer-ma treasures. At eighteen he took refuge at Ri-bo-che with Nam-mkha' rGyal-po, who named him Nam-mkha' rDo-rje. Having received the 'Ba'-ra bKa'-brgyud teachings, he put them into practice. With Padma Gling-pa as his root guru, he cleared away all confusion and matured his understanding. Las-'phro Gling-pa eventually became one of the three Heart Sons of Padma Gling-pa. At twenty-one he was advised by the Dharma protectors to proceed to Mon Dom-tshang-rong in the region of Bhutan.

There in the cave where Ye-shes mTsho-rgyal had practiced Hayagrīva sādhanas, the ḍākinīs actually appeared and handed him a list of gTer-ma treasures to bring forth. At Zla-ba Phug Moon Cave, he found the first of many treasures, followed by discoveries in numerous powerful sacred places: sPa-gro sTag-tshang Tiger Den in Bhutan, one of the eight great practice places of Padmasambhava; mKhar-chu, the power place associated with the Enlightened Mind of the Guru; lHo-skyer-chu, one of Srong-btsan sGam-po's temples; mKha'-'gro gSang-phug, a secret ḍākinī cave; sGrags Yang-rdzong, the sacred site associated with the Enlightened Body of the Guru; bSam-yas mChims-phu, associated with the Enlightened Speech of the Guru; mChod-rten dKar-po, the White Stupa at bSam-yas; Sham-po mountain, where one of Tibet's most powerful mountain gods resides; and other sites.

The precious treasures he found included eight heruka practices, guru sādhanas, Avalokiteśvara practices, powerful mantras, and Vajrakīla texts, healing practices, and other sādhanas, all of which he himself practiced. Able to train and liberate beings in innumerable ways, he filled the rest of his days with enlightened actions.

The family lineage continued into later times, famous as a line of Vidyādharas. Though at first increasing and spreading, his teaching lineage gradually disappeared. Fortunately, the Avalokiteśvara cycle came to 'Jam-dbyangs mKhyen-brtse in a Close Lineage, and Kong-sprul Blo-gros mTha'-yas was able to preserve three texts in the Rin-chen gTer-mdzod.

གཏེར་སྟོན་པདྨ་ཀུན་སྐྱོང་གླིང་པ

gTer-ston Padma Kun-skyong Gling-pa
late 14th–mid-15th C.E.
2 texts, 12 pages, Rin-chen gTer-mdzod: 2 texts

The subsequent reincarnation of the great rDo-rje Gling-pa (1346–1405), and an incarnation of Vairotsana, Padma Kun-skyong Gling-pa was born in the Shangs district at lHa-phu Bi-rdzing. His father was dPal-'byor rGyal-mtshan-mgon and his mother was an incarnation of Tārā known as bDe-mchog dPal-mo. He remembered his earlier lives at a very young age and hardly needed to be instructed in Dharma. Uninterested in children's play, he had an obviously pure and holy nature. Time and again he had visions of Padmasambhava, Dharma King Khri-srong lDe'u-btsan, and Padma's disciples, from whom he received prophecies and instructions on discovering gTer-ma.

When he was fourteen, the treasure list came into his hands that led him to Shangs Zab-bu-lung. There, where Ye-shes mTsho-rgyal had resided for ten years as she perfected the realization of Padmasambhava's closest disciples, he began to discover gTer-ma. His treasure troves were immense, including the eight heruka practices, Dharma protector texts, and mKha'-'gro-snying-thig teachings. He located treasures reconcealed by rDo-rje Gling-pa, ten cycles of rDzogs-chen teachings and Yamāntaka practices, and other teachings. At the White Stupa at bSam-yas he again discovered innumerable treasures. As his fame increased, he was able to lead many beings to happiness and liberation.

His disciples included his own son, dPang-chen Nyi-zla bZang-po, and masters of all schools such as mKhyen-rab Chos-rje, 'Gos Lo-tsā-ba, Khrus-khang Lo-chen, Kun-mkhyen Tshul-rgyal, and Kun-mkhyen-ba Lu-'i Me-tog-pa. To the Mantra-Holder of Glo-bo, 'Jam-dbyangs Rin-chen rGyal-mtshan, he gave the prediction of the birth of two famous sons, who would be mNga'-ris Paṇ-chen and Legs-ldan rDo-rje. The transmission of his treasure texts, especially the rDor-sems-snying-thig, continued, and Kong-sprul Blo-gros mTha'-yas was able to preserve two texts associated with these teachings in the Rin-chen gTer-mdzod. Two additional works are in other sections of Great Treasures.

gTer-ston bSam-gtan bDe-chen Gling-pa
late 14th–mid-15th century C.E.
Rin-chen gTer-mdzod: 2 texts

An incarnation of 'Brog-mi dPal-gyi Ye-shes and gYu-sgra sNying-po, bSam-gtan bDe-chen Gling-pa was born in Lang-po 'Jim-gang. He lived as a Vajradhara and upholder of the Mantrayāna. Since he was famous as Kong-po Nyang-kha bDe-chen Gling, it is clear he founded the center of Kong-po Nyang-kha.

In lower Byar at Jo-bo Brag-dkar, he discovered treasure teachings on the three roots (guru, deva, and ḍākinī), eight heruka practices, and Dharma protector rites. But these teachings gradually disappeared. Later, 'Jam-dbyangs mKhyen-brtse was able to recover the heruka teachings and give them to Kong-sprul to preserve in the Rin-chen gTer-mdzod. Some sources say he lived during the latter part of Sangs-rgyas Gling-pa's life, and some say he lived at a later time.

བགོས་ལོ་ཙྭ་བ་གཞོན་ནུ་དཔལ།

'Gos Lo-tsā-ba gZhon-nu-dpal
1392–1481 C.E.
1 text, 246 pages

Born as the son of 'Gos-ston 'Byung-gnas rDo-rje and Srid-thar-skyid, gZhon-nu-dpal was ordained by sPyan-g.yas mKhan-chen and received Bodhisattva vows from the Karmapa bDe-bzhin gShegs-pa. His masters included rNgog Byang-chub-dpal and the great paṇḍita Vanaratna, who bestowed upon him the empowerments of the Anuttara Tantras. He received the rNying-ma teachings of the Inner Yogas from sGrol-ma-ba bSam-'grub's son Sangs-rgyas Rin-chen. Blessed by this guru with all the empowerments and explanations, 'Gos Lo-tsā-ba became a master of the Tantras of the Ancient School. In turn he transmitted the rNying-ma teachings to the Karmapa Chos-grags rGya-mtsho, and he ordained and transmitted rNying-ma teachings to the Zhwa-dmar-pa Chos-kyi Grags-pa, who regarded 'Gos Lo-tsā-ba as his root guru. Great Treasures of Ancient Teachings contains the Blue Annals, his renowned work on the history of the Dharma and the teaching lineages in Tibet.

# གཏེར་ཁོ་པ་མཁས་གྲུབ་ཡེ་ཤེས་རྒྱལ་མཚན་

## Kaḥ-thog-pa mKhas-grub Ye-shes rGyal-mtshan
### 1395 C.E.
### 1 text, 236 pages

The incarnation of gNyags Jñānakumāra, Ye-shes rGyal-mtshan was born in Bu-'bor in Khams. Studying Sūtra and Mantra, he focused especially on the Anuyoga and Mahāyoga with Bra'o Chos-kyi Bum-pa. He clarified the commentaries on the gSang-ba'i-snying-po, the 'Dus-pa'i-mdo, and the three sections of rDzogs-chen. A prolific author, he wrote commentaries, outlines, and synopses of Mahāyoga, which seem to have been lost, and a commentary on Kaḥ-dam-pa bDe-gsheg's Exposition of the Vehicles (Theg-pa-spyi-bcing), which is preserved in Great Treasures of Ancient Teachings.

This great master was the thirteenth regent of Kaḥ-thog after the founder, Kaḥ-dam-pa bDe-gshegs, and up through his time, Kaḥ-thog had housed one hundred and eighty thousand monks, and established a bShad-gra, and numerous retreat centers. During the era of the Thirteen Gurus, of which he was the last, Kaḥ-thog was the shining light of eastern Tibet, promoting the Inner Tantras of the Ancient School in a period when they were in some decline in central Tibet.

Ye-shes rGyal-mtshan's disciples included rMog-ston rDo-rje dPal-bzang-po, the renowned author and Vidyādhara who attained the level of deathlessness. This great disciple received from Ye-shes rGyal-mtshan the Anuyoga teachings, which he transmitted to rDo-rje rNam-rgyal, creating a stream that became famous as the Khams tradition of the dGongs-pa-'dus-

196

pa'i-mdo. Later this lineage went to central Tibet where gTer-bdag Gling-pa received it. Other disciples of Ye-shes rGyal-mtshan were Kha-ba dKar-po-ba Nam-mkha' rGya-mtsho, author of commentaries and synopses of the major Mahāyoga Tantra (the gSang-ba'i-snying-po), Kun-dga' Zla-ba, Phyogs-med Byang-sems, and Lab-ston Nam-mkha' Rin-chen. Ye-shes rGyal-mtshan benefited disciples from all over Khams. His visionary experience, learning, and yogic accomplishment were confirmed by prophecies from ḍākinīs who predicted his attainment of Buddhahood. Great Treasures of Ancient Teachings contains one work by this master.

གཏེར་སྟོན་ཆེན་པོ་རཏྣ་གླིང་པ

## gTer-ston Chen-po Ratna Gling-pa
### 1403–1479 C.E.
1,351 texts, 5,903 pages, Rin-chen gTer-mdzod: 69 texts

A reincarnation of Padmasambhava's disciple Lang-gro dKon-mchog-'byung-gnas, Ratna Gling-pa was born at Gru-shul in lHo-brag as the son of mDo-sde-dar. He mastered all fields of Buddhist learning and due to his fierce devotion, obtained so many gTer-ma that he is said to have completed the work of three lifetimes. Thus he was known as Zhig-po Gling-pa, 'Gro-'dul Gling-pa, and Ratna Gling-pa. At lHo-brag gNam-skas-can and other places, he discovered twenty-five great treasures including peaceful and wrathful guru sādhanas, rDzogs-chen teachings, Avalokiteśvara practices, Hayagrīva and Vajravārāhī practices, practices dedicated to the three roots (guru, deva, ḍākinī), Mahāmudrā texts, longevity prac-tices, Dharma protector rites, and many others.

At this time, the bKa'-ma transmission of the rNying-ma Tantras was endangered because copies of the texts were so

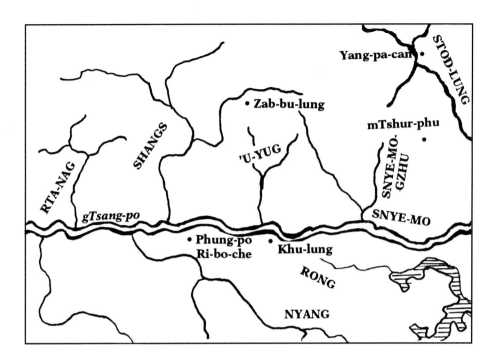

rare. In order to keep these highest Tantras distinct from general Buddhist teachings, they had not been included in the bKa'-'gyur, but existed in private libraries and monasteries throughout Tibet. Ratna Gling-pa searched for the texts and the holders of the oral traditions, finally locating the condensed body of the texts at Zur 'Ug-pa-lung, the residence of Zur-po-che. He then found the aged master Mes-sgom bSam-gtan bZang-po, the sole remaining holder of the complete oral tradition of the rNying-ma Tantras, and received the lineage from him. At lHo-mdo-mkhar lHun-grub palace in Gru-shul, his own residence, he assembled this collection of texts into the rNying-ma'i-rgyud-'bum, the Hundred Thousand rNying-ma Tantras, which survives today in several editions.

Ratna Gling-pa's disciples were said to fill Tibet from Mount Kailaśa in the west to rGyal-mo-rong in the east. His principal disciples were his four Heart Sons, whose descendents were the Son Lineage and the Disciple Lineage, both of which have continued unbroken to the present time. The next incarnation of Ratna Gling-pa was sPrul-sku sNa-tshogs Rang-grol (1494–

1560), who founded the monastery of Dar-rgyas Chos-sdings. Thirteen hundred and fifty-one texts by Ratna Gling-pa are preserved in Great Treasures of Ancient Teachings, together with another sixty-nine works in the Rin-chen gTer-mdzod section.

གཏེར་སྟོན་མགོན་པོ་རིན་ཆེན་

## gTer-ston mGon-po Rin-chen
### late 14th–mid-15th century C.E.

An incarnation of lHa-lcam Legs-bzher, the daughter of Prince Mu-tig (Sad-na-legs), mGon-po Rin-chen was born into the clan of Shud-bu in lHo-brag gTam-shul. This master was also known as Jo-bo rTse-mo and Shud-bu Chos-grags. His inclination toward the Dharma became evident at a very early age. When thirteen years old, he received numerous Dharma teachings from mKhan-chen Phyag-na rDo-rje. He then traveled throughout all of lHo-brag, dBus, and gTsang studying with one master after another and living as an anchorite.

Though he discovered a gTer-ma list at Bum-thang in Bhutan when he was a young man, he was not able to find the exact location of the texts until he was fifty years old. At that time, he discovered many treasures, including a rDzogs-chen gTer-ma at Mon mTsho-sna in Bhutan. Having practiced the teachings until the signs of accomplishment became manifest, mGon-po Rin-chen met the great gTer-ston Ratna Gling-pa and received his teachings and blessings.

Until the age of eighty, he brought benefits to beings in southern districts of lHo-brag, Gru-shul, and mTsho-sna; his enlightened activity was unceasing. His descendents continued to be renowned, but the Dharma lineage disappeared in the following centuries. No texts by this master have been located in recent times.

# གཏེར་སྟོན་བསྟན་གཉིས་གླིང་པ

gTer-ston O-rgyan bsTan-gnyis Gling-pa
Padma Tshe-dbang rGyal-po
late 14th–mid-15th century C.E.
86 texts, 557 pages, Rin-chen gTer-mdzod: 4 texts

Padma Tshe-dbang rGyal-po was born in gTsang-rong at Bya-bzang bKra-shis-sdings as the son of Master Nor-bu and rGyal-mo-skyid. He was known as an incarnation of the daughter of King Khri-srong lDe'u-btsan (lHa-lcam), who took birth with the blessings of Vairotsana. Having received the Triple Vajra Saṁvara vows from mKhan-po Sangs-rgyas dPal-bzang, he studied and practiced at 'Bras-yul sKyed-tshal and at gSer-mdog-can until his knowledge of the Sūtras, Prajñāpāramitā, and Logic was refined. He studied 'Brug-pa bKa'-brgyud teachings and Mahāmudrā with the master Ra-lung sPos-skyar Chos-rje mChog-ldan.

Following various predictions, he discovered gTer-ma lists in the valley where Zur-po-che had worked, at 'U-yug in the Gos-sngon temple and on the banks of the nearby river. So he proceeded to many holy sites: Shangs Zab-bu-lung, where mTsho-rgyal had taught the disciples; bSam-bzang Cave; Phung-po Ri-bo-che, where Padmasambhava had meditated in a secret cave known as the Secret Treasure Site of Tshe-spungs; the Zur-mkhar Stupas, which King Khri-srong lDe'u-btsan had built in the eighth century; Ārya Pālo; Ri-bo bKra-bzang, the sacred mountain north of gCung Ri-bo-che associated with the Northern Treasures; and sPa-ro sTag-tshang, the Tiger Den in Bhutan where Padmasambhava had practiced.

His many discoveries included Yamāntaka texts and Sangs-rgyas-dgongs-'dus teachings. bsTan-gnyis Gling-pa spent many years in central Tibet bringing benefits to countless beings. Especially in the role of guru to the ruler of mNga'-ris Gung-thang, he was able to accomplish enlightened actions for the sake of others. At Mang-yul Ri-bo dPal-'bar before a great crowd of people, he discovered a treasure that had been reconcealed by Rig-'dzin rGod-ldem, and became very famous. In this way his ability to benefit others continually increased.

His two major disciples, gTsang-pa Tshe-bdag and Rong-pa Tshe-bdag, guarded the transmission, which continued unbroken for several centuries down to O-rgyan gTer-bdag Gling-pa. Unfortunately, many treasures had disappeared by the time of Kong-sprul Blo-gros mTha'-yas, except for the Rig-'dzin rGod-ldem treasure and a few others. His precious relics were preserved at Khams-gsum Zangs-khang-gling. Three texts are preserved in the Rin-chen gTer-mdzod and eighty-six texts by him and those in his lineage appear in the Collected Works section of the Ancient Treasures.

གཏེར་སྟོན་སྐལ་ལྡན་རྡོ་རྗེ

gTer-ston sKal-ldan rDo-rje
late 14th–mid-15th century C.E.?

An incarnation of 'Brog-mi dPal-gyi Ye-shes, sKal-ldan rDo-rje was born in gNyal and lived as a holder of Mantrayāna vows. At Mount Sham-po south of Yar-lung, he found many treasures, especially Cakrasaṁvara sādhanas, gCod teachings, and powerful sacred objects associated with the mountain god lHa-chen Yar-lha Sham-po and relics of 'Brog-mi Lo-tsā-ba. The lineage of these teachings remained unbroken in E and gNyal for many years, and the gCod section spread very widely, but by the time of Kong-sprul Blo-gros mTha'-yas, nothing remained.

201

ᨧᨧᨧ

Mang-rong gTer-ston 'Jam-dpal rDo-rje
late 14th–mid-15th century C.E.?

An incarnation of sNa-nam bDud-'joms rDo-rje, 'Jam-dpal rDo-rje discovered Avalokiteśvara teachings at Yer-pa, southwest of lHa-sa, in the mountainsides where siddhas and yogis had practiced under the guidance of Padmasambhava. Over the next centuries his treasure teachings were transmitted continuously from master to disciple and were received by O-rgyan gTer-bdag Gling-pa in the seventeenth century.

Mang-rong gTer-ston founded the monastery of Gangs-ra Nges-gsang rDo-rje-gling in gTsang, which was subsequently cared for first by Zhig-po Gling-pa's Dharma inheritor, Nyi-zla Grags-pa, and then by his nephew, Lo-chen Ngag-gi dBang-po. The latter's nephew, in turn, gZhan-phan rDo-rje, succeeded as abbot at the monastery. After this, the Great Fifth Dalai Lama entrusted rDo-rje-gling to Blo-mchog Rig-pa'i rDo-rje. It appears that the treasures did not continue into the nineteenth century, for Kong-sprul found nothing to include in the Rin-chen gTer-mdzod.

ᨧᨧᨧ

Yol-mo-ba sNgags-'chang
Śākya bZang-po
late 14th–mid-15th century C.E.
1 text, 15 pages

An incarnation of 'Gos Padma Gung-btsan, King Khri-srong lDe'u-btsan's great Dharma minister, Śākya bZang-po was born in southern La-stod at Gram-pa lJongs into a family of great Vajradharas. A key link in the transmission of the

Northern Treasures, he studied both rNying-ma and gSar-ma teachings, and became knowledgeable in both bKa'-ma and gTer-ma, achieving success in all his practices.

At Yol-mo Gangs-kyi Ra-ba, he discovered Avalokiteśvara precepts; at bSam-yas, the ḍākinīs gave him predictions; and at the Red Stupa at bSam-yas he found the treasure text on the Bya-rung-kha-shor Stupa at Boudha in Nepal. This text, in which Guru Padmasambhava describes the history, ruin, and restoration of the stupa, had been discovered centuries earlier by lHa-btsun sNgon-mo, who reconcealed a copy in the Red Stupa. Śākya bZang-po proceeded to lHa-sa where he discovered some of the works of Srong-btsan sGam-po, the great Dharma King who was an incarnation of Avalokiteśvara.

With the blessings and support of Kong-po dKar-chen Kun-dga' Grags-pa, Rig-'dzin Chen-po Padma Gling-pa, and 'Bri-gung Kun-dga' Rin-chen, he then went to Nepal where he restored the great stupa. Thus he fulfilled a vow made by 'Gos Padma Gung-btsan in the presence of Padmasambhava and King Khri-srong lDe'u-btsan. Śākya bZang-po studied with Kong-chen Nam-mkha' dPal-ldan, Mes-ston Nam-mkha' rGyal-mtshan, Rig-'dzin Sangs-rgyas bsTan-pa, gTsang-ston O-rgyan dPal-bzang, and other great masters, hearing the majority of the bKa'-ma and gTer-ma transmissions available in his time. mNga'-ris Paṇ-chen and Legs-ldan rDo-rje were both his disciples, on whom he bestowed the complete teachings of the Northern Treasures.

He greatly benefited the people of mNga'-ris and Gung-thang with his enlightened actions. Following a prediction given him by mChog-ldan mGon-po, he returned to Yol-mo Gangs-ra-ba, where he founded and supported the monastery of Tsūḍa dGon at Padma'i Tshal. His later incarnations included Yol-mo sPrul-sku bsTan-'dzin Nor-bu. His treasure text on the stupa at Boudha and the Srong-btsan sGam-po texts are preserved in Great Treasures of Ancient Teachings.

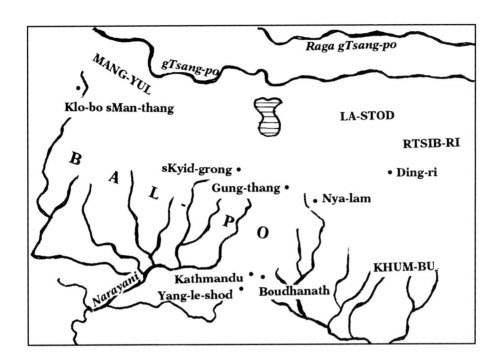

གཏེར་ཆེན་ཨོ་རྒྱན་པདྨ་གླིང་པ

gTer-chen O-rgyan Padma Gling-pa
1450–1521 C.E.
737 texts, 4,266 pages, Rin-chen gTer-mdzod: 23 texts

Padma Gling-pa was the fourth of the Five Great gTer-ston Kings. The final incarnation of Padma gSal, the daughter of King Khri-srong lDe'u-btsan, he had been the incomparable Klong-chen-pa in a previous life. Born in Mon Bum-thang as the son of gNyos Don-grub bZang-po and Grong-mo dPal-'dzom, he awoke to enlightened awareness during childhood.

At age twenty-seven, he obtained a list of locations of one hundred and eight gTer-ma from Padmasambhava, and there-after discovered over fifty texts and ritual objects. His first dis-covery was in Bhutan at Me-'bar lake, east of Bum-thang. Before a crowd of witnesses, he stepped into the lake holding aloft a lighted lantern and surfaced later with a huge chest of rDzogs-chen treasures, the lantern still lit.

His other important discoveries included rDzogs-chen teachings from mChims-phu, the power place in the valley above bSam-yas associated with the Enlightened Speech of the Guru; texts on the eight heruka sādhanas; Avalokiteśvara practices; longevity and healing practices; Vajrakīla and Vajrapāṇi teachings; and many others. Padma Gling-pa restored the temple of lHo-skyer-chu in Bhutan at sPa-gro, and discovered precious objects belonging to King Khri-srong lDe'u-btsan and his royal family.

His lineages were continued by his many disciples, including six great sons, the six accomplished masters, and six incarnations. The Son Lineage began with his physical son Zla-ba, an incarnation of Avalokiteśvara. The lineage of his speech incarnation, known as the gSung-sprul Lineage, began with bsTan-'dzin Grags-pa. These two lineages continued at Gu-ru lHa-khang in lHo-brag. Later the monastery of Theg-mchog Rab-rgyas-gling at lHa-lung became an important seat for the holders of Padma Gling-pa's treasures.

His spiritual sons included Jo-nang-pa Tshul-khrims dPal-'byor, Nang-so rGyal-ba Don-grub, and rDo-rje Gling-pa sPrul-sku mChog-ldan mGon-po. Later masters of Padma Gling-pa's doctrines included sNa-tshog Rang-grol and Don-grub dPal-'bar. His teachings spread throughout southern and central Tibet, to eastern Tibet, and to the kingdom of Bhutan. Great Treasures of Ancient Teachings preserves seven hundred and thirty-seven texts in his collected works, with twenty-three more in the Rin-chen gTer-mdzod section.

# སྤྱན་སྔ་རིན་པོ་ཆེ་ཞྭ་དམར་པ་ཆོས་ཀྱི་གྲགས་པ

sPyan-snga Rinpoche Zhwa-dmar-pa Chos-kyi Grags-pa

1453–1524 C.E.

Chos-kyi Grags-pa was born in Tre-shod Khang-dmar in Tre'o in Khams. He was first ordained at Zur-mang by the Seventh Karmapa Chos-grags rGya-mtsho. 'Gos Lo-tsā-ba gave him complete ordination and the teachings of the rNying-ma school. He also mastered the Tantras of the gSar-ma tradition. He received teachings directly from Padmasambhava in dreams and composed numerous commentaries, Tantric practice texts, and treatises based on the works of Maitreya. His writings were renowned for their refined meaning. He transmitted the rNying-ma teachings to the great master 'Bri-gung Rin-chen Phun-tshogs.

# ཀཿཐོག་པ་བསོད་ནམས་རྒྱལ་མཚན

Kaḥ-thog-pa bSod-nams rGyal-mtshan

1466–1540 C.E.

4 texts, 268 pages

This Kaḥ-thog master of the fifteenth and sixteenth centuries composed a text analyzing all the vehicles of the Dharma, and also wrote an autobiography. Further research into these texts will bring out the details of his life story. Four of his works are preserved in Great Treasures of Ancient Teachings.

# མངའ་རིས་པཎྜི་ཏ་ཆེན་པོ་པདྨ་དབང་རྒྱལ

mNga'-ris Mahāpaṇḍita Padma dBang-rgyal
1487–1542 C.E.
90 texts, 491 pages, Rin-chen gTer-mdzod: 10 texts

An incarnation of King Khri-srong lDe'u-btsan, and the ninth incarnation of rGyal-sras lHa-rje, Padma dBang-rgyal was born in Glo-bo Thang in present-day Nepal. His father was an incarnation of Mar-pa, known as 'Jam-dbyangs Rin-chen rGyal-mtshan, and his mother was the lady 'Bro-lcam Khrom-pa-rgyan. As a youth, Padma dBang-rgyal studied the precious mDo-sgyu-sems subjects of the bKa'-ma with his father from whom he also received Bodhisattva vows. From Nor-bstan bZang-po he received teachings in Vinaya and Sūtra and the bKa'-gdams-pa precepts.

By the age of twenty Padma dBang-rgyal was already a master of Madhyamaka, Logic, and Prajñāpāramitā. 'Jam-dbyangs Chos-skyong and Tshul-khrim-dpal bestowed Yamāntaka empowerments upon him, and Glo-bo Lo-tsā-ba gave him the Lam-'bras teachings. Fully ordained at bSam-'grub-gling by bSod-nams lHun-grub, Padma dBang-rgyal became the foremost holder of the Vinaya in that era. He also mastered grammar and gSar-ma Tantras under the tutelage of rNam-rgyal dPal-bzang of Gu-ge. Under Śākya bZang-po he studied and practiced the Northern Treasures.

He made a pilgrimage to Kathmandu valley where he studied with Tibetan and Newari masters. Having resolved to restore the teachings in central Tibet, Padma dBang-rgyal proceeded to lHa-sa where he received inspiring prophecies; he then went to bSam-yas where he remembered his previous life as the Dharma King. He met and received teachings from eminent masters of the day such as Kaḥ-thog-pa bSod-nams rGyal-mtshan, Phreng-so O-rgyan Chos-bzang, Kong-chen Nam-mkha' dPal-ldan, the descendents of Guru Chos-dbang, and

Nam-mkha'i rNal-'byor of rJe'u at lHo-brag. He restored the Dharma traditions of lHo-brag, and together with his brother Legs-ldan rDo-rje and 'Bri-gung Rin-chen Phun-tshogs, reconsecrated the great monastery of bSam-yas.

At bSam-yas Padma dBang-rgyal discovered the sādhanas for the gSol-'debs Le'u bDun-ma, the Seven-Chaptered Prayer, which are widespread even today. He composed a treatise on the three vows of Hīnayāna, Mahāyāna, and Vajrayāna, a jewel ornament in the tradition of the Ancient Ones. Altogether ninety texts of his are preserved in Great Treasures, as well as ten additional texts in the Rin-chen gTer-mdzod section. His immediate reincarnation was the Northern Treasures lineage holder, bKra-shis sTobs-rgyal Chos-rgyal dBang-po'i-sde.

སྤྲུལ་སྐུ་མཆོག་ལྡན་མགོན་པོ

sPrul-sku mChog-ldan mGon-po
mid-15th–early 16th century C.E.
1 text, 126 pages, Rin-chen gTer-mdzod: 1 text

The gTer-ston mDo-sngags Gling-pa mChog-ldan mGon-po was an incarnation of Vairotsana and the rebirth of Kun-skyong Gling-pa and rDo-rje Gling-pa. He was born in lHo-brag at 'Phyongs-lung, which is a subdivision of Ban-pa. His father was Sum Dar-rgyas of the clan of rGya, and his mother was Bu-chung sMan. Even as a small child he had great wisdom and an ascetic manner; he knew reading and writing without being taught. After his mother died, he entered the monastery of Khyung-tshang, where he studied with Chos-rje gTsang-pa and took lay vows.

With the blessings of Guru Rinpoche, he located lists of gTer-ma. At Chag Byang-chub-gling, the holder of Padma Gling-pa's lesser gTer-ma entrusted gTer-ma lists to him and bestowed teachings on him. Then at bSam-yas he met the master dKar-chen Kun-dga' Grags-pa, who gave him teachings and predictions. At Tsā-ri he had Pure Visions, in Kong-po he discovered treasures, and in Dwags-po he worked for the benefit of beings. When he met Padma Gling-pa, the great gTer-ston recognized him as the incarnation of rDo-rje Gling-pa and granted him many teachings. At gYas-ru gTsang Gram-pa, he discovered gTer-ma, but the obstacles were too great for the treasures to be established.

Nonetheless, he was invited far and wide by the finest masters of the day such as Dwags-po rTse-le Rig-'dzin, and nearly every leader in dBus and gTsang honored him. His enlightened actions were immensely powerful. For example, he turned back armies from lHa-sa with his magical abilities. In the last year of his life in lHo-brag just east of mKhar-chu, he founded Ban-pa Drug-ral lHa-khang and erected a large golden statue of Guru Padmasambhava.

This master passed away at thirty-five before being able to fulfill all his intentions to spread the teachings. His rebirth, who was known as mDo-sngags Gling-pa, did obtain some of the gTer-ma lists but was not able to accomplish much benefit. The next incarnation, Yang-dag rGya-mtsho, founded the monastery of gSang-sngags Chos-gling at sPu-bo rBa-kha. The next incarnation, rBa-kha sPrul-sku Rig-'dzin Chos-kyi rGya-mtsho, was the Dharma heir of the great gTer-ston 'Ja'-tshon sNying-po and the guru of Karma Chags-med and rDzogs-chen Padma Rig-'dzin. The stream of incarnations has continued to the present time.

Not all of mChog-ldan mGon-po's gTer-ma survived, but fortunately 'Jam-dbyangs mKhyen-brtse'i dBang-po received the Hayagrīva discoveries as Pure Vision treasures and Kong-sprul included these in the Rin-chen gTer-mdzod. Other sections of Great Treasures of Ancient Teachings have preserved his biography and songs of realization.

རྒྱ་མ་མི་འགྱུར་ལས་འཕྲོ་གླིང་པ་ཀུན་དགའ་དཔལ་བཟང་

rGya-ma Mi-’gyur Las-’phro Gling-pa Kun-dga’ dPal-bzang
mid-15th–early 16th century C.E.
Rin-chen gTer-mdzod: 1 text

An incarnation of Lady Shel-dkar-bza’ mGon-skyid, Kun-dga’ dPal-bzang was born at rGya-ma in upper dBus, the district where King Srong-btsan sGam-po had been born nearly one thousand years earlier. Kun-dga’ dPal-bzang and ’Bri-gung Rin-chen Phun-tshogs were each disciple and master to the other. This gTer-ma master was also the Dharma inheritor of mNga’-ris Rig-’dzin Chen-po Legs-ldan. From Mi-’gyur Chos-’byung rock, he withdrew treasure teachings, precious substances, and protective rites. The lineage of these teachings was transmitted through ’Bri-gung Rin-chen Phun-tshogs, but it had largely disappeared by the time of Kong-sprul Blo-gros mTha’-yas. ’Jam-dbyangs mKhyen-brtse recovered a few of these teachings, and Kong-sprul preserved one work in the Rin-chen gTer-mdzod.

གདོང་དཀར་ལ་ཁབ་ཚེ་རིང་རྡོ་རྗེ་སྤ་གྲོ་གཏེར་སྟོན་

gDong-dkar La-khab Tshe-ring rDo-rje sPa-gro gTer-ston
mid-15th–early 16th century C.E.
Rin-chen gTer-mdzod: 1 text

The incarnation of gSal-ba’i sGron-ma, the servant of lHa-lcam Nus-’byin Sa-le, Tshe-ring rDo-rje was born in sPa-gro in the region now called Bhutan. He became known as sPa-sgro gTer-ston and as gDong-dkar La-khab. At Brag-dmar north of rTsis-gnas-gsar, the land-taming temple built by Srong-btsan sGam-po, he discovered precious rDzogs-chen teachings belonging to the sPyi-ti cycle. At gNas-gsar, he discovered sacred substances. Then after finding numerous treasure texts at sPa-gro in Bhutan, he benefited many beings in the southern districts and in gTsang at Nyang and rTa-nag as did his incarnations and descendents. His rDzogs-chen teachings became renowned because some who practiced them achieved the Body of Light ('Od-lus), and the lineage did not decline. Kong-sprul was able to receive these teachings and preserved a large text in the Rin-chen gTer-mdzod.

གཏེར་སྟོན་སྣང་གསལ་རིག་འཛིན་བཀྲ་ཤིས་རྒྱ་མཚོ

## gTer-ston sNang-gsal Rig-'dzin bKra-shis rGya-mtsho
### mid-15th–early 16th century C.E.

An incarnation of Ācārya Sa-le, the practice partner of Ye-shes mTsho-rgyal, and of Ras-chung-pa, bKra-shis rGya-mtsho met Padmasambhava in Pure Visions and received the Hearing Lineage of precious teachings relating to Amitābha. These teachings flowed through Zur Chos-dbyings Rang-grol and 'Bri-gung Chos-kyi Grags-pa, spreading widely at first, but did not seem to continue down to the time of Kong-sprul. Therefore, no texts were preserved in the Rin-chen gTer-mdzod, and no other works composed by this master have been found in recent times.

# Part Six


# Era of Phreng-po
# gTer-chen and rTse-le
# sNa-tshogs Rang-grol

ཕྲེང་པོ་གཏེར་ཆེན་ཀུན་མཁྱེན་ཤེས་རབ་འོད་ཟེར་སྒྲོ་འདུལ་གླིང་པ།

Phreng-po gTer-chen Kun-mkhyen Shes-rab 'Od-zer

# Sixteenth and Early
# Seventeenth Centuries

The sixteenth century saw the founding of the rNying-ma monastery of dPal-ri Theg-chen-gling by Phreng-po gTer-chen. It remained the most important monastery of the Ancient School in central Tibet until rDo-rje-brag and sMin-grol-gling were built in the mid-seventeenth century.

In this era, the fortunes of the gTsang-pa princes, former ministers to the Rin-spungs-pa, increased as rTse-brtan rDo-rje and two successors ruled central Tibet (1565–1642). The title of Dalai Lama traces to this century, when the Mongol lord Altan Khan and bSod-nams rGya-mtsho met in 1578. During this period, the Mongols began converting to Buddhism in large numbers, inspired by Tibetan Buddhist teachers.

As Buddhist masters from Tibet brought the Dharma into Sikkim and Bhutan, the first regimes became established in these kingdoms. The first Westerners reached the Land of Snow in 1603, and Jesuit missionaries arrived in 1624.

# འབྲི་གུང་གཏེར་སྟོན་ཆོས་རྒྱལ་རིན་ཆེན་ཕུན་ཚོགས

'Bri-gung gTer-ston Chos-rgyal Rin-chen-phun-tshogs
1509 C.E.
141 texts, 794 pages, Rin-chen gTer-mdzod: 6 texts

An incarnation of Guru Humkāra and King Khri-srong lDe'u-bstan's son Mu-khri, Rin-chen Phun-tshogs was born at 'Bri-gung into the sKyu-ra clan. His father was Chos-rgyal bsTan-pa'i rGyal-mtshan and his mother was bSod-nams sGron-ma. As a child he could remember his past lives, and his inclination toward the Dharma became evident. sPyan-snga Rinpoche Zhwa-dmar Karmapa Chos-kyi Grags-pa gave him Triple Vajra Saṁvara vows. Later Zhwa-dmar-pa, mNga'-ris Paṇ-chen, and Legs-ldan rDo-rje bestowed on him the teachings of the Inner Tantras. Intent on practicing in ancient holy places, Rin-chen Phun-tshogs proceeded to gZho Ti-sgro near 'Bri-gung, where he met Vajranātha, a master from India who granted him the teachings of Javāripa.

In accord with a prophecy made by the ḍākinīs, Rin-chen Phun-tshogs became a White Sangha yogin instead of a monk and began his career as a gTer-ston. Northwest of lHa-sa at Yangs-pa-can, where the seat of the Karmapas had been founded not long before (1490), Rin-chen Phun-tshogs received Pure Vision gTer-ma teachings and located a gTer-ma list. This led him northeast of lHa-sa back to Ti-sgro to the caves where Padmasambhava and Ye-shes mTsho-rgyal meditated; there he found precious treasure texts. In Pure Visions he traveled to Zangs-mdog dPal-ri, where he received empowerments and precious teachings directly from Padmasambhava.

Rin-chen Phun-tshogs became a master of both bKa'-ma and gTer-ma, completely comprehending the Inner Tantras, and becoming expert in the gSar-ma Tantras as well. His knowledge was especially profound regarding all types of the eight heruka teachings, the Upper and Lower Treasures, the

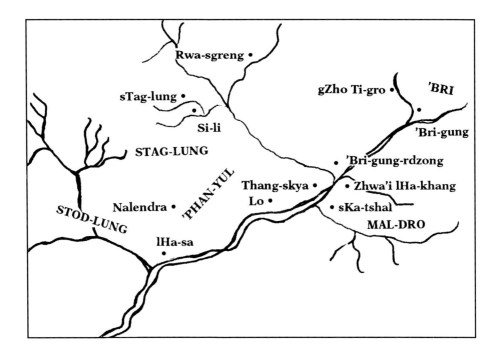

sNying-thig-ya-bzhi, and the works of Kun-mkhyen Klong-chen-pa, who appeared to him in visions.

His disciples could be found everywhere, from La-dwags and mNga'-ris in the west, to dBus and gTsang in central Tibet, to mDo-khams in the east and even in Mongolia. They transmitted a combined gSar-ma and rNying-ma tradition, which remains unbroken today.

The main Mahāyoga transmission flowed through Rin-chen Phun-tshogs to his disciple Rang-grol Nyi-zla Sangs-rgyas to Tshe-dbang Nor-rgyas, who taught his son 'Khon-ston dPal-'byor lHun-grub. He in turn taught Zur-chen Chos-dbyings Rang-grol, who was the master of the Great Fifth Dalai Lama. Rin-chen Phun-tshogs' gTer-ma lineages have been continued by 'Bri-gung-pa masters. Kong-sprul Blo-gros mTha'-yas included seven texts in the Rin-chen gTer-mdzod. One hundred and forty-one other treasures and works composed by 'Bri-gung Rin-chen Phun-tshogs are preserved in Great Treasures of Ancient Teachings.

# མངའ་རིས་རིག་འཛིན་ཆེན་པོ་ལེགས་ལྡན་རྡོ་རྗེ

mNga'-ris Rig-'dzin Chen-po Legs-ldan rDo-rje
1512–1625 C.E.
1 text, 5 pages, Rin-chen gTer-mdzod: 5 texts

An incarnation of sNa-nam bDud-'joms rDo-rje and reincarnation of Rig-'dzin rGod-ldem, Legs-ldan rDo-rje transmitted and protected the Northern Treasures for a hundred years. He was born in mNga'-ris Glo-bo as the son of 'Jam-dbyangs Rin-chen rGyal-mtshan and the younger brother of mNga'-ris Paṇ-chen in accord with the predictions made by Kun-skyong Gling-pa. His father was his first teacher, giving him numerous Inner Yoga empowerments and practices which he perfected. His virtues and knowledge grew immeasurable. His root guru was Śākya bZang-po, who bestowed the precious Northern Treasures on him. He studied with many other great masters of both bKa'-ma and gTer-ma until he was filled with an ocean of Dharma. Legs-ldan rDo-rje was an important link in the transmission of the Anuyoga teachings, which he received from his father and transmitted in turn to sKyi-ston Tshe-ring dBang-po in a lineage that descended to Rig-'dzin Padma 'Phrin-las.

At bSam-yas, together with his older brother mNga'-ris Paṇ-chen, Legs-ldan rDo-rje discovered gTer-ma teachings, which were transmitted to Rin-chen Phun-tshogs. At 'On-phu sTag-tshangs, one of Padmasambhava's three Tiger Den meditation sites, and in Sikkim at lHa-ri Rin-chen sNying-po rock, he located more hidden teachings. His discoveries included Avalokiteśvara, Mañjuśrī, and Vajrapāṇi practices, as well as longevity practices and others. Later in his life, he resided at gSang-sngags Theg-mchog-gling, holding the Lion Throne and teaching tirelessly. He lived one hundred and thirteen years before departing to the Dharmakāya. His next incarnation was Ngag-gi dBang-po. Five of his texts are included in the Rin-chen gTer-mdzod section together with another work in Great Treasures of Ancient Teachings.

ཕྲེང་པོ་གཏེར་ཆེན་ཀུན་མཁྱེན་ཤེས་རབ་འོད་ཟེར་འགྲོ་འདུལ་གླིང་པ

Phreng-po gTer-chen Kun-mkhyen Shes-rab 'Od-zer
'Gro-'dul Gling-pa
1518–1584 C.E.
64 texts, 167 pages, Rin-chen gTer-mdzod: 19 texts

An incarnation of Vairotsana, Shes-rab 'Od-zer was an essential link in the sNying-thig lineage descending from Klong-chen-pa through Rin-chen Phun-tshogs. He was born in the land of Byang Ngom-chen. Even as a child he had a natural revulsion towards samsara, a deep compassion for others, and a profoundly penetrating understanding, for the heart of a genuine follower of the Great Vehicle had awakened within him. He took lay vows from Slob-dpon Tshul-khrims 'Od-zer and Triple Vajra Saṃvara vows from gSer-mdog Paṇ-chen's disciple rDo-rje rGyal-ba. He studied Sūtrayāna texts with dGa'-dan Khri-chen bsTan-dar-ba, and Kālacakra and Sa-lugs Tantras with rDo-rje rGyal-ba, and became a learned master.

Shes-rab 'Od-zer was the disciple of 'Bri-gung Rin-chen Phun-tshogs, and master and disciple had great faith in one another. He received 'Bri-gung and Karma bKa'-brgyud teachings, mDo-sgyu-sems rNying-ma Inner Tantra teachings, the mKha'-'gro-snying-thig, and other precious gTer-ma teachings. After becoming expert at Sūtra and Tantra, he spent long years on retreat at Grogs-ri Rin-chen-spungs cave until he achieved limitless samādhis and the dawning of profound realization.

Inspired by repeated visions of Guru Padmasambhava, at six locations he discovered precious gTer-ma, such as the Grol-

219

tig-dgongs-pa-rang-grol, Buddha relics, and statues. 'Bri-gung Rin-chen Phun-tshogs assisted him in establishing these teachings, which later became one of the major practices of 'Jigs-med Gling-pa. He received the Bla-ma-dgongs-'dus teachings of Sangs-rgyas Gling-pa and many other teachings from the lineage holder Nyi-ma rGyal-mtshan. Again on retreat, he was blessed with visions of Padmasambhava and composed extra-ordinarily clear explanations of profound teachings. Shes-rab 'Od-zer became known as Śāntapurīpa, the spiritual son of Padmasambhava. Devoted to the teachings of Klong-chen-pa, he arranged the printing of the Ngal-gso-skor-gsum and its commentary and widely promoted its study and practice.

At dPal-ri, he refounded the monastery of dPal-ri Theg-chen-gling and supported it with the help of patron Hor bSod-nams Thobs-rgyas. This became the leading rNying-ma monastery for the next one hundred years until the founding of sMin-grol-gling and rDo-rje-brag in the mid-seventeenth century. His enlightened activity filled all of dBus, gTsang, and Khams. His biography and accounts of his gTer-ma discoveries were arranged by Karma Kun-bzang, and the lineage remains un-broken to the present time. Great Treasures of Ancient Teachings includes sixty-four of his works, while the Rin-chen gTer-mdzod section contains another nineteen.

གནས་གསར་བ་མཁྱེན་བརྩེའི་དབང་ཕྱུག་མདོ་སྔགས་གླིང་པ

gNas-gsar-ba mKhyen-brtse'i dBang-phyug

mDo-sngags Gling-pa

1524–1587 C.E.

Rin-chen gTer-mdzod: 2 texts

The Bhū-rlung teachings of Padmasambhava, which grant the attainment of the Body of Light, were taught in India by the Great Guru appearing as the Siddha Mahā Nātha. His disciple was Lord of Yogins, Dza-hā-bhīr, who obtained the Light Body of pristine awareness ('Od-lus Ye-shes-kyi-sku). Among his eight foremost disciples (all with the name Nātha), was Ma-ṇi-ka Nātha, who came to Tibet. He bestowed the root teachings on gNas-gsar-ba mKhyen-brtse'i dBang-phyug, a master of the Sa-skya lineages, whose teachings were later held in high esteem by the Fifth Dalai Lama.

Another disciple of Dza-hā-bhīr, Vajra Nātha, arrived in Tibet and granted the complete teachings, commentaries, explanations, and empowerments to 'Bri-gung Rin-chen Phun-tshogs. Altogether there were three streams of these teachings: the stream through Rin-chen Phun-tshogs, the one through gNas-gsar-ba, and a third stream later that flowed through Nyi-zla Klong-gsal.

Rin-chen Phun-tshogs in turn taught the Dza-bhīr teachings to rDzogs-chen-pa Tshul-khrims Sangs-rgyas. He perfected their practice and obtained power over breath and mind and many magical accomplishments. Tshul-khrims Sangs-rgyas taught mNga'-ris-pa 'Od-gsal mChog-ldan, a great gSar-ma and rNying-ma master, who received the blessings of Dza-hā-bhīr and had many Pure Visions. He lived one hundred and fifty-seven years.

In turn, 'Od-gsal mChog-ldan bestowed the teachings on Bres-gshongs-pa 'Jam-dbyangs Chos-rgyal rDo-rje (1602–1677), who was born in Bres-gshongs in gTsang. Guided by Gong-ra Lo-chen and others, he developed extraordinary knowledge of both gSar-ma teachings and rNying-ma bKa'-ma and gTer-ma traditions. Bres-gshongs-pa practiced with utter fierceness and strength until he obtained understanding. His knowledge of the three times and his virtues were almost beyond belief. His disciples included Nyi-zla Klong-gsal. Four texts containing the teachings of all three streams were preserved by Kong-sprul in the Rin-chen gTer-mdzod.

གཏེར་སྟོན་ཆེན་པོ་ཡོངས་འཛིན་ངག་དབང་གྲགས་པ

gTer-ston Chen-po Yongs-'dzin Ngag-dbang Grags-pa
early 16th–mid-16th century C.E.
18 texts, 167 pages

Born in Bhutan at sPa-sgro Kun-bzang-gling, Ngag-dbang Grags-pa belonged to the clan of the descendents of Klongchen-pa. Having received the highest rDzogs-chen teachings, he contemplated them and practiced them to perfection. He manifested signs of accomplishment, such as flying like a bird in the sky. At various locations he discovered gTer-ma teachings of wrathful guru cycles and others, but the streams of these teachings did not continue down through the centuries. It was this great accomplished practitioner who was the root guru of Sog-bzlog-pa.

None of his gTer-ma texts were preserved in the Rin-chen gTer-mdzod, but eighteen works can be found in the Collected Works section of Great Treasures, including his biography and his rDzogs-chen teachings.

ཞིག་པོ་གླིང་པ་གར་གྱི་དབང་ཕྱུག

Zhig-po Gling-pa Gar-gyi dBang-phyug
1524–1583 C.E.
81 texts, 350 pages, Rin-chen gTer-mdzod: 31 texts

An incarnation of King Khri-srong lDe'u-btsan's middle son, lHas-sras Dam-'dzin Rol-pa Ye-shes-rtsal, Gar-gyi dBang-phyug was born at sTod-lung sNang-rtse in the valley northwest of lHa-sa. His father was Nam-mkha' dBang-chen Phun-tshogs, and his mother was Tshe-dbang brTan-ma. rJe sMan-chu-ba Nam-mkha' Rin-chen gave him vows and the name Tshe-dbang rGyal-po. In sacred power places he found numerous treasures: At Zang-yag rock, the Padmasambhava cave at Ri-bo rTse-lnga, the Five-Peaked Mountain sacred to Mañjuśrī not far south of lHa-sa; at Zur-mkhar-mdo, where Dharma King Khri-srong lDe'u-btsan built stupas; at Zhwa'i lHa-khang, the temple built by Myang Ting-nge-'dzin in the ninth century; at gZho Ti-sgro near 'Bri-gung, where Padmasambhava and Ye-shes mTsho-rgyal practiced; and at lHa-sa and bSam-yas. His discoveries included Avalokiteśvara practices, rDzogs-chen teachings, Hayagrīva sādhanas, Gu-ru-drag-po teachings, and many others.

Zhig-po Gling-pa served and honored all the rNying-ma masters of the day, and became the primary lineage holder of all the bKa'-ma and gTer-ma teachings. His chief disciples included Thams-cad mKhyen-pa dKon-mchog Yan-lag, the Sa-skya bDag-chen Kun-dga' Rin-chen, rTse-gdong bDag-chen Kun-dga' bSam-'grub, and 'Brug-pa Zhabs-drung Mi-pham Chos-rgyal. Because disciples flocked to him from Khams, Kong-po, Dwags-po, E, gNyal, lHo-brag, Mon-yul, dBus and gTsang, his enlightened activities greatly extended the vitality of the rNying-ma traditions.

Zhig-po Gling-pa, Sog-bzlog-pa Blo-gros rGyal-mtshan, and Gong-ra Lo-chen gZhan-phan rDo-rje were known as the Three Mountains (gangs-gsum): During their lifetimes the lineages of the Ancient School flourished. The stream of Zhig-po Gling-pa's gTer-ma teachings flowed through eight disciples named "Padma" including sTag-bla Padma Mati. But in later times, his works became rare, and Kong-sprul had to search to acquire them. Great Treasures of Ancient Teachings includes over thirty texts in the Rin-chen gTer-mdzod section and eighty-one texts in the Collected Works section.

བྱང་པ་བདག་པོ་ཆོས་རྒྱལ་དབང་པོ་སྡེ་བཀྲ་ཤིས་སྟོབས་རྒྱལ

Byang-pa bDag-po Chos-rgyal dBang-po-sde
bKra-shis sTobs-rgyal
1550–1602 C.E.
1 text, 239 pages, Rin-chen gTer-mdzod: 3 texts

A reincarnation of mNga'-ris Paṇ-chen Padma dBang-rgyal (and thus of King Khri-srong lDe'u-bstan, and the tenth rGyal-sras lHa-rje), bKra-shis sTobs-rgyal was one of the major lineage holders of the Northern Treasures. He was born in upper gYas-ru as the son of the nobleman Nam-mkha' Rin-chen, who was related to the kings of Mi-nyag. His mother was Chos-skyong 'Dzom-chen.

rJe-btsun Kun-dga' 'Grol-mchog bestowed the name bKra-shis sTobs-rgyal dBang-po'i-sde upon the child. His early teachers included this master, as well as Lo-chen Ratnabhadra, gNubs dGon-pa Byams-pa Chos-kyi rGyal-mtshan, Rig-'dzin Legs-ldan-pa, and 'Bri-gung Chos-rgyal Rin-chen Phun-tshogs. Under their guidance, he studied Sūtras and rNying-ma and gSar-ma Tantras. In particular he studied the gTer-ma teachings of earlier masters and composed a famous prayer to the lineage. His devoted study and practice led to extraordinary abilities to subdue forces opposed to enlightenment.

At bSam-yas in the temple of Ārya Pālo, he discovered gTer-ma. In gTsang-rong he flew up to a secret practice cave high atop lHang-lhang rock where he found more treasures. In the golden stupa at lHo-brag 'Jod-pa, he found more priceless texts and ritual objects. bKra-shis sTobs-rgyal's teachings filled dBus and gTsang, Kong-po and Khams, and those who practiced them attained profound results. Working in mDo-khams, he set many individuals on the path of liberation.

During his lifetime, the community of Northern Treasures practitioners, which was known as E-wam lCog-sgar, was forced to wander from place to place because of hostility from the rulers of gTsang. In the next generation, bKra-shis sTobs-rgyal's son, Byang-bdag Rig-'dzin Ngag-gi dBang-po, founded the monastery of rDo-rje-brag, where the Northern Treasures community would reside. bKra-shis sTobs-rgyal's younger brother, Yid-bzhin Nor-bu, founded the monastery of Srid-gsum rNam-rgyal at Zang-zang lHa-brag, where Rig-'dzin rGod-ldem had discovered the dGongs-pa-zang-thal. This monastery was later overseen by rDo-rje-brag and became the residence of Klu-sgrub sPrul-sku. Kong-sprul was able to find several texts by bKra-shis sTobs-rgyal, which he preserved in the Rin-chen gTer-mdzod; Great Treasures also contains the biography of Padmasambhava discovered by this gTer-ston.

## གཁས་གྲུབ་ཆེན་པོ་སོག་བཟློག་པ་བློ་གྲོས་རྒྱལ་མཚན་

mKhas-grub Chen-po Sog-bzlog-pa Blo-gros rGyal-mtshan
1552–1624 C.E.
27 texts, 453 pages, Rin-chen gTer-mdzod: 5 texts

An incarnation of gNyags Jñānakumāra, Blo-gros rGyal-mtshan was born into the lDong clan in Thag gDong-khar in gTsang. As a young man he studied the five arts and sciences, and especially medicine, and became known as the Physician of gDong-khar. After being ordained, he studied with Grags-pa Rin-chen, Yongs-'dzin Ngag-dbang Grags-pa, Zla-ba rGyal-mtshan (Padma Gling-pa's spiritual son), gTer-chen Zhig-po Gling-pa, and rDo-rje Seng-ge. Learned in Sūtra and Mantra, bKa'-ma and gTer-ma, Blo-gros rGyal-mtshan became expert in Atiyoga and mastered the transformation of dreams.

Traveling to pure lands, this master received teachings from Bodhisattvas; employing his extraordinary magical powers, he defended Tibet from invading armies. Thus he became known as Sog-bzlog-pa, One Who Turns Back the Hordes. Together with his disciple Gong-ra Lo-chen and his master Zhig-po Gling-pa, he was known as one of the Three Mountains, in whose time rNying-ma lineages were strong and widespread.

Sog-bzlog-pa resided at sKyid-sbug in lower Nyang where he taught and guided disciples in ways suited to the abilities of each. He composed exegeses, texts on history, answers to critics of rNying-ma, and explanations of sādhanas. To preserve the texts of the Ancient School, he had golden copies made of the rGyud-bcu-bdun, the Bi-ma-snying-thig, the bDe-gshegs-'dus-pa and others. He published many bKa'-ma and gTer-ma texts during his long lifetime.

He lived until at least seventy-three years of age. His major disciples included Gong-ra Lo-chen (1595–1655), who prepared three sets of the rNying-ma-rgyud-'bum in the mid-seventeenth century. These two masters were essential links in the transmission of the Anuyoga teachings. Great Treasures of Ancient Teachings preserves twenty-seven of Sog-bzlog-pa's texts, with five additional texts in the Rin-chen gTer-mdzod section.

གཏེར་སྟོན་གར་དབང་ལས་འཕྲོ་གླིང་པ

gTer-ston Gar-dbang Las-'phro Gling-pa
early 16th–mid-16th century C.E.
Rin-chen gTer-mdzod: 1 text

An incarnation of Lo-chung dKon-mchog-'od and the tenth incarnation of rGyal-sras lHa-rje, Las-'phro Gling-pa was born at E-yul sPe-cog. His family belonged to the Nephew Lineage of Ratna Gling-pa that traced back to Lo-tsā-ba Khegad 'Khor-lo. At the age of six, Las-'phro Gling-pa received vows, and even as a child displayed marvelous acts. At seventeen, he proceeded to Yar-lung Shel-brag, a powerful holy site

226

on Padma brTsegs mountain associated with the Enlightened Qualities of the Guru. There he discovered seven precious sections of Avalokiteśvara teachings, yi-dam and ḍākinī sādhanas, eight heruka texts, Amitābha practices and many others. At 'Od-de Gung-rgyal, a mountain peak 6,000 meters tall located in 'Ol-kha, Las-'phro Gling-pa also discovered more precious treasures including longevity practices, Yamāntaka practices, and Dharma protector sādhanas.

gTer-ston Las-'phro Gling-pa received numerous bKa'-ma and gTer-ma teachings, which he studied and practiced until signs of accomplishment and supernormal powers manifested unobstructedly. It is said that on occasion he actually flew like a bird through the sky. The lords of the Yar-lung valley at Phying-ba sTag-rtse paid him great honor. This gTer-ston protected and benefited the inhabitants of dBus and Yar-'brog, E-yul and Dwags-po. His family and Dharma lineages were continued at E-yul sPe-cog, and the stream of some gTer-ma teachings flowed to gTer-bdag Gling-pa. Though they had disappeared by the time of Kong-sprul, fortunately, the great 'Jam-dbyangs mKhyen-brtse was able to recover one teaching, which was preserved in the Rin-chen gTer-mdzod.

## 'Khon-ston dPal-'byor lHun-grub
### 1561–1637 C.E.

An incarnation of sGro-sbug-pa, dPal-'byor lHun-grub was a key link in the Mahāyoga lineages that flowed from Rin-chen Phun-tshogs to the Fifth Dalai Lama. He was the son of Tshe-dbang Nor-rgyas, who was a disciple of Rin-chen Phun-tshogs' disciple Rang-grol Nyi-zla Sangs-rgyas. dPal-'byor lHun-grub was ordained as a novice by bSod-nams rGya-mtsho and studied with masters of both rNying-ma and gSar-ma traditions. His own father transmitted to him the Mahāyoga teachings and especially the works of Kun-mkhyen Klong-chen-pa, and Nyi-zla Sangs-rgyas bestowed rDzogs-chen instructions upon him.

Extremely learned in the Sūtras, he taught at rTse-thang (founded in 1352 by Sa-skya Bla-ma Dam-pa bSod-nams rGyal-mtshan), at Sang-phu (founded in 1073 by rNgog Legs-pa'i Shes-rab), and at Se-ra (founded in 1419 by Byams-chen Chos-rje Śākya Ye-shes). dPal-'byor lHun-grub bestowed teachings on both Zur Chos-dbyings Rang-grol and the Fifth Dalai Lama. He composed numerous works on philosophy and on the worldly sciences, but they are no longer to be found.

གཏེར་སྟོན་བདེ་ཆེན་གླིང་པ

gTer-ston bDe-chen Gling-pa
1562–1622 C.E.
Rin-chen gTer-mdzod: 1 text

An incarnation of 'Brog-mi dPal-gyi Ye-shes, bDe-chen Gling-pa was born in southern Tibet between gNyal and Lo-ro in Gru-shul at Khyung-chen-lding. His father was dPal-'byor rGyal-mtshan, who was related to the family of Ratna Gling-pa, and his mother was Padma mTsho. In his youth bDe-chen Gling-pa had visions of Ye-shes mTsho-rgyal and Padmasambhava, both of whom bestowed blessings and initiations upon him.

Soon he discovered Yamāntaka gTer-ma, sacred substances, and ritual objects at Khyung-chen rock. He found more precious treasures in numerous practice caves such as Nam-mkha'i sNying-po's favorite practice site at Zil-chen secret cave; Gangs-bar Phug-mo-che; mGon-po gDong-gi-brag;

228

sMan-chu-brag; rNa-ring dMar-gyi Pho-brang; Dom-tshang bde-mchog cave; and mDa'-tshe-zer cave. He proceeded to lHo-brag Khom-mthing temple, Ban-pa Chu-mig dMar-po, Khar-kha cave, lHo-brag sNa-bo rock, lHo-brag gTam-shul, and Srin-mo Nag-po rock, and in each place he made more discoveries. At E gZer-po rock, E-rong Khrab-la-kha, 'Ja'-tshon rock, and Tshe-lam mountain, he found still more treasures.

His gTer-ma included statues, ritual objects, precious substances, and many precious teachings such as the eight heruka practices and the complete Sanskrit text of the 100,000-line Prajñāpāramitā. It was predicted that he would have numerous disciples, but the conditions were not quite right and not all gathered. His major disciples were Byang-chub Gling-pa sNa-tshogs Rang-grol and dKar-po bsTan-'dzin Nor-bu.

The next incarnation of bDe-chen Gling-pa was born at Kong-po Bu-chu, the natural power site where Srong-btsan sGam-po built a land-taming temple in the seventh century. This incarnation was the disciple of rGyal-dbang dBang-phyug rDo-rje, with whom he took refuge. He was also the student of Phreng-po gTer-chen, Zhig-po Gling-pa, and 'Bri-gung Chos-rgyal Rin-chen Phun-tshogs. Again the conditions were not quite fitting, and he did not live to forty. The next incarnation was born at Mon-mel-po.

gTer-ma discoveries of these three incarnations included six volumes of the mKha'-'gro-dgongs-pa-'dus-pa, but this lineage did not continue. In the nineteenth century mChog-gyur Gling-pa and 'Jam-dbyangs mKhyen-brtse restored the essential part of these teachings, and Kong-sprul preserved one work in the Rin-chen gTer-mdzod.

གཏེར་སྟོན་རིག་འཛིན་ངག་གི་དབང་པོ

gTer-ston Rig-'dzin Ngag-gi dBang-po
1580–1639 C.E.
Rin-chen gTer-mdzod: 1 text

The third incarnation of the great Rig-'dzin rGod-ldem, and the immediate reincarnation of Legs-ldan-rje, Ngag-gi dBang-po was the founder of rDo-rje-brag monastery, which became the major center for the Northern Treasures. Renowned as the Axis of the Ancient School during the late sixteenth century, he was born as the son of Byang-bdag bKra-shis sTobs-rgyal and lHa-lcam Yid-bzhin dBang-mo, who belonged to the divine clan of Za-hor.

Taking refuge with 'Bri-gung Chos-rgyal Rin-chen Phun-tshogs, Ngag-gi dBang-po began to follow the path of the Bodhisattvas. He received the name Ngag-dbang Rig-'dzin rDo-rje Chos-rgyal bsTan-pa'i rGyal-mtshan dPal-bzang-po. From his father he received rNying-ma bKa'-ma and gTer-ma teachings until he himself became an ocean of Dharma. Upholding the three vows, he lived as a great Vajradhara of the Mantrayāna. At Yar-lung Shel-brag, the power place associated with the Enlightened Qualities of the Guru, and at other ancient holy sites where gTer-ma had been found, he practiced one-pointedly; eventually he beheld many deities and protectors, who served him, and developed incomparable supernormal powers that enabled him to benefit beings.

A deeply compassionate and immensely powerful yogi, Ngag-gi dBang-po brought his influence to bear to mediate disputes, resolving difficulties between kingdoms in eastern Tibet, bringing peace and happiness to many beings. Proceeding to central Tibet, in 1632 he founded the monastery of Thub-bstan rDo-rje-brag along the north banks of the gTsang-po river west of bSam-yas. As this monastery became the chief center for the Northern Treasures, the long-range benefits from the Dharma

230

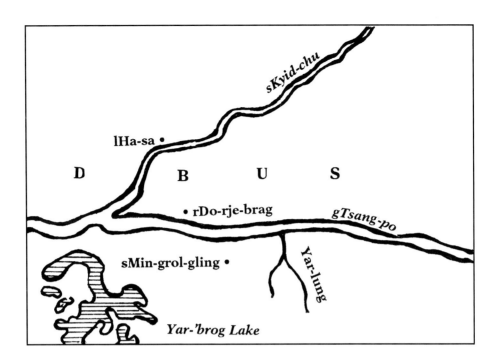

work of Ngag-gi dBang-po can hardly be measured. Ngag-gi dBang-po was admired and honored by the Fifth Dalai Lama, whom he had blessed at birth. The Great Fifth later composed the biography of Ngag-gi dBang-po.

At the end of his life Ngag-gi dBang-po entrusted rDo-rje-brag monastery to Yol-mo sPrul-sku bsTan-'dzin Nor-bu, his primary Heart Son. The lineages of this monastery have been continued unbroken to the present time through the incarnations of Rig-'dzin rGod-ldem and the other great masters of the Northern Treasures, such as rDo-brag Rig-'dzin Padma 'Phrin-las, who was Ngag-gi dBang-po's incarnation. One text of Ngag-gi dBang-po's, elaborating on the gTer-ma discoveries of bKra-shis sTobs-rgyal, is preserved in the Rin-chen gTer-mdzod. His biography is also included in the Great Treasures of Ancient Teachings.

རིག་འཛིན་ཆེན་པོ་འཇའ་ཚོན་ཆེན་སྙིང་པོ་

Rig-'dzin Chen-po 'Ja'-tshon sNying-po
1585–1656 C.E.
314 texts, 1,897 pages, Rin-chen gTer-mdzod: 9 texts

Rig-'dzin Chen-po 'Ja'-tshon sNying-po was an incarnation of Myang Ting-nge-'dzin, one of the one hundred and eight disciples of Padmasambhava who attained the untainted Body of Light. He was born in Kong-po at Wa-ru gNam-tshal as the son of Chos-skyong mGon-po and Nam-lung Bu-khrid. He was also known as Hūṁ-nag Me-'bar and gTer-ston Las-'phro Gling-pa. As a youth he studied the traditional arts and sciences, especially medicine, and took refuge with Mi-pham bKra-shis Blo-gros. He mastered the rNying-ma and gSar-ma traditions under the guidance of Nor-bu brGyan-pa, 'Brug-pa Thams-cad mKhyen-pa, and lHa-rtse-ba, who gave him full ordination.

'Ja'-tshon sNying-po then spent seventeen years on retreat. It was not until he was thirty-five that he began to discover gTer-ma at sacred sites: Brag-lung Hom-'phrang in Kong-po; Kong-po Bu-chu, a land-taming temple built by Srong-btsan sGam-po in the seventh century; Byang-'phreng-mdzes, the entrance to the sacred place of lJong-po-lung; sNye-mo lHa-ri, a sacred mountain; Zhwa'i lHa-khang, the temple built by Myang Ting-nge-'dzin; and other places. His gTer-ma include the famous Gathering of Precious Jewels (dKon-mchog-spyi-'dus), as well as Avalokiteśvara teachings, Hayagrīva and Vajravārāhī practices, peaceful and wrathful deities sādhanas, longevity practices, rDo-rje-gro-lod practices, Dharma protector rites, and a guide to the hidden valley of Padma-bkod.

Most of his discoveries were made in public, inspiring thousands of people with faith in the Dharma. While maintaining the way of the monk, this gTer-ma master had extraordinary magical abilities and supernormal powers that allowed him to guide innumerable disciples to liberation.

At Bang-ri 'Jog-po in Kong-po, 'Ja'-tshon sNying-po established a monastery where he attracted many disciples, including his teacher Nor-bu brGyan-pa, the Karmapas, 'Bri-gung Chos-kyi Grags-pa, rDo-rje-brag Rig-'dzin Ngag-gi dBang-po, lHa-btsun Nam-mkha'i 'Jigs-med, Rig-'dzin Phrin-las lHun-grub, rTse-le sNa-tshogs Rang-grol, gTer-chen bDud-'dul rDo-rje, sTag-bla Padma Mati, sPu-bo rBa-kha sPrul-sku, and many others. The enlightened activity of 'Ja'-tshon sNying-po's gTer-ma teachings has continued unbroken down to the present day. Three hundred and fourteen texts by him are preserved in Great Treasures of Ancient Teachings, as well as nine in the Rin-chen gTer-mdzod section.

ཡོལ་མོ་སྤྲུལ་སྐུ་བསྟན་འཛིན་ནོར་བུ

## Yol-mo sPrul-sku bsTan-'dzin Nor-bu
### 1589–1668 C.E.
### 10 texts, 220 pages

An incarnation of sNgags-'chang Yol-mo sPrul-sku Śākya bZang-po, and the chief disciple and Heart Son of Ngag-gi dBang-po, bsTan-'dzin Nor-bu was born in Kong-po at Klung-rgyas-grong. He was the son of Rig-'dzin 'Phrin-las dBang-phyug and Lady Kun-bzang dBang-mo. While very young, he recalled his previous incarnations, exhibited remarkable abilities, and had inspired visions. Taking lay vows with Zhwa-dmar Karmapa Chos-kyi dBang-phyug, he received the name Karma Thub-bstan sNying-po rNam-par rGyal-ba'i-sde. He relied on masters of the Karma 'Brug-pa school and Lo-chen 'Gyur-med bDe-chen. After completing his studies at Nying-gling, he was invited by the ruler of Yam-bu to come to the kingdom of Nepal. There he consecrated and restored the great Stupa of Bya-rung-kha-shor at Boudhanath. When he taught the Dharma at Ngam-ring, the local gTsang-pa prince revered and honored him.

Then at sMan-thang he met Rig-'dzin Ngag-gi dBang-po, who expelled all his intellectualizing and granted him the rNying-ma teachings. As a holder of the rNying-ma lineages, bsTan-'dzin Nor-bu proceeded to Mang-yul, where he established a practice center at Ri-bo dPal-'bar. After receiving Pure Visions and predictions, he discovered treasures at rGyang Yon-po-lung. When he returned to dBus, he came back to his master Ngag-gi dBang-po, who shortly before passing away entrusted him with the care of rDo-rje-brag monastery.

Later at rTa-nag in Tārā cave, Yol-mo sPrul-sku received gTer-ma teachings from the ḍākinīs in Pure Visions, but he reached the end of his life without the conditions becoming suitable for bringing forth these treasures. This master was also known as sTobs-ldan Shugs-'chang-rtsal. Great Treasures of Ancient Teachings preserves ten of his works, including a history of the Boudhanath Stupa.

 སྟག་བླ་པདྨ་མ་ཏི།

sTag-bla Padma Mati
1591–1637 C.E.
4 texts, 198 pages, Rin-chen gTer-mdzod: 1 text

Disciple of Zhig-po Gling-pa and 'Ja'-tshon sNying-po, Padma Mati (Padma Blo-gros) was a master of Kaḥ-thog monastery and an essential link in the transmission of the rNying-ma bKa'-ma lineages. He received Mahāyoga teachings and especially the Klong-chen-pa commentary (Phyogs-su-mun-sel) from the great Chos-dbyings Rang-grol, who was the

234

master of the Fifth Dalai Lama. Padma Mati transmitted these Mahāyoga lineages to lHo-brag gSung-sprul, the Padma Gling-pa incarnation. Padma Mati bestowed on Chos-dbyings Rang-grol the Anuyoga teachings, together with their texts, initiations, and practices. He also granted him the practices of the mandala of the eight herukas.

His disciples included Gong-ra Lo-chen, who was the nephew of Rig-'dzin Ngag-gi dBang-po and the teacher of gTer-bdag Gling-pa's father. Though he himself was apparently not a gTer-ston, Padma Mati received the gTer-ma lineages of Zhig-po Gling-pa. Padma Mati composed precious explanations of rDzogs-chen teachings, a work containing replies to crucial questions about rNying-ma teachings, and advice on advanced practices. Four texts by this master are preserved in Great Treasures of Ancient Teachings, together with a text in the Rin-chen gTer-mdzod.

## Gong-ra Lo-chen gZhan-phan rDo-rje
### 1595–1655 C.E.

Gong-ra Lo-chen gZhan-phan rDo-rje was born in Sikkim at bKra-shis-gling as the son of dBon-chen, the younger brother of Lo-chen Ngag-gi dBang-po. Ordained by Zhwa-dmar-pa Chos-kyi dBang-phyug, he became learned in the science of language under the guidance of his uncle and later was known as the great translator (Lo-chen) of Gong-ra lHun-grub-sding. He studied the bKa'-ma and gTer-ma of the rNying-ma school under Sog-bzlog-pa, gSung-sprul Tshul-khrims rDo-rje, rTse-le sNa-tshogs, Kaḥ-thog-pa Padma Mati, and others. gZhan-phan rDo-rje was a key link in the Anuyoga lineage that he had received from his master Sog-bzlog-pa. Brilliant and fearless, he reached the limits of realization and dedicated all his energies toward nonworldly concerns.

Together with Sog-bzlog-pa and Zhig-po Gling-pa, he was known as one of the Three Mountains, whose presence in the world guaranteed the strength and firmness of the traditions of the Ancient School. In particular, Gong-ra Lo-chen had three sets of the precious rNying-ma-rgyud-'bum texts prepared for Khams, Kong-po, and central Tibet. His achievements in teaching, yogic attainment, and Dharma work were extensive. His major disciple was gSang-bdag Phrin-las lHun-grub, the father of gTer-bdag Gling-pa. No works by this master have been located in recent times.

འབྲི་གུང་པ་རིག་འཛིན་ཆེན་པོ་ཆོས་ཀྱི་གྲགས་པ

'Bri-gung-pa Rig-'dzin Chen-po Chos-kyi Grags-pa

1595 C.E.

187 texts, 1,400 pages, Rin-chen gTer-mdzod: 18 texts

An incarnation of 'Bri-gung Rin-chen Phun-tshogs, Chos-kyi Grags-pa was the twenty-first lineage holder of the bKa'-brgyud monastery of 'Bri-gung. Master of the five sciences, an expert in the gSar-ma teachings of Cakrasaṁvara, he was a Vidyādhara who held many gTer-ma lineages. He was the disciple of many lamas, especially 'Ja'-tshon sNying-po. Chos-kyi Grags-pa was a master of the eight heruka practices and the 'Bri-gung-pa dGongs-gcig teachings, on which he composed a commentary. He received longevity practices as Pure Vision Treasures and extensive teachings on Yamāntaka as Realization Treasures, which soon spread widely. Kong-sprul Blo-gros mTha'-yas was able to locate and receive his gTer-ma teachings, which he preserved in the Rin-chen gTer-dzod as eighteen texts. One hundred and eighty-seven additional texts have been collected in Great Treasures of Ancient Teachings.

ལྷ་བཙུན་ཆེན་པོ་རིག་འཛིན་ནམ་མཁའ་འཇིགས་མེད

lHa-btsun Chen-po Rig-'dzin Nam-mkha' 'Jigs-med
1597–1650 C.E.
185 texts, 1,722 pages, Rin-chen gTer-mdzod: 18 texts

An incarnation of Vimalamitra and Klong-chen-pa, lHa-btsun Nam-mkha'i 'Jigs-med was born at Byar-yul in southern Tibet in the lHa-btsad-po lineage of the Dharma kings. Receiving the Triple Vajra Saṁvara vows at gSungs-nyan hermitage from O-rgyan dPal-'byor, he received the name Kun-bzang rNam-rgyal. At Thang-'brog college he studied many subjects, including the eight heruka practices, the Bla-ma-dgongs-'dus, and sNying-thig teachings. These last he received from rDzogs-chen-pa bSod-nams dBang-po and practiced intensively on retreat in many holy places, making pilgrimages throughout central Tibet. There are even stories of his traveling to India, where he converted a heretic ruler.

Reaching the stage of a realized siddha, he attained unsurpassed yogic accomplishments. Using his miraculous powers, he enlisted non-human forces to restore the ancient monastery of bSam-yas. Every word he spoke was refined and full of meaning. Pure Visions descended to him often as he practiced in remote sacred places like Zab-bu-lung in Shang, which 'Jam-dbyangs mKhyen-brtse called the most important meditation place in all of western Tibet. He also resided at Yar-lung Shel-ri lHa'i-lding and Padma 'Ja'-'od Shel-rdzong in Sikkim. Through profound meditation, he discovered a remarkable Realization Treasure known as the rDo-rje-snying-po-sprin-gyi-tho-glu'i-chos-skor, which is said to condense all the inner instructions of the gTer-ma lineages.

At the urging of 'Ja'-tshon sNying-po and bDud-'dul rDo-rje, lHa-btsun Nam-mkha'i 'Jigs-med proceeded to Sikkim in 1646, and there he founded a temple in the most sacred place of lHa-ri 'Od-gsal sNying-po. While in Sikkim, he again received

237

precious Realization gTer-ma, the renowned Rig-'dzin-srog-sgrub teachings of the Atiyoga. He taught rDzogs-chen extensively in a lineage famous as 'Bras-longs (Sikkim) rDzogs-chen. His lineages have been passed down unbroken to the present time, especially in Sikkim. His reincarnation, lHa-btsun sPrul-sku, was born in 1682. Various sections of the Great Treasures of Ancient Teachings preserve one hundred and eighty-five texts, while the Rin-chen gTer-mdzod section contains another eighteen.

## པད་གླིང་གསུམ་པ་ཚུལ་ཁྲིམས་རྡོ་རྗེ

### Pad-gling gSum-pa Tshul-khrims rDo-rje
### 1598–1669 C.E.
### Rin-chen gTer-mdzod: 1 text

The lineages of Padma Gling-pa flowed through two major streams: the incarnations of Padma Gling-pa, known as gSung-sprul or as Pad-gling sPrul-sku Lineage, and the incarnations of his son Zla-ba rGyal-mtshan, known as the Thugs-sras or Heart Son Lineage.

Padma Gling-pa gSum-pa, the third gSung-sprul Rinpoche, was the great scholar mKhas-grub Chen-po Tshul-khrims rDo-rje. He and the Fourth Thugs-sras-sprul bsTan-'dzin 'Gyur-med rDo-rje lived at the same time, and both masters resided at Guru lHa-khang. Guru lHa-khang, which had been the residence of Guru Chos-kyi dBang-phyug, was entrusted to the lineage of Padma Gling-pa.

Tshul-khrims rDo-rje and other Padma Gling-pa incarnations were essential links in the lineage of the rNying-ma-rgyud-'bum that descended from Ratna Gling-pa. This stream flowed from Ratna Gling-pa's son Tshe-dbang Grags-pa to Tshe-dbang Grags-pa's younger brother, and then to the younger brother's son Ngag-dbang Nor-bu. He bestowed the lineage on an emanation of Vimalamitra known as Nor-bu Yongs-grags, who in turn taught rGyas-sras Nor-bu dBang-rgyal. It was he who transmitted the rNying-ma-rgyud-'bum lineage to Tshul-khrims rDo-rje.

Tshul-khrims rDo-rje bestowed this lineage on Gar-dbang Tshul-khrims rGyal-mtshan, who in turn taught the fourth Pad-gling Thugs-sras, bsTan-'dzin 'Gyur-med rDo-rje, and the great gTer-bdag Gling-pa.

bsTan-'dzin 'Gyur-med rDo-rje transmitted the lineage to the Fourth Padma Gling-pa gSung-sprul, Ngag-dbang Kun-bzang rDo-rje. He in turn gave it to the Fifth Padma Gling-pa Thugs-sras, 'Gyur-med mChog-grub dPal-'bar. His disciple was Padma Don-grub Grags-pa, who taught Kun-bzang bsTan-pa'i rGyal-mtshan, the sixth gSung-sprul incarnation. He taught rBa-kha Kun-bzang Rig-'dzin rDo-rje, who in turn transmitted the lineage to Kun-bzang bsTan-pa'i Nyi-ma, the eighth gSung-sprul. He instructed rBa-kha Rig-'dzin Khams-gsum Yongs-grol, who taught O-rgyan rNam-grol rGya-mtsho. This master in turn transmitted the lineage to dGe-'dun rGya-mtsho, who bestowed it on the twentieth-century master bDud-'joms Rin-poche 'Jigs-bral Ye-shes rDo-rje.

Tshul-khrims rDo-rje composed a condensed explanation of a cycle of teachings discovered by Padma Gling-pa, the rDzogs-chen Kun-bzang-dgongs-pa-kun-'dus. Kong-sprul was able to preserve this text in the Rin-chen gTer-mdzod, but other works by this great scholar have not yet been located.

ལྡི་རི་ཨོ་རྒྱན་ཆོས་ཀྱི་གྲགས་པ

lDi-ri O-rgyan Chos-kyi Grags-pa
mid-16th–early 17th century C.E.
177 texts, 447 pages, Rin-chen gTer-mdzod: 4 texts

Born in gSer-thal north of Khams, lDi-ri Chos-grags was contemporary with Mati Ratna. At 'Brong-ru rMug-po mountain, he discovered Mahākāla teachings that had been concealed by Vairotsana in the eighth century. Great Treasures of Ancient Teachings preserves one hundred and seventy-seven of his texts in the Collected Works section and a few additional works in the Rin-chen gTer-mdzod section.

གཏེར་སྟོན་མ་ཏི་རཏྣ

gTer-ston Mati Ratna
mid-16th–early 17th century C.E.
82 texts, 269 pages, Rin-chen gTer-mdzod: 2 texts

An incarnation of mKhar-chen dPal-gyi dBang-phyug, Mati Ratna was born on the border of rTa-shel and mDo-smad. He discovered guru sādhana gTer-ma in the river running through the pine forests of Shel-khog. His monastery and Dharma lineages continued at least through the days of Kong-sprul, especially in the mDo-smad region. The sādhanas that he discovered were followed at dPal-yul monastery for centuries. Kong-sprul received the lineages and preserved two texts in the Rin-chen gTer-mdzod, while eighty-two additional works are in Great Treasures of Ancient Teachings.

# འཁྲུལ་ཞིག་དབང་དྲག་རྒྱ་མཚོ

'Khrul-zhig dBang-drag rGya-mtsho
mid-16th–early 17th century C.E.?
45 texts, 146 pages

A contemporary of master Mati Ratna, 'Khrul-zhig dBang-drag rGya-mtsho belonged to the lineages that would flow in the next generation to the great monastery of dPal-yul (which Kun-bzang Shes-rab would found in 1665). He was said to be an incarnation of Lo-chen Vairotsana and Shud-bu dPal-gyi Seng-ge. His next incarnation was gNam-chos Mi-'gyur rDo-rje, the marvelous young gTer-ma master whose gNam-chos teachings became the specialty of dPal-yul. 'Khrul-zhig dBang-drag rGya-mtsho composed forty-five works, which are preserved in Great Treasures of Ancient Teachings.

# མཁས་གྲུབ་བཀྲ་ཤིས་རྣམ་རྒྱལ

mKhas-grub bKra-shis rNam-rgyal
mid-16th–early 17th century C.E.
1 text, 24 pages

A disciple of the Dharma master of the Northern Treasures, Ngag-gi dBang-po, bKra-shis rNam-rgyal composed a brilliant work clarifying the tenets of the rNying-ma school. This text is preserved in Great Treasures of Ancient Teachings.

# རབ་ཞི་གཏེར་སྟོན་རིག་འཛིན།

Ra-zhi gTer-ston Padma Rig-'dzin
mid-16th–early 17th century C.E.
Rin-chen gTer-mdzod: 1 text

The eleventh rebirth of rGyal-sras lHa-rje, and also said to be an incarnation of both Vairotsana and Padma Gling-pa, Padma Rig-'dzin was born at sBu-bor Ra-zhi in eastern Tibet between 'Ba'-thang and Li-thang. From bDud-ri gNam-lcags rock, he removed gTer-ma teachings on peaceful and wrathful deities. He also discovered treasures associated with the Bla-ma-dgongs-'dus teachings. He uncovered precious teachings at sGrags Yang-rdzong near bSam-yas, which is the sacred place associated with the Enlightened Body of the Guru; at lHo-brag mKhar-chu, the powerful sacred place connected to the Enlightened Mind of the Guru; at gNam-skas-can in lHo-brag; and at Zab-bu-lung in gTsang, where Ye-shes mTsho-rgyal resided while perfecting the understanding of Guru Padmasambhava's disciples. He bestowed his gTer-ma teachings on the Karmapa Chos-dbyings rDo-rje and on the seventh Zhwa-dmar Karmapa and made them his Dharma heirs. One of his gTer-ma texts is preserved in the Rin-chen gTer-mdzod.

Padma Rig-'dzin was the Dharma heir of the great 'Ja'-tshon sNying-po. It was he who ordained rTse-le sNa-tshog Rig-'dzin and gave him the name Padma Legs-grub, bestowing upon him some of his own gTer-ma teachings. Ra-zhi gTer-ston's lineage holders resided at sPu-bo rBa-kha gSang-sngags Chos-gling. After Ra-zhi gTer-ston Padma Rig-'dzin, the next incarnation of rGyal-sras lHa-rje was Chos-rje Gling-pa, who was the incarnation just preceding 'Jigs-med Gling-pa. By the time of Kong-sprul Blo-gros mTha'-yas, Ra-zhi gTer-ston's treasure texts were difficult to find. Only one text is preserved in the Rin-chen gTer-mdzod section of Great Treasures.

ལོང་པོ་ལྕགས་སྡེ་པའི་སྔགས་འཆང་བཀྲ་ཤིས་ཚེ་བརྟན་

Long-po lCag sDe-pa'i sNgags-'chang bKra-shis Tshe-brtan
mid-16th–early 17th century C.E.
Rin-chen gTer-mdzod: 1 text

L ong-po lCags sDe-pa'i sNgags-'chang bKra-shis Tshe-brtan
discovered precious sādhana texts at the meditation place
known as Zang-mdog dPal-ri, named after the Copper-Colored
Mountain of Padmasambhava. While these teachings spread
for a while, by the days of Kong-sprul, they could no longer be
easily found. bKra-shis Tshe-brtan lived at the time of 'Ja'-
tshon sNying-po, and he both gave and received teachings from
this great master. bDud-'dul rDo-rje regarded bKra-shis Tshe-
brtan as his root guru and called him Supreme Father, Pha-
mchog Manga Ā-yuḥ. He was clearly an incarnation of a powerful individual though his whole biography is not known. One
of his texts is preserved in the Rin-chen gTer-mdzod.

གཏེར་སྟོན་བཟང་པོ་རྡོ་རྗེ་

gTer-ston bZang-po rDo-rje
mid-16th–early 17th century C.E.

T he gTer-ston bZang-po rDo-rje was born in lower E-yul
Rig-pa 'Byung-gnas as the son of the rNying-ma mantrin
A-bo Chos-mdzad, who descended from the lineage of the
Dharma kings, and his wife dBang-'dzin rGyal-mo. He was the
reincarnation of sGam-po Nor-bu-rgyan, who had been the
very next incarnation of the great Dwags-po bKra-shis rNam-
rgyal. bKra-shis rNam-rgyal was the incarnation of Guru
Padmasambhava, Kha-che Paṇ-chen Vimalamitra, and Dwags-
po lHa-rje (sGam-po-pa). From this extraordinary stream arose

bZang-po rDo-rje, who was recognized as an incarnate master by 'Ja'-tshon sNying-po. He took refuge with this master, who gave him the religious name A-ba-dhuti-pa 'Gyur-med rDo-rje rGyal-mtshan dPal-bzang-po.

bZang-po rDo-rje received many teachings, both rNying-ma and gSar-ma. He took lay vows and then complete ordination with Kun-mkhyen Blo-bzang rGya-mtsho. From sPyan-snga Rin-chen rDo-rje and others he received the bKa'-brgyud teachings of sGam-po-pa; from rTse-le sNa-tshogs Rang-grol he received many instructions on a wide range of philosophical systems. He practiced intensively at sGam-po Zangs-lung and near there began his work as a gTer-ston, discovering treasures as predicted in the gTer-ma of 'Ja'-tshon sNying-po.

At a cave in Dwags-po where Ye-shes mTsho-rgyal had practiced and at other places, he discovered phur-pas and other sacred objects, holy water and medicines, and Yamāntaka treasures. As the circumstances were not completely right, he reconcealed some gTer-ma and so their transmission did not continue. The great O-rgyan gTer-bdag Gling-pa received some of his teachings.

Having continuously turned the Dharma wheel of both gSar-ma and rNying-ma teachings, he departed from this world at Mon-mkhar rNam-sras-gling, where his next incarnation, Kun-bzang Nges-don dBang-po, was born. The succeeding rebirth was rDo-rje rGyal-po, who was born into the clan of the lords of E, as the son of the nobleman of lHa-rgya-ri. No gTer-ma found by bZang-po rDo-rje were preserved in the Rin-chen gTer-mdzod, and no other works by this master have recently been located.

ཟུར་ཆེན་ཆོས་དབྱིངས་རང་གྲོལ

# Zur-chen Chos-dbyings Rang-grol
## 1604–1669 C.E.

This great lineage holder was born as the son of an emanation of Kumārādza known as Zur-chen gZhon-nu Don-
grub, a member of the Zur clan. He received teachings from his
father and prophecies from Rig-'dzin Ngag-gi dBang-po, who
proclaimed that he would greatly benefit the Ancient School.
He intensively studied and practiced the Inner Yogas with
sNang-gsal Rinpoche Ngag-dbang Ye-shes Grub-pa, and did
retreat at Zing-pa sTag-mgo. By the age of seventeen, he had a
profound realization of rDzogs-chen.

Chos-dbyings Rang-grol sought out the rNying-ma master
dPal-'byor lHun-grub, who bestowed upon him Mahāyoga
empowerments and teachings. In his early twenties he began to
teach the gSang-ba'i-snying-po Tantra at rTse-thang. He gave
Mahāyoga teachings to sTag-bla Padma Mati of Kaḥ-thog, who
then transmitted these teachings to lHo-brag gSung-sprul (the
Padma Gling-pa incarnation), so that these precious doctrines
continued without interruption. Padma Mati granted bKa'-
brgyad teachings to Chos-dbyings Rang-grol in return.

As guru of the Fifth Dalai Lama, Chos-dbyings Rang-grol
transmitted to him the key practices of Vajrakīla, the eight
heruka sādhanas, and the sNying-thig teachings. He was also
master of Rig-'dzin Padma Phrin-las and Phrin-las lHun-grub,
the father of gTer-bdag Gling-pa. Works by this lineage holder
have not been located in recent times.

# རྩེ་ལེ་རིག་འཛིན་ཆེན་པོ་སྣ་ཚོགས་རང་གྲོལ

rTse-le Rig-'dzin Chen-po sNa-tshogs Rang-grol
1608 C.E.
129 texts, 1,477 pages, Rin-chen gTer-mdzod: 1 text

An incarnation of the translator Pa-gor Vairotsana, rTse-le sNa-tshog was born on the border of Kong-po and Dwags-po. He was soon recognized as an incarnation of the renowned 'Brug-pa bKa'-'brgyud master rGod-tshang-pa mGon-po rDo-rje (1189–1258) and Mi-la Ras-pa. His previous birth had been as bsTan-'dzin rDo-rje, abbot of rTse-le monastery in Dwags-po and the founder of Thang-'brog monastery in Kong-po.

As a young boy rTse-le sNa-tshogs took refuge with Ra-zhi gTer-ston Padma Rig-'dzin, who gave him the name Padma Legs-grub. Becoming the disciple of 'Ja'-tshon sNying-po, the Third dPa'-bo Rinpoche, and Gong-ra Lo-chen, he grew learned in Sūtra and the Tantras of both the rNying-ma and gSar-ma schools. He completely comprehended all the teachings of the eight great practice lineages of Tibet.

One of his major residences was in Dwags-po at rTse-le dGon-gsar, founded by Rig-'dzin bSod-nams rNam-rgyal. In later life he retired to the practice caves of rGod-tshang-pa in the cliffs of the rTsib-ri mountains in southern La-stod near rTsib-ri rGod-tshang monastery. There he continually deepened his realization of Mahāmudrā and rDzogs-chen. His disciples included sGam-po-pa bZang-po rDo-rje, Chos-rje Mi-pham-pa, and rTa'u Padma Blo-gros. His works are regarded as outstanding guides to the philosophical perspective of the Vajrayāna. His expositions of Mahāmudrā and rDzogs-chen are among his greatest works. Great Treasures of Ancient Teachings preserves one hundred twenty-nine texts.

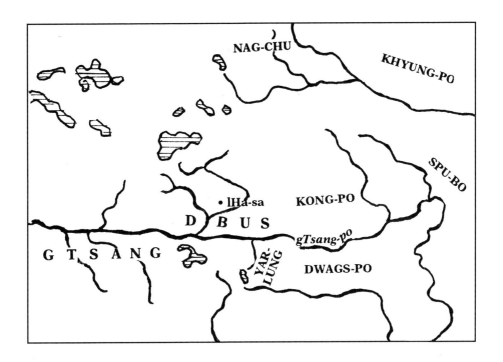

ཀྱིས་སྟོན་རིག་འཛིན་ཆེན་པོ་ཕྲིན་ལས་ལྷུན་གྲུབ

Myos-ston Rig-'dzin Chen-po Phrin-las lHun-grub

1611–1662 C.E.

6 texts, 275 pages, Rin-chen gTer-mdzod: 1 text

A reincarnation of both gNubs-chen Sangs-rgyas Ye-shes and Dran-pa Nam-mkha', Phrin-las lHun-grub was born at Chag Byang-chub-gling as the son of mDo-sngags bsTan-'dzin, who was an accomplished master of the Nyos clan five generations after Padma Gling-pa. He trained especially in the works of Klong-chen-pa as well as the worldly arts and sciences. From his father he received many teachings and practices, in particular the three essential gTer-ma cycles of guru sādhanas, rDzogs-chen teachings, and Avalokiteśvara practices (Bla-rdzogs-thugs-gsum).

After being ordained by gTsug-lag rGya-mtsho, he studied with thirty masters of both gSar-ma and rNying-ma schools.

247

His rNying-ma teachers included: gSung-sprul Tshul-khrims rDo-rje, Gong-ra Lo-chen gZhan-phan rDo-rje, lHa-btsun Kun-bzang rNam-rgyal, rDzogs-chen-pa 'Brug-sgra bZang-po, Bon-lung-pa Tshul-khrims rGyal-mtshan, Zur Chos-dbyings Rang-grol, and 'Khrul-zhig Nor-bu Chos-brtan.

Phrin-las lHun-grub was especially important in the trans-mission of the Anuyoga. He held both the Zur and Khams tra-ditions, and received empowerment from Gong-ra Lo-chen. In solitary hermitages, he then practiced in accord with the teach-ings until he cut through all illusory appearance. Free of all selfishness, he was filled with compassion so powerful that he continuously taught the Dharma to anyone aspiring for free-dom. Blessed by Padmasambhava, he received Pure Visions, which were put into writing.

His main seat was Dar-rgyas Chos-sding in Grwa-nang. His spiritual son was his own son gTer-bdag Gling-pa, to whom he granted the entirety of his teachings. Other close disciples included Lo-chen Chos-rgyal bsTan-'dzin (1631–1708), to whom he transmitted the Anuyoga lineage, and who later joined gTer-bdag Gling-pa in transmitting this lineage at sMin-grol-gling. Great Treasures of Ancient Teachings preserves one text in the Rin-chen gTer-mdzod as well as several other texts and the biography of this outstanding lineage holder.

ཌཁས་གྲུབ་ཆེན་པོ་ཀརྨ་ཆགས་མེད་

mKhas-grub Chen-po Karma Chags-med
1613–1678 C.E.
214 texts, 2,867 pages, Rin-chen gTer-mdzod: 104 texts

An incarnation of both Cog-ro Klu'i rGyal-mtshan and lHa-sras Sad-na-legs, Karma Chags-med was born at Ngom-yul as the son of an upholder of the Mantrayāna traditions named Padma dBang-drag. As a child he learned reading, writing, and astrology with ease. As he matured, he clearly understood the real nature of mind. His father gave him all the rNying-ma teachings he had received. At Zur-mang he took refuge with Kun-dga' rNam-rgyal and received teachings. At 'Phan-yul Za-dam he studied Sūtra and Tantras. Karma Chags-med relied on the Sixth Karmapa Gar-dbang Chos-kyi dBang-phyug as his root guru. This master ordained him and bestowed on him the doctrines of Nāropa and Mahāmudrā. From many leading gSar-ma and rNying-ma masters he received empowerments, transmissions, and instruction.

Karma Chags-med built his own retreat center at gNas-mdo dPal-ri rTse, where he devoted himself to the practices of the three roots of guru, deva, ḍākinī. After spending many years on retreat, he received blessings, signs of accomplishment, and visions of Guru Rinpoche, and discovered treasures in a visionary manner. Karma Chags-med recognized and enthroned the young gTer-ma master gNam-chos Mi-'gyur rDo-rje and then worked closely with him to recover the gNam-chos gTer-ma. Possessing wondrous supernormal powers, Karma Chags-med was able to bring tremendous benefits to beings. He composed extensive commentaries and offered empowerments in both the gNam-chos and Ratna Gling-pa treasures, which were attended by thousands of fortunate people.

Lineages of his disciples continued at gNas-mdo beginning with gSang-phu Padma Kun-dga' and brTson-grus rGya-mtsho. His foremost disciples were the founder of rDzogs-chen monastery, Padma Rig-'dzin, and the founder of dPal-yul monastery, Kun-bzang Shes-rab. Their combined efforts spread Karma Chags-med's teachings far and wide. His incarnation line began with mChog-sprul Phrin-las dBang-phyug. The fourth incarnation of Karma Chags-med was a contemporary of Kong-sprul and bestowed upon him the gTer-ma of Karma Chags-med. The Collected Works section of Great Treasures of Ancient Teachings contains two hundred and fourteen works; another one hundred texts are in the Rin-chen gTer-mdzod section.

# གཏེར་ཆེན་རིག་འཛིན་བདུད་འདུལ་རྡོ་རྗེ

gTer-chen Rig-'dzin bDud-'dul rDo-rje
1615–1672 C.E.
606 texts, 2,080 pages, Rin-chen gTer-mdzod: 23 texts

An incarnation of Guru Padmasambhava's disciple 'Brog-mi Khye'u-chung Lo-tsā-ba, bDud-'dul rDo-rje was born at dNgul-phu-nang in sDe-dge as the son of Klu-grub. Klu-grub was a renowned doctor in the Gling clan and bDud-'dul rDo-rje studied medicine with him from childhood. Beginning at a young age, he resided at the monastery of lHun-grub-steng, where he took refuge with Kun-dga' rGya-mtsho, the incarnation of Rig-'dzin rGod-ldem. At rMug-sang he studied rDzogs-chen teachings with 'Dren-pa dKon-mchog rGyal-mtshan and achieved realization. In central Tibet, he met bKra-shis Tshe-brtan and was inspired to go on retreat, abandoning all food and relying on alchemy. At Ngor and Sa-skya monasteries, he studied the Sa-skya Path and Fruit teachings. At Bang-ri in Kong-po, 'Ja'-tshon sNying-po bestowed empowerments and instructions on him, together with his own gTer-ma teachings.

Receiving a prophecy that he would become a gTer-ston, he proceeded to sPu-bo, where he practiced Ratna Gling-pa's phur-pa teachings intensively. In visions, he met Guru Rinpoche, who blessed him with teachings; he spent a full month in a vision of Zangs-mdog dPal-ri, Padmasambhava's Copper-Colored Mountain. His major discovery was the dGongs-pa-yongs-'dus, which he found at bDe-chen secret cave along the 'Dod-chu river in sPu-bo. His many other discoveries are said to be supplements to this great one.

bDud-'dul rDo-rje opened up pilgrimage places in remote and powerful locations in central Tibet, foremost among them being Padma-bkod, the hidden valley in the bend of the gTsang-po river inhabited by wild hill tribes. As the river turns south here, it flows in deep gorges toward India as the Brahmaputra river. Padmasambhava and the twenty-five disciples practiced in Padma-bkod, as did sGam-po-pa. But until bDud-'dul rDo-rje tamed the land, it was inaccessible to ordinary pilgrims.

bDud-'dul rDo-rje's patrons included the ruler of sDe-dge, Byams-pa Phun-tshogs, and the ruler of Gling-tshang. He established his main residences at bDe-chen-thang and gYu-ri sGang-'go in sPu-bo. At the end of his life, this master's body dissolved almost entirely in light.

bDud-'dul rDo-rje was closely associated with two great gTer-stons, Karma Chags-med and gNam-chos Mi-'gyur rDo-rje. His disciples included other great gTer-ma masters such as lHa-btsun Nam-mkha'i 'Jigs-med and Klong-gsal sNying-po, as well as rBa-kha sPrul-sku Chos-kyi rGya-mtsho, rDzogs-chen Padma Rig-'dzin, Grub-chen Padma Norbu, Kun-bzang Khyab-brdal lHun-grub, and others. bDud-'dul rDo-rje's lineage continued through rGyal-sras Nor-bu Yongs-grags. Twenty-three texts are included in the Rin-chen gTer-mdzod, and six hundred and six texts are preserved in other sections of Great Treasures of Ancient Teachings.

གུན་མཁྱེན་རྒྱལ་དབང་ལྔ་པ་ཆེན་པོ་ངག་དབང་བློ་བཟང་རྒྱ་མཚོ

lNga-pa Chen-po Ngag-dbang Blo-bzang rGya-mtsho
1617–1682 C.E.
167 texts, 2,647 pages, Rin-chen gTer-mdzod: 18 texts

The activity incarnation of King Khri-srong lDe'u-btsan and the embodiment of Avalokiteśvara, Blo-bzang rGya-mtsho was born into the royal family of Za-hor in 'Phyongs-rgyas in central Tibet. His father was bDud-'dul-brtan and his mother was Khri-lcam Kun-dga' lHa-mdzes. Ngag-gi dBang-po, the lineage holder of the Northern Treasures, blessed him at birth.

Recognized as the incarnation of the Fourth Dalai Lama, he studied with many teachers, including the Paṇ-chen Blo-bzang Chos-kyi rGyal-mtshan, dPal-'byor lHun-grub of Pha-bong-kha, Zhwa-lu bSod-nams mChog-grub, Zur-chen Chos-dbyings Rang-grol, and sMan-lung-pa Blo-mchog rDo-rje.

The greatest rNying-ma master of the century, gTer-bdag Gling-pa, was both disciple and teacher of the Great Fifth. Descriptions of his extensive studies fill four volumes of gSan-yig. As a gTer-ma Master he was renowned as rDo-rje Thogs-med-rtsal. He bestowed his visionary gTer-ma discoveries, known as the gSang-ba-rgya-can, on gTer-bdag Gling-pa and Rig-'dzin Padma 'Phrin-las.

With the support and veneration of the Mongol lord Gushri Khan, the Fifth Dalai Lama became the temporal ruler of Tibet in 1642 and was greatly honored in Peking by the second Manchu emperor in 1652. He founded countless monasteries, including the Potala Palace in lHa-sa at dMar-po-ri, where Srong-btsan sGam-po had erected the White Palace in the seventh century. An extraordinarily learned scholar, he composed commentaries on religious and worldly subjects, writing biographies, ornate formal poetry in the Kavya style, and a well-known history of Tibet.

The Fifth Dalai Lama was a key link in the transmission of the Mahāyoga lineages as the disciple of Zur-chen Chos-dbyings Rang-grol. His associates and disciples included most of the important teachers of the time: the abbots and masters of Sa-skya, 'Bri-gung, sTag-lung, and 'Brug, dGa'-ldan Khri Rinpoche, gTer-bdag Gling-pa, Northern Treasures master Padma Phrin-las, and Southern Treasures master bsTan-'dzin 'Gyurmed rDo-rje. Great Treasures of Ancient Teachings preserves one hundred and sixty-seven texts in addition to eighteen works within the Rin-chen gTer-mdzod.

ཀཿཐོག་གཏེར་ཆེན་རིག་འཛིན་ཀློང་གསལ་སྙིང་པོ

Kaḥ-thog gTer-chen Rig-'dzin Klong-gsal sNying-po
1625–1692 C.E.
228 texts, 1,261 pages, Rin-chen gTer-mdzod: 51 texts

The incarnation of Padmasambhava's disciple Lang-gro Lo-tsā-ba dKon-mchog 'Byung-gnas, Klong-gsal sNying-po was clearly predicted in the gTer-ma of bDud-'dul rDo-rje and others. He was born near Ka-bo-gnas as the son of the Mantra-yāna practitioner Kun-dga' Don-grub. His mother was dKon-mchog sGron-ma, who was blessed by White Tārā. He received teachings from Grub-dbang bsTan-pa rGya-mtsho, who gave him the name dBang-drag rGya-mtsho. As a child his inclination toward the Dharma began to manifest, and by the time he was twenty-two, he set out to enter the Dharma at Kaḥ-thog monastery. On the way he received empowerments and teachings at sGa-rje Khams-gong monastery from Chos-skyong rGya-mtsho. At Kaḥ-thog, dKon-mchog rGyal-mtshan gave him numerous instructions in the rDzogs-chen Gongs-pa-zang-thal. Returning to his homeland, he undertook a vow to practice austerities until he reached a high level of accomplishment.

Though he had received various predictions that he would discover treasures, he was not able to locate any gTer-ma. Approaching sPu-bo Rig-'dzin Chen-po, he received advice on how to proceed. At the age of thirty-two, while practicing at mKha'-klong hermitage, he met Guru Rinpoche in the form of a yogin who gave him treasure lists. After two years of intense practice, he made the first of sixteen great discoveries. Klong-gsal sNying-po found teachings of the three essential cycles of guru sādhanas, rDzogs-chen, and Avalokiteśvara practices (Bla-rdzogs-thugs gsum), as well as Mahāyoga texts concealed by Kah-dam-pa bDe-gshegs in the twelfth century, teachings of Vimalamitra, longevity practices, texts associated with the gSang-ba'i-snying-po Tantra, Dharma protector rites, predictions, and many precious substances, statues, and prayers. He was able to establish most of these teachings and practiced each one until the signs of accomplishment came forth.

The benefit and protection this gTer-ston afforded beings are immeasurable. He was famous under several different names, including Hūṁ Nag Me-'bar and O-rgyan mDo-sngags Gling-pa. He was venerated by numerous nobles of Tibet and by Mongol princes. His principal residence was at Kah-thog, where enlightened Dharma activity was greatly enhanced by the work of both bDud-'dul rDo-rje and Klong-gsal sNying-po. After their time, as the bKa'-ma transmission began to decline, Klong-gsal sNying-po's son bSod-nams lDe'u-btsan, who was the reincarnation of bDud-'dul rDo-rje, received the bKa'-ma lineages from gTer-bdag Gling-pa and restored this transmission at Kah-thog monastery.

Klong-gsal sNying-po's chief disciples were bSod-nams lDe'u-btsan, dBon bKra-shis 'Od-zer, Kun-bzang Khyab-bdal lHun-grub, and Ta Bla-ma Padma Nor-bu. His gTer-ma teachings spread very widely in Khams. Kong-sprul Blo-gros mTha'-yas received the major lineages of these gTer-ma, preserving more than fifty works in the Rin-chen gTer-mdzod. Great Treasures of Ancient Teachings contains an additional two hundred and twenty-eight texts.

# རྫོགས་ཆེན་པདྨ་རིག་འཛིན་

rDzogs-chen Padma Rig-'dzin

1625–1697 C.E.

1 text, 30 pages

An incarnation of both the siddha Kukkurāja and Kha-che Paṇ-chen Vimalamitra, Padma Rig-'dzin was born in Ri-bo-che. A disciple of Karma Chags-med and the nephew of Rig-'dzin Kun-bzang Shes-rab, he became a learned scholar and accomplished yogin of great dignity. He received teachings from gTer-chen bDud-'dul rDo-rje and was a chief lineage holder. At rBa-kha hermitage in sPu-bo, he obtained the rDzogs-chen mKha'-'gro-snying-thig teachings from Rig-'dzin Chos-kyi rGya-mtsho, a disciple of bDud-'dul rDo-rje.

In central Tibet, Padma Rig-'dzin made great efforts to restore the temples at bSam-yas. There he heard teachings from thirteen masters including the Fifth Dalai Lama, gTer-chen 'Gyur-med rDo-rje, lHo-brag gSung-sprul, and Thugs-rje sGam-po bZang-po. Practicing at ancient holy places, such as Yer-pa lHa-ri, mChims-phu, Shangs Zab-bu-lung, and Byang gNam-mtsho, he perfected his realization.

At the request of the Great Fifth Dalai Lama, he returned to Khams in 1685, where he established the retreat center of bSam-gtan Chos-gling in the valley of Ru-dam sKyid-khram. The renowned rNying-ma monastery of rDzogs-chen grew up around this center. The three chief spiritual sons of Padma Rig-'dzin were Nyi-ma-grags, who was the incarnation of 'Khon Klu'i-dbang-po, Nam-mkha' 'Od-gsal, who was the rein-carnation of Me-long rDo-rje, and Zhe-chen Rab-'byams bsTan-pa'i rGyal-mtshan. One important work that appears to have been authored by Padma Rig-'dzin is preserved in Great Treasures of Ancient Teachings.

གཏེར་སྟོན་རྒྱལ་སྲས་བསྟན་པའི་འབྱུང་གནས

gTer-ston rGyal-sras-bsTan-pa'i 'Byung-gnas
mid-17th–late 17th century C.E.

An essential link in the incarnation lineage of mChog-ldan mGon-po, rGyal-sras bsTan-pa'i 'Byung-gnas was born after rBa-kha sPrul-sku Rig-'dzin Chos-kyi rGya-mtsho. He resided at 'Phyongs-rgyas, where he practiced intently, obtaining yogic powers and profound knowledge. In Pure Visions he discovered gTer-ma teachings that brought extensive benefits to beings. The stream of these teachings continued down to gTer-bdag Gling-pa and the Fifth Dalai Lama.

The following incarnation was sPrul-sku mDo-sngags 'Byung-gnas, who lived at Yar-'brog Yon-po-do, where he built a magnificent monastery. Although the treasures he discovered were not well-established, he brought immeasurable good to sentient beings. No texts by these masters have been located.

ཡོངས་དགེ་གཏེར་སྟོན་མི་འགྱུར་རྡོ་རྗེ

Yongs-dge gTer-ston Mi-'gyur rDo-rje
1628 C.E.
64 texts, 540 pages, Rin-chen gTer-mdzod: 2 texts

An incarnation of lHa-sras Mu-khri bTsad-po, the son of Khri-srong lDe'u-btsan, Mi-'gyur rDo-rje Drag-po Nus-ldan-rtsal was born in the region of Zal-mo-sgang, the mountainous region of Khams where the 'Bri-chu river flows. His father, a leader of one of the nomad communities, was known as Chief Yongs-dge, and his mother was Ber-mo. He took refuge at mDzo-'dzi monastery with Zur-mang Drung-chen Kun-dga' rNam-rgyal, who bestowed on him the name Karma bSam-'grub. Mi-'gyur rDo-rje studied extensively with this great yogi and with 'Dzi-sgar bSod-nams rGya-mtsho. He also met the Karmapa Chos-dbyings rDo-rje.

Inspired and blessed by visions of Karma Pakṣi and Guru Padmasambhava, he discovered treasures, including rDo-rje-gro-lod sādhanas, longevity practices, and others, said to number one hundred and eight. However, the conditions for these teachings to spread were not all fulfilled. Mi-'gyur rDo-rje then received the blessings of rGyal-dbang Ye-shes rDo-rje at mTshur-phu and departed for the wild pasturelands, where he practiced intensely until great accomplishments and yogic powers manifested. He was able to cure ailments and illnesses of all kinds, turn back armies, and protect many beings. After he met the young Lord Si-tu 'Byung-gnas, he was able to completely establish the gTer-ma teachings he had discovered.

When his activity for others had come to an end, he took birth as Kun-bzang Chos-kyi rDo-rje, an unusual individual who was able to discover Realization Treasures. The continuing incarnations in this stream resided at sGar-shul and protected the transmission. Both the Zhwa-dmar and Zhwa-nag Karmapas were important gTer-ma lineage holders, as well as Si-tu Chos-kyi 'Byung-gnas. Padma Nyin-'byed dBang-po promoted these teachings, and the practices soon spread widely. Several texts were preserved in the Rin-chen gTer-mdzod, as well as sixty-four texts in the Collected Works section of the Great Treasures of Ancient Teachings.

ལོ་ཆེན་ཆོས་རྒྱལ་བསྟན་འཛིན་

# Lo-chen Chos-rgyal bsTan-'dzin
## 1631–1708 C.E.

A disciple of Phrin-las lHun-grub and an important link in the transmission of the Anuyoga, Chos-rgyal bsTan-'dzin was born in E-'dam sNgon-po. He was recognized as the rebirth of the abbot of Dwags-stod-gling monastery in the land of Dwags-po. At dPal-ri in 'Phyongs-rgyas, where he was ordained as a novice by bSod-nams Rin-chen, he studied especially the works of Klong-chen-pa. There he met Phrin-las lHun-grub, who bestowed upon him the empowerments for the Anuyoga according to the Zur tradition and the Khams tradition. Later, Chos-rgyal bsTan-'dzin received the teachings of Zhig-po Gling-pa, the bKa'-brgyad practices, the Bi-ma-snying-thig, and other essential rNying-ma doctrines. He was blessed with teachings from lHa-btsun Nam-mkha' 'Jigs-med and gSung-sprul Tshul-khrims rDo-rje before returning to his monastery in Dwags-po. It was this master who transmitted the Anuyoga teachings to gTer-bdag Gling-pa, having been invited to sMin-grol-gling for this specific purpose. No works by this lineage holder have been located in recent times.

གྲུབ་ཆེན་ཉི་ཟླ་ཀློང་གསལ་

Grub-chen Nyi-zla Klong-gsal
mid-17th century C.E.
Rin-chen gTer-mdzod: 1 text

A disciple of the Sikkim master Bres-gshongs-pa Chos-rgyal rDo-rje (1602–1677), Nyi-zla Klong-gsal had been served and blessed by ḍākinīs since his youth. Chos-rgyal rDo-rje bestowed upon him the empowerments, teachings, and explanations of rDzogs-chen, followed by the complete Dza-bhīr instructions. For years he undertook austerities, renouncing ordinary food, practicing bCud-len to extract essential nourishment from the environment, and eventually learning to live off the wind itself. The ḍākinīs faithfully cared for him, clearing away inner obstacles and bringing forth the benefits of his practice. At last he had many days of visions in which the master Dza-bhīr bestowed teachings on him in a Close Lineage. Thus he achieved a stage of profound accomplishment.

Nyi-zla Klong-gsal established twenty sections of Dza-bhīr precepts and numerous other teachings that he received in Pure Visions. These teachings descended to 'Jam-dbyangs mKhyen-brtse, who bestowed them on Kong-sprul. His main seat was at gYang-chos Padma lHun-sdings on the north branch of the gTsang-po river. His main lineage holder was the incarnation of Gar-dbang rDo-rje, the Vajradhara Kun-bzang Chos-dbang. Both a Son Lineage and a Disciple Lineage continued through the time of Kong-sprul. The monastery, which in times of war was hidden from sight by the Dharma protectors and never allowed to come to harm, preserved the majority of Gar-dbang rDo-rje's gTer-ma teachings. Other than the Dza-bhīr precepts preserved in the Rin-chen gTer-mdzod, no other works by Nyi-zla Klong-gsal have been located.

# Part Seven

# Era of gTer-bdag Gling-pa and Lo-chen Dharmaśrī

གཏེར་ཆེན་ཨོ་རྒྱན་གཏེར་བདག་གླིང་པ

gTer-chen O-rgyan gTer-bdag Gling-pa

# Seventeenth Century

The era of the sMin-gling brothers gTer-bdag Gling-pa and Lo-chen Dharmaśrī marked a period of intense creativity and expansion of the Ancient School. rDo-rje-brag, sMin-grol-gling, dPal-yul, and rDzogs-chen monasteries were founded, and the texts of the bKa'-ma were preserved. The older streams of the sNying-thig, Upper and Lower Treasures, Northern Treasures, and the discoveries of the great Gling-pas continued to flow as gTer-stons brought forth still new treasures.

This period marks the beginning of the regime of the Dalai Lamas in central Tibet. With the support of the Mongols, the influence of the Fifth Dalai Lama, who was both master and disciple of rNying-ma lamas, encompassed not only the spiritual but also the temporal realms. A cultural renaissance blossomed, with the founding of the Potala, the building roads and bridges, and the promotion of the arts and sciences and Sanskrit studies. Widely respected throughout Asia, the Great Fifth supported trade and international relations with India, Kashmir, China, and Mongolia.

# དཔལ་ཡུལ་རིག་འཛིན་ཆེན་པོ་ཀུན་བཟང་ཤེས་རབ

## dPal-yul Rig-'dzin-chen-po Kun-bzang Shes-rab
### 1636–1698 C.E.
### 1 text, 60 pages

Kun-bzang Shes-rab belonged to the stream of incarnations
that included sPrul-sku dGa'-rab rDo-rje, Śrī Siṁha,
Guru Padmasambhava's disciple La-gsum rGyal-ba Byang-
chub, Zur-chen, sTag-lung Thang-pa, and Me-long rDo-rje. He
was born at A-'khyog in Bu-'bor not far from Kaḥ-thog and
dPal-yul monasteries. His father was descended from a long
line of lamas associated with Kaḥ-thog. The child received lay
vows from sGar-rje Chos-skyong rGya-mtsho and was given the
name Tshul-khrims rGya-mtsho. His early teachers included
Chos-nyid rGya-mtsho, Kaḥ-thog-pa sTag-bla Padma Mati,
Padma Mati's disciple dKon-mchog bKra-shis, Kaḥ-thog-pa
Rin-chen rDo-rje, 'Khrul-zhig sTon-pa rGyal-mtshan, and
Shes-rab rGya-mtsho. From these masters and others, he
received the bKa'-'gyur, rNying-ma bKa'-ma and gTer-ma, the
Lam-'bras teachings, and other gSar-ma teachings.

In lHa-sa, he met gTer-ston gNam-chos Mi-'gyur rDo-rje, in
whom he had immediate and complete faith. The gTer-ston
bestowed teachings upon him that perfected his realization of
rDzogs-chen. Later in life, this great gTer-ston made Kun-
bzang Shes-rab his principal Dharma holder. Kun-bzang Shes-
rab was ordained by Karma Chags-med, who transmitted to
him the teachings of Ratna Gling-pa and other great gTer-ma
masters, granted him further rDzogs-chen teachings, and made
him the principal recipient and regent of his own teachings.

When lHa-chen 'Byams-pa Phun-tshogs, the ruler of sDe-
dge, sponsored the building of dPal-yul monastery in 1665, he
asked Kun-bzang Shes-rab to be the first abbot. He greatly
admired the gTer-ma of Klong-gsal sNying-po and bDud-'dul
rDo-rje, and made them essential parts of the dPal-yul tradi-

tion. His disciples came from near and far to study at dPal-yul, which developed a reputation for great purity and intensive retreat practice. Kun-bzang Shes-rab established annual sGrub-chen ceremonies and created a graduated series of practices from the first vows of refuge to the level of Vajrayāna Master, a system that has continued to the present time. He composed a commentary on the three vows (sdom-gsum), which is preserved in Great Treasure of Ancient Teachings.

His disciples erected over a hundred monasteries and retreat centers. His principal disciple was Padma lHun-grub rGya-mtsho (1660–1727), who became the second throne holder at dPal-yul. The dBon-brgyud Nephew Lineage that began with Karma bKra-shis (1728–1791) and Karma 'Gyur-med Nges-don (1794–1851) made dPal-yul their seat. The incarnations of Padma Nor-bu, who was the Heart Son of Padma lHun-grub rGya-mtsho, also resided at dPal-yul.

མངའ་རིས་གཏེར་སྟོན་པདྨ་གར་དབང་རྩལ

### mNga'-ris gTer-ston Padma Gar-dbang-rtsal
### 1640–1685 C.E.
233 texts, 889 pages, Rin-chen gTer-mdzod: 1 text

An incarnation of gNyags Jñānakumāra and Nam-mkha'i sNying-po, Gar-dbang Zla-ba rGyal-mtshan, also known as Padma Gar-dbang-rtsal, was a master of the Byang-gter or Northern Treasures. Born in mNga'-ris at Nub-ri-yam in Gung-thang, he displayed remarkable qualities and propensities even as a child, practicing Avalokiteśvara sādhanas and receiving encouragement from ḍākinīs. At the secret valley of sKyid-mo-lung, he discovered a Vajrasattva treasure text that had been reconcealed by the great gTer-ston Rig-'dzin rGod-ldem. He promulgated these teachings, which have remained strong

265

until the present time, bringing benefits to many beings. He then discovered Avalokiteśvara three roots practices, Vajrakīla rites, rDzogs-chen teachings, and other wonderful treasures in 'Phags-pa Wa-ti in Nepal. Putting these teachings into practice, this gTer-ma master developed magical abilities and vast psychic powers. He met with O-rgyan gTer-bdag Gling-pa, who had complete confidence in his Dharma work, for it benefited all living beings.

Padma Gar-dbang-rtsal's activity for beings came to an end when he was in his forties. His next incarnation was Kun-mkhyen Chos-dbang rDo-rje 'Dzin-pa, the son of the yogin Nyi-zla Klong-gsal. Chos-dbang rDo-rje 'Dzin-pa became the disciple of gTer-bdag Gling-pa and Lo-chen Dharmaśrī and resided a long time at sMin-grol-gling monastery. After devoted study of the worldly arts and sciences, Sūtra, and Mantra, his knowledge grew vast, and he composed extensive practice explanations for the works of Padma Gar-dbang-rtsal.

This lineage continued at gSang-chos Padma-lhun-sdings north of the gTsang-po river. Kong-sprul Blo-gros mTha'-yas received some of Padma Gar-dbang-rtsal's teachings from 'Jam-dbyangs mKhyen-brtse and preserved one text in the Rin-chen gTer-mdzod. In addition two hundred and thirty-three works are preserved in Great Treasures of Ancient Teachings.

རྡོ་བྲག་རིག་འཛིན་ཆེན་པོ་པདྨ་ཕྲིན་ལས།

rDo-brag Rig-'dzin Chen-po Padma Phrin-las
1641–1717 C.E.
84 texts, 1,055 pages, Rin-chen gTer-mdzod: 24 texts

Padma Phrin-las was a major Byang-gter lineage holder belonging to the reincarnation stream of Rig-'dzin rGod-ldem, Legs-ldan-rje, and Rig-'dzin Chen-po Ngag-gi dBang-po.

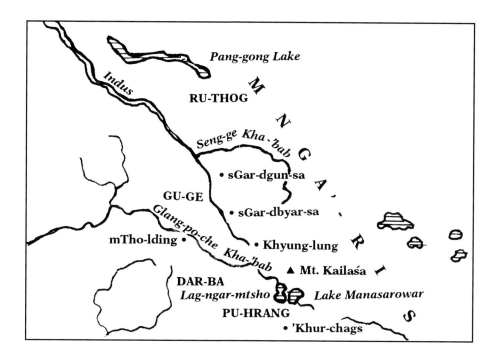

He was born in Mon-mkhar rNam-sras-gling as the son of
Karma Phun-tshogs dBang-po of the Bya-nag clan. At the age
of six, Padma Phrin-las was enthroned at rDo-rje-brag by Zur
Chos-dbyings Rang-grol, who transmitted to him the entire
body of bKa'-ma and gTer-ma. He was ordained by the Great
Fifth Dalai Lama and received from him many teachings.
Other teachers included gSar-ma master gNas-gsar mGon-po
bSod-nams mChog-ldan (1603–1659), from whom he received
innumerable instructions.

Padma Phrin-las practiced extensively at rDo-rje-brag, at
sGrags Yang-rdzong, the sacred power place associated with
the Guru's Enlightened Body, and at Chu-bo-ri, the mountain
on the south bank of the gTsang-po where one hundred and
eight springs rose up after Padmasambhava blessed the land.
While he discovered some gTer-ma that appear not to have
continued, his major contribution to the gTer-ma lineage was
to protect and expand the existing lineages.

Inspired by the Fifth Dalai Lama, Padma Phrin-las composed an important work on the main text of the Anuyoga and bestowed the empowerments for this Tantra on many fortunate individuals. He created distinctive arrangements and explanations of the practices related to the Northern Treasures. He transmitted the complete teachings and empowerments of the Kālacakra and empowerments of the Mahāyoga to Lo-chen Dharmaśrī. To the great lama O-rgyan gTer-bdag Gling-pa, he offered Anuyoga empowerments and instructions and greatly advanced these teachings.

It was a tremendous misfortune for Tibet that this master was killed by the Dzungar Mongols when they destroyed rDo-rje-brag in 1717. Renowned as the Sun of the Ancient School and the Axis of the Mantrayāna teachings, Padma Phrin-las' work had restored the vitality of both the bKa'-ma and gTer-ma transmissions. Eighty-four of his texts are preserved in Great Treasures of Ancient Teachings, together with more than twenty texts in the Rin-chen gTer-mdzod section.

gTer-chen gNam-chos Mi-'gyur rDo-rje
1645–1667 C.E.
159 texts, 2,287 pages, Rin-chen gTer-mdzod: 48 texts

A reincarnation of Vairotsana's and Padmasambhava's direct disciple Shud-bu dPal-gyi Seng-ge, and the next incarnation of 'Khrul-zhig dBang-drag rGya-mtsho, Mi-'gyur rDo-rje was born in Ngom. His father was mGon-po Tshe-brtan, who belonged to the ancient lineage of the Dharma kings. As a small child he described his past lives, performed yogic exercises, and had visions. When he met the great gTer-ston Karma Chags-med, who blessed him and gave him teachings, his psychic abilities blazed forth.

Karma Chags-med bestowed upon him the teachings of Ratna Gling-pa, Karma Gling-pa, the mKha'-'gro-snying-thig, the eight heruka teachings, and many others. When Mi-'gyur rDo-rje entered retreat with Karma Chags-med, he was blessed with visions of Buddha Amitābha, Guru Padmasambhava, and Samantabhadra. Over the next ten years, the teachings he received in continuing visions were written down in thirteen volumes that became known as gNam-chos, Treasures of Space. Karma Chags-med composed numerous explanations of these precious teachings.

Mi-'gyur rDo-rje met with the great gTer-ston bDud-'dul rDo-rje and the two exchanged teachings. He visited Kaḥ-thog, Nang-chen, sDe-dge, sMar-khams, Nang-chen, Sa-ngan, and many places in Khams, turning the wheel of the teachings. While residing at rMugs-sangs, he bestowed his treasures on Kun-bzang Shes-rab, who founded dPal-yul monastery.

Mi-'gyur rDo-rje practiced each of the treasures he had received and granted teachings and empowerments to chief disciples including Kun-bzang Shes-rab, Karma Chags-med, Padma Rig-'dzin, and Phrin-las Don-grub. While his innumerable disciples came from all over Tibet, his teachings were practiced especially at Kaḥ-thog, dPal-yul, gNas-mdo, and the Karmapa's monasteries. Though it was predicted that he would also discover many earth gTer-ma, the conditions were not suitable, and Mi-'gyur rDo-rje passed away in his early twenties amidst many miraculous events. Stupas containing his relics became precious objects of refuge at dPal-yul and other monasteries. His continuing incarnations, including rMog-grub Nam-mkha' Chos-dbang and 'Jigs-'bral Chos-dbyings rDo-rje, extended the teachings of the Ancient School.

Kong-sprul Blo-gros mTha'-yas preserved forty-eight treasures associated with gNam-chos Mi-'gyur rDo-rje in the Rinchen gTer-mdzod, while other sections of Great Treasures of Ancient Teachings contain one hundred and fifty-nine works.

# གཏེར་ཆེན་ཨོ་རྒྱན་གཏེར་བདག་གླིང་པ

gTer-chen O-rgyan gTer-bdag Gling-pa

1646–1714 C.E.

522 texts, 4,027 pages, Rin-chen gTer-mdzod: 143 texts

The incarnation of Vairotsana, O-rgyan gTer-bdag Gling-pa was born at Dar-rgyas Chos-sding as the son of Rig-'dzin Phrin-las lHun-grub, a member of the gNyos clan who was an incarnation of gNubs Sangs-rgyas Ye-shes. His mother was lHa-'dzin dBangs-can sGrol-ma, an incarnation of Shel-dkar rDo-rje-'tsho, one of the disciples of Guru Padmasambhava and Lady Ye-shes mTsho-rgyal who had assisted in completing mTsho-rgyal's biography.

gTer-bdag Gling-pa studied rNying-ma teachings extensively, learning the sādhanas, ceremonies, and rituals as a very young man. His father granted him all of his teachings, and he took refuge with the Fifth Dalai Lama, these two being his principal teachers. He then studied with sixteen other masters, receiving rNying-ma and gSar-ma Tantras, the Tripiṭaka, the works of Klong-chen-pa, and the bKa'-ma lineages, and all the empowerments and oral instructions.

O-rgyan gTer-bdag Gling-pa and his brother sMin-gling Lo-chen Dharmaśrī both held the Vinaya lineage transmitted through Śāriputra, Rāhula, Rāhulabhadra, Nāgārjuna, Bhāvaviveka, and Śāntarakṣita. gTer-bdag Gling-pa also held the Bodhisattva lineage that descended through Mañjuśrī, Nāgārjuna, Candrakīrti, and Jo-bo-rje Atīśa.

gTer-bdag Gling-pa mastered the developing and completion stages of meditation, thoroughly embodying the Three Kāyas of the Buddha and never straying from continuous contemplation. In visions he received teachings and blessings from the greatest masters of India and Tibet, including Guru Padmasambhava, Vimalamitra, Hūṁkāra, Buddhaguhya,

270

Vairotsana, Ye-shes mTsho-rgyal, Nyang-ral Nyi-ma 'Od-zer, and Klong-chen-pa. He practiced at gYa'-ma-lung, one of the eight most powerful retreat places blessed by Guru Padma-sambhava, and at mChims-phu, the sacred power place associated with the Enlightened Speech of the Guru. A great gTer-ston, he discovered Yamāntaka practices, wrathful guru sādhanas, Vajrasattva and Avalokiteśvara practices, and Atiyoga teachings at gYa'-ma-lung, Yar-lung Shel-brag, Bying-mda' O-dkar-brag, and Sha-'ug lTag-sgo in the Mon region in the south.

gTer-bdag Gling-pa taught disciples from all over Tibet, in particular the Great Fifth Dalai Lama, Regent Sangs-rgyas rGya-mtsho, Sa-skya and bKa'-brgyud masters, rNying-ma-pa masters of Kaḥ-thog and rDzogs-chen monasteries, Rig-'dzin Padma Phrin-las, and many others. His true spiritual disciple was his brother Lo-chen Dharmaśrī. His leading disciples included his three sons, Padma 'Gyur-med rGya-mtsho, Yid-bzhin Legs-grub, Rin-chen rNam-rgyal, and his daughter Mi-'gyur dPal-sgron.

Together with Lo-chen Dharmaśrī, gTer-bdag Gling-pa collected the texts of the bKa'-ma and compiled the rNying-ma sādhanas, adding a written guide for each one to clarify the details of practice. On root texts of the Mahā, Anu, and Atiyoga Tantras, he wrote extensive commentaries. To ensure the preservation of important texts, this master directed the carving and printing of the bKa'-'gyur, as well as many rNying-ma commentaries and other texts. gTer-bdag Gling-pa's efforts restored the rNying-ma teachings to their original prominence and united the bKa'-ma and gTer-ma traditions. In 1676 in Grwa-phyi valley south of the gTsang-po river, he founded and then supported the monastery of O-rgyan sMin-grol-gling, which has remained one of the six major rNying-ma centers down to the present time.

Over five hundred texts by this master are preserved in the Great Treasures of Ancient Teachings, as well as another one hundred and forty-three in the Rin-chen gTer-mdzod section.

 རིག་འཛིན་ཆེན་པོ་ཉི་མ་གྲགས་པ

Rig-'dzin Chen-po Nyi-ma Grags-pa
1647–1710 C.E.
50 texts, 290 pages

Born in Nang-chen at sGom-sde, Rig-'dzin Chen-po Nyi-ma-grags was the disciple of Grub-dbang Rinpoche, gTer-chen bDud-'dul rDo-rje, and Padma Rig-'dzin. Under their guidance, he became an accomplished scholar. At twenty-three years of age, he found gTer-ma lists at the hidden valley of Tsā-ri, which led him to Srin-rdzong. There, when he was twenty-six years old, he discovered oceans of treasure texts. In 1693 he established the monastery of Stag-mo-sgang in the 'Dzin-pa area of sDe-dge. Later he founded the monastery of Char Nyi-grags, which was known as 'Od-gsal sGrub-sde. His disciples included bsKal-bzang dBang-ldan and Bla-ma Blo-gros rGya-mtsho. His incarnations continued to transmit his teachings. Great Treasures of Ancient Teachings includes fifty texts by this master.

རིག་འཛིན་ཟིལ་གནོན་དབང་རྒྱལ་རྡོ་རྗེ

Rig-'dzin Zil-gnon dBang-rgyal rDo-rje
1647 C.E.
7 texts, 135 pages

This seventeenth-century master composed five large bio-graphical works recording his various visionary experiences and work for the Dharma. These texts, together with two others written by Rig-'dzin Zil-gnon, are preserved in Great Treasures of Ancient Teachings. Further research into these texts will make the details of his life story available.

སྨིན་གླིང་ལོ་ཆེན་དྷརྨ་ཤྲཱི

sMin-gling Lo-chen Dharmaśrī
1654–1717 C.E.
180 texts, 2,986 pages, Rin-chen gTer-mdzod: 41 texts

An emanation of Vairotsana's disciple gYu-sgra sNying-po, Lo-chen Dharmaśrī was the major disciple of his brother, O-rgyan gTer-bdag Gling-pa, and a revitalizer of the rNying-ma traditions in the seventeenth century. Ordained by the Fifth Dalai Lama, he also carried the Lower Vinaya lineage of the rNying-ma school from Kha-rab Zhal-snga-nas dKon-mchog bsTan-'dzin. He studied Vinaya, Abhidharma, Prajñāpāramitā, Madhyamaka, as well as grammar, linguistics, writing, translation, astrology, divination, sacred dance, and iconography. From his brother, who was his root teacher, he received the teachings of Klong-chen-pa, the lineages of Zur and Rong-zom, and the entire transmission of the rNying-ma Inner Yogas, both the bKa'-ma and gTer-ma. In all, Lo-chen studied with twenty-two masters, including Sangs-rgyas Chos-dar, Gung-

273

thang Paṇ-chen, mKhas-grub Chos-skyong rGyal-mtshan, and Rig-'dzin Padma Phrin-las.

Lo-chen Dharmaśrī ordained hundreds of monks and taught continuously, especially Vinaya, Abhidharma, Prajñā-pāramitā, and sDom-gsum, as well as gTer-ma teachings. To some disciples, he even taught ordinary arts and sciences. Using the three means of teaching, debate, and composition, he revealed the depths of rNying-ma teachings to many. The great Sa-skya lord Ngag-dbang Kun-dga' bKra-shis was his disciple, as were 'Phags-pa-lha rGyal-ba rGya-mtsho, Zhi-ba bZang-po, and Ngag-dbang sPrul-sku in Cham-do.

Lo-chen Dharmaśrī transmitted the precious rNying-ma bKa'-ma lineage to rGyal-sras Rin-chen rNam-rgyal, the son of gTer-bdag Gling-pa; he in turn bestowed the lineage on mKhan-chen Oḍḍiyāna, O-rgyan bsTan-'dzin rDo-rje. From these two the sMin-grol-gling lineage of the bKa'-ma spread to Kaḥ-thog, Zhe-chen, dPal-yul, and rDzogs-chen in Khams, to 'Gu-log, and to rGyal-mo-rong. It was a tragedy for Tibet when this outstanding master died in 1717 at the hands of the Dzungar Mongols in the midst of their campaign of deliberate destruction of rNying-ma monasteries and lineage holders.

Lo-chen Dharmaśrī's collected works include important commentaries on the Mahāyoga and Anuyoga, a commentary on mNga'-ris Paṇ-chen's sDom-gsum-rnam-par-nges-pa, works on astrology, poetry, iconography, divination, sādhana instructions, and ritual texts. Great Treasures of Ancient Teachings preserves one hundred and eighty works by this master, in addition to more than forty texts preserved in the Rin-chen gTer-mdzod section.

གཏེར་ཆེན་སྟག་ཤམ་ནུས་ལྡན་རྡོ་རྗེ

gTer-chen sTag-sham Nus-ldan rDo-rje

1655 C.E.

680 texts, 4,458 pages, Rin-chen gTer-mdzod: 35 texts

Born in the nomadic pasture lands of southern sPar-shod, Nus-ldan rDo-rje was the son of gCod-pa bKra-shis, who descended from the Zur clan, and his wife Lod-skyid. During childhood, self-arisen awareness emerged in Nus-ldan rDo-rje's heart, and he felt an intense renunciation of samsaric activities and a deep compassion for others. At the age of eleven he began to have visions and received predictions from the ḍākinīs. At seventeen years of age, after studying with many learned and holy masters, Nus-ldan rDo-rje set out to begin a retreat, but he encountered a yogin (actually Guru Padmasambhava), who bestowed upon him teachings and precious advice. Thereafter he recalled his past lives and soon began to discover treasures. His first discovery was made in Vairotsana's practice cave at Glang-lung sKu-gsum-brag, where he found Vajrasattva and Vajrakīlaya treasures.

At twenty he was ordained as a monk and received the name bSam-gtan rDo-rje. Altogether he made seventeen great discoveries, including Ye-shes mTsho-rgyal's biography and a Padmasambhava biography that he found at Yang-le-shod at Phar-ping in Nepal. His discoveries included Yi-dam-dgongs-'dus sādhanas, peaceful and wrathful deity practices, Dharma protector rites, Hayagrīva treasures, Avalokiteśvara practices, and oral teachings of Ye-shes mTsho-rgyal. In visions, Nus-ldan rDo-rje met the master of earlier times, mChog-ldan rDo-rje, and received teachings that reestablished that lineage.

He gave these precious teachings to his chief lineage holder, Chos-rje Gling-pa, his nephew Nam-mkha' rDo-rje, and bSam-gtan bsTan-'dzin. From Chos-rje Gling-pa, these teachings descended to the Karmapas and many other disciples.

Nus-ldan rDo-rje was also known as bSam-gtan Gling-pa, and his major seats were at sPar-stod bSam-gtan-gling and dGa'-ba-lung in sPu-bo. His teachings spread all over Khams and were transmitted especially at sPu-bo through an incarnation lineage and a disciple lineage. Six hundred eighty texts are preserved in Great Treasures of Ancient Teachings, as well as thirty-five texts in the Rin-chen gTer-mdzod section.

 རོང་སྟོན་པདྨ་བདེ་ཆེན་གླིང་པ

Rong-ston Padma bDe-chen Gling-pa

1663 C.E.

Rin-chen gTer-mdzod: 10 texts

The heart incarnation of Lo-chen Vairotsana, Padma bDe-chen Gling-pa was born on the border of mDo-smad and gSer-rdo. His father was dKon-mchog and his mother was gZungs Thar-ma, who gave him the name Śākya Thar. From the age of three, he was clearly inclined toward the Dharma, always wishing that others be happy and spontaneously singing prayers to the gurus. As he matured, his compassion grew so intense that he could not bear the suffering of others. At this time, he received teachings from Bla-ma Ye-shes rGyal-mtshan.

As a young man he made a pilgrimage to holy places in central Tibet. From gSer-pa Bla-ma Ye-shes rGyal-mtshan, he received teachings and spent seven years practicing intensively, until understanding dawned. When he was twenty-five years old, he proceeded to rGyal-mo-rong, where he discovered mKha'-'gro-snying-thig cycles at the holy and powerful mountain of dMu-rdo.

From many masters he received gSar-ma and rNying-ma teachings, both bKa'-ma and gTer-ma. At Kaḥ-thog he met the great Klong-gsal sNying-po, to whom he had been deeply connected in the past, and became his chief regent. Soon he also met sTag-sham rDo-rje at bTsan-ri and received his entire teachings, his understanding mingling completely with the great master's. From Ta Bla-ma Padma Nor-bu and Brag-dmar Kun-bzang Khyab-brdal lHun-grub, he received many oral lineages. In return he offered these two masters the teachings he had discovered.

At Tre-phu-brag and bTsan-ri he found more precious ḍākinī cycles, but was unable to obtain all the treasures predicted to be his. In the later part of his life, he made his residence at bTsan-ri, teaching the common people and bringing inconceivable benefits to beings until the end of his life.

His son Padma dBang-rgyal was his disciple and also the disciple of sMin-gling Lo-chen Dharmaśrī and gTer-bdag Gling-pa. An accomplished yogin and a learned scholar, Padma dBang-rgyal transmitted the gTer-ma treasure teachings to the tenth Zhwa-dmar Karmapa and Kun-mkhyen bsTan-pa'i Nyin-byed. Padma dBang-rgyal's chief regent was the renowned Kaḥ-thog Rig-'dzin Tshe-dbang Nor-bu. Ten of Padma bDe-chen Gling-pa's treasures are preserved in the Rin-chen gTer-mdzod, but as yet no other works by this master have been located in recent times.

lHo-brag Gro-bo-lung Blo-bzang lHa-mchog
1672–1747 C.E.
1 text, 50 pages

Belonging to the lineage of Nam-mkha'i sNying-po, dGe-slong lHa-mchog composed his own biography, which is preserved in Great Treasures of Ancient Teachings. Research into this text will provide details of his life story.

277

རྡོ་དམར་ཞབས་དྲུང་མི་འགྱུར་རྡོ་རྗེ

rDo-dmar Zhabs-drung Mi-'gyur rDo-rje

1675 C.E.

63 texts, 390 pages

Belonging to the lineage that flowed through Yol-mo-ba Śākya bZang-po and Zil-gnon dBang-rgyal rDo-rje, rDo-dmar Zhabs-drung was a master of the Northern Treasures. This lineage was strong in mNga'-ris sKor-gsum in western Tibet and in the borderlands of Nepal, but was not well known in central Tibet or in Khams in the east. Great Treasures preserves sixty-three texts by this master.

ལྷ་བཙུན་སྤྲུལ་སྐུ་སྐུ་འཇིགས་མེད་དཔའ་བོ

lHa-btsun sPrul-sku 'Jigs-med dPa'-bo

1682 C.E.

3 texts, 247 pages

A reincarnation of lHa-btsun Chen-po Rig-'dzin Nam-mkha'i 'Jigs-med, 'Jigs-med dPa'-bo transmitted the lineages that became known as the 'Bras-ljongs rDzogs-chen in Sikkim. This lineage has continued unbroken to the present time. The collected works section of Great Treasures of Ancient Teachings contains three texts by this master.

གུ་རུ་དཔོན་གསས་ཁྱུང་ཐོག

## Guru dPon-gsas Khyung-thog
### mid-17th–late 17th century C.E.
### Rin-chen gTer-mdzod: 2 texts

An incarnation of Lo-chen Vairotsana, Guru dPon-gsas Khyung-thog was born near lHa-rtse in gTsang. He lived as a Mantrayāna practitioner known as La-stod sTag-mo gTer-ston. He studied Sa-skya teachings and then recieved the Northern Treasures from rNying-ma lineage holders. Near his birthplace, at rGyang Yon-po-lung, he discovered gTer-ma including rDzogs-chen teachings, which were later preserved by Kong-sprul in the Rin-chen gTer-mdzod. At Ras-chung-phug in dBu, he met the great master Chos-rje Gling-pa and worked with him to discover treasure teachings concealed in the Yar-lung valley.

རིག་འཛིན་ཆེན་པོ་ཆོས་རྗེ་གླིང་པ

## Rig-'dzin Chen-po Chos-rje Gling-pa
### 1682–1726 C.E.
### 144 texts, 521 pages, Rin-chen gTer-mdzod: 42 texts

The twelfth incarnation of rGyal-sras lHa-rje, who was the immediate reincarnation of King Khri-srong lDe'u-btsan, Chos-rje Gling-pa was born at Klu-mkhar-gdong in Dwags-po into the family of rDo-rje Grags-pa. He was known as Chos-rje 'Dzam-gling rDo-rje, O-rgyan Rog-rje Gling-pa, bDe-ba'i rDo-rje, and dBon-rje Gling-pa. bZang-po rDo-rje proclaimed him the incarnation of Zhabs-drung Rin-chen rDo-rje, and the Zhwa-dmar Karmapa Ye-shes sNying-po recognized him as the incarnation of 'Chi-med dBang-po, Ras-chung-phug sPrul-sku. He took vows from gNas-brtan 'Jam-dbyangs Grags-pa, while dGa'-ldan Khri-chen Blo-bzang Dar-rgyas later ordained him and gave him the religious name Ngag-gi dBang-po Blo-bzang Chos-dbyings dPal-bzang-po.

Chos-rje Gling-pa gained comprehensive understanding of the Sūtras and Tantras and became a Kalyaṇamitra of great expertise. Later in life, after he began to discover gTer-ma, he took lady bDe-chen Phrin-las mTsho-mo as his sacred consort. Residing at Yar-lung Ras-chung-phug, the residence of the great siddha gTsang sMyong Chen-po, he received extensive teachings from Byang-chub Gling-pa Yon-tan rGya-mtsho and from dGe-bshes Don-ldan. Through the blessings of rGyal-dbang Ye-shes rDo-rje, he received the Mahāmudrā teachings. Rig-'dzin sTag-sham Nus-ldan rDo-rje bestowed his gTer-ma treasures upon Chos-rje Gling-pa, which gave rise to his complete comprehension of the rDzogs-chen teachings. These last two were his root gurus.

In association with sTag-mo gTer-ston dPon-gsas Khyung-thog, Chos-rje Gling-pa located treasure at Yum-bu Bla-sgang and Srong-bstan Bang-so, but these he mostly reconcealed. At the secret mountain in Tsā-ri, he found precious practices for the three roots. At sPu-bo Bya-rgod gShong, rMa-kung-lung lake, 'Dod-chu temple, and other places, he discovered guru sādhanas, Avalokiteśvara and Bla-ma Rig-'dzin teachings, and others. In Pure Visions, he made further discoveries of sādhanas that have been transmitted to the present time. This great master spent his final years traversing the secret valley of Padma-bkod, making it a safe haven during a period of intense unrest in central Tibet.

His major disciples were rGyal-dbang Byang-chub rDo-rje, Zhwa-dmar dPal-chen Chos-kyi-don-grub, Tre'o Chos-kyi-dbang-po, 'Bri-gung dKon-mchog Phrin-las bZang-po, Dwags-po Zhabs-drung sPrul-sku lHun-grub Nges-don dBang-po, 'Brug Thams-cad mKhyen-pa dPag-bsam dBang-po, rTsib-ri Grub-chen, and lHo-pa Grub-chen. His closest disciple was Rwa-ston sTobs-ldan rDo-rje, and he seems to have also been associated with Rig-'dzin Padma Phrin-las and sMin-gling rGyal-sras Padma 'Gyur-med rGya-mtsho. The next incarnation of Chos-rje Gling-pa was the incomparable 'Jigs-med Gling-pa. One hundred and forty-four texts composed or discovered by Chos-rje Gling-pa are preserved in Great Treasures of Ancient Teachings, as well as more than forty additional texts in the Rin-chen gTer-mdzod section.

སྨིན་གླིང་རབ་འབྱམས་པ་ཆོས་གྲགས་རྒྱ་མཚོ

sMin-gling Rab-'byams-pa Chos-grags rGya-mtsho
mid-17th–late 17th century C.E.
3 texts, 191 pages

Author of a commentary on the major Mahāyoga Tantra, the gSang-ba'i-snying-po, this master apparently lived in the seventeenth century and was closely associated with the monastery and lineages of sMin-grol-gling. More research will be necessary to confirm the details of his biography. Great Treasures of Ancient Teachings includes three works by Rab-'byams-pa Chos-grags.

ར་སྟོན་སྟོབས་ལྡན་རྡོ་རྗེ་པདྨ་ཚེ་དབང་རྩལ

Rwa-ston sTobs-ldan rDo-rje Padma Tshe-dbang-rtsal
mid-17th–late 17th century C.E.
2 texts, 25 pages, Rin-chen gTer-mdzod: 3 texts

An incarnation of Rlangs-chen dPal-gyi Seng-ge, Rwa-ston sTobs-ldan rDo-rje, also known as Padma Tshe-dbang-rtsal, was born at gTsang rGyang-rtse into a family that had descended from Rwa Lo-tsā-ba (eleventh century). Rwa-ston studied at Zur-sde Grwa-tshang in rGyang-rtse. Receiving all the teachings of the master Chos-rje Gling-pa, Rwa-ston became the chief lineage holder for his gTer-ma.

After the passing of Chos-rje Gling-pa, Rwa-ston departed for wild regions in the Indian borderlands and Sikkim where he practiced austerities. At 'On-phu sTag-tshang he discovered precious treasures including Vajrakīla and Che-mchog cycles, which have been preserved through the centuries in unbroken lineages to the present time.

While staying in sPu-bo, he met bsTan-pa'i Nyin-byed, who had also received the gTer-ma of Chos-rje Gling-pa, and the two masters shared their teachings. Both the Zhwa-dmar and the Zhwa-nag Karmapas, gNas-gsar-pa Ngag-dbang Kun-dga' Legs-pa'i 'Byung-gnas, and eminent Sa-skya masters were among his disciples. In the later part of his life, Rwa-ston was venerated by the political leader Pho-lha-gnas bSod-nams sTobs-rgyas (1689–1747), who controlled central Tibet after a period of civil war in 1728.

In the time of Kong-sprul Blo-gros mTha'-yas, Rwa-ston sTobs-ldan rDo-rje's descendents still resided in rGyang-rtse Brag-dmar Bla-brang. Kong-sprul preserved several of his texts in the Rin-chen gTer-mdzod, while an additional two works have been located and placed in another section of Great Treasures of Ancient Teachings.

# ཉ་པ་གཏེར་སྟོན་ངག་གི་རྡོ་རྗེ

Ja-pa gTer-ston Ngag-gi rDo-rje
mid-17th–late 17th century C.E.
Rin-chen gTer-mdzod: 2 texts

An incarnation of the Dharma King Khri-srong lDe'u-btsan, Ngag-gi rDo-rje was born in sGom-sde in Nang-chen. He was also known as Ja-pa gTer-ston and Bya-btang sKu-mchog. He lived as a holder of Mantrayāna vows. From lHo Rinpoche and other holy masters, he received Dharma teachings. At an early age he was deeply interested in meditation and sādhana practice. Ngag-gi rDo-rje had visions of Padmasambhava and repeatedly received predictions from ḍākinīs and Dharma protectors that he would become a gTer-ston.

At last Rig-'dzin Mi-'gyur rDo-rje and lHo Rinpoche urged him to bring forth gTer-ma. At Ja-pa Brag-dkar, where one hundred Buddha images had spontaneously arisen, he discovered precious teachings, which he practiced himself. As a result of his devoted efforts, Vajrapāṇi, the Lord of Secrets, bestowed blessings upon him, after which he developed magical abilities. Biographies do not note his various enlightened activities.

His Dharma heir was Bla-ma Blo-gros rGya-mtsho, who increased the spread of his gTer-ma teachings. Two hundred years later, Kong-sprul Blo-gros mtha'-yas received them and was able to preserve several texts in the Rin-chen gTer-mdzod. An incarnation lineage remained intact until recent times at Ja-pa monastery in Nang-chen.

# རོང་པ་གཏེར་སྟོན་བདུད་འདུལ་གླིང་པ

## Rong-pa gTer-ston bDud-'dul Gling-pa
## d. 1705 C.E.
### Rin-chen gTer-mdzod: 3 texts

An incarnation of Guru Padmasambhava's disciple Lo-tsā-ba rGyal-ba mChog-dbyangs, bDud-'dul Gling-pa was born in gTsang-rong at lDum-ra. He was also known as Rong-pa gTer-ston. He first resided at sKyed-tshal-'od monastery where he studied the Tripiṭaka.

After he received and practiced rNying-ma teachings, marvelous signs of accomplishment arose. One treasure of the Protectress Tārā that had been discovered three hundred years earlier by gYag-phyar sNgon-mo Rin-chen rGyal-po and been reconcealed by him was now unearthed by Rong-pa bDud-'dul Gling-pa. But once again the gTer-ston hid the treasure.

This young master discovered numerous other gTer-ma teachings, and the benefits had just began to spread when his life was cut short by the invasion of lHa-bzang Khan in 1705. Thus most of this stream of teachings did not survive. The next incarnation of bDud-'dul Gling-pa was Zung-mkhar Theg-chen Gling-pa.

The Tārā teachings were rediscovered by 'Jam-dbyangs mKhyen-brtse and bestowed upon Kong-sprul Blo-gros mTha'-yas, who preserved them in the Rin-chen gTer-mdzod. A few texts on Vajrakīla practices were also preserved.

པད་གླིང་བརྒྱད་པ་བསྟན་པའི་ཉི་མ།

Pad-gling brGyad-pa bsTan-pa'i Nyi-ma
mid-17th–late 17th century C.E.?
Rin-chen gTer-mdzod: 2 texts

The eighth incarnation of gTer-chen Padma Gling-pa was born in the seventeenth century. bsTan-pa'i Nyi-ma played a crucial role in the continuous transmission of the rNying-ma-rgyud-'bum. He received this transmission from rBa-kha Kun-bzang Rig-'dzin rDo-rje, the disciple of the sixth incarnation of Padma Gling-pa. bsTan-pa'i Nyi-ma in turn instructed rBa-kha Rig-'dzin Khams-gsum Yongs-grol. This lineage eventually flowed to bDud-'joms Rin-poche. bsTan-pa'i Nyi-ma composed several important explanations of phur-pa and Vajrapāṇi practices that are preserved in the Rin-chen gTer-mdzod.

ཨོ་རྒྱན་རྣམ་གྲོལ།

O-rgyan rNam-grol
mid-17th–late 17th century C.E.
4 texts, 50 pages, Rin-chen gTer-mdzod: 1 text

A lineage-holder of sMin-grol-gling who appears to have lived in the time of gTer-bdag Gling-pa, O-rgyan rNam-grol composed preliminary practices for the Atiyoga, detailed description of Vajrakīla practices, and several other texts on practice and ceremonies used at sMin-grol-gling. These works are preserved in Great Treasures of Ancient Teachings. Further research is necessary to discover the details of the life and work of O-rgyan rNam-grol.

གཏེར་སྟོན་ཏའུ་རོག་རྗེ་གླིང་པ་འགྲོ་འདུལ་རྩལ

gTer-ston Ta'u Rog-rje Gling-pa 'Gro-'dul-rtsal
mid-17th–late 17th century C.E.
Rin-chen gTer-mdzod: 1 text

Said to be another incarnation of Vairotsana and perhaps the next rebirth of Rong-ston Padma bDe-chen Gling-pa, Rog-rje Gling-pa was born at Ta'u-rong. In three different locations, he discovered three gTer-ma treasures connected to Hayagrīva and Vajravārāhī sādhanas. Because this master lived as a hidden yogi and the teachings were transmitted secretly, they spread very little. 'Jam-dbyangs mKhyen-brtse was able, however, to receive his Hayagrīva gTer-ma and transmit it to Kong-sprul Blo-gros mTha'-yas. Thus one text has been preserved in the Rin-chen gTer-mdzod.

ཁམས་པ་ཀུན་དགའ་བསྟན་འཛིན

Khams-pa Kun-dga' bsTan-'dzin
1680 C.E.
Rin-chen gTer-mdzod: 1 text

A manifestation of the blessings of Padmasambhava, the Great Guru of Oḍḍiyāna, Khams-pa Rinpoche Ngag-dbang Kun-dga' bsTan-'dzin took birth in dBus at bDe-skyid-gling in Gongs-dkar rDzong. Mi-pham Chos-kyi dBang-phyug gave him refuge vows. Relying on the 'Brug-pa Father and Son, sGam-po bZang-po rDo-rje, gTer-bdag Gling-pa, and Lo-chen Dharmaśrī, he studied gSar-ma teachings and the bKa'-ma and gTer-ma of the rNying-ma tradition. He became so expert that it seemed there were no doctrines that Khams-pa

Rinpoche had not received. He also became knowledgeable in the worldly sciences and completely mastered the medical arts.

In Khams he practiced at many different retreat places. At gZe-rgyal-mgo he actually met Vimalamitra in visions and received rDzogs-chen teachings from him. With the blessings of Padmasambhava, he began to discover gTer-ma, including practices related to the mountain god rMa-chen sPom-ra and Realization Treasures associated with the Bla-ma-gsang-'dus and the dKon-mchog-spyi-'dus teachings. Based on Pure Vision treasures that he received, he created arrangements of ceremonial chants and dances that became known as the Khams-pa sādhanas.

Turning the wheel of the bKa'-ma and gTer-ma teachings, Kun-dga' bsTan-'dzin reached the stage of a great Vidyādhara of the Ancient School, while also having a deep influence on the 'Brug-pa bKa'-'brgyud tradition. His disciples included Kun-mkhyen Chos-kyi 'Byung-gnas and Rig-'dzin Rol-pa'i rDo-rje. His next incarnation was bsTan-'dzin Chos-kyi Nyi-ma, the brother of the Heart Son of Chos-kyi 'Byung-gnas. This line of bKa'-rnying teachings has remained strong down to recent times. One text is preserved in the Rin-chen gTer-mdzod.

Rig-'dzin Chen-po Rol-pa'i rDo-rje
mid-17th–late 17th century C.E.
Rin-chen gTer-mdzod: 44 texts

An incarnation of Slob-dpon Hūṁkāra and mKhon Klu'i dBang-po, Rol-pa'i rDo-rje was born in the southern districts of mDo-khams at Ke-rong. His father was Tshe-ring rDo-rje and his mother was called lHa-mo. dKon-mchog lHun-grub, as he was known, possessed a deeply compassion-

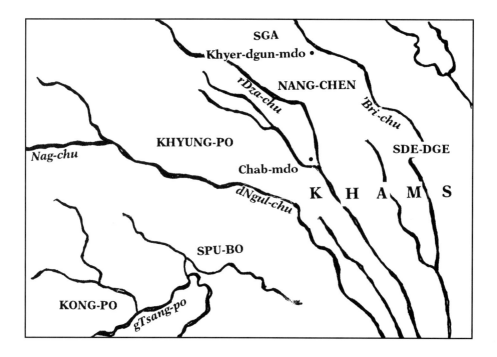

ate heart that could not bear the suffering of others. With the
blessings of the fearless Vidyādharas, he could bring illness to
an end and make rain fall during droughts by simply speaking
words of truth. His holy deeds inspired faith in many people.
Having attained certain understanding of śūnyatā, he naturally
manifested the heart of Enlightenment.

Rol-pa'i rDo-rje received the gSar-ma and rNying-ma teachings from bsTan-pa rNam-rgyal, Che-tshang Rig-'dzin gSung-
rab rGya-mtsho, and Khams-pa Ngag-dbang Kun-dga' bsTan-
'dzin, and then practiced all the teachings he had received.
Blessed again and again with visions of Guru Padmasambhava
and Hūṃkāra, he discovered gTer-ma of many kinds.

At Chab-mdo in eastern Tibet, Rol-pa'i rDo-rje met the great
gTer-ma master sTag-sham Nus-ldan rDo-rje and received the
complete transmission of the Yi-dam-dgongs-'dus and other
gTer-ma, becoming the main lineage holder of these teachings.
'Dren-mchog Ye-shes rDo-rje bestowed upon Rol-pa'i rDo-rje
precious teachings whose lineages have continued to the pres-

288

ent. As a lineage holder of many great gTer-ma transmissions, Rol-pa'i rDo-rje was an axis for both the bKa'-brgyud and the rNying-ma teachings in the seventeenth century.

Among Rol-pa'i rDo-rje's disciples were Gar-dbang Chos-skyong rNam-rgyal, Tshe-bhūm Karma bsTan-'phel, and O-rgyan lHun-grub, who transmitted the teachings to Si-tu Chos-kyi 'Byung-gnas. This lineage came to Kong-sprul, who preserved over forty texts in the Rin-chen gTer-mdzod. The succession of Rol-pa'i rDo-rje's incarnations resided at Zur-mang monastery, but in later times this lineage disappeared.

གནམ་ལྕགས་རྩ་གསུམ་གཏེར་བདག་གླིང་པ

gNam-lcags rTsa-gsum gTer-bdag Gling-pa
mid-17th–late 17th century C.E.
451 texts, 2,665 pages, Rin-chen gTer-mdzod: 1 text

An incarnation of gNubs-chen Sangs-rgyas Ye-shes, rTsa-gsum gTer-bdag Gling-pa was born into the 'Gru-chen Rlangs clan in Upper Nang-chen at lHo-zla. This gTer-ston was also known as Gar-dbang gNam-lcags rDo-rje. He received lay vows from a dGe-lugs Dharma master, an incarnation of rNgog Blo-ldan Shes-rab, who gave him the religious name bKra-shis Phun-tshogs. When gTer-chen sTag-sham Nus-ldan rDo-rje came to Nang-chen, rTsa-gsum gTer-bdag Gling-pa received teachings from him.

Later rTsa-gsum gTer-bdag Gling-pa traveled to 'Bri-gung where he was the disciple of dKon-mchog Phrin-las bZang-po. For three years, he received the Dza-bhīr sNyan-brgyud, which he intensively practiced until his realization became profound. He began to discover gTer-ma texts first at bSam-yas mChims-phu, the sacred power place associated with the Enlightened Speech of the Guru, and then at gZho Ti-sgro near 'Bri-gung, where Ye-shes mTsho-rgyal practiced, and at sPu-bo in the

Secret Grove of Padma. His numerous discoveries included teachings of all types in lineages that have remained unbroken down to the present day.

rTsa-gsum gTer-bdag Gling-pa resided in Khyung-po and in sPu-bo where he built the monastery Khrom-gzigs rNgams-chen. There he received innumerable students and accomplished enlightened activity for the Dharma. After his passing, his Body incarnation, Rong sMyon O-rgyan Rig-'dzin, resided at Khrom-gzigs monastery; his Speech incarnation, Kun-bzang 'Chi-med Nor-bu, resided at sPu-bo dGa'-ba-lung; and his Mind incarnation, Rig-'dzin Mi-'jigs rDo-rje, resided at Khyung-po. Both the Body and Mind streams of incarnations have continued unbroken to the present day.

The major disciple of this great gTer-ma master was the Heart Son Thugs-mchog rDo-rje, who in turn taught Zung-mkhar Theg-chen Gling-pa (Dri-med Gling-pa). Other important disciples were dKon-mchog Seng-ge Paṇḍita, rJe Kun-dga' Blo-gros, and Ye-shes rGyal-mtshan. Great Treasures of Ancient Teachings contains four hundred and fifty-one texts by this master, while the Rin-chen gTer-mdzod section includes one of his gTer-ma.

Thugs-mchog rDo-rje Hūṁ-nag 'Gro-'dul
mid-17th–late 17th century C.E.
Rin-chen gTer-mdzod: 5 texts

An incarnation of Nubs Nam-mkha'i sNying-po and mChims Śākya Prabha, Thugs-mchog rDo-rje was born below mChims-phu at sKyid-mo-grong. He resided at dPal-ri monastery. Since he was learned in both worldly sciences and Dharma, he was called sKyid-grong Chos-mdzad. He was also known as Ngag-dbang bSlab-gsum and Kun-bzang Phrin-las rDo-rje. He received the rDzogs-chen Yang-ti-nag-po teachings from Kong-po rTsub-ri Siddha Kun-bzang Rang-grol and practiced them until realization arose. From that lama, he and Rig-'dzin Tshe-dbang Nor-bu together received the Bla-ma-dgongs-'dus teachings. Thugs-mchog rDo-rje was also the disciple of Chos-rje Gling-pa, Rwa-ston sTobs-ldan rDo-rje, and rTsa-gsum gTer-bdag Gling-pa, and they blessed him with Dharma teachings like filling a vase to overflowing.

Practicing in remote places, Thugs-mchog rDo-rje perfected his understanding and began to discover gTer-ma. At 'On-phu sTag-tshang, one of the three famous Tiger Dens of Guru Padmasambhava, he found Vajrakīla teachings. At 'Phyongs-rgyas Bangs-so dMar-po, the tomb of Srong-btsan sGam-po, he found teachings associated with the three roots (guru, deva, ḍākinī). At bSam-yas mChims-phu, the sacred power place associated with the Enlightened Speech of the Guru, he found numerous treasures.

Though it was predicted that he would discover many gTer-ma, Thugs-mchog rDo-rje met with unfortunate circumstances and ran afoul of a wicked local ruler who obstructed his work. Later on, many great lamas and most of the government officials of central Tibet and Kong-po revered him for the profundity and transforming power of his teachings. His major disciples included Rig-'dzin 'Jigs-med Gling-pa, Theg-gling 'Gro-don mThar-phyin (Dri-med Gling-pa), Kun-bzang bDe-chen rGyal-po, and the incarnation of gNubs Nam-mKha'i sNying-po, mThu-chen Kra-tis Ngags-'chang Karma Rig-'dzin. Five texts are preserved in the Rin-chen gTer-mdzod.

གཏེར་སྟོན་རྡོ་རྗེ་རྒྱལ་པོ

gTer-ston rDo-rje rGyal-po

17th century C.E.?

Following in the stream of incarnations of sGam-po-pa, two
births after bZang-po rDo-rje, rDo-rje rGyal-po was born
into the clan of the lords of E, as the son of a nobleman of
lHa-rgya-ri. He was able to recover some of the treasures that
rDo-rje rGyal-po had reconcealed, but these teachings do not
appear to have been preserved, for they are not found in the
Rin-chen gTer-mdzod.

གླིང་ཚང་རྫོང་མགོ་གཏེར་སྟོན་པདྨ་དབང་ཕྱུག

Gling-tshang rDzong-mgo gTer-ston Padma dBang-phyug

17th century C.E.

An incarnation of Vairotsana, Gling-tshang rDzong-mgo
gTer-ston Padma dBang-phyug met Rig-'dzin Klong-gsal
sNying-po and received from this great gTer-ston teachings
and lists of treasures to be discovered. Near the seventh-
century temple to Tārā founded by Dharma King Srong-btsan
sGam-po in Gling-tshang, Padma dBang-phyug discovered precious rDzogs-chen teachings. At Khro-ri Zil-khrom he found
rDzogs-chen rTsa-gsum-snying-thig teachings. From within the
great cave at rGya-stod, he took out the three essential practices of guru sādhanas, rDzogs-chen teachings, and Avalokiteśvara practices (Bla-rdzogs-thugs-gsum), which soon grew
famous. After this discovery, Padma dBang-phyug became
quite highly regarded.

Although his enlightened activity was renowned, Padma
dBang-phyug did not have great disciples. His own son O-rgyan

gZhan-phan was first in a lineage that transmitted the rTsa-gsum-snying-thig teachings. In the time of Kong-sprul Blo-gros mTha'-yas, the texts and empowerments of these teachings existed, but no gTer-ma were preserved in the Rin-chen gTer-mdzod. No works by this master have been located.

གཏེར་སྟོན་ཁྱུང་གྲགས་རྡོ་རྗེ་ཨོ་རྒྱན་ཕུན་ཚོགས

## gTer-ston Khyung-grags rDo-rje O-rgyan Phun-tshogs
### 17th century C.E.?
### Rin-chen gTer-mdzod: 1 text

An incarnation of Lo-tsā-ba gYu-sgra sNying-po, O-rgyan Phun-tshogs attended upon Yongs-dge gTer-ston Mi-'gyur rDo-rje and later received his lineages of gTer-ma. But first he proceeded to Kaḥ-thog where he met Klong-gsal sNying-po. There he received blessings in the presence of this great master and training in the practices of gTer-stons. O-rgyan Phun-tshogs discovered treasure texts related to rDzogs-chen, the three roots of guru, deva, ḍākinī, the eight heruka sādhanas, and other practices. These precious teachings remained in circulation in the days of Kong-sprul Blo-gros mTha'-yas.

At the urging of Mi-'gyur rDo-rje, O-rgyan Phun-tshogs proceeded to Sa-ngan in Khams, where he was able to accomplish much benefit for beings. He used every offering he received for enlightened Dharma work. His disciples included lHa-steng 'Ja'-mo sPrul-sku, sGa Dam-tshig sPrul-sku, and others. He brought out many volumes of bKa'-ma and gTer-ma by the leading rNying-ma masters, and his impressive work had great influence. A statue with his relics remained for many years in the temple in his birthplace of Khyung-po. Unfortunately, only one gTer-ma text discovered by this master has been preserved in the Rin-chen gTer-mdzod.

# གཡབ་ཆེན་པདྨ་འགྱུར་མེད་རྒྱ་མཚོ

mKhan-chen Padma 'Gyur-med rGya-mtsho
1686–1718 C.E.
5 texts, 213 pages, Rin-chen gTer-mdzod: 8 texts

One of the four children of gTer-bdag Gling-pa, Padma 'Gyur-med rGya-mtsho was an emanation of Hayagrīva. His mother was Yon-tan sGrol-ma. From his early childhood, his father and his uncle, Lo-chen Dharmaśrī, poured their precious wisdom into him like filling a vase with holy water. At the age of twenty he received complete ordination. Chos-rje gZhan-phan dBang-po gave him instruction in Vinaya, Abhidharma, Madhyamaka, and Prajñāpāramitā, and endless explanations of major texts. He studied gSar-ma teachings, śāstras, and poetry commentaries, Mahāyoga, and many other teachings. Padma 'Gyur-med rGya-mtsho became a superb Mantrayāna practitioner, utterly fearless and completely pure in his practice. As his great father's regent, he was one of the key lineage holders of the Ancient School.

Padma 'Gyur-med rGya-mtsho composed a number of important works. Two texts on Mahāyoga rites, apparently authored by his brother Yid-bzhin Legs-grub, were completed or edited by him. He wrote a commentary on the gSang-ba'i-snying-po, the major Mahāyoga tantra, a commentary on the Abhisamāyalaṃkāra, and a commentary on mNga'-ris Paṇ-chen's famous text on the three trainings (sDom-gsum).

When the Dzungar Mongol armies invaded central Tibet in 1717 as fanatical protectors of the dGe-lugs-pa, they destroyed the major rNying-ma monasteries of rDo-rje-brag, sMin-grol-gling, and dPal-ri Theg-mchog-gling and killed the lineage holders. In these violent struggles, Padma 'Gyur-med rGya-mtsho was deliberately murdered. At his passing, the Haya-grīva statue in the main temple of bSam-yas neighed in grief and tumbled to the ground. Fortunately, a few of this master's

294

texts were preserved in the Rin-chen gTer-mdzod, and five more texts have been located and included in Great Treasures of Ancient Teachings.

 སྨིན་གླིང་ཁྲི་ཆེན་རྒྱལ་སྲས་རིན་ཆེན་རྣམ་རྒྱལ

**sMin-gling Khri-chen III rGyal-sras Rin-chen rNam-rgyal**

**late 17th–mid-18th century C.E.**

**4 texts, 44 pages, Rin-chen gTer-mdzod: 6 texts**

An emanation of Vimalamitra, Rin-chen rNam-rgyal was the son of the renowned master gTer-bdag Gling-pa and the younger brother of Padma 'Gyur-med rGya-mtsho. Through his early years, he received constant teachings and blessings from his father and his uncle, Lo-chen Dharmaśrī. His father granted him in particular the special lineages of the Sems-sde and Klongs-sde as well as the sNying-thig teachings of the Atiyoga tradition.

Having been carefully sequestered at Nyag-rong lCags-mdud in Khams during the Dzungar invasion, he was able to return to sMin-grol-gling. After the death of his brother, Padma 'Gyur-med rGya-mtsho, Rin-chen rNam-rgyal became the Third Throne Holder and worked to restore the badly damaged monastery. He was honored by Pho-lha-nas (1689–1747), who held power in central Tibet after 1728.

Rin-chen rNam-rgyal lived sixty-five years, departing this realm in the mid-eighteenth century. His major disciple was his own son, mKhan-chen Oḍḍiyāna (O-rgyan bsTan-'dzin rDo-rje), to whom he transmitted the sMin-grol-gling lineages of the bKa'-ma. His other son was 'Gyur-med Padma bsTan-'dzin, who became the Fourth sMin-gling Throne Holder. His son, 'Gyur-med 'Phrin-las rNam-rgyal, in turn, became the Fifth sMin-gling Throne Holder. The children of the Fifth Throne Holder were 'Gyur-med Padma dBang-rgyal, who became the

Sixth Throne Holder, mKhan-chen O-rgyan Chos-'phel, and the lady Phrin-las Chos-sgron. Rin-chen rNam-rgyal composed several texts on the practices of Yamāntaka and Vajrakīla, which are included in Great Treasures of Ancient Teachings, as well as six texts preserved in the Rin-chen gTer-mdzod.

སྨིན་གླིང་རྗེ་བཙུན་མི་འགྱུར་དཔལ་གྱི་སྒྲོན་མ།

sMin-gling rJe-btsun Mi-'gyur dPal-gyi-sgron-ma
1699–1769 C.E.
6 texts, 45 pages, Rin-chen gTer-mdzod: 2 texts

An emanation of Ye-shes mTsho-rgyal, Mi-'gyur dPal-gyi sGron-ma was born as the daughter of the eminent gTer-bdag Gling-pa. She received teachings throughout her childhood and youth from her father and her uncle Lo-chen Dharmaśrī. In particular, her father bestowed upon her and her brother Rin-chen rNam-rgyal the special lineages of the Sems-sde and Klongs-sde, as well as the sNying-thig teachings of the Atiyoga tradition. From Mi-'gyur dPal-sgron, the sMin-grol-gling Atiyoga transmission passed first to mKhan-chen Oḍḍiyāna and from him to sMin-grol-gling Throne Holder Phrin-las rNam-rgyal, who taught the lady Phrin-las Chos-sgron. She in turn was one of the masters of 'Jam-dbyangs mKhyen-brtse'i dBang-po the First.

A brilliant teacher, Mi-'gyur dPal-sgron composed several important treatises on Atiyoga practice, a commentary on the dKon-mchog-spyi-'dus treasures discovered by gTer-chen 'Ja'-tshon sNying-po, and a work on 'Pho-ba (consciousness transfer at the time of death). After the death of her brother Padma 'Gyur-med rGya-mtsho and the enthronement of her brother Rin-chen rNam-rgyal at sMin-grol-gling, she made enormous efforts to restore the monastery, which had been totally devastated by the Dzungar Mongols in 1717–1718.

She lived to the age of seventy-one. Among her disciples was Khyung-po Ras-pa, who under her guidance became an outstanding master of Atiyoga. Six works by Mi-'gyur dPal-sgron are preserved in Great Treasures of Ancient Teachings together with her biography.

## དབ་དབང་འོད་གསལ

Ngag-dbang 'Od-gsal
late 17th–mid-18th century C.E.
1 text, 16 pages

Ngag-dbang 'Od-gsal was a disciple of sMan-mthing-pa Padma Las-'brel-rtsal, who had been a disciple of rDo-rje-brag Rig-'dzin Chen-mo (1580–1639). Ngag-dbang 'Od-gsal composed an explanation of the 'Jam-dpal dMar-po practices, which is preserved in Great Treasures of Ancient Teachings.

## རིག་འཛིན་ཐུགས་ཀྱི་རྡོ་རྗེ་ཕྲིན་ལས་འདུས་པ་རྩལ

Rig-'dzin Thugs-kyi rDo-rje Phrin-las 'Dus-pa-rtsal
late 17th–mid-18th century C.E.
Rin-chen gTer-mdzod: 12 texts

An emanation of Dharma King Khri-srong lDe'u-btsan, Thugs-kyi rDo-rje was also known as rDo-rje Drag-po Phrin-las 'Dus-pa-rtsal. He was born in the southern districts of mDo-khams at sTag-gzigs. Recognized as the fourth incarnation of the yogin bSod-nams rGya-mtsho, he was installed at the traditional residence of 'Dzi-dgon bKra-shis Chos-gling. He took refuge with Si-tu Chos-kyi 'Byung-gnas, who gave him the name bKa'-brgyud Phrin-las rNam-par rGyal-ba'i-sde. In addition to Si-tu Chos-kyi 'Byung-gnas, his other teachers included 'Brug-chen Thams-cad mKhyen-pa, Yongs-'dzin 'Jam-dpal dPa'-bo, Khams-pa Rinpoche bsTan-'dzin Chos-kyi Nyi-ma, and other masters.

From Rig-'dzin rTa-mgrin mGon-po, Thugs-kyi rDo-rje received the precious teachings of Ratna Gling-pa, especially the Vajrakīla practices, which he mastered to perfection. He was blessed with many visions and developed splendid spiritual power that allowed him to protect many beings from difficulties.

He proceeded to the sacred powerful place of Tsā-ri where he discovered Realization Treasures, teachings on Tārā and Vajrakīla, and others. He transmitted these gTer-ma to the rGyal-dbang Karmapa bDud-'dul rDo-rje (1733–1797), 'Brug-chen Chos-kyi sNang-ba, Si-tu Rinpoche Padma Nyin-byed dBang-po (1774–1853), and others. Through these masters the gTer-ma teachings flowed into the Karma and 'Brug-pa traditions. Kong-sprul Blo-gros mTha'-yas received the teachings of Thugs-kyi rDo-rje and was able to preserve twelve works in the Rin-chen gTer-mdzod.

## gTer-ston rMog-grub Nam-mkha' Chos-dbang
## late 17th–mid-18th century C.E.

The next incarnation of gNam-chos Mi'-'gyur rDo-rje was Lung-gis-'dzin-pa rMog-grub Nam-mkha' Chos-dbang, a renowned practitioner, who also discovered numerous gTer-ma teachings, statues, and sacred substances. But the conditions were not completely right for establishing these treasures, and the texts did not all survive the later centuries. The remarkable statues still existed in the nineteenth century, while the sacred substances were preserved at Kaḥ-thog.

rMog-grub Nam-mkha' Chos-dbang discovered Realization Treasures. Kong-sprul Blo-gro mTha'-yas had heard of some of these, but he was not able to locate texts to include in the Rin-chen gTer-mdzod. Later incarnations included 'Jigs-bral Chos-dbyings rDo-rje, a master who accomplished the benefit of others and furthered the teachings of the Ancient School.

སྣེ་ལུང་རྗེ་དྲུང་བཞད་པའི་རྡོ་རྗེ

Sle-lung rJe-drung bZhad-pa'i rDo-rje
1697–1737 C.E.
453 texts, 3,748 pages

The fifth incarnation of lHo-brag Grub-chen Las-kyi rDo-rje (1326–1401), bZhad-pa'i rDo-rje was born in Zangs-ri. This dGe-lugs-pa dGe-bshes was known as the gSar-ma gTer-ston and was well-educated in the gSar-ma traditions. He was ordained by the Sixth Dalai Lama and received teachings from bDe-gshegs Dam-pa Chos-bzang-po and sNgags-smyon Blo-gsal rGya-mtsho. He was attracted to the teachings of O-rgyan gTer-bdag Gling-pa, which he was fortunate to receive from this great master's disciples.

Becoming a lineage holder for these teachings, he composed commentaries and created sādhanas for gTer-bdag Gling-pa gTer-ma, especially the gSang-ba-ye-shes cycle. His consort lHa-mo Nyi-ma gZhon-nu was renowned for her yogic practice, which transformed her into an actual deity. Great Treasures of Ancient Teachings contains his collected works, numbering four hundred and fifty-three texts and filling sixteen Tibetan volumes.

# Part Eight

# Era of Tshe-dbang Nor-bu and 'Jigs-med Gling-pa

རིག་འཛིན་ཀུན་མཁྱེན་འཇིགས་མེད་གླིང་པ

Rig-'dzin Kun-mkhyen 'Jigs-med-gling-pa

# Eighteenth Century

Since the days of the Dharma Kings, rNying-ma masters had refrained from exerting influence on Tibetan politics, unlike the leaders of other schools. But even noninvolvement offered no protection from the politics of this century. Tibet lost the great learned sDe-srid, murdered in 1705 by lHa-bzang Khan, who entered lHa-sa with Mongol troops. In 1717 the Dzungars killed lHa-bzang and in their fanatic support for other schools began a campaign of destruction, assassinating rNying-ma lineage holders and damaging rNying-ma monasteries. Kang-chen-nas and Pho-lha-gnas expelled the Mongols, but soon the Manchus began to interfere in Tibetan politics.

At times in Tibetan history, religion has suffered at the hands of politics, and internal weakness has supported invitations to external powers to interfere. It is hard to understand how Buddhist leaders could encourage acts that cause so much misery and damage to the Dharma. Though such events are difficult to disclose, a complete picture of Tibet's past will have to include an understanding of how these episodes occur.

# ཀ༔ཐོག་པ་རིག་འཛིན་ཚེ་དབང་ནོར་བུ

Kaḥ-thog-pa Rig-'dzin Tshe-dbang Nor-bu
1698–1755 C.E.
204 texts, 1,404 pages, Rin-chen gTer-mdzod: 38 texts

The Heart incarnation of the great gNubs-chen Nam-mkha'i sNying-po, Tshe-dbang Nor-bu was born in mDo smad Sa-ngan bSo-ba. His father was rDu-pa A-ti-mgon-po, and his mother was sGo-bza' rDo-rje-'tsho. His uncle Padma bDe-chen Gling-pa recognized him as the rebirth of the siddha Padma Nor-bu, took him to gNas-nang monastery, and became his root guru. Tshe-dbang Nor-bu easily learned reading, writing, worldly arts and sciences, and all fields of Buddhist philosophy. Receiving and implementing the practical instructions of his root guru, he cultivated a deepening realization. He took lay vows with Kaḥ-thog rGyal-sras and heard teachings from Zur-mang Che-tshang gSung-rab rGya-mtsho. He lived in the manner of a Vajradhara, an upholder of Mantrayāna vows.

Tshe-dbang Nor-bu eventually traveled to Kong-po and sPu-bo and to dBus and gTsang, studying with masters of all traditions, both gSar-ma and rNying-ma. From Chos-rje Kun-bzang dBang-po, he received the entire Jo-nang-pa tradition, and his efforts significantly improved the longevity of these precious teachings. During Tshe-dbang Nor-bu's time, the Pho-lha family ruled central Tibet, and they honored this master as their royal teacher because of his unobscured vision of the past, present, and future and his yogic powers. He was a peacemaker and mediator of great skill.

Rig-'dzin Tshe-dbang Nor-bu discovered Earth Treasures, Pure Vision Treasures, and Realization Treasures. He practiced all over Tibet, and in sPu-bo, Kong-po, and mNga'-ris he founded new monasteries. A prolific and eclectic author, he composed histories, numerous practice instructions and sād-hanas, works on astrology, letters, songs of realization, and prayers. His learning maintained the eminence of Kaḥ-thog monastery during the eighteenth century.

Tshe-dbang Nor-bu journeyed three times to Nepal, where he restored the stupa at Boudha and the stupa at Swayambhu. His major disciples were the Karmapas, 'Brug Thams-cad mKhyen-pa, and rJe Chos-kyi 'Byung-gnas; his students could be found throughout mNga'-ris in the west, gTsang and dBus in central Tibet, and mDo-khams in the east. The stream of his teachings has flourished down to the present time. Kong-sprul Blo-gros mTha'-yas was able to preserve thirty-eight works in the Rin-chen gTer-mdzod, while two hundred and four additional texts can be found in various sections of Great Treasures of Ancient Teachings.

མདོ་ཁམས་འབའ་རྩེ་ར་གཏེར་སྟོན་པདྨ་ཆོས་རྒྱལ།

**mDo-khams 'Ba' rTse-ra gTer-ston Padma Chos-rgyal**
**late 17th–mid-18th century C.E.**

The master known as mDo-khams 'Ba'-rtse-ra gTer-ston Padma Chos-rgyal obtained many precious treasures. He was renowned in Khams for his unusual powers, abilities, and blessings. He met Tshe-dbang Nor-bu and received teachings from him. During the nineteenth century, his monastery was still intact and in use, and a few of his teachings continued. Kong-sprul Blo-gros mTha'-yas preserved one work in the Rin-chen gTer-mdzod, a small text written by Kaḥ-thog Chos-kyi rDo-rje, with whom this master is associated. No other works by Padma Chos-rgyal have been located in recent times.

མཁན་ཆེན་ཨོ་རྒྱན་ཆོས་འཕེལ་

mKhan-chen O-rgyan Chos-'phel
late 17th–mid-18th century C.E.
2 texts, 8 pages

O-rgyan Chos-phel, the son of sMin-gling Khri-chen V 'Gyur-med Phrin-las rNam-grol, was the brother of Khri-chen VI 'Gyur-med Padma dBang-rgyal and Lady Chos-sgron. He authored a commentary on the major Mahāyoga Tantra, the gSang-ba'i-snying-po, which is preserved in Great Treasures of Ancient Teachings, together with another work. The details of his life story require further research.

ཁྱུང་པོ་རས་པ་འགྱུར་མེད་འོད་གསལ་

Khyung-po Ras-pa 'Gyur-med 'Od-gsal
late 17th–mid-18th century C.E.
1 text, 47 pages

Khyung-po Ras-pa 'Gyur-med 'Od-gsal composed a text on Atiyoga, following the presentation of his teacher, Mi-'gyur dPal-sgron, the daughter of gTer-bdag Gling-pa. This work is preserved in Great Treasures of Ancient Teachings, but no other texts by this author have yet been located.

गटेर-སྟོན་དྲི་མེད་གླིང་པ

gTer-ston Dri-med Gling-pa
1700–1775 C.E.
27 texts, 693 pages, Rin-chen gTer-mdzod: 2 texts

The incarnation of Padmasambhava's disciple Lo-tsā-ba rGyal-ba mChog-dbyangs, Dri-med Gling-pa was the next birth of Rong-pa gTer-ston bDud-'dul Gling-pa. He was born at Zung-mkhar Theg-chen Gling into the family of gTer-ston bDe-chen Gling-pa. He first took vows with the Twelfth Karmapa Byang-chub rDo-rje (1703–1732), who gave him the name Karma 'Gro-don mThar-phyin. Residing with the Tantric community at sGrags, he received gSar-ma and rNying-ma teachings from Bla-ma mNyan-pa dGe-legs. From Thugs-mchog rDo-rje, he received rDzogs-chen teachings, which he practiced intently until his understanding grew profound and his super-normal powers vast.

Recalling his previous lives as Me-long rDo-rje, bDe-chen Gling-pa, and bDud-'dul Gling-pa, he determined to practice intently in remote places. As his throat chakra opened fully like a flower, he expressed the depths of his experience in beautiful songs of realization.

Encouraged and instructed by Thugs-mchog rDo-rje, who recognized him as his Dharma heir, Dri-med Gling-pa began to discover treasures. At sGrags Yang-rdzong, the sacred power place associated with the Enlightened Body of the Guru, he found two precious teachings. At Zur-mkhar-rdo where King Khri-srong lDe'u-btsan had erected stupas, he found another, but reconcealed it. So widely respected was this gTer-ston that the Seventh Dalai Lama bsKal-bzang rGya-mtsho (1708–1757) requested from Dri-med Gling-pa special ceremonies to protect the people of Tibet.

Dri-med Gling-pa's main disciple was lCags-zam-pa Ye-shes lHun-grub, an incarnation of gYu-sgra sNying-po. He continued the lineage of his master's gTer-ma, which passed to Kong-sprul Blo-gro mTha'-yas. Dri-med Gling-pa's family lineage remained at Grung-mkhar lHa-sdings at least through the nineteenth century. Two of his texts were preserved in the Rin-chen gTer-mdzod and another twenty-seven texts, including a biography and songs of realizations, were included in other sections of Great Treasures of Ancient Teachings.

གཏེར་སྟོན་ང་ཕོད་པདྨ་དགྱེས་པ

gTer-ston Nga-phod Padma dGyes-pa

late 17th–mid-18th century C.E.

Rin-chen gTer-mdzod: 2 texts

The rebirth of dGe-sbyong Blo-gsal rGya-mtsho, who belonged to the heart stream of gTer-bdag Gling-pa, Nga-phod dGe-rgan Padma dGyes-pa heard many teachings from the disciples of sMin-grol-gling lineage holder Rin-chen rNam-rgyal. Becoming expert in the worldly arts and sciences, as well as in Sūtra and Tantra, he practiced the path of the Vajrayāna and developed siddhis. In Pure Visions, this outstanding practitioner discovered treasure teachings of Padmasambhava, which he transmitted to future generations. Kong-sprul preserved two works in the Rin-chen gTer-mdzod.

གནུབས་བན་བསྟན་འཛིན་ཡེ་ཤེས་ལྷུན་གྲུབ

gNubs-ban bsTan-'dzin Ye-shes lHun-grub
late 17th–mid-18th century C.E.
Rin-chen gTer-mdzod: 5 texts

The lama known as bsTan-'dzin Ye-shes lHun-grub, also
known as lCags-zam-pa, was one of 'Jigs-med Gling-pa's
gurus. His own masters included Dri-med Gling-pa (1700–
1775) and the great scholar Mang-thos Tshe-dbang Mi-'gyur
rDo-rje, who had been a disciple of both Padma Phrin-las and
of gTer-bdag Gling-pa and his sons. Mang-thos Mi-'gyur rDo-
rje was a gTer-ston who had received Cakrasaṁvara treasure
teachings in a Pure Vision. He bestowed this treasure upon
Ye-shes lHun-grub, who continued the stream of these teachings. Ye-shes lHun-grub composed several texts on guru sādhanas and other works, which Kong-sprul Blo-gros mTha'-yas
preserved in the Rin-chen gTer-mdzod. No other texts by this
author have been located in recent times.

མཁན་ཆེན་ཨོ་རྒྱན་ཨོ་རྒྱན་བསྟན་འཛིན

mKhan-chen Oḍḍiyāna O-rgyan bsTan-'dzin
c. 1718? C.E.
Rin-chen gTer-mdzod: 3 texts

An incarnation of both Lo-chen Dharmaśrī and gYu-sgra
sNying-po, O-rgyan bsTan-'dzin was born into the gNyos
clan as the son of sMin-gling rGyal-sras Rin-chen rNam-rgyal.
His brother was sMin-gling Khri-chen IV 'Gyur-med Padma
bsTan-'dzin. O-rgyan bsTan-'dzin studied worldly arts and sciences, all the Sūtras and the śāstra subjects of Vinaya, Abhidharma, Madhyamaka, Logic, and Prajñāpāramitā, as well as

the three vows and trainings related to the Three Vehicles (sdom-gsum), and the teachings of the Tantras.

Both Mi-'gyur dPal-sgron and Rin-chen rNam-rgyal were O-rgyan bsTan-'dzin's teachers, bestowing upon him the sMin-grol-gling Atiyoga lineage. He in turn transmitted these precious teachings to his nephew Phrin-las rNam-rgyal, who taught the lady Phrin-las Chos-sgron, who in turn taught 'Jam-dbyangs mKhyen-brtse'i dBang-po.

mKhan-chen Oḍḍiyāna played a crucial role in the sMin-grol-gling lineage of the bKa'-ma that had passed from gTer-bdag Gling-pa to Lo-chen Dharmaśrī, from him to rGyal-sras Rin-chen rNam-rgyal, and from him to mKhan-chen Oḍḍiyāna. From mKhan-chen Oḍḍiyāna and his father, the lineage spread to the rNying-ma monasteries in Khams such as Kaḥ-thog, Zhe-chen, dPal-yul, and rDzogs-chen, as well as to rNying-ma centers in 'Gu-log and rGyal-mo-rong. This transmission has remained unbroken to the present time.

In particular, mKhan-chen Oḍḍiyāna transmitted the bKa'-ma to sMin-gling Khri-chen V Phrin-las rNam-rgyal, who was his nephew. This master in turn transmitted it to his own son, Khri-chen VI 'Gyur-med Padma dBang-rgyal. Khri-chen VI bestowed the lineage on sMin-gling Khri-chen VII Sangs-rgyas Kun-dga'. This transmission then passed to mDo-sngags bsTan-'dzin Nor-bu, who passed it to 'Gyur-med Phan-bde 'Od-zer, the master of bDud-'joms 'Jigs-bral Ye-shes rDo-rje.

Three texts by mKhan-chen Oḍḍiyāna are preserved in the Rin-chen gTer-mdzod. One text by mKhan-chen 'Gyur-med gSang-sngags bsTan-'dzin, brother of sMin-gling Khri-chen V, is also preserved in the Great Treasures collection.

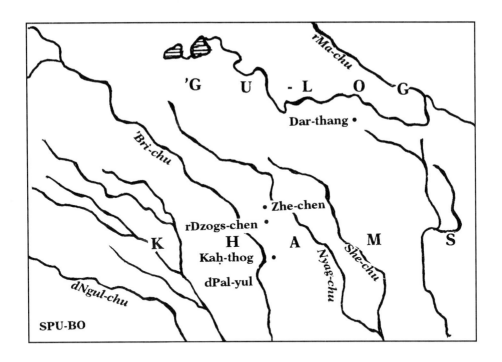

རྗེ་མཁན་ཆེན་བསྟན་འཛིན་ཆོས་རྒྱལ་

rJe-mkhan-chen bsTan-'dzin Chos-rgyal

1700–1767 C.E.

1 text, 62 pages

Ruler of the kingdom of Bhutan in the eighteenth century, bsTan-'dzin Chos-rgyal was both king and scholar. This master belonged to the lineage of Padma Gling-pa's teachings. He composed a biography of sGang-steng sPrul-sku, the reincarnation of the son of Zla-ba rGyal-mtshan (the son of Padma Gling-pa). This text is preserved in the Great Treasures of Ancient Teachings collection.

ཞེ་ཆེན་རབ་འབྱམས་གཉིས་པ་འགྱུར་མེད་ཀུན་བཟང་རྣམ་རྒྱལ

# Zhe-chen Rab-'byams gNyis-pa
## 'Gyur-med Kun-bzang rNam-rgyal
### 1713–1769 C.E.
### 3 texts, 80 pages

The second incarnation of Zhwa-dmar Rab-'byams-pa Chen-po, 'Gyur-med Kun-bzang was born into the same family as the rDzogs-chen Rinpoche. Clearly unusual even as a child, he recalled his previous births, and so was invited to O-rgyan Chos-rdzong. His five major teachers were rGyal-sras Theg-mchog bsTan-'dzin, Byang-pa Rig-'dzin mChog-sprul sKal-bzang Padma dBang-phyug, mKhan 'Gyur-med sKal-bzang 'Phel-rgyas, and his uncle 'Gyur-med sKal-bzang bsTan-'phel. Three other important masters were Ngor mKhan-chen dPal-ldan Chos-skyong, mDo-khams-pa Kun-dga' bsTan-'dzin, and Kaḥ-thog rGyal-sras Dri-med Zhing-skyong.

He studied the Tripiṭaka, the Tantras, and the worldly arts and sciences, practicing very intensively. Blessed with visions and predictions, he came to possess knowledge, compassion, and virtuous qualities so vast as to be nearly incredible. In 1735 he established Zhe-chen bsTan-gnyis Dar-rgyas-gling, which became one of the six major rNying-ma monastries. Its traditions have continued unbroken until recent times.

Zhe-chen Rab-'byams' major disciples included Padma gSang-sngags bsTan-'dzin Chos-rgyal (b. 1760), Kun-bzang sNyan-grags rGya-mtsho, Sib-sprul Kun-bzang Padma dBang-rgyal, Grub-dbang Sangs-rgyas Rab-brtan, Phu-gung Bla-ma Padma Rin-chen, 'Ju Bla gSang-sngags, Zhe-drung Padma rNam-dag, Khrom-bza' Ngag-dbang Padma, and many others. Other outstanding rNying-ma masters who received teachings from him included the rDzogs-chen Rinpoches, Kaḥ-thog Dri-med Zhing-skyong, rJe-dbon Padma Kun-grol rNam-rgyal, and Bla-ma bKra-shis rGya-mtsho, as well as important masters of other schools. Great Treasures of Ancient Teachings includes three texts by this master, one of which is a dkar-chag (table of contents) for the Seven Treasures of Klong-chen-pa.

འཇིགས་མེད་འཕྲིན་ལས་རྣམ་རྒྱལ།

'Jigs-med 'Phrin-las rNam-rgyal

1717 C.E.

1 text, 45 pages

The eighteenth-century master 'Jigs-med Phrin-las rNam-rgyal was the disciple of lHa-ri Rig-'dzin 'Jigs-med dPa'-bo and Chu-bzang mKhan-chen Nam-mkha' Klong-yangs of rDo-rje-brag. He composed a text on a gTer-ma teaching that had been discovered by Sle-lung rJe-drung bZhad-pa'i rDo-rje (1697–1737). This work is preserved in Great Treasures of Ancient Teachings.

རྡོ་རྗེ་བྲག་རིག་འཛིན་ལྔ་པ་བསྐལ་བཟང་པདྨ་དབང་ཕྱུག

rDo-rje-brag Rig-'dzin lNga-pa

bsKal-bzang Padma dBang-phyug

1720–1770 C.E.

2 texts, 202 pages, Rin-chen gTer-mdzod: 2 texts

The fifth incarnation of the great gTer-ma master Rig-'dzin rGod-ldem, and the next immediate incarnation of Padma Phrin-las, Padma dBang-phyug was born into the lHa clan in Nyag-rong lCags-mdud in the Bu-bor-sgang region of southeastern Tibet. He was recognized and installed as the lineage holder of the Northern Treasures traditions of rDo-rje-brag monastery.

In 1717, three years before his birth, the Dzungar Mongols had destroyed rDo-rje-brag. As a young man, Padma dBang-phyug took on the enormous task of rebuilding the monastic center, which, once revitalized, became a major center for the rNying-ma traditions for the next two hundred years. He clarified and articulated the teachings of the Ancient School, supporting and protecting the rNying-ma tradition during the eighteenth century.

In Pure Visions, Padma dBang-phyug received precious longevity teachings, which he later bestowed on Grub-dbang Chos-kyi Nyi-ma. This master transmitted the teachings to Jam-dbyangs mKhyen-brtse, who gave them to Kong-sprul. This text and another were preserved by Kong-sprul in the Rin-chen gTer-mdzod; Padma dBang-phyug's autobiography is contained in another section of the Great Treasures of Ancient Teachings collection.

ষ্ণ্ঠ্ংংশংৃংংংং

Sle-slung Thugs-sras gYung-mgon rDo-rje-dpal
1721–1769 C.E.
1 text, 42 pages

Heart Son of the master Sle-slung rJe-drung, gYung-mgon rDo-rje-dpal was an incarnation of 'Brug-pa Kun-legs (b. 1455), one of the greatest siddhas in the history of the bKa'-brgyud tradition. gYung-mgon rDo-rje-dpal composed a biography of the guru of 'Brug-pa Kun-legs, lHa-btsun Kun-dga' Chos-kyi rGya-mtsho (fourteenth century). This work is preserved in Great Treasures of Ancient Teachings.

རིག་འཛིན་ཀུན་མཁྱེན་འཇིགས་མེད་གླིང་པ

Rig-'dzin Kun-mkhyen 'Jigs-med Gling-pa
1730–1798 C.E.
259 texts, 3,042 pages, Rin-chen gTer-mdzod: 158 texts

The All-knowing 'Jigs-med Gling-pa belonged to the stream of incarnations that included King Krikrī in the time of Kaśyapa Buddha; Nanda, the Buddha's half-brother; King Dri-med Kun-dga'; mKhan-chen Vimalamitra; Dharma King Srong-btsan sGam-po; rGyal-sras lHa-rje; Dwags-po lHa-rje sGam-po-pa; rJe-btsun Grags-pa rGyal-mtshan; O-rgyan Gling-pa; Klong-chen-pa; Byang-bdag bKra-shis sTobs-rgyal; mNga'-ris Paṇ-chen; and 'Bri-gung Rin-chen Phun-tshogs.

'Jigs-med Gling-pa was born into the rGya-brag-pa family, whose members were among the Heart Sons of Chos-rje 'Brug-pa. His birthplace was near the monastery of dPal-ri in 'Phyongs-rgyas in central Tibet. He took refuge with mTsho-rgyal sPrul-sku Nga-dbang Blo-bzang Padma and received from him the name Padma mKhyen-brtse'i 'Od-zer. Ngag-dbang Kun-dga' Legs-pa'i 'Byung-gnas gave him novice vows. He studied with gNas-brtan Kun-bzang 'Od-zer, and took as his root guru Rig-'dzin Thugs-mchog rDo-rje. His other masters included Dri-med Gling-pa, Zhang-sgom Dharmakīrti, Grub-dbang Śrīnātha of sMin-grol-gling, bsTan-'dzin Ye-shes lHun-grub, Thang-'brog dBon Padma mChog-grub, and Mon rDza-dkar Bla-ma Dar-rgyas. He received all the most important bKa'-ma and gTer-ma of the rNying-ma tradition, as well as the Tantras of the gSar-ma school.

During intensive retreat at dPal-ri, 'Jigs-med Gling-pa made a visionary journey to the great stupa at Boudhanath, where he received the Klong-chen-snying-thig cycle. He then proceeded to bSam-yas mChims-phu, where he received the blessings of Klong-chen-pa in visions, and perfected his mastery of the Klong-chen-snying-thig. He first taught fifteen disciples at bSam-yas and thereafter extensively spread these precious enlightened teachings.

In the region just south of the tomb of King Srong-btsan sGam-po, he rebuilt the hermitage of Tshe-ring-ljongs Padma 'Od-gsal Theg-mchog-gling, which he then took as his residence. Disciples came from every region of Tibet, eager to hear both the "old tradition" of Kun-mkhyen Klong-chen-pa's sNying-thig-ya-bzhi and the "new tradition" of 'Jigs-med Gling-pa's Klong-chen-snying-thig. The precious instructions of the Klong-chen-snying-thig spread everywhere and are ardently practiced to the present day.

Unable to bear the possibility that the efforts of the Dharma Kings had been in vain, 'Jigs-med Gling-pa set out to protect the longevity of the texts of the Ancient School, which were growing more rare with each passing generation. He therefore had copies made in fine calligraphy of the rNying-ma Tantras found at sMin-grol-gling, and wrote a catalogue for the texts and a history of their transmission. According to the advice of 'Jigs-med gling-pa, the rNying-ma-rgyud-'bum texts were separately carved at sDe-dge, in addition to the sDe-dge bKa'-'gyur.

'Jigs-med Gling-pa's disciples included masters of all the schools, and most of the rNying-ma teachers from Khams. His spiritual son was Grub-dbang 'Jigs-med Phrin-las 'Od-zer, and his close disciples were 'Jigs-med Kun-grol and 'Jigs-med rGyal-ba'i Myu-gu. The Padma Gling-pa gSung-sprul incarnations and the rDo-rje-brag incarnations were also his devoted students, as were masters of all schools: Sa-skya Khri-chen, the 'Bri-gung-pa Rinpoches, the Bo-dong lineage holder sByor-ra sPrul-sku, Mon mTsho-sna dGon-rtse sPrul-sku, and Ri-bo dGa'-ldan masters.

'Jigs-med Gling-pa's collected works in nine Tibetan volumes include his Klong-chen-snying-thig gTer-ma together with commentaries on them, the gTer-ma Phur-pa-rgyud-lugs, and the Yon-tan-rin-po-che'i-mdzod, a comprehensive description of the entire path, also a Realization Treasure bestowed

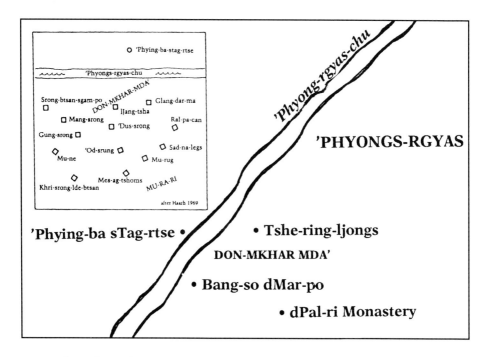

Map labels:
○ 'Phying-ba-stag-rtse
'Phyongs-rgyas-chu
Strong-btsan-sgam-po    □ Glang-dar-ma
DON-MKHAR-MDA'
□ Mang-srong    □ lJang-tsha
□ 'Dus-srong    Ral-pa-can ○
Gung-srong □
◇ 'Od-srung □    □ Sad-na-legs
Mu-ne    □ Mu-rug
◇ Mes-ag-tshoms
Khri-srong-lde-btsan    MU-RA-RI
after Haarh 1969

'PHYONGS-RGYAS

'Phying-ba sTag-rtse •    • Tshe-ring-ljongs

DON-MKHAR MDA'

• Bang-so dMar-po

• dPal-ri Monastery

upon him by Klong-chen-pa. These works, together with others totaling two hundred and fifty-nine texts, are preserved in Great Treasures of Ancient Teachings. Another one hundred and fifty works are in the Rin-chen gTer-mdzod section.

གུན་བཟང་བདེ་ཆེན་རྒྱལ་པོ་སྨོན་ལམ་རྡོ་རྗེ

## Kun-bzang bDe-chen rGyal-po sMon-lam rDo-rje
### 1736 C.E.
6 texts, 50 pages, Rin-chen gTer-mdzod: 1 text

An incarnation of Ācārya dPal-dbyangs and the immediate rebirth of Rwa-ston gTer-ston, Kun-bzang bDe-chen rGyal-po was born at bSam-yas rGod-dkar-la. Even as a young child, he performed ascetic practices and had unusual powers. He listened to the teachings of the Buddha at bSam-yas and at 'Phyongs-rgyas dPal-ri, and received many instructions from rTsub-ri Siddha. His root guru was Thugs-mchog rDo-rje.

317

A list of treasures came into his hands when he was only eleven years old, but it was not until he was twenty-six that he began to discover gTer-ma. In the region of Upper Kong-po and Lower Dwags-po he made his first discoveries of teachings associated with the five Buddha families. In sPu-bo dGa'-ba-lung he found teachings, statues, and precious substances. Near rGyang-rtse at the Tārā temple he found teachings concealed by Jo-bo rJe Atīśa. His most famous treasure was the Hayagrīva and Vārāhī teachings. Altogether he made eighteen discoveries of practices and teachings, which he himself mastered, developing magical powers to assist others.

In central Tibet, rGyal-tshab De-mo Rinpoche (r. 1757) honored him as Ti-śī, State Teacher. He performed the reconsecration of bSam-yas in 1770. In Kong-po, Chos-gling sPrul-sku offered him the monastery of 'Brug-thang, and there he worked until the end of his life, planting the seeds of liberation in numerous beings. His discoveries were not all continuously transmitted, but Kong-sprul received the lineage of one text and preserved it in the Rin-chen gTer-mdzod. Six other works have been located and placed in Great Treasures. His spiritual son was O-rgyan bsTan-'dzin, who was the teacher of Chos-rgyal Ngag-gi dBang-po.

Rig-'dzin Kun-bzang rDo-rje
1738–1805 C.E.
1 text, 174 pages

Born near gTing-skyes in gTsang as the son of bsTan-srung rNam-rgyal, Kun-bzang rDo-rje was the reincarnation of Zil-gnon dBang-rgyal rDo-rje. He took as his gurus Rig-'dzin mThu-stobs rDo-rje and bsKal-bzang Kun-dga' Rig-'dzin. His next incarnation was Rig-'dzin Kun-bzang rGyal-mtshan, born in 1811 at Glang-mthong. Kun-bzang rDo-rje's autobiography is preserved in Great Treasures of Ancient Teachings.

སྨིན་གྲིང་ཁྲི་ཆེན་དྲུག་པ་པདྨ་དབང་རྒྱལ

sMin-gling Khri-chen Drug-pa Padma dBang-rgyal
late 17th–mid-18th century C.E.
3 pages, Rin-chen gTer-mdzod: 2 texts

An incarnation of the incomparable gTer-bdag Gling-pa, Padma dBang-rgyal was born as the son of Phrin-las rNam-rgyal, who was the grandson of Rin-chen rNam-rgyal, gTer-bdag Gling-pa's son. Thus Padma dBang-rgyal was the great-great grandson of gTer-bdag Gling-pa. His sister was Phrin-las Chos-sgron, who bestowed the sMin-grol-gling lineages on the great 'Jam-dbyangs mKhyen-brtse.

From his father, sMin-gling Khri-chen V, he received the entire bKa'-ma tradition of sMin-grol-gling. After the passing of his father, he was enthroned as sMin-gling Khri-chen VI, presiding over the great monastery of sMin-grol-gling at the end of the eighteenth century in the time of 'Jigs-med Gling-pa.

Padma dBang-rgyal composed a text on the ceremonies of the major Mahāyoga Tantra, the gSang-ba'i-snying-po. He arranged several texts, which were preserved in the Rin-chen gTer-mdzod, one of which was transcribed by his renowned sister, Phrin-las Chos-sgron. These three texts are contained in Great Treasures of Ancient Teachings.

319

འཇི་སྒར་གཏེར་སྟོན་རྡོ་རྗེ་དྲག་པོ་རྩལ།

'Dzi-sgar gTer-ston rDo-rje Drag-po-rtsal
1740–1798 C.E.
60 texts, 348 pages

Born in the mid-eighteenth century, this gTer-ston received Realization Treasures for practices of wrathful deities, Tārā sādhanas, and rites for Dharma protectors and local divinities. He also discovered prayers to King Ge-sar of Gling, as well as practices and prayers for healing and pacifying beings in different realms. More research is required to ascertain the details of his life story. Sixty texts by this master are contained in Great Treasures of Ancient Teachings.

རྡོ་གྲུབ་ཆེན་འཇིགས་མེད་ཕྲིན་ལས་འོད་ཟེར།

rDo-grub-chen 'Jigs-med Phrin-las 'Od-zer
1745–1821 C.E.
19 texts, 196 pages, Rin-chen gTer-mdzod: 2 texts

An emanation of King Khri-srong lDe'u-btsan's son, Prince Mu-rum bTsad-po, 'Jigs-med Phrin-las 'Od-zer was clearly prophesied in Sangs-rgyas Gling-pa's gTer-ma. Born into the rMug-po gDong clan in the land of rDo in 'Gu-log, he was also known as rDo-bla Kun-bzang gZhan-phan. He was an obviously unusual child whose orientation toward the Dharma was clear from a young age. From dPal-yul and bKa'-brgyud masters he received Mahāmudrā and rDzogs-chen instructions, which he understood in great depth. He took refuge vows with Zhe-chen Rab-'byams II 'Gyur-med Kun-bzang rNam-rgyal, who gave him the name Kun-bzang gZhan-phan.

He took up a pure way of life, spending seven years in retreat absorbed one-pointedly in meditation. At Dwags-lha sGam-po he received many teachings from Grub-chen Dam-chos dBang-phyug. He also received instructions from dPal-yul Karma bKra-shis, Zhe-chen 'Gyur-med Kun-bzang rNam-rgyal, Kaḥ-thog Dri-med Zhing-skyong, rJe-dpon Padma Kun-grol rNam-rgyal, Nges-don bsTan-'dzin bZang-po, and others. Altogether, twenty masters transmitted to him the major rNying-ma teachings.

At Tshe-ring-ljongs, 'Jigs-med Phrin-las 'Od-zer met 'Jigs-med Gling-pa, the incarnation of King Khri-srong lDe'u-btsan, who recognized him as the incarnation of Prince Mu-rum. 'Jigs-med Gling-pa cherished him as a father loves an only son and empowered him as the lineage holder for the sNying-thig transmission.

In sDe-dge, 'Jigs-med Phrin-las 'Od-zer became the chief teacher of the queen. To all the masters and disciples of the rNying-ma monasteries of Kaḥ-thog, Zhe-chen, and rDzogs-chen, he taught everything he had received from the great 'Jigs-med Gling-pa: the rNying-ma Tantras, the "old and new" sNying-thig, and the Seven Treasures of Klong-chen-pa.

'Jigs-med Phrin-las 'Od-zer founded a monastery in rDza-chu-kha where 'Jigs-med rGyal-ba'i Myu-gu later resided. He then founded Shugs-chen sTag-mgo in rDo valley, and another monastery known as Yar-lung Padma-bkod in gSer-stod, where he remained for the rest of his days. Disciples and great leaders from Khams, sDe-dge, Amdo, 'Gu-log, rGyal-mo-rong, and Kokonor gathered around him like clouds.

Masters of all the eight practice lineages came to him for teachings. His major disciples included Kun-mkhyen mChog-gi sPrul-sku, gZhan-phan mTha'-yas, Grub-dbang Dam-tshig rDo-rje, and rDo-bla 'Jigs-med sKal-bzang. These lineage holders transmitted the teachings of 'Jigs-med Gling-pa in an unbroken stream down to the present day.

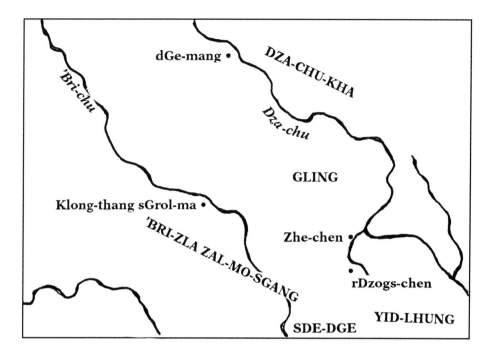

With the blessings of the Great Guru Padmasambhava, rDo-grub-chen Rinpoche discovered Realization Treasures, which are preserved in Great Treasures of Ancient Teachings, together with other works totaling twenty-one titles.

གཏེར་སྟོན་རྡོ་རྗེ་ཐོགས་མེད་བསྟན་འཛིན་ཟླ་འོད་རྡོ་རྗེ

gTer-ston rDo-rje Thogs-med bsTan-'dzin Zla-'od rDo-rje
1746–1796 C.E.
173 texts, 1,262 pages, Rin-chen gTer-mdzod: 1 text

An incarnation of gYu-sgra sNying-po, rDo-rje Thogs-med or bsTan-'dzin Zla-'od rDo-rje was born in Kong-po mTsho-chu Dar-ma-brag as the son of the Dwags-brgyud siddha 'Jam-dbyangs. Even as a child he performed ceremonies and while very young, discovered gTer-ma treasures. But he reconcealed them because conditions were not appropriate.

After meeting with sGam-po sPrul-sku, he discovered more gTer-ma following the treasure list he had located at sPu-bo 'Dod-chu temple. Some of these treasures he took from concealment in public, generating great faith in crowds of people. His discoveries included longevity practices and numerous practices to the three roots of guru, deva, and ḍākinī.

At Padma-bkod Byang-gling bTsan-phyug, he founded a hermitage and remained there for the rest of his life. The precious longevity practices were transmitted by his consort, the yoginī Zla-'od dBang-mo, who achieved the Rainbow Body. Kong-sprul received the essentials of these teachings from 'Jam-dbyangs mKhyen-brtse'i dBang-po. Great Treasures of Ancient Teachings contains one hundred and seventy-three texts by this great yogin.

## སེམས་དཔའ་ཆེན་པོ་འཇིགས་མེད་རྒྱལ་བའི་མྱུ་གུ

### Sems-dpa' Chen-po 'Jigs-med rGyal-ba'i Myu-gu
### ca. 1750–1825 C.E.
### 1 text, 89 pages

A chief disciple of 'Jigs-med Gling-pa, 'Jigs-med rGyal-ba'i Myu-gu was a great Bodhisattva known as Khra-ma Bla-ma. He practiced intensively at Tsā-ri and other places. After reaching profound realization under the guidance of the All-Knowing 'Jigs-med Gling-pa, he retired to Khra-ma in the rDza Valley, where he remained for twenty years, perfecting his understanding.

His most famous teaching is the Kun-bzang-bla-ma'i-zhal-lung, which was written down by his disciple, dPal-sprul Rinpoche. This text is dPal-sprul's record of the oral commentary on 'Jigs-med Gling-pa's sNying-thig Preliminary Practice made by his beloved master rGyal-ba'i Myu-gu, whom he regarded as Samantabhadra Buddha in person. The Kun-bzang-bla-ma'i-zhal-lung and the biography of this Bodhisattva are preserved in the Great Treasures of Ancient Teachings collection.

ཀཿཐོག་པ་ཀུན་བཟང་ངེས་དོན་དབང་པོ

Kaḥ-thog-pa Kun-bzang Nges-don dBang-po
mid-18th–early 19th century C.E.?
Rin-chen gTer-mdzod: 1 text

An incarnation of Padmasambhava's disciple gNubs-chen Sangs-rgyas Ye-shes, Kun-bzang Nges-don dBang-po was renowned as a great scholar. Though 'Jigs-med Gling-pa clearly indicated that he was a gTer-ma master, Kun-bzang Nges-don did not wish to live in the manner of a Tantric yogin, as most gTer-ma masters do, and so numerous treasures did not actually come to him. Nonetheless, he was blessed with Pure Vision treasures and Realization Treasures, a few of which Kong-sprul Blo-gros mTha'-yas received and was able to preserve in the Rin-chen gTer-mdzod.

# རྗེ་བཙུན་མ་འཕྲིན་ལས་ཆོས་སྒྲོན་

rJe-btsun-ma 'Phrin-las Chos-sgron
mid-18th–early 19th century C.E.
Rin-chen gTer-mdzod: 3 texts

The daughter of sMin-gling Khri-chen V 'Gyur-med Phrin-las rNam-rgyal, 'Phrin-las Chos-sgron was born toward the end of the eighteenth century in the time of 'Jigs-med Gling-pa. She was ordained as a nun and received from her father the precious sMin-grol-gling Atiyoga lineage that traced back to gTer-bdag Gling-pa. 'Phrin-las Chos-sgron bestowed these teachings on the great 'Jam-dbyang mKhyen-brtse dBang-po.

She composed explanations of the 'Pho-ba teachings on the transference of consciousness at death, and on Yamāntaka teachings discovered originally by Nyang-ral Nyi-ma 'Od-zer and preserved in the sMin-grol-gling tradition. She also assisted her brother, Khri-chen VI Padma dBang-rgyal, in composing explanations of Hayagrīva practices. These works are preserved in the Rin-chen gTer-mdzod.

# རྡོ་རྗེ་བྲག་རིག་འཛིན་དྲུག་པ་ཁམས་གསུམ་ཟིལ་གནོན་

rDo-rje-brag Rig-'dzin Drug-pa Khams-gsum Zil-gnon
mid-18th–early 19th century C.E.
Rin-chen gTer-mdzod: 1 text

Khams-gsum Zil-gnon was the sixth master in the lineage of the Vidyādharas who guided rDo-rje-brag. He belonged to the renowned succession that began with Rig-'dzin rGod-ldem and passed through Legs-ldan rDo-rje, Ngag-gi dBang-po, Padma Phrin-las, and sKal-bzang Padma dBang-phyug (1719–

1770). In Pure Visions, Khams-gsum Zil-gnon received precious longevity practices, which were preserved in the Rinchen gTer-mdzod by Kong-sprul Blo-gros mTha'-yas, but no other works by this master have recently been located.

པདྨ་ཕྲིན་ལས་བདུད་འཇོམས

## Padma Phrin-las bDud-'joms
mid-18th–early 19th century C.E.
6 texts, 139 pages

A disciple of Tshe-dbang Nor-bu, the outstanding polymath of Kaḥ-thog monastery, Padma Phrin-las bDud-'joms was the teacher of Brag-dkar rTa-so sPrul-sku and Tshe-dbang 'Chi-med mGon-po. He authored two works explicating the Vajrakīla practices of the Northern Treasures tradition and several texts on rituals. These works are preserved in the Great Treasures of Ancient Teachings, together with his biography, written by his disciple Tshe-dbang 'Chi-med mGon-po.

མདོ་ཆེན་པ་ཚེ་དབང་འཆི་མེད་མགོན་པོ

## mDo-chen-pa Tshe-dbang 'Chi-med mGon-po
1755–1807 C.E.
23 texts, 347 pages

Tshe-dbang 'Chi-med mGon-po was born at sKyid-grong in western Tibet as the son of Śrīnātha dPal-gyi mGon-po and Gyang-'dzom Bu-khrid. He received teachings from his father and from other rNying-ma and bKa'-brgyud masters. In particular he studied with Tshe-mchog-gling Yongs-'dzin Ye-shes rGyal-mtshan and Phrin-las bDud-'joms. The tradition that flowed through Tshe-dbang 'Chi-med mGon-po was known as the mDo-chen bKa'-brgyud or Ma-bdun tradition. 'Chi-med mGon-po composed the biography of his master Phrin-las bDud-'joms; his own biography was later completed by Brag-dkar rTa-so sPrul-sku. Twenty-three texts in the mDo-chen tradition are in Great Treasures of Ancient Teachings.

སྒམ་པོ་ཨོ་རྒྱན་འགྲོ་འདུལ་གླིང་པ་

sGam-po O-rgyan 'Gro-'dul Gling-pa
1757 C.E.
12 texts, 223 pages

The fifth incarnation of Dwags-lha sGam-po sPrul-sku, 'Gro-'dul Gling-pa was born in rGya-ri Sa-skyong Pho-brang as the son of 'Jigs-med dPal-bzang and Sri-thar dPal-joms. Enthroned as a young boy at sGam-po, he studied the worldly arts and sciences, gSar-ma teachings, and the bKa'-ma and gTer-ma of the rNying-ma school. He received teachings from gTer-chen bDe-chen rGyal-po at 'Brug-thang in Kong-po, and from other masters.

Frequenting the hidden valleys in central Tibet, he discovered numerous Avalokiteśvara teachings and other precious gTer-ma, including texts related to those discovered by rDo-rje Thogs-med. His teachings were continued by the incarnations of sGam-po sPrul-sku and the Son Lineage of rGyal-sras bDe-chen Gling-pa. Twelve works by this master are preserved in Great Treasures of Ancient Teachings.

ཤོག་པོ་དགེ་བཤེས་བསྟན་དར་བ

Sog-po dGe-bshes bsTan-dar-ba

1759 C.E.

1 text, 154 pages

A disciple of rDo-grub-chen 'Jigs-med Phrin-las 'Od-zer, Sog-po dGe-bshes bsTan-dar-ba composed a commentary on 'Jigs-med Gling-pa's Yon-tan-rin-po-che'i-mdzod. This text is included in the Great Treasures of Ancient Teachings in the collected works of Kun-mkhyen 'Jigs-med Gling-pa.

གཏེར་སྟོན་རང་གྲོལ་ཏིང་འཛིན་རྒྱལ་པོ་ཟླ་བའི་འོད་ཟེར

gTer-ston Rang-grol Ting-'dzin rGyal-po Zla-ba'i 'Od-zer

mid-18th–early 19th century C.E.

Rin-chen gTer-mdzod: 5 texts

A n incarnation of rGyal-sras lHa-rje, Zla-ba'i 'Od-zer was born in sGrags at Phu-skyu-ru-can as the son of Theg-gling 'Gro-don mThar-phyin (Dri-med Gling-pa) and a noble lady whose family belonged to the lineage of gNubs. His father bestowed vast gTer-ma teachings upon him and then passed away when Zla-ba'i 'Od-zer was only six. From lCags-zam-pa Ye-shes lHun-grub and Padma bsTan-'dzin rGya-mtsho he received the majority of the rNying-ma bKa'-ma and gTer-ma.

Zla-ba'i 'Od-zer entered the Dharma at dPal-ri monastery, taking refuge vows with the mTsho-rgyal sPrul-sku Padma Chos-'byor rGya-mtsho. In Pure Visions, Mandāravā blessed him with precious myrobalan seeds, and thereafter he became expert in the healing arts. He received teachings from Grub-chen Ngag-dbang Chos-grags and fulfilled his vow to practice intensively for five years at mChims-phu. After this, the teachings from his father began to blossom forth.

In visionary journeys he went to Nga-yab Padma 'Od and met with Thang-stong rGyal-po, whose blessings evoked abundant Pure Visions. Locating a treasure list at Brag-dmar mGrin-bzang, the birthplace of King Khri-srong lDe'u-btsan, he discovered gTer-ma at mChims-phu, including precious statues and texts. He practiced these teachings for seven years and then began to teach and offer empowerments and explanations to others. His major disciples included mKhyen-rab mThu-stobs, the Fourth rDzogs-chen Rinpoche Mi-'gyur Nam-mkha'i rDo-rje, and Shes-rab Blo-gros.

Honored by the government of central Tibet as a great incarnate gTer-ma master, Zla-ba'i 'Od-zer was able to bring about benefits for the people of the Land of Snow. Warding off evil influences, he repaired and reconsecrated sacred sites, taming the land and uplifting living beings. His next incarnation was born in Khams and resided at mChims-phu, spreading and increasing the teachings of Zla-ba'i 'Od-zer. Five texts by this master were preserved by Kong-sprul Blo-gros mTha'-yas in the Rin-chen gTer-mdzod.

དཔལ་རི་སྤྲུལ་སྐུ་པདྨ་ཆོས་འབྱོར་རྒྱ་མཚོ

dPal-ri sPrul-sku Padma Chos-'byor rGya-mtsho
mid-18th–early 19th century C.E.
Rin-chen gTer-mdzod: 2 texts

An incarnation of Ye-shes mTsho-rgyal, Padma Chos-'byor was a disciple of 'Jigs-med Gling-pa. He resided at dPal-ri Theg-mchog-gling and was known as dPal-ri mTsho-rgyal sPrul-sku. He bestowed teachings on gTer-ston Zla-ba'i 'Od-zer Ting-'dzin rGyal-po.

In Pure Visions Padma Chos-'byor discovered treasure teachings, such as the lHa-mo Tsaṇḍalī cycle of longevity practices. These precious practices passed from him to Zhabs-drung rDo-rje sNying-po, and then in succession to mTshung-ston bDe-chen rDo-rje, rJe gSang-sngags bsTan-'dzin (one of Zhe-chen Rab-'byams' main disciples), and 'Jam-dbyangs mKhyen-brtse. Kong-sprul preserved this text in the Rin-chen gTer-mdzod, as well as a text by gSang-sngags bsTan-'dzin.

gTer-ston Gar-dbang 'Chi-med rDo-rje
1763 C.E.
Rin-chen gTer-mdzod: 3 texts

Gar-dbang 'Chi-med rDo-rje was born in Mon as the son of sNgags-'chang dKon-mchog and the lady rGyal-sde. As a young child, his behavior was so remarkably holy that the local people were amazed by him. He was taken to sPu-bo rBa-kha monastery where he began his training. 'Brug-thang gTer-chen gave him refuge vows and named him Kun-bzang 'Od-zer Gar-dbang bsTan-pa'i Nyi-ma.

At sPu-bo rBa-kha monastery he came into the possession of treasure lists and proceeded to discover gTer-ma in the hidden valleys of Padma-bkod. For twelve years, he privately practiced these teachings, telling no one of his discoveries. The first person to whom he disclosed the teachings was sGam-po sPrul-sku, followed by sByor-ra Thams-cad mKhyen-pa, the holder of Bo-dong lineages and a disciple of 'Jigs-med Gling-pa. This treasure and another he discovered in dBus have been transmitted down to the present time.

Working in concert with Dwags-po gTer-ston, Gar-dbang 'Chi-med rDo-rje opened up major places in the great hidden valley, building stupas and temples in key locations and performing sādhanas in each place. He protected and benefited the people of the wild borderland regions of Mon and Glo. His incarnation lineage resided there in the hidden valley. Kong-sprul received his gTer-ma teachings and preserved three works in the Rin-chen gTer-mdzod.

མཁས་གྲུབ་ཆེན་པོ་ཀཿཐོག་དགེ་རྩེ་འགྱུར་མེད་ཚེ་དབང་མཆོག་གྲུབ

mKhas-grub Chen-po Kaḥ-thog dGe-rtse
'Gyur-med Tshe-dbang mChog-grub
1764 C.E.
8 texts, 745 pages

An incarnation of gNyags Jñānakumāra, Kaḥ-thog dGe-rtse Mahāpaṇḍita 'Gyur-med Tshe-dbang mChog-grub made an enormous contribution to the rNyingma School by cataloguing the sDe-dge edition of the rNying-ma-rgyud-'bum. After the texts had been assembled according to the advice of 'Jigs-med Gling-pa, the great Mahāpaṇḍita composed the dKar-chag. This outstanding scholar of Kaḥ-thog monastery also composed a commentary on the major Mahāyoga Tantra (the gSang-ba'i-snying-po), a commentary on an important text by Guru Padmasambhava on the stages of the Mantrayāna path, and several other works. Eight texts are contained in Great Treasures of Ancient Teachings.

331

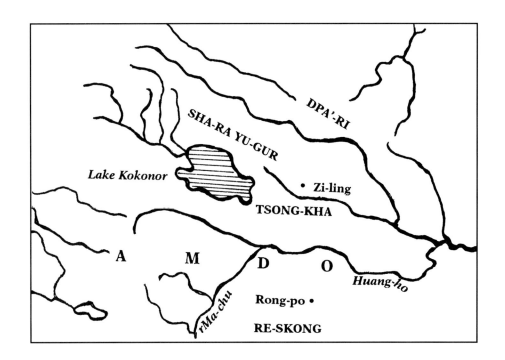

ཕྲག་དཀར་རྟ་སོ་སྤྲུལ་སྐུ་མི་ཕམ་ཚོས་ཀྱི་དབང་ཕྱུག

Brag-dkar rTa-so sPrul-sku
Mi-pham Chos-kyi dBang-phyug
1775 C.E.
42 texts, 490 pages

Disciple of Padma Phrin-las bDud-'joms, Mi-pham Chos-kyi dBang-phyug composed works associated with the cycles of the Northern Treasures, a biography of Tshe-dbang Nor-bu, and several other texts on lineage holders, together with collected practice explanations. Forty-two texts are preserved in Great Treasures of Ancient Teachings.

# ཚོས་རྒྱལ་ངག་གི་དབང་པོ

Chos-rgyal Ngag-gi dBang-po
18th century C.E.
2 texts, 259 pages

Considered an incarnation of Mar-pa Lo-tsā-ba, Ngag-gi dBang-po was a Mongolian prince of Kokonor descended from Gushri Khan. Because his uncle rDo-rje Pha-lam (d. 1770) died without a son to inherit his lands, Ngag-gi dBang-po succeeded him. But Ngag-gi dBang-po abandoned this domain to enter the Dharma, becoming a rNying-ma lineage holder of great learning and meditative accomplishment.

Knowledgeable in both gSar-ma and rNying-ma teachings, he received sNying-thig teachings from rDo-grub-chen Kun-bzang gZhan-phan. From gTer-ston Kun-bzang bDe-chen's disciple, O-rgyan bsTan-'dzin, he received Hayagrīva and Vārāhī treasure teachings, which he passed to Zhabs-dkar Tshogs-drug Rang-grol. He composed a lengthy explanation of rDzogs-chen, preserved in Great Treasures of Ancient Teachings.

# སེམས་དཔའ་ཆེན་པོ་ཞབས་དཀར་ཚོགས་དྲུག་རང་གྲོལ

Sems-dpa' Chen-po Zhabs-dkar Tshogs-drug Rang-grol
1781–1850 C.E.
29 texts, 1,403 pages

An incarnation of Atiyoga Vidyādhara Mañjuśrīmitra and of Mi-la Ras-pa, Tshogs-drug Rang-grol was born in the Rebkong area of A-mdo in the far northeast. He was dedicated to the Dharma from an early age and spent his childhood days reciting prayers and mantras. By the age of sixteen he had undertaken a one-year retreat; at twenty he received ordination. He heard teachings from 'Jam-dpal rDo-rje and 'Jam-dbyangs rGya-mtsho. As his root guru, he relied upon Chos-rgyal Ngag-gi dBang-po, who bestowed upon him all the essential instructions of the rNying-ma and gSar-ma traditions.

A wandering yogin, Zhabs-dkar spent years in solitary retreat, residing at rMa-chen sPom-ra in 'Gu-log, in Tsā-ri in southern Tibet, and at Mount Kailaśa in the west. He traveled to Nepal's Kathmandu valley where he covered the spire of the Boudhanath stupa in gold. Devoted to the teachings of Guru Padmasambhava, Atīśa, and Tsong-kha-pa, he envisioned all Dharma teachings as a perfect whole. His spiritual songs and life story and his lucid Dharma explanations have inspired generations of practitioners. Great Treasures of Ancient Teachings preserves twenty-nine works by this master.

Rig-'dzin Chos-rgyal rDo-rje
1789–1859 C.E.
27 texts, 287 pages, Rin-chen gTer-mdzod: 6 texts

An incarnation of King Khri-srong lDe'u-btsan's son, lHa-sras Mu-khri bTsad-po, Chos-rgyal rDo-rje was born in the nomad camps at mDo-stod dGe-rgyal. He was first a follower of the 'Brug-pa bKa'-brgyud tradition, receiving teachings from 'Brug-chen Rinpoche. The yogin and gTer-ston lHun-grub Rab-brtan (Rig-'dzin rNam-rgyal rDo-rje) gave him the distinctive teachings of the rNying-ma tradition. Chos-rgyal rDo-rje especially focused on the practices that gTer-ston Yongs-dge Mi-'gyur rDo-rje had discovered.

Chos-rgyal rDo-rje discovered gTer-ma in Pure Visions, as Realization Treasures, and also as Earth Treasures, which he located in the Black Stupa at bSam-yas. He found the relics of Lang-gro Lo-tsā-ba and other precious substances that brought wonderful benefits to sentient beings.

The teachings of this master continued to flourish until recent times. His disciples included mChog-gyur bDe-chen Gling-pa, mKhan-chen Zla-bzang Rinpoche, and his chief lineage holder Tshogs-gnyis Padma Dri-med 'Od-zer. Kong-sprul received gTer-ma teachings from Chos-rgyal rDo-rje himself and preserved six texts in the Rin-chen gTer-mdzod. An additional twenty-seven texts are contained in Great Treasures of Ancient Teachings.

འཁྲུལ་ཞིག་ཨོ་རྒྱན་རྣམ་རྒྱལ

'Khrul-zhig O-rgyan rNam-rgyal
mid-18th–early 19th century C.E.?
1 text, 68 pages

The master 'Khrul-zhig O-rgyan rNam-rgyal lived in the time of Zhabs-dkar sNa-tshogs Rang-grol and was associated with the stream of his teachings. He composed a work of several hundred folios explicating various practices especially connected to this lineage. This text is preserved in Great Treasures of Ancient Teachings.

# མཁས་གྲུབ་ངག་དབང་རྡོ་རྗེ་

mKhas-grub Ngag-dbang rDo-rje
mid-18th–early 19th century C.E.?
Rin-chen gTer-mdzod: 1 text

Born in E-yul at Rig-pa'i 'Byung-gnas, Ngag-dbang rDo-rje was associated with a rNying-ma monastery there known as E-ne Ring-nub, which followed the sMin-grol-gling traditions. His learning in Dharma and worldly subjects and his enlightened activity were extensive. Through the blessings of the lineage, he discovered Realization Treasure teachings on the three roots of guru, deva, and ḍākinī.

The Bo-dong master sByor-ra Thams-cad mKhyen-pa and Dwags-po sPrul-sku heard his gTer-ma teachings and bestowed them on others. Kong-sprul received some of these teachings and preserved one text in the Rin-chen gTer-mdzod.

རྫོགས་ཆེན་བཞི་པ་འཁྲུལ་ཞིག་མི་འགྱུར་ནམ་མཁའི་རྡོ་རྗེ

# rDzogs-chen bZhi-pa
## 'Khrul-zhig Mi-'gyur Nam-mkha'i rDo-rje
### 1793 C.E.

Mi-'gyur Nam-mkha'i rDo-rje guided the monastery of rDzogs-chen in the beginning of the nineteenth century. He was born in lDan-yul, the fourth in a particular series of emanations of Paṇ-chen Vimalamitra that began with rDzogs-chen Padma Rig-'dzin (1625–1679), the founder of rDzogs-chen monastery. Inspired by visions and predictions and guided by supernormal powers, Mi-'gyur Nam-mkha'i rDo-rje received gTer-ma teachings in Pure Visions, which he bestowed on fortunate disciples on many occasions. mChog-gyur bDe-chen Gling-pa continued these teachings, which are preserved in the Rin-chen gTer-mdzod.

# Part Nine


# Era of ’Jam-dbyangs mKhyen-brtse and ’Jam-mgon Kong-sprul

བགའ་བབས་བདུན་ལྡན་འཇམ་ད་དྱངས་མཁྱེན་བརྩེའི་དབང་པོ།

'Jam-dbyangs mKhyen-brtse'i dBang-po

# Nineteenth Century

Under the auspices of the "Two 'Jam-mgon," 'Jam-dbyangs mKhyen-brtse'i dBang-po and 'Jam-mgon Kong-sprul Blo-gros mTha'-yas, the teachings of the Ancient Ones were strengthened and revitalized during the nineteenth century. Inspiring a nonsectarian (ris-med) vision of Dharma especially in eastern Tibet, they were instrumental in training outstanding masters of all schools.

This era saw the appearance of a remarkable number of great rNying-ma leaders. Scholars, yogins, and masters of bKa'-ma and gTer-ma composed texts, founded monasteries, established philosophical colleges, fostered sacred art, and preserved the lineages during this century. The texts of the bKa'-ma were printed and essential gTer-ma texts were collected together and printed for the first time. The work of the great lamas of the nineteenth century made it possible for the teachings of the Ancient School to be successfully transmitted to the present day.

གཁས་གྲུབ་ཆེན་པོ་རྒྱལ་སྲས་གཞན་ཕན་མཐའ་ཡས

mKhas-grub Chen-po rGyal-sras gZhan-phan mTha'-yas
1800 C.E.
41 texts, 379 pages, Rin-chen gTer-mdzod: 1 text

An emanation of the seventeenth-century master gTer-bdag Gling-pa, rGyal-sras gZhan-phan mTha'-yas was the founder of Śrī Siṁha College, located at rDzogs-chen monastery. He was a disciple of 'Jigs-med rGyal-ba'i Myu-gu, and held the sNying-thig lineage as well as the complete teachings of gTer-bdag Gling-pa. Abbot of rDzogs-chen monastery and a leader of the scholastic tradition, gZhan-phan mTha'-yas revitalized the study and practice of Vinaya and encouraged the study of Sūtras and śāstras. It was due to his efforts that Śrī Siṁha College became a major center for rNying-ma teachings during the nineteenth century. His disciples included dPal-sprul Rinpoche and 'Jam-dbyangs mKhyen-brtse'i dBang-po.

gZhan-phan mTha'-yas was instrumental in preserving the texts and practices of the bKa'-ma tradition of sMin-grol-gling. Forty-one of gZhan-phan mTha'-yas's own works are preserved in Great Treasures of Ancient Teachings in addition to one text in the Rin-chen gTer-mdzod section.

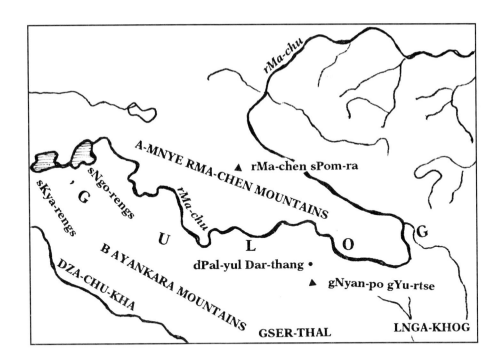

ཁས་གྲུབ་ཆེན་པོ་མདོ་མཁྱེན་བརྩེ་ཡེ་ཤེས་རྡོ་རྗེ

mKhas-grub Chen-po mDo-mkhyen-brtse Ye-shes rDo-rje

1800–1859 C.E.

54 texts, 429 pages

Born in 'Gu-log at the beginning of the nineteenth century, mDo-mkhyen-brtse Ye-shes rDo-rje was regarded as an incarnation of 'Jigs-med Gling-pa. This great siddha and gTer-ma master was also known as 'Ja'-lus rDo-rje. He was the disciple of the first rDo-grub-chen 'Jigs-med Phrin-las 'Od-zer.

mDo-mkhyen-brtse Ye-shes rDo-rje was the teacher of outstanding lamas, including dPal-sprul Rinpoche, the second rDo-drup-chen 'Jigs-med Phun-tshogs 'Byung-gnas, and Nyag-bla Padma bDud-'dul. His own sister Da-ki Blo-gsal dBang-mo and his son Sras Ral-gri were also his disciples. Fifty-four texts by this enlightened master, including his

343

gTerma treasures and autobiography, are preserved in the Great Treasures of Ancient Teachings collection.

སེམས་དཔའ་ཆེན་པོ་དཔལ་སྤྲུལ་ཨོ་རྒྱན་འཇིགས་མེད་ཆོས་ཀྱི་དབང་པོ

Sems-dpa' Chen-po dPal-sprul O-rgyan 'Jigs-med
Chos-kyi dBang-po
1808–1887 C.E.
112 texts, 911 pages, Rin-chen gTer-mdzod: 1 text

An incarnation of 'Jigs-med Gling-pa and also of Śāntideva, dPal-sprul O-rgyan 'Jigs-med Chos-kyi dBang-po was born in rDza-chu-kha in Khams. His teachers included 'Jigs-med rGyal-ba'i Myu-gu, gZhan-phan mTha'-yas, and mDo-mkhyen-brtse Ye-shes rDo-rje.

dPal-sprul Rinpoche was holder of the sNying-thig rTsa-lung practices of 'Jigs-med Gling-pa's lineage and the Hearing Lineage of the Ye-shes-bla-ma, 'Jigs-med Gling-pa's summary of the teachings of Klong-chen-pa. He transmitted these two lineages under rather special circumstances. Because dPal-sprul's mother was aged, he asked the great A-'dzom 'Brug-pa to guide her consciousness through the bar-do, and in return he offered A-'dzom Rinpoche these two precious oral lineages.

dPal-sprul Rinpoche was Dharma brother with the great 'Jam-dbyangs mKhyen-brtse, both having studied with Zhe-chen mThu-stobs rNam-rgyal. dPal-sprul Rinpoche sometimes resided at dGe-kong and rDzogs-chen, though he spent most of his life as a wandering yogin.

Among dPal-sprul's disciples were Lama Mi-pham, sNyo-shul Lung-rtogs, O-rgyan bsTan-'dzin Nor-bu, mKhan-po Kun-bzang dPal-ldan, and mKhan-po Yon-tan rGya-mtsho. His six Tibetan volumes of collected works include outlines and commentaries on key Madhyamaka, Abhidharma, Prajñāpāramitā,

344

and sDom-gsum works, commentaries on Maitreya texts, 'Jigs-med Gling-pa's Yon-tan-mdzod, the vehicles and stages of the Bodhisattva path, rDzogs-chen theory and practice, and many other subjects. One hundred and twelve works are preserved in Great Treasures of Ancient Teachings. Excerpts from some of his writings have been translated and published in *Footsteps on the Diamond Path* (Dharma Publishing, 1992).

འཇམ་མགོན་ཀོང་སྤྲུལ་བློ་གྲོས་མཐའ་ཡས་

'Jam-mgon Kong-sprul Blo-gros mTha'-yas
1813–1899 C.E.
886 texts, 7,993 pages, Rin-chen gTer-mdzod: 725 texts

An incarnation of Vairotsana, 'Jam-mgon Kong-sprul was clearly prophesied in the Sūtras and by Padmasambhava. He was born in the hidden valley of Rong-rgyab 'Bri-zla Zal-mo-sgang in Khams. His father was bsTan-'dzin gYung-drung of the Khyung-po clan. His mother was bKra-shis-mtsho.

Blo-gros mTha'-yas studied the traditional arts and sciences and the Sūtrayāna texts with Paṇḍita 'Gyur-med mThu-stobs rNam-rgyal of Zhe-chen monastery and T'ai Si-tu Padma Nyin-byed dBang-po. With fifty spiritual masters, the foremost among them being 'Jam-dbyangs mKhyen-brtse'i dBang-po, he pursued all eight practice lineages.

An extraordinary master of the Tibetan language, Kong-sprul composed hundreds of texts, which were gathered into five large collections known as the Five Treasures (mDzod-lnga): the Treasure that Embraces All Knowledge (Shes-bya-kun-la-khyab-pa'i-mdzod), the Treasure of Precious Instruction (gDams-ngag-mdzod), the Treasure of Mantra Lineages of Transmitted Precepts (bKa'-brgyud-sngags-mdzod), the

345

Treasure of Precious gTer-ma (Rin-chen gTer-mdzod), and the Extensive Treasure (rGya-chen-mdzod).

Kong-sprul resided at Tsa-'dra Rin-chen-brag near dPal-spungs monastery in sDe-dge. His activity was truly inconceivable. In his Chos-'byung, bDud-'joms Rinpoche describes Kong-sprul's life as if it were four lifetimes condensed into one: His career as an author was so vast that it seems he spent his entire life writing; his career as a teacher makes it appear that his entire life was spent giving instruction; his career as a practitioner gives the impression that all his days were spent on retreat; and likewise for his efforts to renovate monasteries, commission statues, and sponsor monastic communities.

Kong-sprul's efforts to search out rare gTer-ma lineages and compile the gTer-ma teachings into the Rin-chen gTer-mdzod were made in conjunction with mChog-gyur Gling-pa and 'Jam-dbyangs mKhyen-brtse. gTer-ston Las-rab Gling-pa also helped locate gTer-ma, while Kong-sprul himself discovered numerous treasures.

His disciples included the leaders of the six major rNying-ma monasteries as well as Sa-skya-pa, dGe-lug-pa, and bKa'-brgyud-pa masters. His foremost disciple was his master 'Jam-dbyangs mKhyen-brtse, and together they were renowned as "the Two 'Jam-mgon." Kong-sprul's entire teachings were passed to the Karmapa, the Ta'i Situ, the Sa-skya-pa master 'Jam-dbyangs Blo-gter dBang-po, rDzong-gsar mNga'-ris Chos-rje Kun-dga' 'Jam-dbyangs, Lama Mi-pham, Las-rab Gling-pa, 'Gyur-med Nges-don dBang-po, rJe-drung Phrin-las Byams-pa'i 'Byung-gnas, and to dGe-lug-pa masters Ye-shes Gong-'phel and Ngag-dbang Dam-chos rGya-mtsho.

Great Treasures of Ancient Teachings preserves eight hundred and eighty-six works by Kong-sprul Blo-gros mTha'-yas, as well as over seven hundred texts he himself composed and added to the Rin-chen gTer-mdzod.

ཨོ་རྒྱན་བསྟན་འཛིན་ནོར་བུ

O-rgyan bsTan-'dzin Nor-bu

early 19th–mid-19th century C.E.

8 texts, 206 pages

A nephew of the great gZhan-phan mTha'-yas and disciple of dPal-sprul Rinpoche, O-rgyan bsTan-'dzin Nor-bu received the sNying-thig lineage from his master. He composed a text on his own yogic experiences and a commentary on a famous prayer by Karma Chags-med, and several other works. Eight texts are preserved in the Great Treasures of Ancient Teachings collection.

མཁན་ཆེན་ལུང་རྟོགས་བསྟན་པའི་ཉི་མ

mKhan-chen Lung-rtogs bsTan-pa'i Nyi-ma

early 19th–mid-19th century C.E.

451 texts, 2,338 pages

The master mKhan-chen Lung-rtogs bsTan-pa'i Nyi-ma was a disciple of dPal-sprul Rinpoche and a holder of the Klong-chen-snying-thig lineage. He was also known as Ngag-chen. The entire nine-volume collected works of mKhan-chen Lung-rtogs is preserved in Great Treasures of Ancient Teachings. His major disciple was Ngag-dbang dPal-bzang.

གསལ་ཆེན་པདྨ་བཛྲ

mKhan-chen Padmavajra

early 19th–mid-19th century C.E.

68 texts, 324 pages

Master of rDzogs-chen monastery, Padmavajra was one of
the chief disciples of gZhan-phan mTha'-yas and transmitted lineages to mKhyen-brtse'i dBang-po and rDo-grub-
chen 'Jigs-med bsTan-pa'i Nyi-ma. Holder of the sNying-thig
lineage, he wrote widely on subjects ranging from Prajñāpāramitā to the Inner Yogas. Great Treasures of Ancient
Teachings contains sixty-eight texts by this master.


གསལ་ཆེན་མི་ཉག་ཀུན་བཟང་བསོད་ནམས་ཐུབ་བསྟན་ཆོས་ཀྱི་གྲགས་པ

mKhan-chen Mi-nyag Kun-bzang bSod-nams

Thub-bstan Chos-kyi Grags-pa

d. 1901 C.E.

2 texts, 28 pages

A scholar from Mi-nyag, Kun-bzang bSod-nams Thub-bstan
was trained in the dGe-lugs-pa tradition and later became
a disciple of dPal-sprul Rinpoche and 'Jam-dbyangs mKhyen-
brtse. He composed two commentaries, one for a Sūtra on the
Three Jewels and another for the Śīlasaṁyukta Sūtra. Both
texts are preserved in Great Treasures of Ancient Teachings.

རིག་འཛིན་ཀུན་བཟང་ངེས་དོན་ཀློང་ཡངས་རྡོ་རྗེ་གསང་བ་རྩལ།

Rig-'dzin Kun-bzang Nges-don Klong-yangs

rDo-rje gSang-ba-rtsal

1814 C.E.

3 texts, 195 pages

Born in Kong-po at the beginning of the nineteenth century, Kun-bzang Nges-don Klong-yangs composed an autobiography and a history of the rNying-ma school, both of which are preserved in Great Treasures of Ancient Teachings.

ཉག་བླ་སྒྲུབ་ཆེན་འཇའ་ལུས་པ་པདྨ་བདུད་འདུལ།

Nyag-bla Grub-chen 'Ja'-lus-pa Padma bDud-'dul

1816–1872 C.E.

350 texts, 920 pages

Born in Nyag-rong west of sDe-dge in Khams, Padma bDud-'dul became an outstanding practitioner, a true siddha. He shared teachings with the Fourth rDzogs-chen Rinpoche Mi-'gyur Nam-mkha'i rDo-rje, mDo-mkhyen-brtse Ye-shes rDo-rje, Kaḥ-thog Situ, dPal-sprul Rinpoche, sNyo-shul Lung-rtogs, A-'dzom 'Brug-pa, and Rin-chen Gling-pa. A master of Bodhisattva practices, Padma bDud-'dul had frequent visions of Padmasambhava. He received the precious Atiyoga sNying-thig lineages, and through perfecting the practices, attained the Rainbow Body, the complete transformation of body, speech, and mind into Enlightenment. Lama Mi-pham and 'Jam-dbyangs mKhyen-brtse confirmed the authenticity of this accomplishment, which took place when Padma bDud-'dul was fifty-six. His collected works, numbering three hundred and fifty texts, are preserved in the Great Treasures of Ancient Teachings collection.

ཨོ་རྒྱན་གཞན་ཕན་མཐའ་ཡས

O-rgyan gZhan-phan mTha'-yas
1817–1875 C.E.
2 texts, 173 pages

A disciple of Tshogs-gnyis Rinpoche, O-rgyan gZhan-phan mTha'-yas composed songs of realization and an autobiography that are preserved in the Great Treasures of Ancient Teachings collection.

པདྨ་ཆོས་འཕེལ

Padma Chos-'phel
early 19th–mid-19th century C.E.
67 texts, 453 pages

This author composed biographies and prayers to the outstanding masters of the dKon-mchog-spyi-'dus lineage. Associated with the lineage of rDo-rje Thogs-med, he composed the biography of the reincarnation of rDo-rje Thogs-med, O-rgyan bDud-'dul dBang-drag. He wrote works on Bodhisattva and Vajrayāna practice. Sixty-seven texts are preserved in Great Treasures of Ancient Teachings.

ཀུན་མཁྱེན་བསྟན་པའི་ཉི་མ

Kun-mkhyen bsTan-pa'i Nyi-ma
early 19th–mid-19th century C.E.?
1 text, 55 pages

Not much is known about the identity of this author, but his commentary on advanced Tantric meditation practices is highly respected and widely studied. This work is preserved in Great Treasures of Ancient Teachings.

བཀའ་བབས་བདུན་ལྡན་འཇམ་དབྱངས་མཁྱེན་བརྩེའི་དབང་པོ

bKa'-babs bDun-ldan
'Jam-dbyangs mKhyen-brtse'i dBang-po
1820–1892 C.E.
411 texts, 4,452 pages, Rin-chen gTer-mdzod: 230 texts

The Fifth gTer-ston King, 'Jam-dbyangs mKhyen-brtse'i dBang-po was an incarnation of 'Jigs-med Gling-pa and King Khri-srong lDe'u-bstan. Born in Dil-mgo near sDe-dge as the son of Rin-chen sBang-rgyal of the gNyos clan, he was ordained by Rig-'dzin bZang-po of sMin-grol-gling. He studied with one hundred and fifty Tantric and academic scholars, mastering all fields of philosophy, rNying-ma and gSar-ma Tantras, and the special teachings of the eight practice lineages. He thoroughly practiced each of the doctrines that he studied, without confusing the methods or theories. mKhyen-brtse Rinpoche founded temples, published texts, erected stupas and statues, and sponsored rituals and prayers, supporting the Sangha in innumerable ways.

'Jam-dbyangs mKhyen-brtse held all the Seven Streams of the rNying-ma teachings: He received the bKa'-ma transmission through the blessings of Guru Padmasambhava. His Earth Treasures included major texts of all kinds, some of which were jointly discovered by mKhyen-brtse and mChog-gyur Gling-pa. Reconcealed Treasures included many texts that he found with the support of Kong-sprul Blo-gros mTha'-yas. Realization Treasures included the teachings of Thang-stong rGyal-po. Memory Treasures included the teachings of lCe-btsun Seng-ge dBang-phyug, the great rDzogs-chen master whom 'Jam-dbyangs mKhyen-brtse had been in the tenth century. 'Jam-dbyangs mKhyen-brtse also discovered Pure Vision Treasures and Hearing Treasures.

Great Treasures of Ancient Teachings contains over four hundred works by 'Jam-dbyangs mKhyen-brtse, in addition to more than two hundred works in the Rin-chen gTer-mdzod section. His precious teachings have come down to the present time through disciples including Kong-sprul Blo-gros mTha'-yas and Lama Mi-pham, and through five incarnation lineages that continue today to benefit living beings.

Tshogs-gnyis Padma Dri-med 'Od-zer

1828 C.E.

40 texts, 268 pages, Rin-chen gTer-mdzod: 3 texts

Chief disciple of Chos-rgyal rDo-rje and the teacher of bDud-'joms Drag-sngags Gling-pa, Tshogs-gnyis Padma Dri-med 'Od-zer was born in Nang-chen. He was also closely associated with mChog-gyur Gling-pa. Forty works composed by him on Tantric practice are preserved in Great Treasures of Ancient Teachings, with several additional texts in the Rin-chen gTer-mdzod section.

# གཏེར་ཆེན་མཆོག་གྱུར་བདེ་ཆེན་ཞིག་པོ་གླིང་པ

gTer-chen mChog-gyur bDe-chen Zhig-po Gling-pa

1829–1870 C.E.

951 texts, 5,987 pages, Rin-chen gTer-mdzod: 267 texts

This outstanding nineteenth-century gTer-ston was born in sGom-sde Grwa-nang at Yer-stod in southern mDo-khams as the son of the Tantric practitioner Padma dBang-phyug in the A-lcags 'Bru lineage. mChog-gyur bDe-chen Gling-pa was an incarnation of Mu-rub bTsad-po, the son of Khri-srong lDe'u-btsan (lHa-sras Dam-'dzin Rol-pa Ye-shes-rtsal).

He was given lay vows by sTag-lung Ma Rinpoche. His first teachers were dPa'-bo gTsug-lag, the Karmapa, the heads of the 'Brug-pa and 'Bri-gung-pa schools, the abbot of Zur-mang, Si-tu Padma Nyin-byed, Karma Nges-don, and Kong-sprul Blo-gros mTha'-yas. He became the close disciple and associate of mKhyen-brtse'i dBang-po and shared with him the authorization over the Seven Streams of the rNying-ma teachings.

The first stream is the bKa'-ma transmission of the Inner Tantras. The second through seventh streams are gTer-ma transmissions: the Earth Treasures, Reconcealed Treasures, Realization Treasures, Memory Treasures, Pure Vision Treasures, and Hearing Treasures. mChog-gyur bDe-chen Gling-pa received the transmissions of most of the bKa'-ma teachings in existence. His major gTer-ma teachings include the rDzogs-chen-sde-gsum, seven cycles of Zhi-byed teachings, Thugs-sgrub-bar-chad-kun-sel, twenty-four meditation guides, and many other priceless teachings. Most of his discoveries were made in public, inspiring thousands of people.

mChog-gyur Gling-pa taught masters and lamas of the Karma bKa'-brgyud-pa, 'Brug-pa, 'Bri-gung-pa, Sa-skya-pa, and sTag-lung-pa schools, as well as the most prominent rNying-ma masters of the six major monasteries. He estab-

353

lished elaborate and powerful ceremonies at dPal-spungs, Kaḥ-thog, and rDzogs-chen monasteries. Kong-sprul Blo-gros mTha'-yas and 'Jam-dbyangs mKhyen-brtse were especially devoted to his teachings.

He resided at Karma Ri in Nang-chen, at gNas-brtan-sgang in Khyung-po, and at rTsi-ke 'Dus-mdo in Nang-chen. At the last two locations, he established philosophical and Tantric colleges. His successors were ten masters who spread his teachings extensively in lineages that have continued to the present. Nine hundred and fifty-one texts are preserved in Great Treasures of Ancient Teachings, with more than two hundred and fifty texts in the Rin-chen gTer-mdzod section.

བླ་མ་གཏེར་བདུད་འཛོམས་གླིང་པ་ཁྲག་འཐུང་ནུས་ལྡན་རྡོ་རྗེ

sGas-gter bDud-'joms Gling-pa
Khrag-'thung Nus-ldan rDo-rje
1835–1904 C.E.
1,121 texts, 3,068 pages

The first bDud-'joms Rinpoche, bDud-'joms Gling-pa, also known as sGas-le gTer-ston, was born in 'Gu-log gSer-thal. He had seven sons, all of whom were famous incarnations, such as rDo-grub-chen bsTan-pa'i Nyi-ma. Thirteen disciples of bDud-'joms Gling-pa became highly accomplished practitioners. During his lifetime, bDud-'joms Gling-pa discovered many hundreds of treasures. One thousand one hundred and twenty-one of his texts are included in the Great Treasures of Ancient Teachings. His next incarnation was bDud-'joms Rinpoche 'Jigs-bral Ye-shes rDo-rje.

ཤུག་གསེབ་རྗེ་བཙུན་མ་ཆོས་ཉིད་བཟང་མོ

Shug-gseb rJe-btsun-ma Chos-nyid bZang-mo
1841–1951 C.E.
1 text, 141 pages

Born near Rewalsar mTsho Padma, Chos-nyid bZang-mo was the disciple of gTer-chen Chos-kyi rGyal-po mDo-sngags Gling-pa, Dharma Seng-ge, Sems-nyid rTogs-ldan Rinpoche of dPal-sprul's lineage, and many other masters. From them she received the bKa'-ma and gTer-ma transmissions, as well as the oral lineages. For much of her life, she remained on retreat at Shug-gseb, where today the lineage holders continue unbroken and a nunnery is very successful. A highly respected master of both Yang-tig-nag-po and sNying-thig teachings, she lived for over one hundred years. Her biography is preserved in Great Treasures of Ancient Teachings.

ཨ་འཛོམ་འབྲུག་པ་རིན་པོ་ཆེ་རིག་འཛིན་སྣ་ཚོགས་རང་གྲོལ

A-'dzom 'Brug-pa Rinpoche
Rig-'dzin sNa-tshogs Rang-grol
1842–1924 C.E.
148 texts, 935 pages

A reincarnation of rMa Rin-chen-mchog, sNa-tshogs Rang-grol took the refuge vows with Zhe-chen mThu-stobs rNam-rgyal, the great lama who had taught 'Jam-dbyangs mKhyen-brtse, Kong-sprul Blo-gros mTha'-yas, and dPal-sprul Rinpoche. With Kaḥ-thog Si-tu he began preliminary practices, followed by intensive study and practice of the teachings of

Klong-gsal sNying-po and bDud-'dul rDo-rje. At dPal-yul monastery, Padma mDo-sngags bsTan-'dzin and other teachers gave him further teachings of great gTer-ma masters, and he began to have visions of Ye-shes mTsho-rgyal. Kaḥ-thog Si-tu and Kaḥ-thog rMog-tsha continued to guide the remarkable young meditator, until at last Si-tu Rinpoche sent him to 'Jam-dbyangs mKhyen-brtse.

The great mKhyen-brtse dBang-po bestowed the lCe-btsun-snying-thig teachings upon A-'dzom 'Brug-pa, and advised him to take up the lifestyle of a gTer-ston in order to make important discoveries. Nyag-bla Padma bDud-'dul gave him the same advice. Later in life he did indeed discover treasures, which have been passed down continuously to the present day.

On thirty occasions, A-'dzom 'Brug-pa received teachings from 'Jam-dbyangs mKhyen-brtse dBang-po. From Kong-sprul he received the entire Rin-chen gTer-mdzod. A-'dzom 'Brug-pa was the sole holder of the oral lineages of 'Jigs-med Gling-pa's Ye-shes Bla-ma, and the sNying-thig-rtsa-lung practices, which he had received from dPal-sprul Rinpoche. 'Jigs-med Gling-pa also appeared to A-'dzom in visions and taught him directly.

Residing at A-'dzom-sgar in Khrom-khog, A-'dzom 'Brug-pa taught Atiyoga to fortunate disciples and gave blessings and guidance to ordinary people. A-'dzom 'Brug-pa and Lama Mi-pham, both disciples of 'Jam-dbyangs mKhyen-brtse, were close friends who admired and inspired one another greatly. Among the numerous masters with whom A-'dzom 'Brug-pa exchanged initiations were Nyag-bla Padma bDud-'dul, Śākya Śrī, Ra-mgo sPrul-sku, rDzogs-chen Thub-bstan Chos-kyi rDo-rje, Zhe-chen rGyal-tshab, Zhe-chen Rab-'byams VI, rDzong-gsar mKhyen-brtse, mDo Rinpoche, Zhe-chen Bai-ro, dGe-mang mKhan-po Yon-dga', and mKhan Rinpoche. The queen of Bhutan and the king of lCag-la came for teachings and blessings, as did the leaders of lHa-sa, 'Gu-log, Ser-thal, sDe-dge, Gling-tshang, Dar-rtse-mdo, and even Khu-nur in India.

His major disciples were his sons, 'Gyur-med rDo-rje and Padma dBang-rgyal. 'Gyur-med rDo-rje received comprehensive transmission of the Inner Yoga lineages from his father. One hundred forty-eight texts by A-'dzom 'Brug-pa are preserved in Great Treasures of Ancient Teachings.

# འཇམ་མགོན་བླ་མ་མི་ཕམ་རྣམ་རྒྱལ་རྒྱ་མཚོ

'Jam-mgon Bla-ma Mi-pham rNam-rgyal rGya-mtsho
1846–1912 C.E.
322 texts, 5,848 pages, Rin-chen gTer-mdzod: 3 texts

Mi-pham 'Jam-dbyangs rNam-rgyal rGya-mtsho, known as Lama Mi-pham and 'Ju Mi-pham, was born at Ya-chu'i-ding-chung on the rDza-chu river as the son of mGon-po Dar-rgyas of the lHa clan of 'Ju. As a young man, he studied at a branch of Zhe-chen monastery. His masters included dPal-sprul and 'Jam-dbyangs mKhyen-brtse, Kong-sprul, Padma Vajra, who was the preceptor at rDzogs-chen monastery, and Blo-gter-dbang-po. 'Jam-dbyangs mKhyen-brtse regarded him as his successor.

Lama Mi-pham discovered no Earth Treasures, but many of his treatises are considered to be Realization Treasures. Inspired by Mañjuśrī, Lama Mi-pham's knowledge was truly comprehensive: He composed thirty-five volumes on such diverse topics as logic, philosophy, astrology, cosmology, painting, sculpture, engineering, chemistry, alchemy, medicine, meditation, and Tantra. His writings can be classified into four general subjects: eulogies and narratives, common arts and sciences, the inner science of Buddhist philosophy, and prayers and benedictions.

His works include a commentary on the ninth chapter of the Bodhicaryāvatāra; a dictionary of Tibetan and Sanskrit equivalents for the philosophical and psychological concepts of rDzogs-chen; a commentary on the Kāvyādarśa; writings on ancient methods of divination; and transcriptions of oral versions of the Ge-sar epic.

Among Lama Mi-pham's principal disciples were rDo-grub-chen 'Jigs-med bsTan-pa'i Nyi-ma, Las-rab Gling-pa, the Fifth rDzogs-chen sPrul-sku Thub-bstan Chos-kyi rDo-rje, rDzogs-chen dGe-mang rGyal-sras, Kaḥ-thog Si-tu Chos-kyi rGya-mtsho, Zhe-chen Rab-'byams sNang-mdzad Grub-pa'i rDo-rje, Zhe-chen rGyal-tshab Padma rNam-rgyal, Kun-bzang dPal-ldan, dPal-yul rGya-sprul, A-'dzom 'Brug-pa, and Grub-dbang rTogs-ldan Śākya Śrī. Great Treasures of Ancient Teachings contains three hundred and twenty-two texts by this outstanding master.

ཉག་བླ་རང་རིག་རྡོ་རྗེ

Nyag-bla Rang-rig rDo-rje
1847–1903 C.E.
2 texts, 92 pages

R ang-rig rDo-rje was born in Nyag-rong. He married into the family of the sMin-grol-gling lineage holders, and his sons were sMin-grol-gling masters. He composed an autobiography that is preserved in the Great Treasures collection.

ཁཁན་ཆེན་ཀུན་བཟང་དཔལ་ལྡན

mKhan-chen Kun-bzang dPal-ldan
early 19th–mid-19th century C.E.
9 texts, 409 pages

Residing in Ge-kong in rDza-chu-kha in Khams, Kun-bzang dPal-ldan, also known as Kun-dpal, was the disciple of dPal-sprul, Lama Mi-pham, dPal-sprul's disciple bsTan-'dzin Nor-bu, and Kaḥ-thog Si-tu Chos-kyi rGya-mtsho. For many years, he served as abbot of the philosophical college at Kaḥ-thog. His major disciples included Bod-pa Tulku, 'Jam-dbyangs mKhyen-brtse Chos-kyi Blo-gros, mKhan-po Nus-ldan, and mKhan-po Ngag-chung. He composed a biography of Lama Mi-pham, a commentary on the Yon-tan-mdzod, and a commentary on the Bodhicaryāvatāra. Nine texts by mKhan-chen Kun-dpal are preserved in Great Treasures of Ancient Teachings.

གྲུབ་དབང་རྟོགས་ལྡན་ཤཱཀྱ་ཤྲཱི

Grub-dbang rTogs-ldan Śākya Śrī
1853–1913 C.E.
72 texts, 180 pages

Disciple of A-'dzom 'Brug-pa, 'Jam-dbyangs mKhyen-brtse, and Lama Mi-pham, the accomplished siddha Śākya Śrī was a well-known master of rDzogs-chen and Mahāmudrā who taught with great success in Bhutan and Tsā-ri. He composed seventy-two texts in Great Treasures of Ancient Teachings.

# ཉག་བླ་བསོད་རྒྱལ་གཏེར་སྟོན་ལས་རབ་གླིང་པ

Nyag-bla bSod-rgyal gTer-ston Las-rab Gling-pa
1856–1926 C.E.
912 texts, 2,942 pages

A disciple of 'Jam-dbyangs mKhyen-brtse'i dBang-po, Kong-sprul, and A-'dzom 'Brug-pa, Las-rab Gling-pa worked with Kong-sprul Blo-gros mTha'-yas and mKhyen-brtse to uncover gTer-ma treasures for the Rin-chen gTer-mdzod. From dPal-sprul's disciple sNyo-shul Lung-rtogs and from 'Jam-dbyangs mKhyen-brtse, he received the Klong-chen-snying-thig lineage. He bestowed his Vajkrakīla lineage on the Thirteenth Dalai Lama. Nine hundred and twelve texts, including his gTer-ma discoveries, are contained in Great Treasures of Ancient Teachings.

# མཁན་ཆེན་འགྱུར་མེད་ཕན་བདེའི་འོད་ཟེར

mKhan-chen 'Gyur-med Phan-bde'i 'Od-zer
early 19th–mid-19th century C.E.
1 text, 139 pages

A n emanation of Vajrapāṇi, 'Gyur-med Phan-bde'i 'Od-zer was the Throne Holder of sMin-grol-gling monastery. He held the sMin-grol-gling lineage of the bKa'-ma, which had been transmitted to him by mDo-sngags bsTan-'dzin Nor-bu, mDo-khams Gyang-mkhar sPrul-sku. He composed an important commentary on the major Mahāyoga Tantra, the gSang-ba'i-snying-po, which is preserved in Great Treasures of Ancient Teachings. He was one of the teachers of 'Jigs-'bral Ye-shes rDo-rje bDud-'joms Rinpoche.

རྡོ་གྲུབ་ཆེན་འཇིགས་མེད་བསྟན་པའི་ཉི་མ།

rDo-grub-chen 'Jigs-med bsTan-pa'i Nyi-ma

1865–1926 C.E.

99 texts, 1,008 pages

Born into the A-lcags 'Bru clan as the son of bDud-'joms Gling-pa, 'Jigs-med bsTan-pa'i Nyi-ma was the Third rDo-grub-chen Rinpoche. He received teachings from dPal-sprul Rinpoche, 'Jam-dbyangs mKhyen-brtse'i dBang-po, and Kong-sprul Blo-gros mTha'-yas. He became learned in the Sūtras and śāstras, and held the Klong-chen-snying-thig lineage.

'Jigs-med bsTan-pa'i Nyi-ma was an outstanding scholar, practitioner, and teacher whose disciples included four famous scholars renowned as the Four mKhan-pos of rDo-grub-chen. He composed a commentary on the major Mahāyoga Tantra, the gSang-ba'i-snying-po. Ninety-nine works are preserved in Great Treasures of Ancient Teachings.

མཁས་གྲུབ་ཆེན་པོ་གཡུ་ཁོག་བྱ་བྲལ་ཆོས་དབྱིངས་རང་གྲོལ།

mKhas-grub Chen-po gYu-khog Bya-bral

Chos-dbyings Rang-grol

c. 1870–c. 1950 C.E.

2 texts, 97 pages

An incarnation of Vimalamitra, gYu-khog Bya-bral was an outstanding master of rDzogs-chen. He was a disciple of the master A-'dzom 'Brug-pa, who transmitted to him the lCe-btsun-snying-thig teachings and oral sNying-thig teachings. He also received blessings and teachings from Las-rab Gling-pa and Lama Mi-pham. gYu-khog Bya-bral resided in gSer-khog, living as a yogin, His disciples focused on Lama Mipham's commentaries and sNying-thig practices. They numbered in the thousands, and all became accomplished yogins and scholars. Among his disciples were 'Jigs-med dPal-ldan (rGya-ngag Bla-ma) and sDzi-rong Bla-ma mChogldan. gYu-khog Bya-bral composed commentaries on the gSang-ba'i-snying-po and wrote sngon-'gro texts. Only a few small works, extraordinary in their depth of understanding, remain today. Two texts are preserved in the Great Treasures collection.

མཁན་ཆེན་གཞན་ཕན་ཆོས་ཀྱི་སྣང་བ

## mKhan-chen gZhan-phan Chos-kyi sNang-ba
### 1871–1927 C.E.
### 35 texts, 913 pages

Incarnation of the great gZhan-phan mTha'-yas, gZhan-phan Chos-kyi sNang-ba was a disciple of bsTan-'dzin Nor-bu, the direct disciple of dPal-sprul Rinpoche. Also known as mKhan-po gZhan-dga', he was an outstanding preceptor of Śrī Siṁha College at rDzogs-chen monastery in the early twentieth century. He created commentaries on thirteen fundamental śāstras based on the works of the great Indian commentators. This non-sectarian collection provided a foundation for Dharma studies, not only for the rNying-ma but for the bKa'-brgyud and Sa-skya as well. He spent the greater part of his life teaching the śāstras at colleges in Khams such as rDzong-gsar. His commentaries and several other texts totaling thirty-five works are preserved in Great Treasures of Ancient Teachings.

# ཞི་ཆེན་རྒྱལ་ཚབ་པདྨ་འགྱུར་མེད་རྣམ་རྒྱལ་

Zhe-chen rGyal-tshab Padma 'Gyur-med rNam-rgyal
1871–1926 C.E.
54 texts, 2,714 pages, Rin-chen gTer-mdzod: 3 texts

Padma 'Gyur-med rNam-rgyal was born in lHo-khog-rdzong. Recognized as a lineage holder of Zhe-chen monastery, he became the disciple of rDzogs-chen mKhan-po, Zhe-chen Rab-'byams, 'Jam-dbyangs mKhyen-brtse, and Kong-sprul Blo-gros mTha'-yas. His other outstanding masters included dPal-sprul Rinpoche, Lama Mi-pham, mChog-gyur Gling-pa, Kaḥ-thog Si-tu, dPal-yul rGya-sprul, Padma Dam-chos 'Od-zer, Khro-shul mKhan-po Tshul-khrims rGya-mtsho, Kun-bzang dPal-ldan, mKhan-po Yong-dga', rMe-ba Chos-grub, bKra-shis Chos-'phel, Karma mKhan-chen bKra-shis 'Od-zer, dPal-ldan Chos-rgyal, mChog-sprul Orgyan Tshe-ring Rig-'dzin, and sMin-gling rJe-bstun-ma 'Gyur-med Chos-sgron.

From these masters he received the Sūtra and Mantra lineages, the bKa'-ma and gTer-ma traditions of the rNying-ma school, the complete teachings of Klong-chen-pa, Rong-zom Mahāpaṇḍita, and gTer-bdag Gling-pa, as well as the doctrines of Mar-pa and Mi-la Ras-pa.

Padma 'Gyur-med rNam-rgyal was an extremely learned master and a profound practitioner. His major disciples included mKhyen-brtse Chos-kyi Blo-gros and Zhe-chen Kong-sprul. Zhe-chen rGyal-tshab composed thirteen volumes of texts, all of which are preserved in Great Treasures of Ancient Teachings. His comprehensive explanation of mind training (blo-sbyong) and Bodhicitta practices has been translated into English as *Path of Heroes* (Dharma Publishing, 1995).

པདྨ་བདེ་བའི་རྒྱལ་པོ།

Padma bDe-ba'i rGyal-po

1873–1933 C.E.

42 texts, 443 pages

Master of rDzogs-pa-chen-po who was born in A-mdo and associated with Brag-dmar Khyung-rdzong hermitage, Padma bDe-ba'i rGyal-po was a lineage holder of bDud-'joms Gling-pa's teachings. He was very successful in mNga'-ris in the western part of Tibet, and his students became accomplished practitioners. Padma bDe-ba'i rGyal-po composed forty-two texts preserved in Great Treasures of Ancient Teachings.

མཁན་ཆེན་ངག་དབང་དཔལ་བཟང༌།

mKhan-chen Ngag-dbang dPal-bzang

1879–1941 C.E.

20 texts, 859 pages

Kaḥ-thog mKhan-po Ngag-dbang dPal-bzang, also known as mKhan-po Ngag-chung and as Padma Las-'brel-rtsal, was an incarnation of Shud-pu dPal-gyi Seng-ge, disciple of Padmasambhava. He was the disciple of Kun-bzang dPal-ldan, Lung-rtog bsTan-pa'i Nyi-ma, and Kaḥ-thog Situ.

A learned philosopher, outstanding scholar, and well-known master of rDzogs-chen, mKhan-po Ngag-chung was the principal teacher at Kaḥ-thog during his lifetime. He gave teachings to the abbot of Dar-thang monastery, mChog-sprul Chos-kyi Zla-ba, and to Bya-bral Sangs-rgyas rDo-rje, among many others. Ngag-dbang dPal-bzang composed commentaries on Madhyamaka and rDzogs-chen, and notes on the

Kun-bzang-bla-ma'i-zhal-lung teachings of rGyal-ba'i Myu-gu. Twenty works by this author are preserved in Great Treasures of Ancient Teachings.

## གཏེར་གི་ཤི་ཏུ་ཆོས་ཀྱི་རྒྱ་མཚོ

### Kaḥ-thog Si-tu Chos-kyi rGya-mtsho
### 1880–1925 C.E.
### 4 texts, 456 pages

Kaḥ-thog Si-tu Chos-kyi rGya-mtsho was a disciple of the First 'Jam-dbyangs mKhyen-brtse and Lama Mi-pham and a teacher of the Second 'Jam-dbyangs mKhyen-brtse. He was a holder of the sMin-grol-gling Vinaya and Bodhisattva lineages, and received 'Jigs-med Gling-pa's Klong-chen-snying-thig lineage from 'Jam-dbyangs mKhyen-brtse'i dBang-po. The finest scholars of dBus and gTsang were impressed with his learning and received teachings from him.

Kaḥ-thog Si-tu composed guides for pilgrimage to holy places and works on the history of the stupas of Nepal. To honor the Great Guru, he rebuilt Padmasambhava's Copper Mountain Monument at Kaḥ-thog. He created a curriculum of Dharma study based on one hundred essential Sūtras, śāstras, and Tantras.

With the blessings of the Vidyādharas, Kaḥ-thog Si-tu was able to recover several important lost teachings. One was an Anuyoga commentary by gNubs-chen Sangs-rgyas Ye-shes, the mDo'i-'grel-pa-mun-pa'i-go-cha. Inspired by a vision, Kaḥ-thog Si-tu located a copy of the text and restored the lineage, which he bestowed on mKhan-po Nus-ldan. Kaḥ-thog Si-tu also located Guru Padmasambhava's own commentary on the gSang-ba'i-snying-po Tantra, which was known as the bKa'-mchims-phu-ma, named after the caves of mChims-phu, where Guru Rinpoche had taught his twenty-five disciples. Over the centuries this text had also been lost. Having found a copy of the text in central Tibet, Kaḥ-thog Si-tu was able to reinstate the transmission.

Kaḥ-thog Si-tu's library was one of the treasures of Tibet. Although some fifteen volumes of his writings seem to have been lost, several of Kaḥ-thog Si-tu's own compositions are preserved in Great Treasures of Ancient Teachings, together with these recovered texts.

དཔལ་ཡུལ་པདྨ་ནོར་བུ་ཐུབ་བསྟན་ཆོས་ཀྱི་གླང་པོ

dPal-yul Padma Nor-bu Thub-bstan Chos-kyi Glang-po
1887–1932 C.E.
305 texts, 1,096 pages

A reincarnation of the first Padma Nor-bu Rinpoche, Thub-bstan Chos-kyi Glang-po was enthroned at the age of seven. He was ordained as a novice by dPal-yul Karma sKu-chen mDo-sngags Chos-kyi Nyi-ma and received all the dPal-yul teachings from mKhan-po Kun-bzang dPal-ldan, mKhan-po Ngag-dbang dPal-bzang, and Kaḥ-thog Si-tu: the works of the gTer-ma masters Ratna Gling-pa, gNam-chos Mi-'gyur rDo-rje, and 'Ja'-tshon sNying-po; the treasures of Karma Gling-pa; the rNying-ma bKa'-ma, the bKa'-'gyur, and the Rin-chen gTer-mdzod; Anuyoga empowerments; and bKa'-brgyad and dGongs-'dus practices.

Khan-po Ngag-dbang dPal-bzang, his root guru, ordained him and also bestowed rDzogs-chen teachings upon him. From A-'dzom 'Brug-pa, he received the sNying-thig lineage. Lama Mi-pham gave him blessings and teachings as did the great Kong-sprul Blo-gros mTha'-yas. Padma Nor-bu gave innumerable empowerments to fortunate disciples. He composed seven Tibetan volumes of works, which are preserved in Great Treasures of Ancient Teachings.

དར་ཐང་མཆོག་སྤྲུལ་འཇམ་དཔལ་དགྱེས་པའི་རྡོ་རྗེ་ཆོས་ཀྱི་ཟླ་བ

Dar-thang mChog-sprul
'Jam-dpal dGyes-pa'i rDo-rje Chos-kyi Zla-ba
1894–1959 A.D.
4 texts

An incarnation of Atīśa, 'Jam-dpal dGyes-pa'i rDo-rje had been predicted by several gTer-ma masters. lHa-sprul Rinpoche (1862–1945), the founder of Dar-thang monastery, discovered the child in rGyal-mo-rong and brought him to Dar-thang monastery.

From Kaḥ-thog Si-tu, he received the sMin-grol-gling Vinaya lineages and the sMin-grol-gling Bodhisattva lineage, and the Bla-ma-dgongs-'dus practices. From 'Jam-mgon Chos-kyi Glang-po, he received the dPal-yul gTer-ma lineages of Ratna Gling-pa, gNam-chos Mi-'gyur rDo-rje, and 'Ja'-tshon sNying-po, the Rin-chen gTer-mdzod, the bKa'-ma, and the bKa'-brgyad teachings. mKhan-po Ngag-chung bestowed the sNying-thig and Ya-bzhi lineages upon him, while Khra-dge-slong gave him the Nā-ro mKha'-spyod-ma teachings. rDo-grub mKhan-po Klu-shul and mGar-klong gTer-ston were also his teachers. Under his care Dar-thang monastery flourished and greatly expanded. A few works on rituals composed by this master have been included in Great Treasures of Ancient Teachings.

# ཀུན་གཟིགས་འཇམ་དབྱངས་མཁྱེན་བརྩེ་ཆོས་ཀྱི་བློ་གྲོས

Kun-gzigs 'Jam-dbyangs mKhyen-brtse Chos-kyi Blo-gros
1896–1959 C.E.
308 texts, 1,479 pages, Rin-chen gTer-mdzod: 9 texts

The Second 'Jam-dbyangs mKhyen-brtse Chos-kyi Blo-gros was born into the lCag-gong clan in the family of gSer-ba gTer-ston. He was raised at Kaḥ-thog monastery by Kaḥ-thog Si-tu, who recognized him as an incarnation of the first mKhyen-brtse Rinpoche. His other teachers included the Third rDo-grub-chen bsTan-pa'i Nyi-ma, Zhe-chen rGyal-tshab, A-'dzom 'Brug-pa, and Sa-skya master Ngag-dbangs Legs-pa.

Later he was enthroned at rDzong-gsar, which had been the original seat of the first mKhyen-brtse Rinpoche. A comprehensive scholar, he possessed knowledge said to be almost equal to that of the first mKhyen-brtse. He held all the major rNying-ma and Sa-skya lineages, and was considered omniscient by his disciples. His vast intellect encompassed the entire scope of Buddhist philosophy and practice. He was also a master of visionary gTer-ma.

A well-known ris-med master, he held all eight practice lineages (shing-rta-brgyad), and the sixteen major lineages, and had disciples from all schools. Chos-kyi Blo-gros sponsored the building of monasteries and the creation of a forty-foot-high Buddha statue at Kaḥ-thog monastery at Thub-chen lHa-khang. At Khams-kyi Bye-ma-thang college, he erected a huge Maitreya statue. Near rDzong-gsar, he founded dKar-mo sTag-tshang, a center for Tantric practices, where he spent some time teaching. He offered two or three initiations or teachings almost every day. Some of his works have been lost, but his collected works of three hundred and eight texts are preserved in Great Treasures of Ancient Teachings, together with additional texts in the Rin-chen gTer-mdzod section.

ཨ་འཛོམ་རྒྱལ་སྲས་མཁས་གྲུབ་ཆེན་པོ་རིག་འཛིན་འགྱུར་མེད་རྡོ་རྗེ

A-'dzom rGyal-sras mKhas-grub Chen-po
Rig-'dzin 'Gyur-med rDo-rje
mid-19th–early 20th century C.E.
2 texts, 100 pages

Incarnation of gTer-bdag Gling-pa recognized by Kong-sprul, A-'gyur Rinpoche rGyal-sras Rig-'dzin 'Gyur-med rDo-rje was the son of A-'dzom 'Brug-pa. He received from his father comprehensive knowledge of the three Inner Yogas of Mahā, Anu, and Ati, as well as all the lineages his father had held. The father had told his son, "I have given you my heart," and people regarded A-'gyur Rinpoche as the equal of A-'dzom 'Brug-pa. His brother, Padma dBang-rgyal, had been recognized as an incarnation of mNga'-ris Paṇ-chen Padma dBang-rgyal. He too was a rDzogs-chen master and a great example of the monk's way of life.

At A-'dzom sGar, A-'gyur Rinpoche taught rDzogs-chen to fortunate students from all across eastern Tibet: Mar-khams, Ka-mdzes, Hor-khog, Nyag-rong, rGyal-mo-rong, Li-thang, Sa-ngan, sDe-dge, Ser-thal, Brag-gyab, Kong-po, sPu-bo, and Dwags-po. Once each year he gave teachings on the Ye-shes Bla-ma, and twice each year sNgon-'gro instructions, attended by three to five hundred yogins, monks, and nuns.

A holder of the sNyan-brgyud, the Oral Explanation Lineage or Realization Lineage, he was accomplished at teaching the sNying-thig according to the quality and state of each individual's consciousness. A-'gyur Rinpoche composed a commentary on an important work by Buddhaguhya (Lam-rim-chen-mo), sādhanas, and prayers to Klong-chen-pa. These works are preserved in Great Treasures of Ancient Teachings.

369

ཀཿ་ཐོག་མཁན་ཆེན་ནུས་ལྡན་ཐུབ་བསྟན་མཁྱེན་བརྩེ་བློ་གྲོས

Kaḥ-thog mKhan-chen Nus-ldan
Thub-bstan mKhyen-brtse Blo-gros
mid-19th–early 20th century C.E.
3 texts, 978 pages

Master of Kaḥ-thog monastery, Kaḥ-thog mKhan-po Nus-ldan was a disciple of Kun-bzang dPal-ldan, Ngag-dbang dPal-bzang, and the siddha and great magician rTsang-pa Grub-dbang Byams-pa Chos-'dzin. Kaḥ-thog Si-tu gave him gNubs-chen gSangs-rgyas Ye-shes' Anuyoga commentary (mDo'i-'grel-pa-mun-pa'i-go-cha), which Si-tu had recovered, and mKhan-po Nus-ldan composed an extensive commentary upon it. He also wrote a commentary on Lama Mi-pham's mKhas-'jug. mKhan-po Nus-ldan held the Klong-chen-snying-thig lineage and was master of the Three Inner Yogas. Three of his texts are preserved in Great Treasures.

དགེ་མང་མཁན་ཆེན་ཡོན་ཏན་རྒྱ་མཚོ

dGe-mang mKhan-chen Yon-tan rGya-mtsho
mid-19th–early 20th century C.E.
7 texts, 558 pages, Rin-chen gTer-mdzod: 1 text

A disciple of dPal-sprul Rinpoche and O-rgyan bsTan-'dzin Nor-bu, Yon-tan rGya-mtsho was a great scholar and practitioner associated with rDzogs-chen monastery and dGe-mang monastery in rDza-chu-kha. He composed a detailed commentary on 'Jigs-med Gling-pa's Yon-tan-mdzod. This work and six others are preserved in Great Treasures of Ancient Teachings.

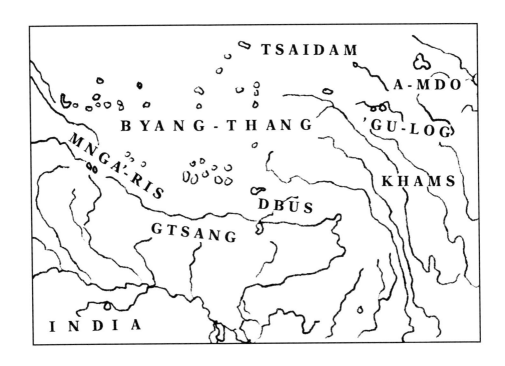

ཁ་མ་སྒྲུབ་ཆེན་པོ་ཁྲ་དགེ་སློང་ཚུལ་ཁྲིམས་དར་རྒྱས

mKhas-grub Chen-po Khra-dge-slong
Tshul-khrims Dar-rgyas
mid-19th–early 20th century C.E.
1 text, 31 pages

A reincarnation of Nāropa, Khra-dge-slong was a siddha, poet, and writer of distinction. He specialized in the Nā-ro-mkha'-spyod-ma teachings, the Vajra Yoginī lineage of Nāropa, and was blessed with visions of the goddess Sarasvatī. Practitioners of this particular lineage were famous for their successful results and Khra-dge-slong and his disciples were no exceptions. He was also very learned in the Cakrasaṁvara Tantra. His chief disciple was Sog-po sPrul-sku Padma Dga'-ba'i rDo-rje (1892–1945). Khra-dge-slong's writings are not available today except for a few texts. One work is preserved in Great Treasures of Ancient Teachings.

ཞེ་ཆེན་ཀོང་སྤྲུལ་མཁས་གྲུབ་པདྨ་དྲི་མེད་ལེགས་པའི་བློ་གྲོས

Zhe-chen Kong-sprul
mKhas-grub Padma Dri-med Legs-pa'i Blo-gros
1901–1958 C.E.
1 text, 91 pages

This learned monk was a great yogic practitioner and rDzogs-chen master, the reincarnation of Kong-sprul Blo-gros mTha'-yas and an incarnation of Vairotsana. He was expert in both bKa'-ma and gTer-ma, the Three Inner Yogas, the works of Lama Mi-pham, and the writings of his teacher, Zhe-chen rGyal-tshab, who had recognized him as Kong-sprul's incarnation. The Sixteenth Karmapa received teachings from him and considered him a master of masters. While he did not devote himself to writing like his predecessor, Zhe-chen Kong-sprul was not different from the first Kong-sprul in his vast intellect, his endless compassion for his students, and his tremendously advanced meditative accomplishments. Great Treasures of Ancient Teachings contains one of his texts.

བོད་པ་སྤྲུལ་སྐུ་ཀུན་གཟིགས་མདོ་སྔགས་བསྟན་པའི་ཉི་མ

Bod-pa sPrul-sku
Kun-gzigs mDo-sngags bsTan-pa'i Nyi-ma
1907–1959 C.E.
3 texts, 205 pages

Born in sPu-bo as the son of a famous gTer-ston, Bod-pa
sPrul-sku was the spiritual heir to the lineages and teachings of Lama Mi-pham. Considered an incarnation of dPal-sprul Rinpoche, Bod-pa sPrul-sku was the most outstanding rNying-ma scholar of the early twentieth century. He had studied for over two decades with Kun-bzang dPal-ldan, the disciple of Lama Mi-pham, and at rDzogs-chen Śrī Siṁha College. Not remaining long in any one location, Bod-pa sPrul-sku taught at Zhe-chen, at Ge-kong, and at many other places. He established a college of philosophical studies at Zhe-chen monastery.

Bod-pa sPrul-sku authored commentaries on the Abhisamayālaṁkāra and Āryadeva's bsTan-bcos bZhi-brgya-pa. He composed a remarkable commentary called the lTa-sgrub-shan-'byed that explained the key distinctions characterizing the views of all the different Buddhist schools and articulated the distinctive approach of the rNying-ma-pa. This work followed the topics of a text by Lama Mi-pham, the Nges-shes-rin-po-che-sgron-ma, which contained seven essential questions to Mañjuśrī, the Bodhisattva of Wisdom. Bod-pa sPrul-sku's root verses provide a critical perspective on the positions of all the schools. These three works are preserved in Great Treasures of Ancient Teachings. It is hoped some of his other writings will be found in the future.

ཞི་ཆེན་རབ་འབྱམས་སྣང་མཛད་གྲུབ་པའི་རྡོ་རྗེ་

Zhe-chen Rab-'byams sNang-mdzad Grub-pa'i rDo-rje
b. 1910 C.E.

This master's family belonged to the rBa-gsar clan, who were well-known heroes in 'Gu-log A-skyong. His incarnation lineage traced back to an accomplished master known as bsTan-pa'i rGyal-mtshan, the First Rab-'byams, a title meaning champion of Dharma. So outstanding was his mastery of the doctrine that bsTan-pa'i rGyal-mtshan was known as Zhwa-lam-pa—one with no rival in learning.

The Sixth Rab-'byams sNang-mdzad Grub-pa'i rDo-rje was the disciple of 'Jam-dbyangs mKhyen-brtse Chos-kyi Blo-gros and Zhe-chen rGyal-tshab. He became a great scholar and influential in sDe-dge, well-known as a diplomat and as an excellent speaker.

He transmitted the lineage of the Rin-chen-gter-mdzod to the leading masters of Tibet in the early twentieth century, bestowing these teachings on the sMin-grol-gling lineage holders at lHa-sa and masters in Khams at bsTan-'phel lCag-mo dGon-pa. sNang-mdzad Grub-pa'i rDo-rje gave teachings and instruction to the incarnation of his teacher, Zhe-chen rGyal-tshab. He supported the philosophical college at Zhe-chen and the sMin-grol-gling lineages, promoting the ceremonies of Guru Padmasambhava and the Great Sādhanas (sgrub-chen). Great Treasures of Ancient Teachings contains a few prayers by this master.

གཅེར་སྟོན་དཔའ་བོ་ནུས་ལྡན་རྡོ་རྗེ་ཀུན་བཟང་ཉི་མ

dPa'-bo Nus-ldan rDo-rje Kun-bzang Nyi-ma
mid-19th century–early 20th century C.E.

The successor of Nyag-bla bSod-rgyal, dPa'-bo Nus-ldan rDo-rje was the son of mKhyen-sprul, a son of bDud-'joms Gling-pa. A gTer-ston who resided in 'Gu-log, he produced thirty volumes of texts, two volumes of which were Hayagrīva gTer-ma. He was also an incarnation of one of the twenty-five disciples of Padmasambhava, rGyal-ba mChog-dbyangs, who had mastered the Hayagrīva teachings. Sog-po sPrul-sku was his chief disciple. Texts by this master have been located for future volumes of Great Treasures of Ancient Teachings.

མགར་ཀློང་གཅེར་སྟོན

mGar-klong gTer-ston
mid-19th century–early 20th century C.E.

Master from 'Gu-log, mGar-klong gTer-ston gave teachings to mChog-sprul Rinpoche of Dar-thang monastery. His incarnations were associated with Dar-thang in succeeding generations. Texts by this master have been located for future volumes of Great Treasures of Ancient Teachings.

# Part Ten


# Additional
# rNying-ma Authors

 སེམས་དཔའ་ཆེན་པོ་དཔལ་སྤྲུལ་ཨོ་རྒྱན་འཇིགས་མེད་ཆོས་ཀྱི་དབང་པོ།

dPal-sprul O-rgyan 'Jigs-med Chos-kyi dBang-po

# Additional
# rNying-ma Authors

Additional rNying-ma masters who are authors in Great Treasures of Ancient Teachings are named in the following lists. Some of these individuals are gTer-stons from the Rin-chen gTer-mdzod about whom very little is known; some are undated authors from other sections of Great Treasures of Ancient Teachings; and some are important masters of the nineteenth and twentieth centuries whose biographies we have not yet completed.

# Undated gTer-stons
# from the Rin-chen gTer-mdzod

གཏེར་སྟོན་ཟླ་བན་གཟི་བརྗིད་འབར།

gTer-ston Zla-ban gZi-brjid-'bar

གཏེར་སྟོན་འབྲོམ་ཆེས་ཀྱི་སྙིང་པོ།

gTer-ston 'Brom-ches-kyi sNying-po

གཏེར་སྟོན་འོད་ཟེར་སྟོན་པ།

gTer-ston 'Od-zer sTon-pa

མེ་ཉག་གྲགས་འབྱུང་།

Me-nyag Grags-'byung
Rin-chen gTer-mdzod: 1 text

གཏེར་སྟོན་ཟླ་བ་རྡོ་རྗེ།

gTer-ston Zla-ba rDo-rje

གཏེར་སྟོན་གཙང་གི་ཉང་སྟོན་ཤེས་རབ་གྲགས་པ།

gTer-ston gTsang-gi Nyang-ston Shes-rab Grags-pa

ཁམས་པ་མེ་ཟོར།

Khams-pa Me-zor
Rin-chen gTer-mdzod: 1 text

གཏེར་སྟོན་གཙང་སྟོན་ཆོས་འབར

gTer-ston gTsang-ston Chos-'bar

གཏེར་སྟོན་སྔགས་འཆང་དབང་ཆེན་བཟང་པོ

gTer-ston sNgags-'chang dBang-chen bZang-po

གཏེར་སྟོན་སར་པོ་བྱའུ་མགོན

gTer-ston Sar-po Bya'u-mgon

སྐྱེས་བུ་ཟངས་གླིང་དབང་ཕྱུག

sKyes-bu Zangs-gling dBang-phyug

ཡན་བོན་རི་ཁྲོད་པ་སེངྒེ

Yan-bon Ri-khrod-pa Seng-ge
Rin-chen gTer-mdzod: 1 text

གཏེར་སྟོན་ལྕང་སྨན་དོན་གྲུབ་དར་རྒྱས

gTer-ston lCang-sman Don-grub Dar-rgyas

གཏེར་སྟོན་འགོས་པདྨ

gTer-ston 'Gos Padma

གཏེར་སྟོན་རང་བྱུང་ཡེ་ཤེས

gTer-ston Rang-byung Ye-shes

གཏེར་སྟོན་བསེ་བན་ཉི་མའི་སྙིང་པོ

gTer-ston bSe-ban Nyi-ma'i sNying-po

གཏེར་སྟོན་ལྷོ་བྲག་པ་ཀུན་དགའ་བཟང་པོ

gTer-ston lHo-brag-pa Kun-dga' bZang-po

གཏེར་སྟོན་ཁམས་པ་འབྲུག་སྒོམ་ཞིག་པོ

gTer-ston Khams-pa 'Brug-sgom Zhig-po

གཏེར་སྟོན་ལྷ་གསུམ་བཟའ་བྱང་ཆུབ་དཔལ་མོ

gTer-ston lHa-gsum-bza' Byang-chub dPal-mo

གཏེར་སྟོན་མ་ཧཱ་བཛྲ

gTer-ston Mahā Vajra

ནམ་མཁའ་བསོད་ནམས

Nam-mkha' bSod-nams

# Undated rNying-ma Authors
# from Great Treasures of Ancient Teachings

རྡོ་རྗེ་བྲག་མཁན་ཟུར་སྟག་ལུང་ཕྲིན་ལས་བཟང་པོ

rDo-rje-brag mKhan Zur-stag-lung Phrin-las bZang-po

6 texts, 11 pages

དཀོན་མཆོག་བཟང་པོ་དྲི་མེད་བློ་ལྡན

dKon-mchog bZang-po Dri-med Blo-ldan

2 texts, 23 pages

འཆི་མེད་སྟོབས་ལྡན་རྡོ་རྗེ

'Chi-med sTobs-ldan rDo-rje

2 texts, 57 pages

ཤེས་རབ་བློ་ལྡན

Shes-rab Blo-ldan

1 text, 100 pages

ཨོ་རྒྱན་བསྟན་འཛིན

O-rgyan bsTan-'dzin

1 text, 64 pages

ཀཿཐོག་པ་ནམ་མཁའ་རྡོ་རྗེ

Kaḥ-thog-pa Nam-mkha' rDo-rje

1 text, 13 pages

ཀརྨ་བཀྲ་ཤིས་འོད་ཟེར

Karma bKra-shis 'Od-zer

1 text

ཆོས་དབྱིངས་བདེ་ཆེན་མཚོ་མོ

Chos-dbyings bDe-chen mTsho-mo

1 text

ངག་དབང་བློ་བཟང་
མདོ་སྔགས་བསྟན་འཛིན་ནོར་བུ

Ngag-dbang Blo-bzang mDo-sngags bsTan-'dzin Nor-bu

1 text

རྣལ་འབྱོར་པ་ཞེ་སྡང་རྡོ་རྗེ

rNal-'byor-pa Zhe-sdang rDo-rje

1 text

ཨོ་རྒྱན་ཀུན་བཟང་བསྟན་འཛིན་རྡོ་རྗེ

O-rgyan Kun-bzang bsTan-'dzin rDo-rje

2 texts

# Dated rNying-ma Authors
# from Great Treasures of Ancient Teachings
# for Further Reasearch

གུ་རུ་བཀྲ་ཤིས་སྟག་སྒང་མཁས་མཆོག་ངག་དབང་བློ་གྲོས་

Gu-ru bKra-shis sTag-sgang mKhas-mchog
Ngag-dbang Blo-gros
1775 C.E.
1 text, 724 pages

གེ་བཅགས་རྟོགས་ལྡན་ཚངས་དབྱངས་རྒྱ་མཚོ

Ge-bcags rTogs-ldan Tshangs-dbyangs rGya-mtsho
mid 18th–early 19th century C.E.
3 texts, 258 pages

འགྱུར་མེད་བསྟན་འཛིན

'Gyur-med bsTan-'dzin
1858–1914 C.E.
1 text, 43 pages

རྡོ་རྗེ་བྲག་རིག་འཛིན་བདུན་པ་ཀུན་བཟང་འགྱུར་མེད་ལྷུན་གྲུབ

rDo-rje-brag Rig-'dzin bDun-pa
Kun-bzang 'Gyur-med lHun-grub
early 19th–mid 19th century C.E.?
Rin-chen gTer-mdzod: 1 text

385

ཨཁན་ཆེན་བདེ་ཆེན་འབར་བའི་རྡོ་རྗེ

mKhan-chen bDe-chen 'Bar-ba'i rDo-rje
1836–1920 C.E.
85 texts, 701 pages


གཀརྨའི་ཨཁན་ཆེན་རིན་ཆེན་དར་རྒྱས

Karma'i mKhan-chen Rin-chen Dar-rgyas
early 19th–mid 19th century C.E.
186 texts, 770 pages
Rin-chen gTer-mdzod: 11 texts


ཚ་བ་ལོ་ཙྭ་བ་རིན་ཆེན་རྣམ་རྒྱལ

Tsha-ba Lo-tsā-ba Rin-chen rNam-rgyal
early 19th–mid 19th century C.E.
2 texts, 136 pages


ངག་དབང་དམ་ཆོས་རྒྱ་མཚོ
བློ་བཟང་བཤད་སྒྲུབ་བསྟན་པའི་ཉི་མ

Ngag-dbang Dam-chos rGya-mtsho
Blo-bzang bShad-sgrub bsTan-pa'i Nyi-ma
early 19th–mid 19th century C.E.
1 text, 30 pages

ཆགས་མེད་བཞི་པ་ཀརྨ་བསྟན་འཛིན་ཕྲིན་ལས

Chags-med bZhi-pa Karma bsTan-'dzin Phrin-las
early 19th–mid 19th century C.E.
Rin-chen gTer-mdzod: 8 texts

ཆགས་མེད་གསུང་སྤྲུལ་ཀརྨ་བདེ་ཆེན་སྙིང་པོ

Chags-med gSung-sprul Karma bDe-chen sNying-po
early 19th–mid 19th century C.E.?
Rin-chen gTer-mdzod: 1 text

མང་དགེ་རྡོ་རྗེ་འཆང་དགེ་ལེགས་ཡར་འཕེལ

Mang-dge rDo-rje-'chang dGe-legs Yar-'phel
early 19th–mid 19th century C.E.?
Rin-chen gTer-mdzod: 1 text

གནས་གསར་ཀརྨ་བཀྲ་ཤིས་ཆོས་འཕེལ

gNas-gsar Karma bKra-shis Chos-'phel
early 19th–mid 19th century C.E.?
Rin-chen gTer-mdzod: 1 text

ཐུགས་སྲས་འགྱུར་མེད་ཚེ་དབང་གྲགས་པ

Thugs-sras 'Gyur-med Tshe-dbang Grags-pa
early 19th–mid 19th century C.E.?
Rin-chen gTer-mdzod: 1 text

གཁན་ཆེན་ཐུབ་བསྟན་རྒྱལ་མཚན་འོད་ཟེར

mKhan-chen Thub-bstan rGyal-mtshan 'Od-zer
early 19th–mid 19th century C.E.?
Rin-chen gTer-mdzod: 2 texts

རྡོ་རྗེ་མཆོག་རབ་རྩལ

rDo-rje mChog-rab-rtsal
early 19th–mid 19th century C.E.?
Rin-chen gTer-mdzod: 1 text

ཛ་ཀ་སྤྲུལ་སྐུ་འཇིགས་མེད་ཀུན་བཟང་རྣམ་རྒྱལ

Dza-ka sPrul-sku 'Jigs-med Kun-bzang rNam-rgyal
early 19th–mid 19th century C.E.?
Rin-chen gTer-mdzod: 1 text

ཛ་སྤྲུལ

Dza-sprul
early 19th–mid 19th century C.E.?
Rin-chen gTer-mdzod: 1 text

རོང་ཕུ་ངག་དབང་བསྟན་འཛིན་ནོར་བུ།

Rong-phu  Ngag-dbang bsTan-'dzin Nor-bu
1867 C.E.
8 texts, 442 pages

བདུད་འཇོམས་དྲག་སྔགས་གླིང་པ།

bDud-'joms Drag-sngags Gling-pa
1871–1936  C.E.
255 texts, 1,128 pages

མཁན་ཆེན་ལྷག་བསམ་བསྟན་པའི་རྒྱལ་མཚན།

mKhan-chen Lhag-bsam bsTan-pa'i rGyal-mtshan
mid 19th–early 20th century
2 texts, 60 pages

རྫོང་གསར་མཁན་པོ་ཀུན་དགའ་དབང་ཕྱུག

rDzong-gsar mKhan-po Kun-dga'dBang-phyug
mid 19th–early 20th century  C.E.
1 text, 17 pages

རག་མགོ་མཆོག་སྤྲུལ་ཐུབ་བསྟན་བཤད་སྒྲུབ།

Rag-mgo mChog-sprul Thub-bstan bShad-sgrub
1890–1973 C.E.
244 texts, 880 pages

པདྨ་ལུང་རྟོགས་རྒྱ་མཚོ།

Padma Lung-rtogs rGya-mtsho
1891–1964 C.E.
37 texts, 514 pages

ཨ་སྐྱེས་མཁའ་སྤྱོད་གླིང་པ།

A-skyes mKha'-spyod Gling-pa
1893–1939 C.E.
6 texts, 121 pages

སེ་ར་མཁའ་འགྲོ་བདེ་བའི་རྡོ་རྗེ།

Se-ra mKha'-'gro bDe-ba'i rDo-rje
1899–1952 C.E.
285 texts, 904 pages

འགྱུར་མེད་བསྟན་འཕེལ།

'Gyur-med bsTan-'phel
mid 19th–early 20th century C.E. ?
1 text, 31 pages

སྨེ་བ་མཁན་ཆེན་བསོད་ནམས་ཆོས་འགྲུབ

rMe-ba mKhan-chen bSod-nams Chos-'grub
mid 19th–early 20th century C.E.
2 texts, 84 pages

ཁྲོ་ཤུལ་མཁན་ཆེན་འཇམ་དཔལ་རྡོ་རྗེ

Khro-shul mKhan-chen 'Jam-dpal rDo-rje
mid 19th–early 20th century C.E.
1 text, 83 pages

ཨོ་རྒྱན་རིན་ཆེན་གླིང་པ

O-rgyan Rin-chen Gling-pa
mid 19th–early 20th century C.E.
22 texts, 156 pages
Rin-chen gTer-mdzod: 3 texts

མཁས་གྲུབ་ཀུན་བཟང་བསྟན་དར

mKhas-grub Kun-bzang bsTan-dar
mid 19th–early 20th century C.E.
1 text, 17 pages

བོད་པ་སྤྲུལ་སྐུ་ཀུན་གཟིགས་མདོ་སྔགས་བསྟན་པའི་ཉི་མ

Bod-pa sPrul-sku Kun-gzigs mDo-sngags bsTan-pa'i Nyi-ma
1907–1959 C.E.
3 texts, 205 pages

རྫོགས་ཆེན་མཁན་པོ་ཐུབ་བསྟན་སྙན་གྲགས

rDzogs-chen mKhan-po Thub-bstan sNyan-grags
mid 19th–early 20th century C.E.
1 text, 93 pages

པདྨ་ཕྲིན་ལས་སྙིང་པོ

Padma Phrin-las sNying-po
mid-19th–early 20th century C.E.
1 text, 106 pages

རྗེ་དྲུང་རིན་པོ་ཆེ་ནམ་མཁའི་རྡོ་རྗེ

rJe-drung Rin-po-che Nam-mkha'i rDo-rje
mid 19th–early 20th century C.E.
446 texts, 2,078 pages
Rin-chen gTer-mdzod: 29 texts

གཏེར་ཆེན་མཁན་ཆེན་དགེ་རྩེ་འགྱུར་མེད་བསྟན་པ་
རྣམ་རྒྱལ་འཇམ་དབྱངས་དགྱེས་པའི་བློ་གྲོས

Kaḥ-thog mKhan-chen dGe-rtse 'Gyur-med bsTan-pa
rNam-rgyal 'Jam-dbyangs dGyes-pa'i Blo-gros
mid 19th–early 20th century  C.E.
2 texts, 215 pages

དར་ཐང་མཁན་པོ་བསྟན་འཛིན

Dar-thang mKhan-po bsTan-'dzin
mid 19th–early 20th century  C.E.
1 text, 6 pages

ཨ་པམ་གཏེར་སྟོན་ཨོ་རྒྱན་ཕྲིན་ལས་གླིང་པ

A-pam gTer-ston  O-rgyan Phrin-las Gling-pa
mid 19th–early 20th century  C.E.
453 texts, 1,354 pages

ཤུགས་ཆུང་སྤྲུལ་སྐུ་ཚུལ་ཁྲིམས་བཟང་པོ

Shugs-chung  sPrul-sku Tshul-khrims bZang-po
mid 19th–early 20th century C.E.
2 texts, 238 pages

དབུལ་སེལ་གླིང་པ་

dBul-sel Gling-pa
mid 19th–early 20th century  C.E.
19 texts, 79 pages

རྭ་ཁྲོ་གཏེར་སྟོན་ཨོ་རྒྱན་འགྲོ་འདུལ་ཀུན་འདུས་གླིང་པ་

Rwa-khro gTer-ston O-rgyan 'Gro-'dul Kun-'dus Gling-pa
mid 19th–early 20th century  C.E.
22 texts, 143 pages

ཆོས་སྐྱོང་གླིང་པ་

Chos-skyong Gling-pa
mid 19th–early 20th century  C.E.
59 texts, 239 pages

རྡོ་རྗེ་ཚེ་རྒྱལ་

rDo-rje Tshe-rgyal
mid 19th–early 20th century  C.E.
14 texts, 73 pages

མཁས་དབང་དགེ་འདུན་ཆོས་འཕེལ་

mKhas-dbang dGe-'dun Chos-'phel
mid 19th–early 20th century  C.E.
8 texts, 528 pages

བདུད་འཇོམས་འཇིགས་བྲལ་ཡེ་ཤེས་རྡོ་རྗེ

bDud-'joms 'Jigs-bral Ye-shes rDo-rje
1904–1987 C.E.
560 texts, 4,102 pages

དིལ་མགོ་མཁྱེན་བརྩེ་མཁས་གྲུབ་རབ་གསལ་ཟླ་བ

Dil-mgo mKhyen-brtse mKhas-grub Rab-gsal Zla-ba
1910–1991 C.E.
318 texts, 3,600 pages
Rin-chen gTer-mdzod: 21 texts

ཡོངས་འཛིན་ངག་གི་དབང་པོ

Yongs-'dzin Ngag-gi dBang-po
mid 19th–early 20th century  C.E.
1 text, 82 pages

ཟླ་བ་གྲགས་པ

Zla-ba Grags-pa
20th century C.E.?
1 text, 21 pages

སྲས་འཕགས་མཆོག་རྡོ་རྗེ

Sras 'Phags-mchog rDo-rje
mid 19th–early 20th century  C.E.
1 text, 80 pages

ལས་རབ་རྡོ་རྗེ

Las-rab rDo-rje
mid 19th–early 20th century  C.E.
1 text, 34 pages

མཁན་པོ་ཟླ་བའི་འོད་ཟེར

mKhan-po Zla-ba'i 'Od-zer
mid 19th–early 20th century  C.E.
1 text, 61 pages

འཁོར་གདོན་གཏེར་ཆེན་ནུས་ལྡན་རྡོ་རྗེ་འགྲོ་ཕན་གླིང་པ

'Khor-gdon gTer-chen Nus-ldan rDo-rje 'Gro-phan Gling-pa
20th century C.E.
276 pages

ཐུབ་བསྟན་བརྩོན་འགྲུས།

Thub-bstan brTson-'grus
20th century C.E.
85 texts, 294 pages


བྱ་བྲལ་སངས་རྒྱས་རྡོ་རྗེ།

Bya-bral Sangs-rgyas rDo-rje
20th century C.E.
1 text, 72 pages

# Part Eleven


# Indian Authors and
# Authors of
# Other Schools

འཇམ་མགོན་ཀོང་སྤྲུལ་བློ་གྲོས་མཐའ་ཡས

'Jam-mgon Kong-sprul Blo-gros mTha'-yas

# Additional Authors

Within the ten sections of Great Treasures of Ancient Teachings are five fields of rNying-ma subjects (see p. xxxi) and five general fields such as the subjects of śāstra study: Logic and Epistemology, Vinaya, Abhidharma, Madhyamaka, and Prajñāpāramitā; sDom-gsum; traditional arts and sciences such as medicine, astrology, poetry, grammar, and art; and history and biography. To support these studies, Great Treasures includes works not only by rNying-ma masters, but contributions by the great śāstra masters of India and outstanding authors of all schools of Tibetan Buddhism.

The following lists give the names of the Indian authors and masters of all Tibetan schools who composed texts included in Great Treasures of Ancient Teachings. In addition, noted here are the names of masters of other schools whom Kong-sprul Blo-gros mTha'-yas listed as gTer-stons in the Rin-chen gTer-mdzod dKar-chag.

# Śāstra Authors

## Prajñāpāramitā

ङ्के'བཙུན་བྱམས་པ་མགོན་པོ་

Maitreyanātha
1 text, 6 pages

སློབ་དཔོན་ཤེར་འབྱུང་བློ་གྲོས་

Prajñākaramati
1 text, 11 pages

སློབ་དཔོན་རྣམ་གྲོལ་སྡེ་

Vimuktasena
2 texts, 189 pages

སློབ་དཔོན་ཆོས་ཀྱི་བཤེས་གཉེན་

Dharmamitra
1 text, 54 pages

སློབ་དཔོན་ཆེན་པོ་སྨྲྀཏི་ཛྙཱ་ན་ཀཱིརྟི་

Smṛtijñānakīrti
1 text, 31 pages

སློབ་དཔོན་གཞོན་ནུ་དཔལ་བཟང་པོ་

Kumāraśrībhadra
1 text, 3 pages

སློབ་དཔོན་སེང་གེ་བཟང་པོ་

Haribhadra
4 texts, 751 pages

སློབ་དཔོན་སངས་རྒྱས་དཔལ་ཡེ་ཤེས་

Buddhaśrījñāna
1 text, 37 pages

སློབ་དཔོན་ཆོས་ཀྱི་གྲགས་པ་

Dharmakīrti
1 text, 57 pages

པ་ཚེན་རིན་ཆེན་གྲགས་པ་

Ratnakīrti
1 text, 36 pages

སློབ་དཔོན་སངས་རྒྱས་དཔལ་ཡེ་ཤེས

Buddhaśrījñāna

1 text, 37 pages

སློབ་དཔོན་ཕྱོགས་ཀྱི་གླང་པོ

Dignāga

1 text, 1 page

སློབ་དཔོན་རིན་ཆེན་འབྱུང་གནས

Ratnākaraśānti

2 texts 151 pages

སློབ་དཔོན
དཀོན་མཆོག་གསུམ་གྱི་འབངས

Triratnadāsa

1 text, 11 pages

སློབ་དཔོན་ཁ་ཆེ་མཁན་པོ་ཆོས་དཔལ

Dharmaśrī

2 texts, 39 pages

སློབ་དཔོན་འཇིག་རྟེན་གནས་པར་བྱུང་བ

Jagaddalanivāsin

1 text, 160 pages

སློབ་དཔོན་ཇོ་བོ་རྗེ་ཨ་ཏི་ཤ

Atīśa

2 texts, 9 pages

སློབ་དཔོན་ཀ་མ་ལ

Kambala

2 texts, 2 pages

སློབ་དཔོན་འཇིགས་མེད
འབྱུང་གནས་སྦས་པ

Abhayākaragupta

1 text, 113 pages

སློབ་དཔོན་བི་མ་ལ་མི་ཏྲ

Vimalamitra

2 texts, 47 pages

སློབ་དཔོན་མཆེ་བ་རྣོ་སེན

Daṃṣṭrāsena

2 texts, 436 pages

སློབ་དཔོན་ཀ་མ་ལ་ཤཱི་ལ

Kamalaśīla

2 texts, 77 pages

403

སློབ་དཔོན་དབྱིག་གཉེན།

Vasubandhu

1 text, 13 pages

སློབ་དཔོན་ཕྱུག་སྡེ་སེན།

Praśāstrasena

1 text, 5 pages

སློབ་དཔོན་ཚོན་མི་ཏྲ།

Jñānamitra

1 text, 3 pages

སློབ་དཔོན་མ་ཧཱ་ཛ་ན།

Mahājana

1 text, 4 pages

སློབ་དཔོན་ཕྱག་ན་རྡོ་རྗེ།

Vajrapāṇi

1 text, 4 pages

Madhayamaka

དཔལ་མགོན་འཕགས་པ་ཀླུ་སྒྲུབ།

Nāgārjuna

20 texts, 109 pages

རྗེ་བཙུན་བྱམས་པ་མགོན་པོ།

Maitreyanātha

1 text, 4 pages

སློབ་དཔོན་འཕགས་པ་ཀླུ་སྒྲུབ་སྙིང་པོ།

Nāgārjunagarbha

1 text, 1 page

སློབ་དཔོན་སངས་རྒྱས་བསྐྱངས།

Buddhapālita

1 text, 61 pages

404

སློབ་དཔོན་འཕགས་པ་ལྷ
Āryadeva
8 texts, 13 pages

སློབ་དཔོན་ཟླ་བ་གྲགས་པ
Candrakīrti
9 texts, 342 pages

སློབ་དཔོན་བྱང་ཆུབ་བཟང་པོ
Bodhibhadra
3 texts, 16 pages

སློབ་དཔོན་གཞན་ལ་ཕན་པ
Parahita
1 text, 19 pages

སློབ་དཔོན་ལེགས་ལྡན་བྱེད
Bhāvaviveka
2 texts, 108 pages 288

སློབ་དཔོན་ཁ་ཆེ་པ་ཆེན་རྒྱལ་བ་ཀུན་དགའ
Jayānanda
2 texts, 183 pages

སློབ་དཔོན་སྐལ་ལྡན
Bhavya
5 texts, 180 pages

སློབ་དཔོན་ཞི་བ་ལྷ
Śāntideva
4 texts, 116 pages

སློབ་དཔོན་ནག་པོ་པ
Kṛṣṇa-pa
5 texts, 38 pages

སློབ་དཔོན་ཤེས་རབ་འབྱུང་གནས་བློ་གྲོས
Prajñākaramati
1 text, 124 pages

སློབ་དཔོན་སྤྱན་གཟིགས
བརྟུལ་ཞུགས་སྒྲུབ
Avalokitavrata
1 text, 481 pages

སློབ་དཔོན་གཤུ་ཆ་ནེ་བ
Kalyāṇadeva
1 text, 44 pages

སློབ་དཔོན་རྣམ་སྣང་སྲུང་

Vairocanarakṣita

2 texts, 42 pages

སློབ་དཔོན་ཀླུའི་བཤེས་གཉེན་

Nāgamitra

1 text, 3 pages

སློབ་དཔོན་གསེར་གླིང་གི་བླ་མཆོས་སྐྱོང་

Dharmapāla

2 texts, 3 pages

སློབ་དཔོན་ཡེ་ཤེས་ཟླ་བ་

Jñānacandra

1 text, 16 pagcs

སློབ་དཔོན་བི་བྷུ་ཏི་ཙནྡྲ་

Vibhūticandra

1 text, 47 pages

སློབ་དཔོན་དཔལ་སྦས་

Śrīgupta

1 text, 2 pages

སློབ་དཔོན་ཡེ་ཤེས་སྙིང་པོ་

Jñānagarbha

3 texts, 8 pages

སློབ་དཔོན་བི་དྱ་ཀ་ར་པྲ་བྷ་

Vidyākaraprabha

1 text, 3 pages

སློབ་དཔོན་ཞི་བ་འཚོ་

Śāntarakṣita

3 texts, 34 pages

སློབ་དཔོན་དགའ་བའི་དཔལ་

Nandaśrī

1 text, 1 page

སློབ་དཔོན་ཀ་མ་ལ་ཤཱི་ལ་

Kamalaśīla

9 texts, 129 pages

སློབ་དཔོན་ཀ་མ་པ་ལ་

Kambala

2 texts, 7 pages

སློབ་དཔོན་ངོ་བོ་ཉིད་མེད་པ

Asvabhāva

1 text, 23 pages

སློབ་དཔོན་འཇིགས་མེད་འབྱུང་གནས་སྦས་པའི་ཞབས

Abhayākaragupta

2 texts, 111 pages

སློབ་དཔོན་སྟོབས་བཅུ་དཔལ་བཤེས་གཉེན

Daśabalaśrīmitra

1 text, 105 pages

སློབ་དཔོན་སངས་རྒྱས་ཡེ་ཤེས་ཞབས

Buddhajñānapāda

1 text, 5 pages

སློབ་དཔོན་དབུམའི་སེང་གེ

Mādhyamikasiṁha

1 text, 3 pages

སློབ་དཔོན་ཚུལ་ཁྲིམས་འཕགས་པ

Udgataśīla

1 text, 1 page

སློབ་དཔོན་དགྲ་ལས་རྣམ་པར་རྒྱལ་བ

Jetāri

3 texts, 30 pages

བཙུན་པ་རབ་འབྱོར་དབྱངས

Subhūtighoṣa

1 text, 4 pages

སློབ་དཔོན་ཙནྡྲ་ཧ་རི

Candrahari-pa

1 text, 3 pages

སློབ་དཔོན་དྲི་མ་ལ་མི་ཏྲ

Vimalamitra

3 texts, 15 pages

སློབ་དཔོན་རྗེ་བོ་རྗེ་ཨ་ཏི་ཤ

Atīśa

26 texts, 154 pages

སློབ་དཔོན་རྟ་དབྱངས

Aśvaghoṣa

2 texts, 1 page

སློབ་དཔོན་སངས་རྒྱས་སྦས་པ

Buddhagupta

1 text, 2 pages

སློབ་དཔོན་ཤེས་རབ་ཐར་པ

Prajñāmokṣa

1 text, 4 pages

སློབ་དཔོན་དགེ་བའི་གོ་ཆ

Kalyāṇavarman

1 text, 1 page

སློབ་དཔོན་ཀཱ་རོ

Karo

1 text, 11 pages

སློབ་དཔོན་ཡེ་ཤེས་གྲགས་པ

Jñānakīrti

1 text, 3 pages

སློབ་དཔོན་རིན་ཆེན་འབྱུང་གནས་ཞབས

Ratnākaraśānti

1 text, 60 pages

སློབ་དཔོན་བློ་གྲོས་ཆེན་པོ

Mahāmati

1 text, 1 page

སློབ་དཔོན་ཆོས་ལྡན་རབ་འབྱོར་དབྱངས

Dhārmika Subhūtighoṣa

1 text, 2 pages

སློབ་དཔོན་ཨ་བ་དྷཱུ་ཏི་པ

Avadhūti-pa

1 text, 1 page

སློབ་དཔོན་ཨཱཪྻ་ཤཱུ་ར

Āryaśūra

1 text, 8 pages

སློབ་དཔོན་སྦྱིན་པ་ཚུལ་ཁྲིམས

Dānaśīla

1 text, 1 page

སློབ་དཔོན་གུ་ཧྱ་རྗེ་ཏཱ་རི

Guhyajetāri

1 text, 1 page

སློབ་དཔོན་ཤཱཀྱ་ཤྲཱི་བཟང་པོ་

Śākyaśrībhadra

2 texts, 2 pages

སློབ་དཔོན་ཤཱཀྱ་ཤྲཱི་

Śākyaśri

1 text, 1 page

སློབ་དཔོན་སངས་རྒྱས་དཔལ་ཡེ་ཤེས་

Buddhaśrījñāna

1 text, 17 pages

སློབ་དཔོན་རཱ་ཧུ་ལ་བྷ་ད

Rāhulabhadra

1 text, 1 page

སློབ་དཔོན་དེ་བ་ཤཱནྟི

Devaśānti

1 text, 1 page

སློབ་དཔོན་སྐྱོན་མེད་རྡོ་རྗེ

Niṣkalaṅkavajra

1 text, 1 page

སློབ་དཔོན་འཇིག་རྟེན་མྒྲི་དྒའ་བྱེད

Jaganmitrānanda

1 text, 1 page

# Cittamātra

རྗེ་བཙུན་བྱམས་པ་མགོན་པོ

Maitreyanātha

5 texts, 34 pages

སློབ་དཔོན་བློ་གྲོས་བརྟན་པ

Sthiramati

4 texts, 378 pages

དཔལ་མགོན་འཕགས་པ་ཐོགས་མེད

Asaṅga

12 texts, 778 pages

སློབ་དཔོན་ཡེ་ཤེས་སྙིང་པོ

Jñānagarbha

1 text, 14 pages

སློབ་དཔོན་དབྱིག་གཉེན

Vasubandhu

13 texts, 223 pages

སློབ་དཔོན་ཡོན་ཏན་འོད

Guṇaprabha

3 texts, 40 pages

སློབ་དཔོན་ངོ་བོ་ཉིད་མེད་པ

Asvabhāva

2 texts, 121 pages

སློབ་དཔོན་རྒྱལ་བའི་སྲས

Jinaputra

3 texts, 162 pages

སློབ་དཔོན་པ་ར་ཧི་ཏ་བྷ་ད

Parahitabhadra

1 text, 5 pages

སློབ་དཔོན་རྒྱ་མཚོ་སྤྲིན

Sāgaramegha

1 text, 170 pages

སློབ་དཔོན་ཛྙ་ན་ཤྲཱི

Jñānaśrī

1 text, 3 pages

སློབ་དཔོན་དུལ་བའི་ལྷ

Vinītadeva

2 texts, 43 pages

སློབ་དཔོན་ས་ཡི་རྩ་ལག
Pṛthivībandhu
1 text, 54 pages

སློབ་དཔོན་ཆོས་ཀྱི་དབང་པོ
Dharmendra
1 text, 1 page

སློབ་དཔོན་གུཎ་མ་ཏི
Guṇamati
1 text, 81 pages

སློབ་དཔོན་རྟུ་ན་ཙྪུ
Jñānacandra
1 text, 1 page

དགེ་སློང་བློ་བཟང་དང་ཚུལ
Sumatiśīla
1 text, 19 pages

སློབ་དཔོན་རཏྣ་ཀིརྟི
Ratnakīrti
2 texts, 5 pages

སློབ་དཔོན་རིན་ཆེན་འབྱུང་གནས་ཞི་བ
Ratnākaraśānti
5 texts, 29 pages

སློབ་དཔོན་ཞི་བ་འཚོ
Śāntarakṣita
1 text, 9 pages

སློབ་དཔོན་ཕྱོགས་ཀྱི་གླང་པོ
Dignāga
1 text, 1 page

སློབ་དཔོན་བྱང་ཆུབ་བཟང་པོ
Bodhibhadra
1 text, 17 pages

# Abhidharma

སློབ་དཔོན་མོཏྒལྱཱཡན་

Maudgalyāyana

3 texts, 114 pages

སློབ་དཔོན་དགེ་སློང་ཞི་གནས་ལྷ་

Śamathadeva

1 text, 190 pages

སློབ་དཔོན་དབྱིག་གཉེན་

Vasubandhu

4 texts, 195 pages

སློབ་དཔོན་ཕྱོགས་ཀྱི་གླང་པོ་

Dignāga

1 text, 59 pages

སློབ་དཔོན་ཁ་ཆེ་དགེ་འདུན་བཟང་

Saṃghabhadra

1 text, 86 pages

སློབ་དཔོན་དྲ་བ་ཙོམ་པ་ཆོས་སྐྱོབ་

Dharmatrāta

1 text, 22 pages

སློབ་དཔོན་གྲགས་པའི་གཤེས་གཉེན་

Yaśomitra

1 text, 331 pages

སློབ་དཔོན་པ་རྫོ་ཐམ་ཅན་

Prajñāvarman

1 text, 199 pages

སློབ་དཔོན་གང་སྐྱེལ་

Pūrṇavardhana

2 texts, 345 pages

དཔལ་མགོན་འཕགས་པ་ཀླུ་སྒྲུབ་

Nāgārjuna

1 text, 1 page

# Vinaya

སློབ་དཔོན་དཔའ་བོ།
Śūra
1 text, pages

སློབ་དཔོན་ཚུལ་ཁྲིམས་བསྐྱངས།
Śīlapālita
1 text, 115 pages

སློབ་དཔོན་ཁྱད་པར་བཤེས་གཉེན།
Viśeṣamitra
1 text, 91 pages

སློབ་དཔོན་ཡོན་ཏན་འོད།
Guṇaprabha
4 texts, 577 pages

སློབ་དཔོན་དྲི་མ་མེད།
Vimalamitra
1 text, 370 pages

སློབ་དཔོན་ཆོས་ཀྱི་བཤེས་གཉེན།
Dharmamitra
1 text, 389 pages

སློབ་དཔོན་སྦྱིན་པ་ཚུལ་ཁྲིམས།
Dānaśīla
1 text, 18 pages

སློབ་དཔོན་ཤེར་འབྱུང་།
Prajñākara
1 text, 357 pages

སློབ་དཔོན་དགེ་བའི་བཤེས་གཉེན།
Kalyāṇamitra
6 texts, 164 pages

སློབ་དཔོན་ས་གའི་ལྷ།
Sagadeva
1 text, 30 pages

སློབ་དཔོན་དུལ་བའི་ལྷ།
Vinītadeva
4 texts, 159 pages

སློབ་དཔོན་ཤཱཀྱ་འོད།
Śākyaprabha
2 texts, 50 pages

དཔལ་མགོན་འཕགས་པ་ཀླུ་སྒྲུབ།

Nāgārjuna

2 texts, 2 pages

སློབ་དཔོན་དབྱིག་གི་བཤེས་གཉེན།

Vasumitra

1 text, 3 pages

སློབ་དཔོན་ཀ་མ་ལ་ཤཱི་ལ།

Kamalaśīla

1 text, 12 pages

སློབ་དཔོན་བྷ་བྱ།

Bhavya

1 text, 4 pages

སློབ་དཔོན་བྱང་ཆུབ་སེམས་དཔའ།

Bodhisattva

1 text, 12 pages

སློབ་དཔོན་སུ་ན་ཤྲཱི།

Sunayaśrī

2 texts, 3 pages

སློབ་དཔོན་བ་ལ་ཤྲཱི་བྷ་ད་ར།

Balaśrībhadra

1 text, 3 pages

སློབ་དཔོན་གསང་བ་བྱིན།

Guhyadatta

1 text, 4 pages

སློབ་དཔོན་ཆོས་ཀྱི་ཚོང་དཔོན།

Dharmaśreṣṭhin

1 text, 1 page

སློབ་དཔོན་ཐུག་པའི་རྡོ་རྗེ།

Śaśvatavajra

1 text, 1 page

# Pramāṇa

སློབ་དཔོན་ཕྱོགས་ཀྱི་གླང་པོ།

Dignāga

7 texts, 45 pages

སློབ་དཔོན་ཤཾཀ་རཱ་མུ་དི་ཏ།

Śaṅkarāmudita

1 text, 146 pages

སློབ་དཔོན་ཆོས་ཀྱི་གྲགས་པ།

Dharmakīrti

9 texts, 152 pages

སློབ་དཔོན་ཉི་མ་སྦས་པ།

Sūryagupta

2 texts, 139 pages

སློབ་དཔོན་ལྷ་དབང་བློ།

Devendramati

1 text, 341 pages

དཔལ་གཤས་པ་ཇ་མཱ་རི།

Jamāri

1 text, 476 pages

སློབ་དཔོན་ཤཱཀྱ་བློ།

Śākyabuddhi

1 text, 325 pages

སློབ་དཔོན་ཆོས་མཆོག

Dharmottara

8 texts, 289 pages

སློབ་དཔོན་ཤེས་རབ་འབྱུང་གནས་སྦས་པ།

Prajñākaragupta

1 text, 295 pages

སློབ་དཔོན་ཡེ་ཤེས་དཔལ་བཟང་པོ།

Jñānaśrībhadra

1 text, 59 pages

སློབ་དཔོན་རྒྱལ་བཅན།

Jina

1 text, 338 pages

སློབ་དཔོན་དུལ་བའི་ལྷ།

Vinītadeva

6 texts, 95 pages

སློབ་དཔོན་ཀ་མ་ལ་ཤི་ལ

Kamalaśīla

2 texts, 284 pages

སློབ་དཔོན་དགེ་སྲུངས

Śubhagupta

5 texts, 6 pages

སློབ་དཔོན་རྒྱལ་བ་བཤེས་གཉེན

Jinamitra

1 text, 1 page

སློབ་དཔོན་སྦྱིན་པ་ཚུལ་ཁྲིམས

Dānaśīla

1 text, 1 page

བྲམ་ཟེ་ཨརྩཊ

Arcaṭa

1 text, 73 pages

སློབ་དཔོན་མུཀྟ་ཀ་ལ་ཤ

Muktākalaśa

1 text, 8 pages

བྲམ་ཟེ་བདེ་བྱེད་དགའ་བ

Śaṅkarānanda

3 texts, 18 pages

སློབ་དཔོན་ཤེས་རབ་འབྱུང་གནས་སྲུང་བ

Prajñākaragupta

1 text, 3 pages

སློབ་དཔོན་ཞི་བ་འཚོ

Śāntarakṣita

2 texts, 116 pages

སློབ་དཔོན་ཛྙཱ་ན་ཤྲི་མི་ཏྲ

Jñānaśrīmitra

1 text, 1 page

སློབ་དཔོན་ཙནྡྲ་གོ་མིན

Candragomin

1 text, 1 page

སློབ་དཔོན་རིན་ཆེན་འབྱུང་གནས་ཞི་བའི་ཞབས

Ratnākaraśānti

2 texts, 4 pages

སློབ་དཔོན་དགྲ་ལས་རྣམ་པར་རྒྱལ་བ

Jetāri

3 texts, 11 pages

སློབ་དཔོན་རྗེ་ནེནྟྲ་མ་ཏི

Jinendramati

1 text, 157 pages

དགེ་སློང་ཐར་པའི་འབྱུང་གནས་

ཀྱིས་སྦས་པ

Mokṣākaragupta

1 text, 16 pages

སློབ་དཔོན་རྫོ་ནྲ་ཤྲི་མི་ཏྲ

Jñānaśrīmitra

1 text, 1 page

སློབ་དཔོན་རིན་ཆེན་རྡོ་རྗེ

Ratnavajra

1 text, 1 page

སློབ་དཔོན་རིན་ཆེན་འབྱུང་གནས་

ཞི་བའིཞབས

Ratnākaraśānti

2 texts, 4 pages

# Authors of Other Schools

## Earth gTer-stons from the Rin-chen gTer-mdzod

ཇོ་བོ་རྗེ་ཨ་ཏི་ཤ

Jo-bo-rje Atīśa
982–1054 C.E.

གཉན་ལོ་ཙཱ་བ་དར་མ་གྲགས

gNyan Lo-tsā-ba
Dar-ma-grags
11th century C.E.

རྒྱ་ལོ་ཙཱ་བ

rGya Lo-tsā-ba
late 10th century C.E.

ཁྲོ་ཕུ་ལོ་ཙཱ་བ་བྱམས་པ་དཔལ

Khro-phu Lo-tsā-ba
Byams-pa-dpal
1173–1225 C.E.

ལྷ་བཙུན་བྱང་ཆུབ་འོད

lHa-btsun Byang-chub-'od
early 11th century C.E.

སྟག་ལུང་པ་སངས་རྒྱས་དབོན་པོ

sTag-lung-pa   Sangs-rgyas
dBon-po
1251–1296 C.E.

## Pure Vision and Realization gTer-stons from the Rin-chen gTer-mdzod

རས་ཆུང་རྡོ་རྗེ་གྲགས

Ras-chung rDo-rje-grags
1084–1161 C.E.

ཁ་ཆེ་པཎ་ཆེན་ཤཱཀྱ་ཤྲཱི

Kha-che Paṇ-chen
Śākya Śrī
1127 C.E.

འཕན་ཡུལ་པ་དཔལ་ལྡན་རྡོ་རྗེ

'Phan-yul-pa
dPal-ldan rDo-rje
15th century C.E.

པཎ་གྲུབ་ཆེན་པོ་ཤྲཱི་བ་ན་རཏྣ

Paṇ-grub Chen-po
Śrī Vanaratna
1384 C.E.

རྒྱལ་དབང་ཆོས་རྗེ་ཀུན་དགའ་དཔལ་འབྱོར

rGyal-dbang Chos-rje Kun-
dga' dPal-'byor
15th century C.E.

ཀརྨ་པ་མཐོང་བ་དོན་ལྡན

Karmapa mThong-ba
Don-ldan
1416–1453 C.E.

རས་ཆེན་དཔལ་འབྱོར་བཟང་པོ

Ras-chen dPal-'byor
bZang-po
15th century C.E.

བོ་དོང་རྟོགས་ལྡན་སངས་རྒྱས་མགོན་པོ

Bo-dong rTogs-ldan Sangs-
rgyas mGon-po
uncertain date

ཀུན་མཁྱེན་པདྨ་དཀར་པོ

Kun-mkhyen
Padma dKar-po
1527–1592 C.E.

བྱམས་མགོན་ཏཱའི་སི་ཏུ་པདྨ་ཉིན་བྱེད་དབང་པོ

Byams-mgon Tā'i Si-tu
Padma Nyin-byed dBang-po
1774–1853 C.E.

དཔའ་བོ་གཙུག་ལག་ཆོས་ཀྱི་རྒྱལ་པོ

dPa'-bo gTsug-lag Chos-kyi
rGyal-po
19th century C.E.

ཇོ་བོ་རྗེ་ཨ་ཏི་ཤ།

Jo-bo-rje Atīśa
982–1054 C.E.
3 texts

རྗེ་མར་པ་ལོ་ཙྪ་བ་ཆོས་ཀྱི་བློ་གྲོས།

rJe Mar-pa Lo-tsā-ba
Chos-kyi Blo-gros
1012–1097 C.E.
1 text

འབྲོམ་སྟོན་རྒྱལ་བའི་འབྱུང་གནས།

'Brom-ston rGyal-ba'i
'Byung-gnas
1005–1064 C.E.
2 texts

རྗེ་བཙུན་མི་ལ་རས་པ།

rJe-btsun Mi-la Ras-pa
1040–1123 C.E.
4 texts

དྲན་པ་ཡེ་ཤེས་གྲགས་པ།

Dran-pa Ye-shes Grags-pa
11th century C.E.
2 texts

བ་རི་ལོ་ཙྪ་རིན་ཆེན་གྲགས།

Ba-ri Lo-tsā Rin-chen-grags
1040 C.E.
4 texts

གཙང་སྟོད་དར་མ་མགོན་པོ།

gTsang-stod
Dar-ma mGon-po
11th–12th century C.E.
4 texts

རྗེ་བཙུན་མ་གཅིག་ལབ་ཀྱི་སྒྲོན་མ།

rJe-btsun Ma-gcig
Lab-kyi sGron-ma
1062–1150 C.E.
2 texts

ཁ་སྒྲུབ་ཆེན་པོ་སྒམ་པོ་པ་
བསོད་ནམས་རིན་ཆེན

mKhas-grub Chen-po
sGam-po-pa
bSod-nams Rin-chen
1079–1153 C.E.
20 texts

ཞང་གཡུ་བྲག་པ་
བརྩོན་འགྲུས་གྲགས་པ་

Zhang gYu-brag-pa
brTson-'grus Grags-pa
1123–1193 C.E.
4 texts

རས་ཆུང་རྡོ་རྗེ་གྲགས་པ་

Ras-chung rDo-rje Grags-pa
1084–1161 C.E.
5 texts

གླིང་ཆེན་རས་པ་པདྨ་རྡོ་རྗེ་

Gling-chen Ras-pa
Padma rDo-rje
1128–1188 C.E.
1 text

གྲུབ་ཐོབ་ཆེན་པོ་ཕ་དམ་པ་
སངས་རྒྱས

Grub-thob Chen-po
Pha-dam-pa Sangs-rgyas
d. 1117 C.E.
7 texts

རྗེ་བཙུན་ཆེན་པོ་
བསོད་ནམས་རྩེ་མོ

rJe-btsun Chen-po
bSod-nams rTse-mo
1142–1182 C.E.
1 text

འགྲོ་མགོན་ཕག་མོ་གྲུ་པ་
རྡོ་རྗེ་རྒྱལ་པོ

'Gro-mgon Phag-mo-gru-pa
rDo-rje rGyal-po
1110–1170 C.E.
31 texts

སྟག་ལུང་ཐང་པ་ཆེན་པོ་
བཀྲ་ཤིས་དཔལ

sTag-lung Thang-pa Chen-po
bKra-shis-dpal
1142–1210 C.E.
2 texts

འབྲི་གུང་སྐྱོབ་པ
འཇིག་རྟེན་མགོན་པོ

'Bri-gung sKyob-pa
'Jig-rten mGon-po
1143–1217 C.E.
21 texts

འཇམ་དབྱངས་ས་སྐྱ་པཎྜི
ཀུན་དགའ་རྒྱལ་མཚན

'Jam-dbyangs
Sa-skya Paṇḍita
Kun-dga' rGyal-mtshan
1182–1251 C.E.
4 texts

རྗེ་བཙུན་ཆེན་པོ
གྲགས་པ་རྒྱལ་མཚན

rJe-btsun Chen-po
Grags-pa rGyal-mtshan
1147–1216 C.E.
10 texts

དབོན་པོ་ཤེས་རབ་འབྱུང་གནས

dBon-po Shes-rab
'Byung-gnas
1187–1241 C.E.
1 text

འགྲོ་མགོན་གཙང་པ་རྒྱ་རས
ཡེ་ཤེས་རྡོ་རྗེ

'Gro-mgon
gTsang-pa rGya-ras
Ye-shes rDo-rje
1161–1211 C.E.
1 text

གྲུབ་ཆེན་རྒོད་ཚང་པ
མགོན་པོ་རྡོ་རྗེ

Grub-chen rGod-tshang-pa
mGon-po rDo-rje
1189–1258 C.E.
1 text

ཁྲོ་ཕུ་ལོ་ཙཱ་བ་བྱམས་པ་དཔལ

Khro-phu Lo-tsā-ba
Byams-pa-dpal
1173–1225 C.E.
3 texts

བྱང་ཆུབ་དངོས་གྲུབ་ལ་ཡག་པ

Byang-chub dNgos-grub
La-yag-pa
12th century C.E.
1 text

གྲུབ་ཆེན་གཱརྨ་པཀྵི

Grub-chen Karma Pakṣi
1204–1283 C.E.
1 text

ཟླ་བ་སེངྒེ

Zla-ba Seng-ge
13th century C.E.
1 text

མཁས་གྲུབ་ཡང་དགོན་པ
རྒྱལ་མཚན་དཔལ

mKhas-grub Yang-dgon-pa
rGyal-mtshan-dpal
1213–1258 C.E.
1 text

སངས་རྒྱས་རིན་ཆེན

Sangs-rgyas Rin-chen
1245–1302 C.E.
1 text

སྤྱན་སྔ་རིན་ཆེན་ལྡན

sPyan-snga Rin-chen-ldan
1202 C.E.
1 text

ཉི་མ་སེངྒེ

Nyi-ma Seng-ge
1251–1287 C.E.
1 text

འགྲོ་མགོན་འཕགས་པ
བློ་གྲོས་རྒྱལ་མཚན

'Gro-mgon 'Phags-pa
Blo-gros rGyal-mtshan
1235–1280 C.E.
1 text

སློབ་དཔོན་གནས་བརྟན
བློ་གྲོས་བརྟན་པ

Slob-dpon gNas-brtan
Blo-gros brTan-pa
1276–1342 C.E.
1 text

ཀུན་མཁྱེན་བུ་སྟོན་རིན་ཆེན་གྲུབ

Kun-mkhyen Bu-ston
Rin-chen-grub
1290–1364 C.E.
27 texts

སྣར་ཐང་དགེ་འདུན་དཔལ

sNar-thang dGe-'dun-dpal
13th century C.E.
1 text

ཀུན་མཁྱེན་དོལ་པོ
ཤེས་རབ་རྒྱལ་མཚན

Kun-mkhyen Dol-po
Shes-rab rGyal-mtshan
1291–1361 C.E.
17 texts

དབུས་པ་བློ་གསལ

dBus-pa Blo-gsal
14th century C.E.
1 text

རྒྱལ་སྲས་ཐོགས་མེད་བཟང་པོ

rGyal-sras Thogs-med
bZang-po
1295–1369 C.E.
1 text

མཆིམས་སྟོན་བློ་བཟང་གྲགས་པ

mChims-ston
Blo-bzang Grags-pa
14th century C.E.
1 text

འུ་ཡུག་པ་རིག་པའི་སེང་གེ

'U-yug-pa Rig-pa'i Seng-ge
13th century C.E.
1 text

བྱང་ཆུབ་རྒྱལ་མཚན

Byang-chub rGyal-mtshan
1302 C.E.
1 text

བོ་དོང་པཎ་ཆེན
ཕྱོགས་ལས་རྣམ་རྒྱལ

Bo-dong Paṇ-chen
Phyogs-las rNam-rgyal
1306–1386 C.E.
12 texts

མ་ཏི་པཎ་ཆེན
འཇམ་དབྱངས་བློ་གྲོས

Ma-ti Paṇ-chen 'Jam-dbyangs
Blo-gros
14th century C.E.
2 texts

འབའ་ར་བ་རྒྱལ་མཚན
དཔལ་བཟང

'Ba'-ra-ba
rGyal-mtshan dPal-bzang
1310–1391 C.E.
4 texts

རྩིས་པ་ཀུན་དགའ་གསལ་བ

rTsis-pa Kun-dga' gSal-ba
14th century C.E.
1 text

ས་སྐྱ་བླ་མ་དམ་པ
བསོད་ནམས་རྒྱལ་མཚན

Sa-skya Bla-ma Dam-pa
bSod-nams rGyal-mtshan
1312–1375 C.E.
2 texts

ཚལ་པ་ཀུན་དགའ་རྡོ་རྗེ

Tshal-pa Kun-dga' rDo-rje
1346 C.E.
1 text

འཇམ་དབྱངས་ཀུན་དགའ་སེངྒེ

'Jam-dbyangs Kun-dga'
Seng-ge
1314–1347 C.E.
1 text

རྗེ་བཙུན་རེད་མདའ་བ་གཞོན་ནུ
བློ་གྲོས

rJe-btsun Red-mda'-ba
gZhon-nu Blo-gros
1349–1412 C.E.
3 texts

ཤྭ་དམར་གཉིས་པ
མཁའ་སྤྱོད་དབང་པོ

Zhwa-dmar gNyis-pa

mKha'-spyod dBang-po

1350–1405 C.E.

3 texts

པཎ་གྲུབ་ཆེན་པོ་ཤྲི་བ་ན་རཏྣ

Paṇ-grub Chen-po

Śrī Vanaratna

1384

རྗེ་འཇམ་དབྱངས
ཙོང་ཁ་པ་ཆེན་པོ

rJe 'Jam-dbyangs

Tsong-kha-pa Chen-po

1357–1419 C.E.

16 texts

རྒྱ་མ་བློས་གྲོས་རྒྱལ་མཚན

rGya-ma-ba

Blos-gros rGyal-mtshan

1390–1448 C.E.

1 text

ཀུན་མཁྱེན་རོང་སྟོན་ཆེན་པོ

Kun-mkhyen Rong-ston

Chen-po

1367–1456 C.E.

12 texts

ངོར་ཆེན་སངས་རྒྱས་ཕུན་ཚོགས

Ngor-chen

Sangs-rgyas Phun-tshogs

15th century C.E.

2 texts

ངོར་ཆེན་ཀུན་དགའ་བཟང་པོ

Ngor-chen

Kun-dga' bZang-po

1382–1456 C.E.

5 texts

སྟག་ཚང་ལོ་ཙཱ་བ་ཤེས་རབ་རིན་ཆེན

sTag-tshang Lo-tsā-ba

Shes-rab Rin-chen

1405 C.E.

2 texts

འབྲུག་ཆེན་གཉིས་པ་རྒྱལ་དབང་
ཀུན་དགའ་དཔལ་འབྱོར

'Brug-chen gNyis-pa
rGyal-dbang
Kun-dga' dPal-'byor
1428–1476 C.E.
2 texts

གཡས་རུ་སྟག་ཚང་པ་
དཔལ་འབྱོར་བཟང་པོ

gYas-ru sTag-tshang-pa
dPal-'byor bZang-po
1434 C.E.
1 text

གསེར་མདོག་པཎ་ཆེན་
ཤཱཀྱ་མཆོག་ལྡན

gSer-mdog Paṇ-chen
Śākya mChog-ldan
1428–1507 C.E.
1 text

ཟུར་མཁར་
མཉམ་ཉིད་རྡོ་རྗེ

Zur-mkhar mNyam-nyid
rDo-rje
1439–1475 C.E.
4 texts

མཁས་གྲུབ་ཆེན་པོ་གོ་བོ་རབ་
འབྱམས་པ་བསོད་ནམས་སེང་གེ

mKhas-grub Chen-po Go-bo
Rab-'byams-pa
bSod-nams Seng-ge
1429–1489 C.E.
20 texts

ས་སྐྱ་བདག་ཆེན་
བློ་གྲོས་རྒྱལ་མཚན

Sa-skya bDag-chen
Blo-gros rGyal-mtshan
1444–1495 C.E.
3 texts

སྤོས་ཁང་པ་རིན་ཆེན་རྒྱལ་མཚན

sPos-khang-pa
Rin-chen rGyal-mtshan
15th century C.E.
1 text

གཙང་སྨྱོན་ཧེ་རུ་ཀ
སངས་རྒྱས་རྒྱལ་མཚན

gTsang-smyon He-ru-ka
Sangs-rgyas rGyal-mtshan
1452–1507 C.E.
1 text

ཀརྨ་པ་ཆོས་གྲགས་རྒྱ་མཚོ

Karmapa Chos-grags
rGya-mtsho
1454–1506 C.E.
1 text

གཉུག་ལ་པཎ་ཆེན
ངག་དབང་གྲགས་པ

gNyug-la Paṇ-chen
Ngag-dbang Grags-pa
1458–1515 C.E.
1 text

རྒྱལ་བ་དགེ་འདུན་རྒྱ་མཚོ

rGyal-ba dGe-'dun
rGya-mtsho
1476–1542 C.E.
1 text

རིན་སྤུངས་ངག་དབང་འཇིག་རྟེན
དབང་ཕྱུག་གྲགས་པ

Rin-spungs Ngag-dbang
'Jig-rten
dBang-phyug Grags-pa
1482–1565 C.E.
5 texts

བསོད་ནམས་ལྷའི་དབང་པོ

bSod-nams lHa'i-dbang-po
1484 C.E.
1 text

སྒམ་པོ་པ་བསོད་ནམས་ལྷུན་གྲུབ

sGam-po-pa bSod-nams
lHun-grub
1488–1552 C.E.
1 text

ལས་ཆེན་ཀུན་དགའ་རྒྱལ་མཚན་

Las-chen Kun-dga'
rGyal-mtshan
1494 C.E.
1 text

ཞང་ཞུང་ཆོས་དབང་གྲགས་པ་

Zhang-zhung
Chos-dbang Grags-pa
15th century C.E.
1 text

རྒོད་ཚང་རས་པ་སྣ་ཚོགས་རང་
གྲོལ

rGod-tshang Ras-pa
sNa-tshogs Rang-grol
1494–1570 C.E.
1 text

གློ་བོ་མཁན་ཆེན་
བསོད་ནམས་ལྷུན་གྲུབ

Glo-bo mKhan-chen
bSod-nams lHun-grub
15th century C.E.
1 text

ངོར་ཆེན་དཀོན་མཆོག་ལྷུན་གྲུབ

Ngor-chen dKon-mchog
lHun-grub
1497–1557 C.E.
5 texts

ནེའུ་པཎྜི་ཏ
གྲགས་པ་སྨོན་ལམ་བློ་གྲོས

Ne'u Paṇḍita
Grags-pa sMon-lam Blo-gros
15th century C.E.
1 text

སྙེ་ཐང་བློ་གྲོས་བརྟན་པ་བཞི་པ

sNye-thang  Blo-gros  brTan-
pa bZhi-pa
15th century C.E.
1 text

མ་ཕམ་རྡོ་རྗེ

Ma-pham rDo-rje
15th century C.E.
1 text

དོན་དམ་སྨྲ་བའི་སེང་གེ

Don-dam sMra-ba'i Seng-ge
15th century C.E.
1 text

ཇོ་ནང་རྗེ་བཙུན
ཀུན་དགའ་གྲོལ་མཆོག

Jo-nang rJe-btsun Kun-dga'
Grol-mchog
1507–1566 C.E.
10 texts

ཟུར་མཁར་བློ་གྲོས་རྒྱལ་པོ
ལེགས་བཤད་འཚོལ

Zur-mkhar Blo-gros
rGyal-po
Legs-bshad-'tshol
fl. 1508 C.E.
5 texts

ཀརྨ་པ་མི་བསྐྱོད་རྡོ་རྗེ

Karmapa Mi-bskyod rDo-rje
1507–1554 C.E.
3 texts

ཚར་ཆེན་བློ་གསལ་རྒྱ་མཚོ

Tshar-chen
Blo-gsal rGya-mtsho
1502–1566 C.E.
6 texts

ལྷ་མཐོང་ལོ་ཙཱ་བ
བཤེས་གཉེན་རྣམ་རྒྱལ

lHa-mthong Lo-tsā-ba
bShes-gnyen rNam-rgyal
1512 C.E.
1 text

དཔའ་བོ་གཙུག་ལག་ཕྲེང་བ

dPa'-bo gTsug-lag Phreng-ba
1504–1566 C.E.
2 texts

དྭགས་པོ་པཎ་ཆེན
བཀྲ་ཤིས་རྣམ་རྒྱལ

Dwags-po Paṇ-chen
bKra-shis rNam-rgyal
1512–1587 C.E.
7 texts

མང་ཐོས་ཀླུ་སྒྲུབ་རྒྱ་མཚོ

Mang-thos Klu-sgrub
rGya-mtsho
1523–1596 C.E.
1 text

རྒྱལ་བ་བསོད་ནམས་རྒྱ་མཚོ

rGyal-ba bSod-nams
rGya-mtsho
1543–1588 C.E.
1 text

པད་དཀར་ཡིད་བཞིན་དབང་པོ

Pad-dkar
Yid-bzhin dBang-po
1525 C.E.
1 text

ཀརྨ་པ་དབང་ཕྱུག་རྡོ་རྗེ

Karmapa dBang-phyug
rDo-rje
1556–1603 C.E.
2 texts

ཞྭ་དམར་ལྔ་པ
དགོན་མཆོག་ཡན་ལག

Zhwa-dmar lNga-pa
dKon-mchog Yan-lag
1525–1583 C.E.
1 text

ས་སྐྱ་པ་ཀུན་དགའ་བཀྲ་ཤིས

Sa-skya-pa
Kun-dga' bKra-shis
1558–1615 C.E.
1 text

ཀུན་མཁྱེན་པདྨ་དཀར་པོ

Kun-mkhyen
Padma dKar-po
1527–1592 C.E.
46 texts

པཎ་ཆེན་བློ་བཟང
ཆོས་ཀྱི་རྒྱལ་མཚན

Paṇ-chen Blo-bzang
Chos-kyi rGyal-mtshan
1570–1662 C.E.
3 texts

རྟག་ལུང་པ་ངག་དབང་རྣམ་རྒྱལ

sTag-lung-pa Ngag-dbang
rNam-rgyal
1571–1626 C.E.
3 texts

ཁམས་སྨྱོན་དྷརྨ་སེངྒེ

Khams-smyon
Dharma Seng-ge
16th century C.E.
10 texts

ངག་དབང་ཆོས་གྲགས

Ngag-dbang Chos-grags
1572–1641 C.E.
1 text

གོང་སྨན་དཀོན་མཆོག
བདེ་ལེགས

Gong-sman dKon-mchog
bDe-legs
15th–16th century C.E.
6 texts

ཇོ་ནང་ཀུན་དགའ་སྙིང་པོ་ཏཱ་ར་ནཱ་ཐ

Jo-nang Kun-dga' sNying-po
Tāranātha
1575 C.E.
49 texts

གོང་སྨན་དཀོན་མཆོག་ཕན་དར

Gong-sman dKon-mchog
Phan-dar
16th century C.E.
1 text

ཞྭ་དམར་དྲུག་པ
གར་དབང་ཆོས་ཀྱི་དབང་ཕྱུག

Zhwa-dmar Drug-pa Gar-
dbang Chos-kyi dBang-phyug
1584–1630 C.E.
1 text

མཁས་མཆོག་ཟུར་འཚོ་བ
ཕྱག་རྡོར་མགོན་པོ

mKhas-mchog Zur-'tsho-ba
Phyag-rdor mGon-po
16th century C.E.
1 text

དཔལ་ཁང་ལོ་ཙཱ་བ
ངག་དབང་ཆོས་ཀྱི་རྒྱ་མཚོ

dPal-khang Lo-tsā-ba Ngag-
dbang Chos-kyi rGya-mtsho
16th century C.E.
2 texts

གཙང་མཁན་ཆེན
འཇམ་དབྱངས་དཔལ་ལྡན་རྒྱ་མཚོ

gTsang-mkhan-chen
'Jam-dbyangs dPal-ldan
rGya-mtsho
1610–1684 C.E.
3 texts

འཇམ་མགོན་ཨ་མྱེས་ཞབས
ངག་དབང་ཀུན་དགའ་བསོད་ནམས

'Jam-mgon A-myes Zhabs
Ngag-dbang
Kun-dga' bSod-nams
16th century C.E.
1 text

ཞ་ལུ་མཁན་ཆེན་རིན་ཆེན་བསོད་
ནམས་མཆོག་གྲུབ

Zha-lu mKhan-chen
Rin-chen
bSod-nams mChog-grub
1642–1721 C.E.
1 text

འདུལ་འཛིན་མཁྱེན་རབ་རྒྱ་མཚོ

'Dul-'dzin
mKhyen-rab rGya-mtsho
16th century C.E.
1 text

སྡེ་སྲིད་སངས་རྒྱས་རྒྱ་མཚོ

sDe-srid Sangs-rgyas
rGya-mtsho
1653–1705 C.E.
10 texts

བཙུན་པ་བྷི་ཀྵུ་རེ་ཤ་ཏི་བྷ་ད་

bTsun-pa Bhikṣu
Sureśamatibhadra
16th century C.E.
1 text

འཛམ་གླིང་པ་བློ་གྲོས་ཆོས་འཕེལ

'Dzam-gling-pa
Blo-gros Chos-'phel
1665–1727 C.E.
1 text

ཕུར་བུ་ལྕོག་བྱམས་པ་རྒྱ་མཚོ

Phur-bu-lcog Byams-pa
rGya-mtsho
1682–1762 C.E.
5 texts

ཀརྨ་རིག་འཛིན་གསུང་རབ་རྒྱ་མཚོ

Karma Rig-'dzin
gSung-rab rGya-mtsho
17th century C.E.
2 texts

བྱ་རིགས་རྣམ་གླིང་པ་པཎ་ཆེན་
དགོན་མཆོག་ཆོས་གྲགས

Bya-rigs rNam-gling-pa
Paṇ-chen dKon-mchog
Chos-grags
fl. 1683 C.E.
1 text

བོད་མཁས་པ་མི་ཕམ་
དགེ་ལེགས་རྣམ་རྒྱལ

Bod-mkhas-pa
Mi-pham dGe-legs
rNam-rgyal
17th century C.E.
11 texts

གྲུབ་དབང་རིག་འཛིན་རྒྱལ་པོ

Grub-dbang
Rig-'dzin rGyal-po
1692 C.E.
1 text

འབྲི་གུང་པ་ཞབས་དྲུང་
དགོན་མཆོག་རིན་ཆེན

'Bri-gung-pa Zhabs-drung
dKon-mchog Rin-chen
17th century C.E.

མདོ་མཁར་ཞབས་དྲུང་ཚེ་རིང་
དབང་རྒྱལ

mDo-mkhar Zhabs-drung
Tshe-ring dBang-rgyal
1697–1763 C.E.
3 texts

ཀརྨ་མི་འགྱུར་དབང་རྒྱལ

Karma Mi-'gyur dBang-rgyal
17th century C.E.
2 texts

དྲུང་ཡིག་རྟ་མགྲིན་དབང་རྒྱལ

Drung-yig rTa-mgrin
dBang-rgyal
17th century C.E.
1 text

ངག་དབང་བསྟན་པའི་ཉི་མ

Ngag-dbang bsTan-pa'i
Nyi-ma
17th century C.E.
2 texts

དར་མོ་སྨན་རམས་པ
བློ་བཟང་ཆོས་གྲགས

Dar-mo sMan-rams-pa
Blo-bzang Chos-grags
17th century C.E.
2 texts

ངག་དབང་དཀོན་མཆོག
བསྟན་རྒྱལ

Ngag-dbang dKon-mchog
bsTan-rgyal
17th or 18th century C.E.
1 text

ངག་དབང་དཔལ་བཟང་པོ

Ngag-dbang dPal-bzang-po
17th century C.E.
2 texts

ཏཱའི་སི་ཏུ་ཆོས་ཀྱི་འབྱུང་གནས
གཙུག་ལག་ཆོས་ཀྱི་སྣང་བ

Tā'i Situ Chos-kyi 'Byung-
gnas gTsug-lag
Chos-kyi sNang-ba
1700–1774 C.E.
10 texts

ངག་དབང་རིག་གནས་རྒྱ་མཚོ་
རྡོ་རྗེའི་དབང་ཕྱུག

Ngag-dbang Rig-gnas rGya-
mtsho rDo-rje'i
dBang-phyug Ngag-dbang
dPal-bzang-po
17th century C.E.
1 text

འབེ་ལོ་ཚེ་དབང་ཀུན་ཁྱབ

'Be-lo Tshe-dbang Kun-khyab
18th century C.E.
1 text

གཀྨ་ངེས་ལེགས་
བསྟན་འཛིན་

Karma Nges-legs
bsTan-'dzin
18th century C.E.
3 texts

ཁམས་སྤྲུལ་བསྟན་འཛིན་
ཆོས་ཀྱི་ཉི་མ་

Khams-sprul bsTan-'dzin
Chos-kyi Nyi-ma
1730–1779 C.E.
1 text

ལྕང་སྐྱ་རོལ་པའི་རྡོ་རྗེ་

lCang-skya Rol-pa'i rDo-rje
1717–1786 C.E.
2 texts

གུང་ཐང་དཀོན་མཆོག་
བསྟན་པའི་སྒྲོན་མེ་

Gung-thang dKon-mchog
bsTan-pa'i sGron-me
1762–1823 C.E.
1 text

ཀུན་དགའ་བློ་གྲོས་

Kun-dga' Blo-gros
1729–1783 C.E.
4 texts

འབྲུག་པ་ཀུན་གཟིགས་
ཆོས་ཀྱི་སྣང་བ་

'Brug-pa Kun-gzigs
Chos-kyi sNang-ba
1768–1822 C.E.
2 texts

ཐུའུབ་ཀྭན་བློ་བཟང་ཆོས་ཀྱི་ཉི་མ་

Thu'ub-kwan
Blo-bzang Chos-kyi Nyi-ma
1737–1802 C.E.
1 text

བསྟན་འཛིན་པདྨའི་རྒྱལ་མཚན་

bsTan-'dzin Padma'i rGyal-
mtshan 'Bri-gung Che-tshang
bzhi-pa
1770 C.E.
1 text

དངུལ་ཆུ་དྷ་རྨ་བྷ་དྲ

dNgul-chu Dharmabhadra
1772–1851 C.E.
1 text

ཏཱའི་སི་ཏུ་པདྨ་ཉིན་བྱེད་དབང་པོ

Tā'i Situ
Padma Nyin-byed dBang-po
1774–1853? C.E.
9 texts

སྟག་ལུང་ངག་དབང་
བསྟན་པའི་ཉི་མ

sTag-lung Ngag-dbang
bsTan-pa'i Nyi-ma
1788 C.E.
1 text

འཇམ་དཔལ་ཆོས་ཀྱི་
བསྟན་འཛིན་འཕྲིན་ལས

'Jam-dpal Chos-kyi
bsTan-'dzin 'Phrin-las
1789–1838 C.E.
1 text

ཀརྨ་ངེས་དོན་བསྟན་འཛིན་
འཕྲིན་ལས་རབ་རྒྱས

Karma Nges-don
bsTan-'dzin
'Phrin-las Rab-rgyas
18th century C.E.
1 text

བསྟན་འཛིན་རྒྱལ་མཚན

bsTan-'dzin rGyal-mtshan
18th century C.E.
4 texts

སྨན་བླ་དོན་གྲུབ་སྨན་ཐང་པ

sMan-bla Don-grub
sMan-thang-pa
18th century C.E.
1 text

དིལ་དམར་དགེ་བཤེས་
བསྟན་འཛིན་ཕུན་ཚོགས

Dil-dmar dGe-bshes
bsTan-'dzin Phun-tshogs
18th century C.E.
4 texts

ཐུའུབ་ཀུན་ཆོས་ཀྱི་རྡོ་རྗེ

Thu'ub-kwan
Chos-kyi rDo-rje
18th century C.E.
1 text

དཔའ་བོ་བརྒྱད་པ་པདྨ་བསྟན་
འཛིན་གྲུབ་མཆོག་རྩལ

dPa'-bo brGyad-pa
Padma bsTan-'dzin
Grub-mchog-rtsal
19th century C.E.
1 text

ཀརྨ་པ་བཅུ་བཞི་པ་
ཐེག་མཆོག་རྡོ་རྗེ

Karmapa bCu-bzhi-pa
Theg-mchog rDo-rje
1797–1867 C.E.
9 texts

འཇམ་དབྱངས་བློ་གཏེར་
དབང་པོ

'Jam-dbyangs Blo-gter
dBang-po
1847–1914 C.E.
7 texts

ཀུན་དགའ་འཕྲིན་ལས་དཔལ་ལྡན

Kun-dga' 'Phrin-las
dPal-ldan
fl. 1800 C.E.
1 text

འབྲི་གུང་པ་ནུས་ལྡན་རྡོ་རྗེ

'Bri-gung-pa Nus-ldan
rDo-rje
1849–1903 C.E.
4 texts

ཞྭ་ལུ་རི་སྦུག་སྤྲུལ་སྐུ་
བློ་གསལ་བསྟན་སྐྱོང

Zhwa-lu Ri-sbug sPrul-sku
Blo-gsal bsTan-skyong
1804–1874 C.E.
9 texts

ཀུན་དགའ་གྲགས་པ་བརྒྱལ་མཚན

Kun-dga' Grags-pa
rGyal-mtshan
19th century C.E.
1 text

ཀརྨ་རཏྣ

Karma Ratna
19th century C.E.
2 texts

འཇམ་དཔལ་རྡོ་རྗེ

'Jam-dpal rDo-rje
19th century C.E.
1 text

ཟུར་མང་མཁན་པོ་པདྨ་རྣམ་རྒྱལ

Zur-mang mKhan-po
Padma rNam-rgyal
19th century C.E.
2 texts

ཀརྨ་ཆོས་རྒྱལ

Karma Chos-rgyal
19th or 20th century C.E.
2 texts

བསྟན་འཛིན་ཆོས་ཀྱི་བློ་གྲོས

bsTan-'dzin Chos-kyi
Blo-gros
1868 C.E.
1 text

སྤྲུལ་སྐུ་ཚེ་དབང་རྡོ་རྗེ

sPrul-sku Tshe-dbang
rDo-rje
19th or 20th century C.E.
1 text

ཀརྨ་པ་བཅོ་ལྔ་པ་མཁའ་ཁྱབ་རྡོ་རྗེ

Karmapa bCo-lnga-pa
mKha'-khyab rDo-rje
1871–1922 C.E.
16 texts

ངོར་ཁང་གསར་མཁན་ཆེན་ངག་དབང

Ngor Khang-gsar
mKhan-chen Ngag-dbang
bSod-nams rGyal-mtshan-
20th century C.E.
2 texts

མཁྱེན་རབ་ནོར་བུ

mKhyen-rab Nor-bu
1883–1963 C.E.
4 texts

# Undated Authors

འབའ་ར་བ་ཨོ་རྒྱན་
ངག་དབང་ཡེ་ཤེས་

'Ba'-ra-ba-O-rgyan
Ngag-dbang Ye-shes
1 text

ཟུར་མང་དྲུང་པ་
ཀུན་དགའ་རྣམ་རྒྱལ་

Zur-mang Drung-pa
Kun-dga' rNam-rgyal
1 text

བོ་དོང་རྟོགས་ལྡན་
སངས་རྒྱས་མགོན་པོ་

Bo-dong rTogs-ldan
Sangs-rgyas mGon-po
1 text

གྲུབ་ཐོབ་ཡེ་ཤེས་བརྩེགས་པ་

Grub-thob
Ye-shes brTsegs-pa
1 text

ཀུན་དགའ་ཆོས་འཕེལ་

Kun-dga' Chos-'phel
1 text

སྙེ་མདོ་བ་བསོད་ནམས་དཔལ་

sNye-mdo-ba
bSod-nams-dpal
1 text

ངམ་རྫོང་སྟོན་པ་
བྱང་ཆུབ་རྒྱལ་པོ་

Ngam-rdzong sTon-pa
Byang-chub rGyal-po
1 text

རྟོགས་ལྡན་བསྟན་འཛིན་རྣམ་དག་

rTogs-ldan bsTan-'dzin
rNam-dag
1 text

440

ཆོས་དཔག་རྡོ་རྗེ

'Od-dpag rDo-rje

15 texts

མཁྱེན་རབ་ཆོས་རྗེ

mKhyen-rab Chos-rje

1 text

ཡེ་ཤེས་དོན་གྲུབ
བསྟན་པའི་རྒྱལ་མཚན

Ye-shes Don-grub
bsTan-pa'i rGyal-mtshan

1 text

གྲགས་པ་རིན་ཆེན

Grags-pa Rin-chen

2 texts

བྱམས་པ་ངག་དབང
བསྟན་འཛིན་སྙན་གྲགས

Byams-pa Ngag-dbang
bsTan-'dzin sNyan-grags

1 text

རྒྱལ་སྲས་དངུལ་ཆུ
ཐོགས་མེད་བཟང་པོ་དཔལ

rGyal-sras dNgul-chu
Thogs-med bZang-po-dpal

1 text

གཞན་ཕན་བྱམས་པའི་གོ་ཆ

gZhan-phan Byams-pa'i
Go-cha

1 text

ཀརྨ་ཚེ་དབང་དཔལ་ལྡན

Karma Tshe-dbang
dPal-ldan

1 text

བློ་གྲོས་རྒྱ་མཚོ

Blo-gros rGya-mtsho

1 text

པདྨ་ཕྲིན་ལས་ཆོས་གྲགས་རྒྱ་མཚོ

Padma Phrin-las Chos-grags
rGya-mtsho

1 text

ग्रम་ངེས་དོན་སྙིང་པོ་
གཞན་ཕན་ཆོས་ཀྱི་དབང་ཕྱུག

Karma Nges-don sNying-po
gZhan-phan Chos-kyi
dBang-phyug
1 text

དཀོན་མཆོག་ངེས་དོན་འཛམ་གླིང་
ཆོས་གྲགས་རྒྱ་མཚོ

dKon-mchog Nges-don
'Dzam-gling
Chos-grags rGya-mtsho
1 text

ग्रम་སངས་རྒྱས་ཆོས་འཕེལ

Karma Sangs-rgyas
Chos-'phel
1 text

སངས་རྒྱས་དར་པོ

Sangs-rgyas Dar-po
1 text

གུ་རུ་རཏྣ

Guru Ratna
1 text

སངས་རྒྱས་འབུམ

Sangs-rgyas 'Bum
4 texts

ཐུབ་བསྟན་ཆོས་གྲགས

Thub-bstan Chos-grags
1 text

ཤཱི་ལ

Shī-la
1 text

དབང་ཕྱུག་རྒྱལ་མཚན

dBang-phyug rGyal-mtshan
1 text

སྡེ་སྣོད་འཛིན་པ་རིན་ཆེན་དཔལ

sDe-snod 'Dzin-pa
Rin-chen-dpal
1 text

ग्राग्स་པ་སེང་གེ

Grags-pa Seng-ge

1 text

སྤེན་ཏ་པ་ཉི་མ་རྒྱལ་པོ

sPen-ta-pa Nyi-ma rGyal-po

1 text

བསམ་རྒྱལ་ཁ་ཆེ

bSam-rgyal Kha-che

1 text

ཨ་ན་རཱ་ཛ

A-na-rā-dza

1 text

རྗེ་ལྷ་དབང་བློ་གྲོས

rJe lHa-dbang Blo-gros

1 text

ཤཱ་ཀྱ་རིན་ཆེན

Shā-kya Rin-chen

2 texts

བྱར་པོ་སྒོམ་ཆེན་ཆོས་རྒྱལ་
བསོད་ནམས་རྒྱལ་མཚན

Byar-po sGom-chen
Chos-rgyal
bSod-nams rGyal-mtshan

1 text

ངག་དབང་ཆོས་ཀྱི་རྒྱལ་པོ

Ngag-dbang Chos-kyi
rGyal-po

1 text

བསོད་ནམས་མཆོག་ལྡན

bSod-nams mChog-ldan

1 text

འབྲུག་པ་ངག་གི་དབང་པོ

'Brug-pa Ngag-gi dBang-po

1 text

རིན་ཆེན་སེང་གེ

Rin-chen Seng-ge

2 texts

གུང་མགོན་པོ་སྐྱབས།

Gung mGon-po sKyabs

1 text

ཤེས་རབ་བཟང་པོ།

Shes-rab bZang-po

3 texts

འཛམ་ཐང་བླ་མ་ངག་དབང་
བློ་གྲོས་གྲགས་པ།

Dzam-thang Bla-ma Ngag-
dbang Blo-gros Grags-pa

1 text

ཀརྨ་རིན་ཆེན་འཕྲིན་ལས་
བསྟན་པའི་རྒྱལ་མཚན།

Karma Rin-chen 'Phrin-las
bsTan-pa'i rGyal-mtshan

1 text

སྟག་ཚང་རས་པ་
ངག་དབང་རྒྱ་མཚོ།

sTag-tshang-ras-pa
Ngag-dbang rGya-mtsho

1 text

འཕྲེང་ཁ་བ་
དཔལ་ལྡན་བློ་གྲོས་བཟང་པོ།

'Phreng-kha-ba
dPal-ldan Blo-gros bZang-po

1 text

ངག་དབང་བསྟན་པའི་ཉིམ།

Ngag-dbang bsTan-pa'i
Nyi-ma

1 text

གཙང་སྨན་དར་མ་མགོན་པོ།

gTsang-sman
Dar-ma mGon-po

64 texts

ཕྲ་ཏི་དགེ་བཤེས་
དཔལ་ལྡན་རྒྱལ་མཚན་

Brang-ti dGe-bshes
dPal-ldan rGyal-mtshan
1 text

སྒ་སྟོད་གནས་བཟང་བ་
དགེ་འདུན་

sGa-stod-gnas bZang-ba
dGe-'dun
1 text

མཁས་དབང་སངས་རྒྱས་རྡོ་རྗེ་

nKhas-dbang   Sangs-rgyas
rDo-rje
1 text

སྒྲུབ་སྤྲུལ་ཕྲིན་ལས་རྒྱ་མཚོ་

sGrub-sprul
Phrin-las rGya-mtsho
1 text

ཟླ་བའི་འོད་ཟེར་རྡོ་རྗེ་དཔལ་ལྡན་

Zla-ba'i 'Od-zer
rDo-rje dPal-ldan
1 text

ལོ་ཙཱ་བ་ནམ་མཁའ་བཟང་པོ་

Lo-tsā-ba
Nam-mkha' bZang-po
1 text

འབྲི་གུང་དཀོན་མཆོག་
འཕྲིན་ལས་བཟང་པོ་

'Bri-gung dKon-mchog
'Phrin-las bZang-po
1 text

ལོ་ཆེན་ངག་དབང་
དཔལ་ལྡན་བཟང་པོ་

Lo-chen Ngag-dbang
dPal-ldan bZang-po
1 text

རྡོ་རམས་པ
བློ་བཟང་ཚུལ་ཁྲིམས་རྒྱ་མཚོ

rDo-rams-pa
Blo-bzang Tshul-khrims
rGya-mtsho
1 text

ཁམས་བྲག་སྤྲུལ་སྐུ་ངག་དབང་
ཀུན་བཟང་རྣམ་རྒྱལ

Khams-brag sPrul-sku
Ngag-dbang
Kun-bzang rNam-rgyal
1 text

དོན་གྲུབ་དབང་རྒྱལ

Don-grub dBang-rgyal
1 text

ལུང་རིགས་བསྟན་དར

Lung-rigs bsTan-dar
2 texts

རིན་ཆེན་རྒྱལ་མཚན

Rin-chen rGyal-mtshan
1 text

ཆོས་གྲགས་རྒྱ་མཚོ

Chos-grags rGya-mtsho
1 text

བཀྲ་ཤིས་ཚེ

bKra-shis-tshe
1 text

མང་ཐོས་རྡོ་རྗེ

Mang-thos rDo-rje
1 text

བློ་གྲོས་རབ་གསལ་པདྨ་བཞད་པ

Blo-gros Rab-gsal Padma
bZhad-pa
1 text

དགེ་བསྙེན་བློ་གྲོས་བཟང་པོ

dGe-bsnyen Blo-gros
bZang-po
1 text

མང་ཐོས་ནམ་མཁའི་ནོར་བུ

Mang-thos
Nam mkha'i Nor-bu
1 text

དམར་སྟོན་ཆོས་རྒྱལ

dMar-ston Chos-rgyal
1 text

ངེས་དོན་རྒྱ་མཚོ

Nges-don rGya-mtsho
1 text

447

# Part Twelve

# Monasteries, Sacred and Historic Sites

འཇམ་མགོན་བླ་མ་མི་ཕམ་རྣམ་རྒྱལ་རྒྱ་མཚོ

'Jam-mgon Bla-ma Mi-pham rNam-rgyal rGya-mtsho

# Sacred Geography

The Dharma entered into Tibetan civilization so deeply that the land itself was transformed into an enlightened realm. Journeying throughout Tibet, the Great Guru and his closest disciple Ye-shes mTsho-rgyal are said to have visited every hill and vale, filling the entire Land of Snow with blessings. As Guru Padmasambhava's lineages later spread across Tibet, hermitages were established and monasteries founded in all of the four directions.

The following list of monasteries, historic places, and sacred sites is a preliminary compilation of important places in the rNying-ma tradition selected from a few histories. These places include power sites associated with Padmasambhava, historic sites in central Tibet from the days of the Dharma Kings, and monasteries and residences of some of the major rNying-ma masters. Preserving the names and locations of these early edifices and sites will support more extensive research in the future.

# bSam-yas and the Six Major
# rNying-ma Monasteries

བསམ་ཡས་མི་འགྱུར་ལྷུན་གྱི་གྲུབ་པའི་གཙུག་ལག་ཁང་

## bSam-yas

On the north bank of the gTsang-po River is bSam-yas monastery, the Inconceivable Unchanging Perfect Creation, the Temple of bSam-yas (Mi-'gyur lHun-gyi Grub-pa'i gTsug-lag-khang). Founded in 762 or 763 by Dharma King Khri-srong lDe'u-btsan, Guru Padmasambhava, and Abbot Śāntarakṣita, bSam-yas was the first monastery in Tibet.

The mandala of bSam-yas revolves around the Central Temple (dBu-rtse Rigs-gsum gTsug-lha-khang), which has three storeys, each built in a different style. It is surrounded by four major and eight minor temples, with the Sun and Moon temples (Nyi-ma and Zla-ba) to the east and west. Four stupas mark the four corners of the Central Temple, while a large wall topped with small stupas encircles the monastery complex.

ཀཿཐོག་རྡོ་རྗེ་གདན་

## Kaḥ-thog rDo-rje-gdan

Founded in 1159 by Kaḥ-dam-pa bDe-gshegs in eastern Tibet in Khams, Kaḥ-thog was maintained in early times by thirteen generations of masters, the last of whom was Ye-shes rGyal-mtshan. Whenever the lineages of the Three Inner Tantras weakened in central Tibet, Kaḥ-thog kept them alive in an uninterrupted stream. In 1656 Kaḥ-thog was revitalized and expanded, and its bKa'-ma lineages restored by Klong-gsal sNying-po's son rGyal-sras bSod-nams lDe-btsan (1679–1723).

ཐུབ་བསྟན་རྡོ་རྗེ་བྲག

## Thub-bstan rDo-rje-brag

Home of the Byang-gter Northern Treasures discovered by Rig-'dzin rGod-ldem. The first foundation of rDo-rje-brag was bKra-shis sTob-rgyal's monastery, E-wam lCog-sgar Grwa-tshang. In 1632 Rig-'dzin Ngag-gi dBang-po founded Thub-bstan rDo-rje-brag at that site. Though badly damaged in 1717–18 by the Dzungar Mongols, the monastery was rebuilt and continued to be one of the major rNying-ma monasteries in central Tibet until the present time.

ཨོ་རྒྱན་སྨིན་གྲོལ་གླིང་

## O-rgyan sMin-grol-gling

The monastery of sMin-grol-gling is located south of the gTsang-po river in the valley of Grwa-phyi. Founded in 1676 by O-rgyan gTer-bdag-gling-pa, it preserved the bKa'-ma lineages, the rNying-ma-rgyud-'bum transmission, and the gTer-ma traditions of gTer-bdag Gling-pa. sMin-grol-gling housed over four hundred monks and three incarnate lamas. Badly damaged by the Dzungar Mongols in 1717–18, sMin-grol-gling was restored and continued to be one of the major rNying-ma monasteries in central Tibet until recent times.

# དཔལ་ཡུལ་རྣམ་རྒྱལ་བྱང་ཆུབ་གླིང་

## dPal-yul rNam-rgyal Byang-chub-gling

Rig-'dzin Kun-bzang Shes-rab (1636–1699) founded the doctrinal school of rNam-rgyal Byang-chub-gling at dPal-yul in 1665 in eastern Tibet. An unbroken stream of his disciples and incarnations continued the activities of dPal-yul. dPal-yul housed six hundred monks and seven incarnate lamas, and had many branch monasteries, the largest being dPal-yul Dar-thang in 'Gu-log founded in 1882.

# རྫོགས་ཆེན་ཨོ་རྒྱན་བསམ་གཏན་ཆོས་གླིང་

## rDzogs-chen

In 1685 the retreat center of rDzogs-chen O-rgyan bSam-gtan Chos-gling was founded near Ru-dam sKyid-khram valley in Khams by Padma Rig-'dzin with the encouragement of the Fifth Dalai Lama. rDzogs-chen housed eight hundred and fifty monks and eleven incarnate lamas. Associated with rDzogs-chen were thirteen retreat centers.

# ཞེ་ཆེན་བསྟན་གཉིས་དར་རྒྱས་གླིང་

## Zhe-chen

Zhe-chen bsTan-gnyis Dar-rgyas-gling was founded near Zhe-chen O-rgyan Chos-rdzong in Khams in 1735 by the Second Zhe-chen Rab-'byams, 'Gyur-med Kun-bzang rNam-rgyal. Zhe-chen housed two hundred monks and nine incarnate lamas, and was well-known for its strict monastic discipline.

# Monasteries, Sacred Places, and Historic Sites

## མཐའ་འདུལ་ཡང་འདུལ་དང་རུ་གནོན་གཙུག་ལག་ཁང་།

### Land-taming temples

mTha'-'dul, Yang-'dul, and Ru-gnon temples were built by Dharma King Srong-bstan sGam-po in the seventh century to tame the land of Tibet. The temples were envisioned as pinning down a demoness who would otherwise create obstacles to establishing the Dharma. The Jo-khang temple was built at the heart of the demoness and the twelve other temples marked key sites in three concentric four-cornered squares: the four inner subduers, the four border subduers, and the distant subduers.

## མལ་རྟོ་སྐ་ཚལ་དང་ཡར་ལུང་ཁྲ་འབྲུག

### sKa-tshal in Mal-dro and Khra-'brug in Yar-lung

These two temples pinned down the right and left shoulders of the demoness, one on the north side of the gTsang-po river east of lHa-sa in Mal-dro, and one on the south side of the gTsang-po in Yar-lung.

## གཙང་གྲམ་དང་གྲམ་པ་རྒྱང་

### Gram in gTsang and Gram-pa-rgyangs

These two temples pinned down the right and left hips and legs of the demoness, both east of lHa-sa. One was in the southern part of gTsang and one in the northern part of gTsang.

## ཀོང་པོ་བུ་ཆུ་དང་ལྷོ་བྲག་ཁོམ་ཐིང་

Kong-po Bu-chu in Kong-po and Khom-thing in lHo-brag

These two temples pinned down the right and left elbows of the demoness, both east of lHa-sa. One was north of the gTsang-po river in Kong-po, and one was south of the gTsang-po in the southern district of lHo-brag.

## སྐ་བྲག་དང་བྲ་དུམ་རྩེ་

sKa-brag and Bra-dum-rtse

These two temples pinned down the right and left knees of the demoness, both west of lHa-sa.

## བྱང་ཚལ་ཀློང་གནོད་དང་ལྡན་ཁོག་སྒྲོལ་མ

Klong-thang sGrol-ma in lDan-khog and
Lung-gnod in Byang-tshal

These two temples pinned down the right and left hands of the demoness, both east of lHa-sa. One was somewhere in the northern plains and the other was in Khams in lDan-khog in the far northeast.

## མང་ཡུལ་བྱམས་སྤྲིན་དང་མོན་ཡུལ་སྤ་རོ་སྐྱེར་ཆུ

Byams-sprin in Mang-yul and sPa-ro sKyer-chu in Mon-yul

These two temples pinned down the feet of the demoness. One was in the far west in Mang-yul and the other was in the south in Bhutan.

# Five Sacred Sites Associated with the Guru

ষ্ক্রণাম'অম'র্ট্র্ন'

### sGrags Yang-rdzong

Associated with the Guru's Body, this power site is located in sGrags. Here thirty-three great yogins achieved realization in the days of the Dharma kings.

বমম'অম'মক্টিমম'ধু

### bSam-yas mChims-phu

Associated with the Guru's Speech, this power site is the location of a meditation cave of Guru Rinpoche and the twenty-five disciples. Here Padmasambhava bestowed initiations for the eight heruka sādhanas on fortunate disciples.

ষ্ট্র'ব্রণা'মঁখর'ক্ত

### lHo-brag mKhar-chu

Associated with the Guru's Heart, this power site in lHo-brag is where Nam-mkha'i sNying-po attained realization.

অম'অুন'শ্বিম'ব্রণা

### Yar-lung Shel-brag

Associated with the Guru's Qualities, this power site is in Yar-lung. Fifty-five great realized ones achieved understanding here in the days of the Dharma Kings.

ཨོན་ཁ་ནེ་རིང་སེང་གེ་རྫོང་

Mon-kha Ne-ring Seng-ge-rdzong

Associated with the Guru's Activity, this power site is located south of lHo-brag in the Bhutan region.

## Three Tiger Dens

ཨོན་ཕུ་སྟག་ཚང་

'On-phu sTag-tshang

Tiger Den in 'On valley in central Tibet where Guru Padmasambhava and Ye-shes mTsho-rgyal practiced.

སྤ་རོ་སྟག་ཚང་

sPa-ro sTag-tshang

Tiger Den in Bhutan near sPa-ro where Guru Padmasambhava and Ye-shes mtsho-rgyal practiced.

ཁམས་སྟག་ཚང་

Khams sTag-tshang

Tiger Den near Kaḥ-thog in eastern Tibet where Guru Padmasambhava and Ye-shes mTsho-rgyal practiced.

# Sacred and Historic Sites
# in dBus and the lHa-sa Area

ར་མོ་ཆེ

## Ramoche

Temple built in the seventh century in lHa-sa by Kong-jo, the Chinese queen of Srong-btsan sGam-po, to house the statue called the Jo-bo Chen-po. Later this temple was the home of the Jo-bo Chung-ba statue.

ར་ས་འཕྲུལ་སྣང་གཙུག་ལྷ་ཁང་

## Ra-sa 'Phrul-snang gTsug-lha-khang

Temple built in the seventh century in lHa-sa by Khri-btsun, the Nepalese queen of Srong-btsan sGam-po, to house the Jo-bo Chung-ba statue. Later this temple was the home of the Jo-bo Chen-po and became renowned as the Jo-khang.

ཕ་བོང་ཁ

## Pha-bong-kha

Site near lHa-sa where Dharma King Srong-btsan sGam-po meditated and performed retreats. One of the twenty-four holy places in the Tantric tradition.

བྲག་ཡེར་པ

Brag Yer-pa

This powerful site northeast of lHa-sa is the location of the practice caves of Dharma King Srong-btsan sGam-po, Padma-sambhava, and the eighty siddhas of Yer-pa. King Khri-srong lDe'u-btsan established a Tantric retreat center here.

རི་བོ་རྩེ་ལྔ།

Ri-bo rTse-lnga

The Five-Peaked Mountain of the Gods associated with the Bodhisattva Mañjuśrī is located south of lHa-sa. A counterpart mountain, known as Wu-t'ai-shan, is in China.

གངས་རི་ཐོད་དཀར

Gangs-ri Thod-dkar

White Skull Mountain is the site of sacred caves where Klong-chen-pa perfected realization, redacted the Ya-bzhi, composed the Seven Treasures, and passed into Nirvana.

བྲག་དམར་ཟང་ཡག་ནམ་མཁའ་རྫོང་

Brag-dmar Zang-yag Nam-mkha'-rdzong

Meditation cave of Padmasambhava near Ri-bo rTse-lnga.

ཨུ་ཤང་རྡོ་དཔེ་མེད་དགེ་འཕེལ

'U-shang-rdo dPe-med dGe-'phel

This nine-storied temple with a famous golden roof was built by the ninth-century Dharma King Ral-pa-can.

དཔལ་ཆུ་བོ་རི

dPal Chu-bo-ri

Powerful sacred place at the confluence of the sKyid-chu and gTsang-po rivers, Chu-bo-ri is where King Khri-srong lDe'u-btsan established a Tantric retreat center, and one hundred and eight great meditators achieved realization in the days of the Dharma Kings. One hundred and eight springs arose here from Padmasambhava's blessings. Guru Padma's practice place of Nam-mkha'-lding is nearby.

ལྕགས་ཟམ་ཆུ་བོ་རི

lCags-zam Chu-bo-ri

Founded by Thang-ston rGyal-po at Chu-bo-ri, this was the residence of lCags-zam sPrul-sku and bsTan-'dzin Ye-shes lHun-grub. It is located north of Yar-'brog Lake.

# Sacred and Historic Sites in the 'Bri-gung Area

ཐང་སྐྱ།

### Thang-skya

This temple was founded near the banks of the sKyid-chu river in the seventh century by King Srong-btsan sGam-po .

རྒྱ་མ་ཁྲི་ཁང་

### rGya-ma Khri-khang

Birthplace of Dharma King Srong-btsan sGam-po.

ཞྭའི་ལྷ་ཁང་

### Zhwa'i lHa-khang

This temple was built in the ninth century by Myang Ting-nge-'dzin, who concealed the Bi-ma-snying-thig teachings here.

གཞོ་ཏི་སྒྲོ

### gZho Ti-sgro

Power place and site of practice caves of Padmasambhava and Ye-shes mTsho-rgyal, Ti-sgro is northeast of lHa-sa near 'Bri-gung. mTsho-rgyal practiced with Ācārya Sa-le and performed numerous retreats at this location.

# Sacred and Historic Sites Near bSam-yas

བྲག་དམར་གཡའ་མ་ལུང་

## Brag-dmar gYa'-ma-lung

This power site north of bSam-yas is where Padmasambhava first gave Dharma instructions to Ye-shes mTsho-rgyal and where Vairotsana went on retreat.

བྲག་དམར་མགྲིན་བཟང་

## Brag-dmar mGrin-bzang

Birthplace of Dharma King Khri-srong lDe'u-btsan, mGrin-bzang was built by his father, King Mes-ag-tshoms.

ཧས་པོ་རི

## Has-po-ri

From this hill near bSam-yas, Guru Padmasambhava descended to first meet King Khri-srong lDe'u-tsan in 762.

## Zur-mkhar-rdo

These five stūpas dedicated to the five Buddha families were erected by King Khri-srong lDe'u-bstan near bSam-yas.

སྒྲགས

sGrags

Birthplace of Ye-shes mTsho-rgyal and gNubs-chen Sangs-rgyas Ye-shes. North of the gTsang-po river and south of lHa-sa.


# Sacred and Historic Sites in the Yar-lung Area

ཡར་ཀླུང་

Yar-lung

The district of Yar-lung is the valley of the Yar-lung river, a tributary of the gTsang-po. Yar-lung was the center of the kingdom of Tibet in the days of the early kings until Srong-btsan sGam-po moved the capital north to lHa-sa.

ཡུམ་བུ་བླ་མཁར་

Yum-bu Bla-mkhar

This castle was built by the first king of Tibet, gNya'-khri bTsan-po, in the third century B.C.

ཚེ་ཆུ་འབུམ་པ

Tshe-chu 'Bum-pa

Near a spring of life-giving water stands this ancient stūpa. Within the stūpa is a rock-crystal image from India given to King Khri-srong lDe'u-bstan by Cog-ro Klu'i rGyal-mtshan.

464

## བཙན་ཐང་གཡུ་ཡི་ལྷ་ཁང་

bTsan-thang gYu yi lHa-khang

This temple was built by Queen Nyang-tshul Byang-chub, wife of one of the Dharma kings.

## བཙན་ཐང་ལྷ་རི་སྒོ་བཞི

bTsan-thang lHa-ri sgo-bzhi

Upon this hill, according to some sources, the first king of Tibet descended into the Land of Snow.

## འཕྱོངས་རྒྱས

'Phyongs-rgyas

The 'Phyongs-rgyas district is the valley of the river 'Phyongs-rgyas that flows into the Yar-lung river.

## པ་གོར

Pa-gor

Residence of Vairotsana in the 'Phyong-rgyas valley.

## འཕྱོངས་རྒྱས་དཔལ་རི་ཐེག་མཆོག་གླིང

'Phyongs-rgyas dPal-ri Theg-mchog-gling

This monastery, founded by Phreng-po gTer-chen Shes-rab 'Od-zer, was the residence of mTsho-rgyal sPrul-sku Rig-'dzin Phrin-las rNam-rgyal and others. Before the founding of sMin-grol-gling in the seventeenth century, dPal-ri was the most important rNying-ma center in central Tibet. It was known as rDor-smin dPal-ri.

ཚེ་རིང་ལྗོངས་པདྨ་འོད་གསལ་ཐེག་མཆོག་གླིང་

Tshe-ring-ljongs Padma 'Od-gsal Theg-mchog-gling

Restored by 'Jigs-med Gling-pa, this hermitage was the residence of his nephew dBon-po 'Od-zer Phrin-las.

འཕྱིང་བ་སྟག་རྩེ་

'Phying-ba sTag-rtse

In this castle, the early kings resided before Srong-btsan sGam-po moved the capital to lHa-sa. It was the birthplace of the Fifth Dalai Lama.

བང་སོ་དམར་པོ་

Bang-so dMar-po

The Red Tomb in 'Phyongs-rgyas is the site of Dharma King Srong-btsan sGam-po's tomb. Nearby are tombs of other kings of the Yar-lung Dynasty.

ཡར་ལྷ་ཤམ་པོ་

Yar-lha Sham-po

One of the most sacred and powerful mountains in Tibet, this peak rises south of Yar-lung valley.

བྱིང་མདའ་འོ་དཀར་བྲག

Byang-mda' 'O-dkar-brag

A meditation place of Padmasambhava west of Yar-lung.

## Sacred and Historic Sites in the Grwa-nang Area

Grwa-nang

Residence of gTer-ston Grwa-pa mNgon-shes.

དར་རྒྱས་ཆོས་སྡིང་

Dar-rgyas Chos-sding

This monastery founded by Ratna Gling-pa sPrul-sku sNa-tshogs Rang-grol transmitted sNying-thig lineages.

Guru Padma'i E-wam lCog-sgar

E-wam lCog-sgar was the community of Byang-gter practition-ers established by bKra-shis sTobs-rgyal. It was the "seed" of rDo-rje-brag monastery founded in later centuries.

ཡར་རྗེ་ལྷ་ཁང་

Yar-rje lHa-khang

Birthplace of Klong-chen-pa in Grwa-nang valley.

## Sacred and Historic Sites in the Lo-ro and Nyal Areas

ཉལ་

Nyal

The district of Nyal was the seat of Rig-'dzin Ngag-gi dBang-po's student Ngag-dbang bKra-shis rNam-rgyal.

ལོ་རོ་

Loro

The district of Lo-ro is where Bo-dong-pa Chos-kyi rGyal-mtshan's incarnation, sByor-ra Thams-cad mKhyen-pa, made his seat. rNying-ma lineage holders also resided here.

# Sacred and Historic Sites in the lHo-brag Area

ལྷོ་བྲག་ཤར་སྨྲ་བ་ཅོག

## lHo-brag-shar sMra-ba-cog

sMra-ba-cog was founded by Nyang-ral Nyi-ma 'Od-zer in the twelfth century in eastern lHo-brag. It became the residence of the sons of Nyang-ral Nyi-ma 'Od-zer and the descendents of Guru Chos-dbang.

གུ་རུ་ལྷ་ཁང

## Guru lHa-khang

This was the residence of Guru Chos-dbang at La-yag in lHo-brag. Given to Padma Gling-pa's son Zla-ba rGyal-mtshan, it became the residence for Padma Gling-pa descendents.

ལྷོ་བྲག་ལྷ་ཁང

## lHo-brag lHa-khang

This temple is also known as  Khom-mthing, the land-taming temple built by Srong-btsan sGam-po in the seventh century.

## gNas-gzhi Zhi-khro lHa-khang

Seat of the descendents of Guru Chos-dbang.

ལྷོ་མདོ་མཁར་ལྷུན་གྲུབ་ཕོ་བྲང་

lHo-mdo-mkhar lHun-grub Pho-brang

Residence of Ratna Gling-pa.

ལྷོ་བྲག་ཆག་བྱང་ཆུབ་གླིང་

lHo-brag Chag Byang-chub-gling

Residence of Byang-chub Gling-pa, disciple of the great Padma Gling-pa, this monastery was administered by sMin-grol-gling.

ལྷོ་བྲག་མཁར་ཆུ་བདུད་འཇོམས་གླིང་

lHo-brag mKhar-chu bDud-'joms-gling

Founded by the Fifth Dalai Lama in the seventeenth century, this monastery's specialties were gTer-kha-gong-'og and the Byang-gter Northern Treasures.

ལྷ་ལུང་མེ་ཏོག་ལྷ་ནང་ཐེག་མཆོག་རབ་རྒྱས་གླིང་

lHa-lung Me-tog lHa-nang Theg-mchog Rab-rgyas-gling

Monastery connected to Guru lHa-khang.

བན་པ་དྲུག་རལ་ལྷ་ཁང་

Ban-pa Drug-ral lHa-khang

Monastery founded by mChog-ldan mGon-po.

sGrub-mtsho Padma Gling

Padma Gling is one of Tibet's four most sacred lakes, with hand- and footprints of Padmasambhava evident nearby.

Yar-'brog Yon-po-de

Founded by gTer-ston mChog-ldan mGon-po's incarnation, this monastery was later taken care of by the descendents of Padma Gling-pa.

## Sacred and Historic Sites in the Mon Area

gDung-bsam Ri-bo bsTan-rgyas-gling

This monastery was founded by Kun-mkhyen 'Jigs-med Gling-pa's disciple 'Jigs-med Kun-grol.

# Sacred and Historic Sites in the 'On and E-yul Areas

## 'On Ke-ru

This temple was built in the days of King Khri-srong lDe'u-btsan in the district of 'On east of bSam-yas.

## Zangs-ri mKhar-dmar

This is the residence of Ma-gcig Lab-sgron-ma in the district of 'Ol-kha near the gTsang-po river.

## rTsa-sgrub-sde

Founded by rDzogs-chen-pa Nam-mkha' 'Brug-sgra bZang-po.

## E sPe-lcog

Residence of Gar-dbang Las-'phro Gling-pa.

བྲག་སྣ་བ།

Brag-sna-ba

Residence of Chos-rje O-rgyan bsTan-'dzin.

ཨེ་ཡུལ་རིགས་པའི་འབྱུང་གནས།

E-yul Rigs-pa'i 'Byung-gnas

At this ancient power site in the district of E is a practice cave of Padmasambhava known as gZar-mo-lung.

## Sacred and Historic Sites in the Dwags-po Area

 རྩེ་ལེ་གོང་འོག

rTse-le Gong-'og

An early monastery was founded by Kun-mkhyen Chos-sku 'Od-zer. A later one was founded by Rig-'dzin bSod-nams rNam-rgyal. Residence of rTse-le sNa-tshogs Rang-grol.

དྭགས་ལྷ་སྒམ་པོ།

Dwags lHa-sgam-po

This monastery was founded by sGam-po-pa Dwags-po lHa-rje in 1122. Disciples of later incarnations of Dwags-po Rin-po-che, such as gTer-chen bZang-po rDo-rje and others, followed rNying-ma teachings.

473

### Tsā-ri

The sacred mountain of Tsā-ri stands southeast of Dwags-po in a hidden valley (sbas-yul) surrounded by wilderness.

## Sacred and Historic Sites in the Kong-po Area

### sNyi-phu bDe-chen bSam-grub

This was the residence of Sangs-rgyas Gling-pa's descendents, including his son Ye-shes rDo-rje.

### Bya-khyung-dgon

The monastery of Bya-khyung was founded by dPal-ldan Seng-ge, a lineage holder of Sangs-rgyas Gling-pa's teachings.

### Thang-'brog-dgon

Founded by bsTan-'dzin rDo-rje, this monastery was the residence of the descendents of his incarnation, rTse-le sNa-tshogs Rang-grol.

Kong-po lHun-grags

Residence of Dri-med-lhun-po.

བང་རི་འཇོག་པོ

Bang-ri 'Jog-po

Residence of 'Ja'-tshon sNying-po.

## Sacred and Historic Sites in the sPu-bo Area

དགའ་བ་ལུང་

dGa'-ba-lung

dGa'-ba-lung was the residence of gTer-ston sTag-sham Nus-ldan rDo-rje and his later incarnations.

གསང་སྔགས་ཆོས་གླིང་

gSang-sngags Chos-gling

Residence of Rig-'dzin Chos-kyi rGya-mtsho's incarnations.

ཪྦ་ཁ་གསང་སྔགས་ཆོས་གླིང་

rBa-kha gSang-sngags Chos-gling

Founded by the mChog-ldan mGon-po incarnation, Yang-dag rGya-mtsho, this monastery was the residence of rBa-kha sPrul-sku.

475

# Sacred and Historic Sites in the gTsang Area

ཁམས་བུ་ལུང་

## Khams-bu-lung

Site in eastern gTsang at Rong-chung with a meditation cave of Guru Padmasambhava.

དུན་པ་ཆུ་ཚན་ཁ་

## Dun-pa Chu-tsan-kha

Birthplace of gTer-ston rGya Zhang-khrom in eastern gTsang.

འུག་པ་ལུང་

## 'Ug-pa-lung

Founded by Zur-po-che and completed by Zur-chung, this monastery was located north of Zhwa-lu near gSer-mdog-can.

བདེ་གྲོལ་གསང་སྔགས་ཆོས་གླིང་

## bDe-grol gSang-sngags Chos-gling

Residence of Mes-ston, an important early lineage holder.

རྒྱ་མཁར་གསང་སྔགས་ཆོས་གླིང་

## rGya-mkhar gSang-sngags Chos-gling

Residence of the descendents of Se-ston Nyi-ma bZang-po.

Gangs-ra Nges-gsang rDo-rje-gling

Founded by Rong-gter 'Jam-dpal rDo-rje, this monastery was the residence of Gangs-ra Lo-chen gZhan-phan rDo-rje.

Phung-po Ri-bo-che

Founded by the Fifth Dalai Lama, and known as bDud-dpung Zil-gnon-gling, this ancient holy place associated with a practice cave of Padmasambhava.

O-rgyan 'Gro-'dren-gling

Founded by Yol-mo-ba'i rNam-sprul Padma bShes-gnyen, this monastery was the residence of his incarnations, including 'Jigs-med dPa'-bo. Located near rGyal-rtse.

Theg-mchog-gling

Founded by 'Brug-pa Padma dKar-po, this monastery was turned into rNying-ma center by the Fifth Dalai Lama.

སྒོ་བཞི་རེ་ཐང་

sGo-bzhi Re-thang

Birthplace of gYu-thog Yon-tan mGon-po, near rGyal-rtse.

477

rTsis-gnas-gsar

This temple in gTsang north of rGyal-rtse, which was built in the days of the Dharma Kings, is sometimes called one of the land-taming temples.

 མང་མཁར་

Mang-mkhar

Region in gTsang where rMa Rin-chen-mchog was born.

རྒྱངས་ཡོན་པོ་ལུང་

rGyangs Yon-po-lung

This is the site of a meditation cave where Padmasambhava practiced in western gTsang near lHa-rtse.

གཉན་ཡོད་བྱ་རྒོད་གཤོང་

mNyan-yod Bya-rgod-gshong

An ancient temple, which is one of the land-taming temples, according to some sources.

# Sacred and Historic Sites
## in the 'U-yug, Shangs, and rTa-nag Areas

'U-yug Lug-gdon

A meditation place of Guru Padmasambhava in 'U-yug.

sNye-mo gZhu

Birthplace of Vairotsana, according to some sources.

ཤངས་ཟབ་བུ་ལུང་

Shangs Zab-bu-lung

An important meditation place in gTsang, Ye-shes mTsho-rgyal trained the disciples of Padmasambhava here for ten years before departing from Tibet. Also spelled Zam-bu-lung.

ཤངས་མདའ་དཔལ་ཆེན་

Shangs-mda' dPal-chen

Meditation place of Zur-chen and Zur-chung.

ཪྟ་ནག་སྒྲོལ་མ་ཕུག

rTa-nag sGrol-ma-phug

Residence of the descendents of sGrol-chen.

## Sacred and Historic Sites in the La-stod Area

གཙང་ལ་སྟོད་ནུབ་དགོན

gTsang La-stod Nub-dgon

This monastery was the residence of Byams-pa Chos-kyi rGyal-mtshan and his disciples and also of Khams-lung-pa Rig-'dzin dbang-rgyal.

ཟང་ཟང་ལྷ་བྲག་སྲིད་གསུམ་རྣམ་རྒྱལ

Zang-zang lHa-brag Srid-gsum rNam-rgyal

Founded by Yid-bzhin Nor-bu, the younger brother of bKra-shis sTobs-rgyal, this monastery was located near the site where Rig-'dzin rGod-ldem discovered gTer-ma. Residence of the incarnations of Nāgarjuna.

གཅུང་རི་བོ་ཆེ

gCung Ri-bo-che

Founded by Thang-ston rGyal-po, this monastery was the residence of Yol-mo gTer-ston bTsan-'dzin Nor-bu and the lineage of his younger brother Phyag-rdor Nor-bu. Located in western gTsang.

480

བཀྲ་བཟང་

## bKra-bzang

Founded by Rig-'dzin rGod-ldem in the fourteenth century, this monastery was near the mountain where he found the key to important gTer-ma. Residence of rNam-rgyal mGon-po, son of Rig-'dzin rGod-ldem, it preserved unbroken the Tantric lineages, especially Byang-gter. Located in western gTsang.


# Sacred and Historic Sites in the sTod-lung Areas

## gZhong-ba lHa-chu

This spring created by Padmasambhava is located in lower sTod-lung west of lHa-sa.

# Alphabetical List of Biographies

mKhar-chen dPal-gyi dbang-phyug, 48

Karma Chags-med, 248

Karma Gling-pa, 178

Karmapa Rang-byung rDo-rje, *see* Rang-byung rDo-rje

mKhas-grub Chen-po Karma chags-med, *see* Karma Chags-med

mKhas-grub Chen-po gYu-khog Bya-bral, *see* gYu-khog Bya-bral

mKhas-grub bKra-shis rNam-rgyal, *see* bKra-shis rNam-rgyal

mKhas-grub Ngag-dbang rDo-rje, *see* Ngag-dbang rDo-rje

mKhas-pa Zangs-gling dBang-phyug, 113

mKha'-'gro-ma Kun-dga'-'bum, *see* Kun-dga'-bum

'Khon-ston dPal-'byor lHun-grub, *see* dPal-'byor lHun-grub

Khra-dge-slong Tshul-khrims Dar-rgyas, 371

Khri-srong lDe'u-btsan, 29

'Khrul-zhig dBang-drag rGya-mtsho, 241

'Khrul-zhig Mi-'gyur Nam-mkha'i rDo-rje, 337

'Khrul-zhig O-rgyan rNam-rgyal, 335

'Khrul-zhig Seng-ge-rgyab, 140

Khu-lung-pa, *see* Yon-tan rGya-mtsho

mKhyen-brtse'i dBang-phyug, 220

Khye'u-chung Lo-tsā, 53

Khyung-grags rDo-rje O-rgyan Phun-tshogs, 293

Khyung-po dPal-dge, 83

Khyung-po Ras-pa 'Gyur-med 'Od-gsal, 306

Klong-chen-pa, 166

Klong-chen Rab-'byams, *see* Klong-chen-pa,

Klong-gsal sNying-po, 253

Kon-mchog 'Byung-gnas, 58

Kong-sprul Blo-gros mTha'-yas, 345

bKra-shis Khye'u-'dren, 65

bKra-shis rNam-rgyal, 241

bKra-shis Tshe-brtan, 243

bKra-shis sTobs-rgyal, 224

Ku-sa sMan-pa Padma-skyabs, 109

Kukkurāja, 9

sPrul-sku La-stod dMar-po, *see* La-stod dMar-po

sPyan-snga Rinpoche Zhwa-dmar-pa Chos-kyi Grags-pa, see Zhwa-dmar Chos-kyi Grags-pa

**R**a-mo Shel-sman Ye-shes bZang-po, 105

Ra-shag gTer-ston Chos-'bar bSod-nams rDo-rje, 101

Ra-zhi gTer-ston Padma Rig-'dzin, 242

Rakṣi sTon-pa, 145

Rang-byung rDo-rje, 152

Rang-grol Ting-'dzin rGyal-po Zla-ba'i 'Od-zer, 328

Ratna Gling-pa, 197

Rig-'dzin Chen-po Chos-rje Gling-pa, *see* Chos-rje Gling-pa

Rig-'dzin Chen-po Nyi-ma Grags-pa, 272

Rig-'dzin Chen-po Rol-pa'i rDo-rje, *see* Rol-pa'i rDo-rje

Rig-'dzin Chos-rgyal rDo-rje, *see* Chos-rgyal rDo-rje

Rig-'dzin bDud-'dul rDo-rje, *see* bDud-'dul rDo-rje

Rig-'dzin rGod-ldem, 175

Rig-'dzin Kun-mkhyen 'Jigs-med Gling-pa, *see* 'Jigs-med Gling-pa

Rig-'dzin Kun-bzang rDo-rje, *see* Kun-bzang rDo-rje

Rig-'dzin Kun-bzang Nges-don Klong-yangs, *see* Kun-bzang Nges-don Klong-yangs

Rig-'dzin Ngag-gi dBang-po, 230

Rig-'dzin Thugs-kyi rDo-rje Phrin-las 'Dus-pa-rtsal, *see* Thugs-kyi rDo-rje

Rig-'dzin Zil-gnon dBang-rgyal rDo-rje, *see* Zil-gnon dBang-rgyal rDo-rje

Rin-chen Gling-pa, 162

Rin-chen rNam-rgyal, 295

Rin-chen Phun-tshogs, *see* 'Bri-gung Rin-chen phun-tshogs

Rlangs dPal-gyi Seng-ge, 44

Rog-ban Shes-rab 'Od-zer, 125

Rol-pa'i rDo-rje, 287

Rong-pa gTer-ston bDud-'dul Gling-pa, *see* bDud-'dul gling-pa

Rong-ston Padma bDe-chen Gling-pa, 276

Rong-zom Mahāpaṇḍita Chos-kyi bZang-po, 87

Rwa-ston sTobs-ldan rDo-rje Padma Tshe-dbang-rtsal, 281

*Sita-Cintāmaṇi Mahākāla*

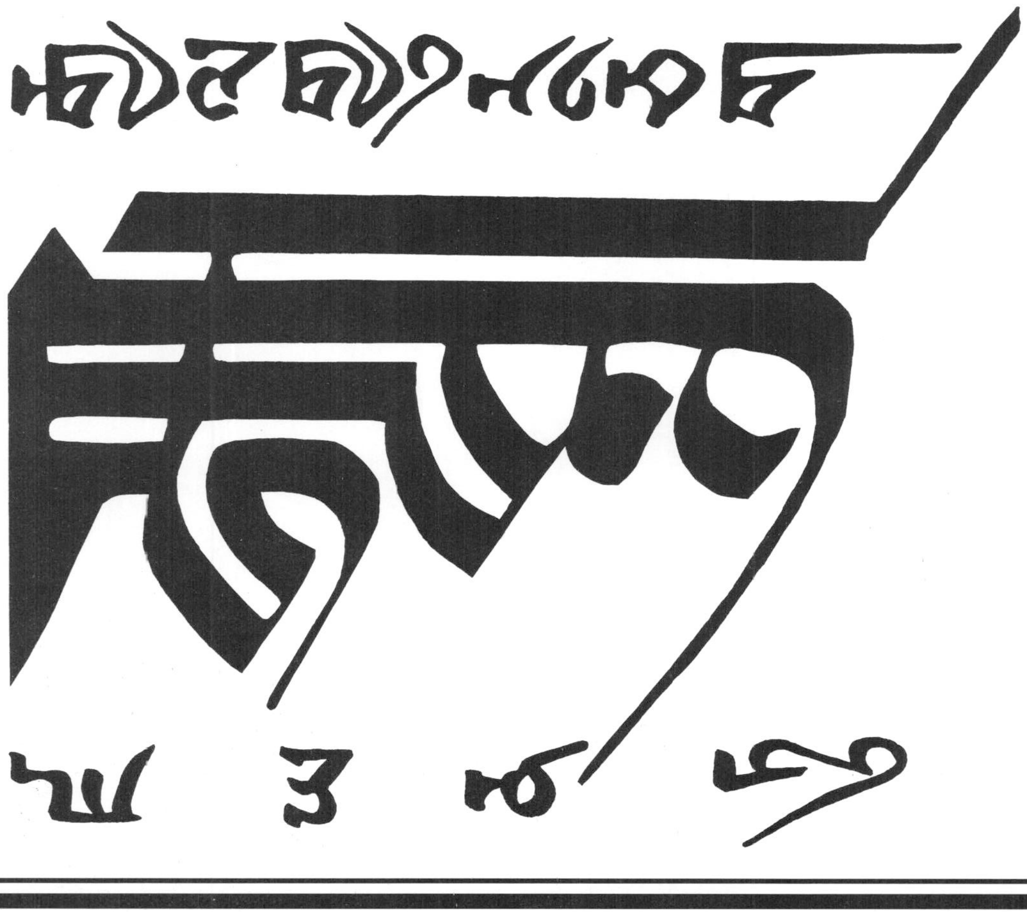

Tarthang Tulku

## About Tarthang Tulku: A Note from the Staff of Dharma Publishing

The creator and general editor of the Crystal Mirror Series is Tarthang Tulku, an accomplished Tibetan lama who has lived and worked in the United States since 1969. For most of his life, in Tibet, in India, and in America, Rinpoche has dedicated his full energy and resources to preserving and transmitting the Dharma. As his students, we have learned to find inspiration in his tireless devotion and profound respect for the Buddha's teachings.

From 1959 to 1966, while teaching at the Sanskrit University in Vārāṇasī, Rinpoche founded Dharma Mudranālaya and began publishing texts he had brought with him from Tibet. He continued this work in America, where he established Dharma

Publishing and Dharma Press, incorporated in 1975 as Dharma Mudranālaya. Under his direction, Dharma Publishing has preserved more than 35,000 Tibetan texts by 1,500 Buddhist masters in 755 large western-style volumes, and Dharma Publishing's books in English, including translations of important Buddhist texts, have been adopted for use in more than five hundred colleges and universities throughout the world.

In addition to his work as a scholar and publisher, Rinpoche has been active as an author and educator. He has written eleven books presenting teachings for the modern world, overseen translations of traditional texts and created and edited *The Nyingma Edition of the bKa'-'gyur and bsTan-'gyur* and *Great Treasures of Ancient Teachings,* the first compilation of the Nyingma Canon together with works by masters of all Tibetan Buddhist traditions. He is founder and president of the Nyingma Institute in Berkeley and its affiliated centers, where several thousand students have come in contact with the Buddhist teachings. Rinpoche has also created and directed the construction and ornamentation of Odiyan, a country center for retreats, study, and extended practice.

In the midst of these activities, Rinpoche serves in the traditional role of teacher for a growing community of Western students. Always willing to experiment, he has established a form of practice for his students in which their work on behalf of the Dharma becomes a path to realization. Although many of his students do not have frequent direct contact with Rinpoche, through the institutions he has established they are able to grow in wisdom and understanding, while developing practical skills that enable them to make their way in the world.

With so many diverse demands on his time, it has not always been possible for Rinpoche to verify the accuracy of every element of the books we produce under his direction, and the staff of Dharma Publishing assumes full responsibility for mistakes that appear in our publications. We only hope that on balance we have succeeded in transmitting some elements of the Dharma tradition.

Those of us who have had the opportunity to work under Rinpoche in the production of Dharma Publishing books are deeply grateful for the example he has set us. His dedication and reliable knowledge, his steady, untiring efforts, his patience and his caring enable us to direct our energy with confidence that despite our imperfections, our work can benefit others, making it possible for us to contribute in some way to the growth of the Dharma in the west.

# Books in the Crystal Mirror Series

**1–3. Footsteps on the Diamond Path**   The writings of great Nyingma masters and modern Nyingma teachings on mind, self-image, and meditation. An inspiring and practical introduction to the Vajrayāna Buddhism of Tibet.

**4. Guru Padmasambhava and Buddhism in Tibet**   Lives of the Great Guru Padmasambhava and his disciples convey the power and scope of the Dharma transmission in Tibet. Includes the teaching of Longchenpa on the Natural Freedom of Mind.

**5. Lineage of Diamond Light**   A richly illustrated presentation of Tarthang Tulku's history of the Buddhist Dharma in India and Tibet, with a special emphasis on the masters and lineages of the Nyingma tradition and translations of two works by Longchenpa.

**6. The Three Jewels and History of Dharma Transmission** A traditional introduction to the Buddha, Dharma, and Sangha, the forms of the Buddha's teachings, and the philosophical schools they inspired.

**7. The Buddha, Dharma, and Sangha in Historical Perspective**   The life of the Buddha, the unfolding of the Dharma, and the growth of the Sangha, framed in the larger sweep of world history. With maps and comparative timelines.

**8. Light of Liberation**   A history of Buddhism in India from the origin of the Śākyas to the twelfth century, based on traditional sources and modern archeological research.

**9. Holy Places of the Buddha**   The origin and value of pilgrimage, expressed in accounts of the eight great places of pilgrimage and the monuments along the ancient routes across India into Afghanistan.

**10. The Buddha and His Teachings**   The path and qualities of the Perfect Buddhas, the life of the Buddha Śākyamuni, and the openings of the Sūtras preserved in the Tibetan Canon.

**11. Masters of the Nyingma Lineage**   Biographies of over 350 masters trace the Mantrayāna lineages from the original transmission of the Dharma to Tibet to the present day. With 31 maps and lists of important monasteries and sacred sites.